Buddhist Hermeneutics

Kuroda Institute
Studies in East Asian Buddhism

Studies in Ch'an and Hua-yen
Robert M. Gimello and Peter N. Gregory

Dōgen Studies
William R. LaFleur

The Northern School and the Formation of Early Ch'an Buddhism
John R. McRae

Traditions of Meditation in Chinese Buddhism
Peter N. Gregory

Sudden and Gradual: Approaches to Enlightenment in Chinese Thought
Peter N. Gregory

Studies in East Asian Buddhism 6

Buddhist Hermeneutics

Edited by
Donald S. Lopez, Jr.

University of Hawaii Press • Honolulu

The Kuroda Institute for the Study of Buddhism and Human Values is a non-profit, educational corporation founded in 1976. One of its primary objectives is to promote scholarship on the historical, philosophical, and cultural ramifications of Buddhism. The Institute serves the scholarly community by providing a forum for conferences and colloquia; to date the Institute has sponsored six conferences in the area of Buddhist Studies. The present volume is the outgrowth of the sixth of these conferences, held in spring of 1984. Other conference volumes, as well as individual monographs, are planned for publication in the present series. In association with the University of Hawaii Press, the Institute also publishes Classics in East Asian Buddhism, a series devoted to the translation of significant texts in the East Asian Buddhist tradition.

Library of Congress Cataloging-in-Publication Data

Buddhist hermeneutics / edited by Donald S. Lopez, Jr.
p. cm. — (Studies in East Asian Buddhism; no. 6)
Includes index.
ISBN 0-8248-1161-5
1. Hermeneutics—Religious aspects—Buddhism. 2. Buddhism—Doctrines. I. Lopez, Donald S., 1952- . II. Series.
BQ4175.B83 1988 87-30175
294.3'8—dc19 CIP

Contents

Preface

The essays included in this volume are the fruition of a conference on Buddhist hermeneutics held at the Kuroda Institute for the Study of Buddhism and Human Values in Los Angeles in the spring of 1984. Major funding for the conference was provided by the National Endowment for the Humanities, whose support is gratefully acknowledged. The meeting in 1984 was very much a working conference in which the participants presented drafts of papers, the final versions of which appear here. The revision of the papers was guided by the stimulating discussion that took place during the four days of the conference. I would like to take this opportunity to thank those participants whose papers are not included here for their contributions to the success of the conference. They are Yuichi Kajiyama of Kyoto University, D. Seyfort Ruegg of the University of Hamburg, Luis Gómez of the University of Michigan, Robert Gimello of the University of Arizona, Jeffrey Hopkins of the University of Virginia, and John Maraldo of the University of North Florida. In addition, I wish to acknowledge the contributions of the three discussants: Alan Sponberg of Stanford University, Carl Bielefeldt of Stanford University, and especially David Tracy of the University of Chicago. Professor Tracy made extensive and astute comments on each of the papers, and did much to ensure the success of the conference.

In addition to the participants of the conference, I would like to thank the Zen Center of Los Angeles for graciously providing accommodations and hospitality. In the preparation of the volume, I have been aided by Robin Miller, who entered the papers onto computer disks. This work was supported by a faculty research grant from Middlebury College. Thanks are also due to the *Buddhist Studies Review* for granting permission to reprint Sara Boin-Webb's translation of Étienne Lamotte's 1949 essay, "La critique d'interprétation dans le bouddhisme." I would also like to thank Stuart Kiang and the staff of the University of Hawaii Press for their expertise in the editing and production of this volume. A final expression of gratitude to Peter Gregory, director of the Kuroda Institute, for his unfailing support and encouragement throughout this project.

Standard abbreviations for collections of scripture cited throughout this volume are as follows:

P Peking edition of the *Tibetan Tripiṭaka*. Tokyo-Kyoto, 1956.
T *Taishō shinshū daizōkyō*. Tokyo, 1914–1922.
ZZ *Dainihon zokuzōkyō*. Revised edition. Tokyo, 1950–.

DONALD S. LOPEZ, JR.

Buddhist Hermeneutics

Introduction

DONALD S. LOPEZ, JR.

> Then the Bhagavan addressed the venerable Ānanda: "It may be, Ānanda, that some of you will think, 'The word of the Teacher is a thing of the past; we have now no Teacher.' But that, Ānanda, is not the correct view. The Doctrine and the Discipline, Ānanda, which I have taught and enjoined upon you is to be your teacher when I am gone."[1]

These last instructions of the Buddha before his passage into nirvāṇa attempt to address the dilemma of a religious community upon the death of its founder. Where, in his absence, shall authority reside? The Buddha instructs Ānanda that it is his teaching that shall be the teacher. But what, exactly, was his teaching and what does it mean for the teaching to be the teacher? It was the contemplation of these questions that led to what can be called Buddhist hermeneutics.

The term "hermeneutics" is heard frequently today in the fields of Biblical studies, philosophy, and literary criticism. It has been variously defined, encompassing notions of translation, exegesis, interpretation, and understanding.[2] For the purposes of this volume, hermeneutics will be broadly conceived as concerned with establishing principles for the retrieval of meaning, especially from a text. Hermeneutics is by no means a new science; sophisticated systems of interpretation were devised by the Talmudic rabbis and by the early Church fathers. However, current interest in hermeneutics is focused primarily on more modern theories of interpretation, a tradition beginning with the work of Friedrich Schleiermacher and continuing into the twentieth century with such figures as Martin Heidegger, Rudolf Bultmann, Hans-Georg Gadamer, and Paul Ricoeur.

The interpretation of sacred scripture is, of course, a concern which is not confined to the Judeo-Christian tradition. It is also a major issue in

Buddhism, where the problems faced by the interpreters of the Buddha's word were somewhat different from those found in the West. First, Buddhism has a vast sacred canon, a fact due both to the length of the Buddha's teaching career and to the posthumous attribution of many discourses to him, especially by the Mahāyāna. Sūtras continued to be composed for over a millennium after the Buddha's death. As philosophical and soteriological problems arose in the unfolding of the tradition, new texts, claiming the authority of the word of the Buddha, were composed to address those problems and to validate certain doctrinal positions. Indeed, it may be that one reason for the relative dearth of hermeneutical strategies in Buddhism when compared to the Jewish and Christian traditions is the size and plastic nature of the Mahāyāna canon. Whereas Origen, for example, had to develop his famous trichotomy of the literal, moral, and spiritual levels of scripture in order to find the truths of pagan philosophy in the Bible, the Buddhists seemed to have simply written a new sūtra or interpolated new material into an existing text. The authority of these texts was not, for the most part, questioned by the Mahāyāna savants, who were continually faced with the problem of interpreting these doctrines in light of myriad others, all in an attempt to have "the teaching be the teacher."

Besides the sheer bulk of the canon (for example, were the Chinese Buddhist canon translated into English, it would require more than 500,000 pages to print), the Buddhist schools of India, Southeast Asia, Tibet, China, Korea, and Japan were confronted with another problem in their attempt to interpret the Buddha's teaching: just as a physician does not prescribe the same medicine to cure all maladies, the Buddha did not teach the same thing to everyone. Or, as Nāgārjuna says in the *Ratnāvalī* (IV.94–96):

> Just as grammarians
> Begin with reading the alphabet,
> The Buddha teaches doctrines
> That students can bear.
>
> To some he teaches doctrines
> For the reversal of sin;
> To some, in order to win merit;
> To some, doctrines based on duality.
>
> To some [he teaches doctrines] based on nonduality.
> To some, the profound, frightening to the fearful,
> Having an essence of emptiness and compassion,
> The means of achieving highest enlightenment.[3]

The Buddha is said to have taught different things to different people based on their interests, dispositions, capacities, and levels of intelligence. Furthermore, the tradition maintained that as a Buddha, an enlightened being, his teachings must be free of error and contradiction. But how is one to harmonize the statement "the self is one's protector" with the statement that "there is no self"? How can the advice that suffering is to be identified, its origin abandoned, its cessation actualized, and the path to that cessation cultivated be seen as compatible with the declaration that "there is no suffering, no origin, no cessation, no path"? And given the enormity of the literature attributed to the Buddha, how is one to interpret the statement "From the night that he attained enlightenment to the night that he passed into nirvāṇa, the Tathāgata did not utter a single word"?

The major schools of Buddhist philosophy in India each set forth its own opinion as to the nature of the Buddha's final view. They were still faced with the difficulty, however, of accounting for those statements that seemed to contradict what they understood the Buddha's final position to be on some point of doctrine. This problem provided the impetus for the development of interpretative formulae in India, the formal beginning of Buddhist hermeneutics. The situation was further complicated by the existence of interpretative guidelines in discourses attributed to the Buddha himself; the Buddha was seen in some instances to provide autocommentaries in which he explained what he meant by some previous teaching, while in other instances he provided rules for the interpretation of his own statements. One such guideline was that found in the *Catuḥpratisaraṇasūtra,* in which the Buddha provided four reliances:

> Rely on the teaching, not the teacher.
> Rely on the meaning, not the letter.
> Rely on the definitive meaning *(nītārtha),* not the interpretable meaning *(neyārtha).*
> Rely on wisdom *(jñāna),* not on [ordinary] consciousness *(vijñāna).*

Another schema is that provided in the seventh chapter of the *Saṃdhinirmocanasūtra,* where the teaching of the Buddha is divided into three stages or wheels of doctrine, with the first two being declared provisional and the third and final stage definitive.

The situation in China was complicated by several factors, beginning with the fact that when the Buddhist teachings entered China during the Han dynasty, they entered a culture quite alien to that of India. Furthermore, the Buddhist sūtras arrived in a haphazard fashion, and the

Chinese were soon bewildered by the conflicting claims to authority made by various texts and teachers. They responded by devising a number of classification systems *(p'an-chiao)* which attempted to order the various sūtras and sūtra genres according to when they were taught by the Buddha and to whom. As was the case in India, a divergence of opinion occurred as to which sūtra constituted the Buddha's highest and final teaching, with the T'ien-t'ai school, for example, placing the *Lotus Sūtra (Saddharmapuṇḍarīka)* atop its hierarchy and the Hua-yen school assigning the *Avataṃsakasūtra* to that position.

The Japanese appropriated the Chinese rubrics at first but came to take a more radical and exclusionary hermeneutical stance during the Kamakura period when the Zen, Pure Land, and Nichiren schools each claimed that their interpretation of the teachings of the Buddha constituted the sole vehicle to enlightenment.

The Tibetans, benefiting from the relatively late propagation of Buddhism in their snowy land, were able to systematize the various interpretative strategies devised in India. They also took over the task of seeking to find meaning and consistency in the often cryptic tantric literature, and developed hermeneutical principles to that end.

The hermeneutical dilemma faced by Buddhism in its various forms is summarized by Robert A. F. Thurman:

> Imagine for a moment that Jesus taught for about fifty years, to close disciples numbering in the thousands; that his pedagogical aim and skill were such that he formulated doctrines to resonate precisely with the abilities and inclinations of each disciple; that while recommending devotionalism to many, he taught others to rely on the intellect, and still others to rely on works motivated by love and compassion; that he constantly demanded critical reflection on the deeper meaning of his teachings; that he sometimes even provided conceptual schemes with which to interpret his own doctrines, which schemes sometimes included dismissal of the ultimate validity of a teaching he had previously set forth unequivocally; that it sometimes happened that two such schemes referred to each other as merely conditional, valid only in that other context; and that in spite of these apparent contradictions he had to be accepted as a supreme authority, incapable of self-contradiction; and finally that different groups of his disciples preserved traditional records of his promulgations in different places, some not even knowing of the existence of the others during certain periods during and after the Teacher's lifetime. It is easy to see that all this would result in the situation for all later generations in which a bewildering profusion of doctrines, all embedded in hallowed scriptural traditions, is presented as uniformly authentic.[4]

The essays in this volume demonstrate the various ways in which Buddhist exegetes dealt with this situation. It is not the purpose of this volume to identify some specific and unique "Buddhist" hermeneutic, but rather to suggest some of the problems encountered by Buddhist scholars in the interpretation of their scriptures, as well as the principles of interpretation that they developed in response to those problems.

It would be difficult to summarize here the salient points of each of the essays in the volume. However, there are a number of recurrent issues that appear central to the hermeneutical enterprise in Buddhism and that warrant brief consideration. These include the use of the doctrine of upāya as a hermeneutical principle, the role of spiritual development in understanding a text, the relationship between hermeneutics and soteriology, and the question of the existence of historical consciousness in Buddhism.

As we have seen, a belief common to the major schools of Buddhist thought in Asia is that the Buddha did not teach the same thing to all, but rather expediently adapted his message to meet the specific needs of his audience. Based on his knowledge of the interests, needs, and capacities of his listeners, he is said to have taught what was most appropriate for each. Furthermore, his approach seems to have been facultative rather than dogmatic with regard to the acceptance of his teachings. He adjured his followers to adopt only what they found to be apodictic:

> Like gold that is melted, cut, and polished,
> So should monks and scholars
> Analyze my words [before] accepting them;
> They should not do so out of respect.[5]

But how should these words be analyzed? It was the conviction of the various Buddhist schools that the Buddha was not an agnostic; moreover, his teachings were never regarded as ultimately contentless forms to be filled by interpretations projected by his followers, as in a Rorschach inkblot. Rather, it was their belief that the antinomic character of his teaching was only apparent and that his final view could be ascertained. Seeking to determine this final view became an overriding concern in Buddhist hermeneutics, and it is not surprising that the doctrine of upāya, of the Buddha's skillful methods in teaching the doctrine, which caused such problems in the interpretation of scripture should itself become a principle by which that interpretation was undertaken. Peter Gregory points out that the various Chinese *p'an-chiao* classifications were based on the notion of upāya, that the Buddha's teaching was bound by context. Upāya also seems to form the basis of textual taxonomies that are as ostensibly disparate as those set forth in the Theravāda *Netti Pakaraṇa* and Kūkai's *Jūjūshinron*. As George Bond shows, the Theravādin exegetes based their hermeneutical strategy on the idea of a gradual path to enlightenment. Hence, they delineated a typology of persons, based on factors such as level of spiritual development and temperament, to whom the Buddha addressed his teaching. They then classified the *suttas* and their appropriate audiences, forming a correlation between types of scriptures and types of personalities. The exegetes were thus able to construe a "hierarchy of means and ends necessary to relate the *dhamma* to a variety of people and yet to maintain the belief in one ultimate goal and one ultimate meaning of the *dhamma.*"

Kūkai's ten stages, discussed by Thomas Kasulis, were far more comprehensive in scope, attempting to encompass all spiritual levels from the ramlike state of ignorance to the enlightened Shingon participation in the dharmakāya, and all the philosophies current in Heian Japan, including Confucianism and Taoism as well as the various Buddhist schools. However, like the Theravāda, Kūkai envisioned a progression from lowest to highest through appropriate spiritual development, ending finally in the experience of enlightenment.

As I note in my essay on the interpretation of the Mahāyāna sūtras in India, upāya did not function simply as a hermeneutic of accommodation, in which all the Buddha's teachings are understood as appropriate; it also served as a hermeneutic of control, whereby rival philosophies are subsumed. Even the Ch'an school, renowned as "a special transmission outside the scriptures," selectively used scripture to uphold sectarian positions, as Robert Buswell demonstrates. Thus, each school placed a different text or teaching at the pinnacle of its hierarchy: for Kūkai it was his own Shingon school; for T'ien-t'ai it was the *Lotus Sūtra,* and for Hua-yen, the *Avataṃsakasūtra.* Candrakīrti looked to the *Akṣayamatinirdeśasūtra* for his understanding of what constitutes the definitive *(nītārtha)* and the interpretable *(neyārtha)* while the *Saṃdhinirmocana* provided those criteria for the Yogācāra. As Lamotte notes, "Each school tends to take literally the doctrinal texts which conform to its theses and to consider those which cause dilemmas as being of provisional meaning." This trend makes the Ch'an and Hua-yen patriarch Tsung-mi's recognition of the danger in the perfect teaching of the interpenetration of phenomena and phenomena *(shih shih wu ai),* as discussed by Peter Gregory, particularly intriguing.

It would be misleading, however, to see the hermeneutical concern with upāya as motivated purely by intersectarian polemic. It is motivated by a more difficult problem: what was the most exalted vision of the Buddha? To what final truth was he leading his disciples with his skillful methods? Robert Buswell correctly identifies the fundamental question of Mahāyāna hermeneutics: what was the content of the Buddha's enlightenment? Korean Ch'an addressed this question by attempting to make the step from the principles by which the truth is explained to the direct experience of that truth, labeling theoretical statements "dead words" and statements that effect realization "live words."

This distinction leads immediately to the question of establishing the Buddha's intention in giving a specific teaching. As I note in my essay, this concern with intention may very well run counter to modern trends in hermeneutics, but its centrality to the Buddhist interpretation of scripture is undeniable. Indeed, Michael Broido remarks that "it seems wholly plausible that we shall be able to make sense of the Buddhist hermeneutical enterprise by seeing it as founded upon intention-ascription." (Broido shows that this is equally true of the tantras as well as of the sūtras.) The various hermeneutical tools devised by the Buddhists, including the categories of the definitive *(nītārtha)* and the interpretable *(neyārtha),* the four special intentions *(abhiprāya)* and the four hidden intentions *(abhisaṃdhi)* (all discussed by Lamotte), as well as the seven ornaments *(alaṃkāra)* and the six alternatives or parameters *(koṭi)* employed in the interpretation of the tantras (discussed by Robert Thurman), are all concerned in some way with determining the intention of a particular statement.

If the goal of Mahāyāna philosophy is to bring oneself and others to the experience of enlightenment, which is nothing more or less than a repetition of the experience of the Buddha, then the attempt to establish the intention of the author, the goal of what Gadamer terms the Romantic endeavor, has strong soteriological overtones for the Buddhist. In this respect, the discussion of the intended audience of a given teaching is not merely a device by which one can relegate one's opponent to the audience of a provisional teaching. Rather, it is a means by which the interpreter attempts to find his own place among the circle surrounding the Buddha.

If the Buddhist interpreters sought in their way to follow Schleiermacher's dictum that to understand the text one must experience the mental processes of the author, then the interpreters were compelled to become enlightened, and that, indeed, would seem to be their ultimate goal. It would follow, then, that it is the experience of the Buddha's enlightenment that provides final validity in interpretation. Étienne Lamotte derives this position from the fact that the last of the four reliances is to rely on wisdom *(jñāna)* and not on ordinary consciousness *(vijñāna)*. For Lamotte, this wisdom "constitutes the single and indispensable instrument of true exegesis." His view is supported by the *Saṃdhinirmocanasūtra* (VIII.24) which says:

> Through a wisdom arisen from [hearing] the doctrine, Bodhisattvas base themselves upon the words [of the sūtras], take the text literally, and do not

> yet understand the intention. . . . Through a wisdom arisen from thinking, Bodhisattvas do not base themselves solely upon the words or take the meaning literally, and understand the intention. . . . Through a wisdom arisen from meditation, Bodhisattvas either base themselves on the words or do not, either take the text literally or do not, but they understand the intention, manifested through the images which are the object of the *samādhi* that accords with the nature of things.[6]

Indeed, meditational and visionary experience have played an important role in the interpretation of religious texts. In the case of Buddhism, there are many examples, such as Shinran's revelation of the implosion of all practice into the *nembutsu* and Tsong-kha-pa's vision in which Buddhapālita placed his commentary on the *Madhyamakaśāstra* upon Tsong-kha-pa's head, thereby signifying that his was the Indian commentary to follow. Sadly, perhaps, the visions and experiences of enlightenment of the exegetes are by no means uniform, raising the question, which Roger Corless takes up, of the line between valid interpretation and misreading—is the manipulation of texts to conform to sectarian viewpoints justified by religious experience? Here, Gershom Scholem's observation that the mystical approach to sacred texts contains two complementary or contradictory elements, the conservative and the revolutionary, seems especially germane. He writes:

> Precisely because they preserve the foundations of the traditional authority for all time, they are able to treat Scripture with the almost unlimited freedom that never ceases to amaze us in the writings of the mystics, a freedom even to despair, as in our metaphor of the wrong keys. Recognition of the unaltered validity of the traditional authority is the price which these mystics pay for transforming the meaning of the texts in their exegesis. As long as the framework is kept intact, the conservative and revolutionary elements in this type of mystic preserve their balance, or perhaps it would be better to say, their creative tension.[7]

Bracketing the question of whether Buddhism is "mystical," it would seem that the tension between the revolutionary and the conservative exists also in Buddhism, a tension that Matthew Kapstein discerns in Buddhist technical terminology between scripture *(āgama)* and realization *(adhigama)*.

Thus, the dictum that enlightenment provides the final criterion for interpretation raises as many questions as it settles, for Buddhism is a tradition that has developed in history, with new interpretations formulated to resolve crises, scriptures used to legitimate these new interpretations, and those interpretations propagated to establish their superiority. (This threefold process is illustrated by David Chappell in the cases of the Ch'an and Pure Land schools in China.)

The question remains, then, whether enlightenment obviates hermeneutics. Nevertheless it seems certain that without enlightenment, there must be hermeneutics—which, as Alan Sponberg noted at the conference, provides the soteric function of serving as a technique for divesting oneself of illusion, a radical hermeneutics of suspicion. Those who are not yet enlightened must interpret. The Buddhist exegete suffers from a displacement, an absence; he did not sit in the circle at the feet of the Buddha and hear the doctrine that was intended especially for him. Now the Buddha is gone, the audience is gone; now the teaching must be the teacher. The exegete is constantly in search of his place in the absent circle, and his hermeneutics provide the compass.

Some have objected to the application of modern hermeneutical theory to Buddhism because Buddhism lacks the historical consciousness that has, in large part, defined the hermeneutical enterprise since Heidegger. But there is historical consciousness in Buddhism, often understood in terms of one's temporal distance from the Buddha, as in the various theories of the degeneration of the doctrine, or in the attempts to account for the late appearance of the Mahāyāna sūtras and the tantras, or the emphasis on lineage in the Ch'an and Tibetan traditions. In his remarks at the conference, Carl Bielefeldt observed that the very fact that there is something called hermeneutics in Buddhism is a sign of alienation, of distance from a tradition that Buddhist thinkers felt the need to somehow recover. He also discussed the tension between the historical and ahistorical as manifested in Chih-i's use of the *Lotus Sūtra.* Chih-i encompassed the doctrine of the Buddha in four teachings: the Hīnayāna sūtras teach being, the early Mādhyamika teaches nonbeing, the tathāgatagarbha teaches both, and the perfect teaching, that of the *Lotus Sūtra,* neither. Chih-i saw these four teachings as unfolding sequentially in the teachings of the Buddha historically and as unfolding in the experience of the practitioner as well. But such a historical system raises an entirely new set of questions, for if we are living in an age in which the perfect teaching has been fully revealed, what is left for us to discover? Such questions suggest that the relationship between the historical and the ahistorical, of the putatively timeless nature of the Buddha's enlightenment and the manifestation of that enlightenment in time, calls for our further reflection.

Among the questions left unexplored in this volume is that of the hermeneutical enterprise not of the ancient Buddhist exegete but of the modern western Buddhologist. Although it is impossible in light of the work of Gadamer to separate the study of Buddhist hermeneutics from the question of the hermeneutics—the principles and presuppositions of interpretation—of the modern scholars who today interpret Buddhist texts, such a separation is attempted here (perhaps naively), with the essays devoted to an evaluation of the dynamic relationship that existed between Buddhist scriptures and their traditional exegetes. An attempt to become aware of the prejudices and preunderstandings that the modern Buddhologist, alienated from his subject by both time and culture, brings to the study of Buddhist texts remains a desideratum.[8]

It is hoped that this study will spur further interest in what is referred to here as Buddhist hermeneutics—interest in defining more precisely the meaning of that term as well as the ways in which the hermeneutical undertaking manifests itself in Buddhist thought, not only to contribute to our understanding of Buddhism but to provide alternative approaches to the problems of hermeneutics in the west.

Notes

1. From the *Mahāparinibbannasutta* (60), translated by Henry Clarke Warren in *Buddhism in Translations* (New York: Atheneum, 1984), 107.

2. For ancient and modern understandings of the term, see Richard Palmer, *Hermeneutics* (Evanston: Northwestern University Press, 1969), 12–45.

3. For the Sanskrit, see P. L. Vaidya, ed., *Madhyamakaśāstra of Nāgārjuna* (Darbhanga: Mithila Institute, 1960), 310.

4. Robert A. F. Thurman, "Buddhist Hermeneutics," *Journal of the American Academy of Religion* 46, no. 1 (January 1978): 22.

5. Cited by Tsong-kha-pa in *Drang nges legs bshad snying po* (Sarnath: Pleasure of Elegant Sayings Press, 1973), 3. Robert A. F. Thurman has located the passage in Śantarakṣita's *Tattvasaṃgraha*; see Thurman, *Tsong-khapa's Speech of Gold in the Essence of True Eloquence* (Princeton: Princeton University Press, 1984), 190 n. 12.

6. For the Tibetan, see Étienne Lamotte, ed., *Saṃdhinirmocana Sūtra: L'Explication des Mystères* (Paris: Adrien Maisonneuve, 1935), 105. Thanks to John Keenan for pointing out this passage.

7. Gershom Scholem, "Religious Authority and Mysticism," in *On the Kabbalah and Its Symbolism* (New York: Schocken Books, 1969), 13.

8. A call for such an undertaking was recently made by John Maraldo in "Hermeneutics and Historicity in the Study of Buddhism," *The Eastern Buddhist* 19, no.1 (Spring 1986): 17–43.

The Assessment of Textual Interpretation in Buddhism

ÉTIENNE LAMOTTE

In *India Antiqua,* a volume of articles published in honor of the eminent archaeologist J. P. Vogel, there is a contribution of mine entitled "La critique d'authenticité dans le bouddhisme."[1] It was concerned with the *Mahāpadeśa* (Discourse on the Great Authorities), in which the rules for the assessment of textual authenticity according to the minds of Buddhist scholars were recorded: for a text to be considered as the "word of the Buddha," it must be based on the authority of the Buddha himself, of a formally constituted community, of one of several particularly learned "elders"; it should further be in harmony with the doctrinal texts *(sūtra),* the disciplinary collections *(vinaya),* and the spirit of Buddhist philosophy.

Once the authenticity of a text has been duly established it remains to supply a correct interpretation of it, to understand what the author is saying and, especially, what he is trying to say; it is to this assessment of interpretation that we wish to devote the present article and offer it in homage and respect to Professor Henri Grégoire, whose splendid discoveries in the fields of Byzantine studies, epic literature and comparative mythology are sealed with the stamp of the most sure assessment and the most penetrating exegesis. While not attaining his incomparable virtuosity, the early Buddhist thinkers attempted to define and apply the rules of sound textual interpretation. Such rules are formulated in the *Catuḥpratisaraṇasūtra* (Sūtra of the Four Refuges), of which we possess several versions in Sanskrit and Chinese. However, while the *Mahāpadeśasūtra,* which deals with the assessment of textual authenticity, appears in the earliest collections of the sūtras and vinayas, the *Catuḥpratisaraṇasūtra,* which is devoted to the assessment of interpretation, is unknown to the canonical literature in its strict sense and seems to have been compiled at a later date. It first appears in compositions pertaining to the Sarvāstivādin-Vaibhāṣika school, such as the *Abhidharmakośa* (trans. L. de la Vallée Poussin, IX.246), the *Abhidharmakośavyākhyā* (ed. U. Wogihara, 704), and the *Mahāvyutpatti* (ed. R. Sakaki, nos. 1546–1549); it is again found in the sūtras and śāstras of the Mādhyamika school, such as the *Akṣayamatinirdeśasūtra* quoted in the *Madhyamakavṛtti* (ed. L. de la Vallée Poussin, 43), the *Mahāprajñāpāramitāśāstra* (translated as *Traité de la Grande Vertu de Sagesse,* 1:536–540), and the *Dharmasaṃgraha* (ed. Max Müller, chap. 53); finally, it is repeated in several treatises of the Yogācāra school, such as the *Bodhisattvabhūmi* (ed. U. Wogihara, 256) and the *Sūtrālaṃkāra* (ed. S. Lévi, 138). Nevertheless, even if the sūtra in question was not given its definitive form until a period after the establishment of the Buddhist sects and schools, the ideas which it contains had already been evolving since the earliest texts of the Buddhist canon.

The *Catuḥpratisaraṇasūtra* posits, under the name of refuges *(pratisaraṇa),* four rules of textual interpretation: (1) the dharma is the refuge and not the person; (2) the spirit is the refuge and not the letter; (3) the sūtra of precise meaning is the refuge and not the sūtra of provisional meaning; (4) (direct) knowledge is the refuge and not (discursive) consciousness.[2] As will be seen, the aim of this sūtra is not to condemn in the name of sound assessment certain methods of interpretation of the texts, but merely to ensure the subordination of human authority to the spirit of the dharma, the letter to the spirit, the sūtra of provisional meaning to the sūtra of precise meaning, and discursive consciousness to direct knowledge.

I. *The doctrine (dharma) is the refuge and not the person (puruṣa).* This first principle merely consists of summarizing the rules of the assessment of textual authenticity which were already formulated in the *Mahāpadeśasūtra:* in order that a text be accepted as the "word of the Buddha" it is not sufficient to call upon the authority of the Buddha himself, upon a religious community *(saṃgha)* which has been formally established, or upon one of several particularly learned elders; the text in question must also be found in the sūtra *(sūtra 'vatarati),* appear in the vinaya *(vinaye saṃdṛśyate),* and not contradict the nature of things *(dharmatāṃ ca na vilomayati).* In other words, adherence to the doctrine cannot be dependent on human authority, however respectable, since experience shows that human evidence is contradictory and changeable; adherence should be based on personal reasoning *(yukti),* on what one has oneself known *(jñāta),* seen *(dṛṣṭa)* and grasped *(vidita).*[3] "By relying on reasoning and not on a person's authority, one does not deviate from the meaning of reality, because one is autonomous, independent of others when confronted with rationally examined truths."[4] Nevertheless, in the case of a beginner who is unable to understand by himself the teaching which has been given to him, faith in the master's word is a provisional necessity: "The [beginner] merely adheres to the profound texts which his intelligence cannot fathom; he tells himself those are truths within reach of the Buddha and not within reach of our intelligence, and he refrains from rejecting them. In this way, he is protected from any fault."[5] To the mind of Buddhists, the judicious application of the *mahāpadeśas* is directed less at supplying the historian with rules for assessment than at making the devotee become indissolubly wedded to the *saddharma*. If he is incapable of grasping it himself, he should at least adhere to it with faith, since "by adhering to the holy dharma, one does not perish."[6]

II. *The spirit (artha) is the refuge and not the letter (vyañjana).* The meaning is single and invariable, while the letter is multiple and infinitely variable. Buddhist exegetes often wondered anxiously whether one and the same entity or one and the same truth was not concealed under different terms. The monks of the Macchikāsaṇḍa debated among themselves in order to know whether the expressions "fetter" *(saññojana)* or "fettering things" *(saññojaniyā dhamma)* designated one and the same thing *(ekattha)* or different things *(nānattha)*.[7] The venerable Godatta thought he knew, from a certain point of view, that the four mental liberations *(cetovimutti)* are identical in meaning but different in expression *(ime dhammā ekatthā vyañjanaṃ eva nānan ti)*.[8] The four noble truths which were expounded in Vārāṇasī have only one acceptable meaning, but they can be explained in an infinity of ways. Hence, with regard to the first truth, "the fact of [universal] suffering is true, not false or changeable, but many are the subtleties and terms, many are the means of explaining that first noble truth of suffering."[9]

Although the spirit takes precedence, the good doctrine is perfect in its spirit and in its letter. This twofold perfection characterizes the dharma which the Buddha expounded; it is also found in a good monk, a good instructor and a student. A formula which is repeated incessantly throughout the canonical writings states that the Buddha expounds a dharma which is "good in the beginning, in the middle and at the end: the meaning is good *(sāttha)* and the letter is good *(savyañjana)*." The *Sūtrālaṃkāra* explains that the meaning is good because it applies to conventional truth and absolute truth, and that its letter is good because the phrases and syllables are intelligible.[10] The early texts laud the perfect monk "who correctly grasps the meaning and correctly applies its terms";[11] his colleagues consider it a gain and an advantage to have a fellow-member who is so expert in the meaning and the formula.[12] Conversely, if a monk has discovered the right formula but misunderstands the meaning, his colleagues should chide him patiently and say to him:

"That formula [which we accept as you do], does it not have this meaning rather than that meaning?"[13]; if a monk correctly grasps the meaning but uses a faulty expression, he should be taxed: "In order to render that meaning [over which we are in agreement], is not this formula more suitable than that formula?"[14] A good speaker is he who is not mistaken over the spirit or the letter,[15] and it is all for the best if he speaks *at length* and *well* and if those listening to him are capable of judging whether he is right or wrong.[16] The talented instructor "teaches the phrases and syllables according to the requisite order; then, once those phrases and syllables have been taught, he explains them from the point of view of their meaning according to the requisite order."[17] It is advantageous for the student to hear the dharma at the appropriate time and to examine its spirit at the appropriate time.[18] Nāgasena, who was a model disciple of Dhammarakkhita, learned in three months, with the help of a single recitation, the word of the Buddha which is contained in the three baskets and, in a further three months, he mastered its meaning.[19]

It ensues from what has just been described that the monk who limits himself to memorizing the texts without attempting to understand them is failing in his duty: "There are some foolish men who learn the *dhamma, suttas, geyas,* and so on by heart but once they have learned it by heart they do not examine the meaning in order to understand the texts. Those texts, the meaning of which they have not examined in order to understand them, do not please them and the only advantage they gain from their memorization is to be able to contradict [their adversaries] and to give quotations; all the same, they do not reach the goal for the sake of which they memorized the *dhamma;* those texts which they do not understand will, for a long time, earn them much sorrow and suffering. Why? Because those texts have not been understood."[20]

Whoever memorizes the *dhamma* like a parrot at least has the merit of being able to transmit it materially in an impeccable form. However, such a monk is one of those who "memorize texts which have not been understood and the phrases and syllables of which are wrongly arranged":[21] such monks conduce to the confusion and destruction of the *saddhamma.*[22] In fact, when the form is faulty, all hope of discovering the correct meaning is lost: "If the phrases and syllables are wrongly arranged, the meaning in turn is impossible to discover."[23]

It is clear that it is far from the intention of the *Catuḥpratisaraṇsūtra* to deny the importance of the letter, but only to subordinate it to the spirit. According to Buddhist concepts, there are cases in which the letter must be sacrificed for the sake of the spirit; its function is to indicate the meaning, but it is never able to express it in an adequate way.

That the letter is not absolutely indispensable is confirmed by the famous meeting between Śāriputra and Aśvajit, one of the Buddha's first five disciples.[24] The latter had just embraced the new religion when he was questioned by Śāriputra about Śākyamuni's teaching. Aśvajit at first attempted to evade Śāriputra by saying: "Friend, I am only a novice and it is not long since I left the world; I only recently embraced this doctrine and discipline. I cannot propound the doctrine to its full extent *(vitthāreṇa dhammam desetem),* but I can briefly indicate its spirit *(api ca saṃkhittena atthaṃ vakkhāmi).*" Then the wandering mendicant Śāriputra said to the venerable Aśvajit: "Let it be so, my friend. Tell me a little or a great deal of it, but speak to me of its spirit; I need only the spirit, so why be so preoccupied with the letter?"[25]

The letter indicates the spirit just as a fingertip indicates an object, but since the spirit is alien to syllables *(akṣaravarjita),* the letter is unable to express it in full. Purely literal exegesis is therefore bound to fail. The theme of the letter which kills and the spirit which enlivens is elaborated several times in the *Laṅkāvatārasūtra,* of which we will merely quote a page here:

> O Mahāmati, the son and daughter of good family should not interpret the spirit according to the letter *(yathārutārthābhiniveśa)* since reality is not connected with syllables *(nirakṣaratvāt tattvasya).* One should not act like those who look at the finger *(aṅguliprekṣaka):* it is as if someone pointed out something with his finger to someone else and the latter persisted in staring at the fingertip [instead of looking at the object indicated]; similarly, just like children, foolish worldlings end their lives as attached to that fingertip which consists of the literal translation and, by neglecting the meaning indicated by the fingertip of literal interpretation, they never reach the higher meaning. It is as if someone were to give some rice to children, for whom it is the customary food, to eat but without cooking it; whoever were to act in such a way should be considered foolish, since he has not understood that the rice must first be cooked; equally, the nonarising and nondestruction [of all things] is not revealed if it has not been prepared; it is therefore necessary to train and not to act like someone who thinks he has seen an object merely by looking at a fingertip. For this reason, one should try and reach the spirit. The spirit, which is in isolation *(vivikta),* is a cause of nirvāṇa, while the letter, which is bound up with discrimination *(vikalpasaṃbaddha)* favors saṃsāra. The spirit is acquired in the company of educated people, and through learning *(bāhaśrutya),* one should be conversant with the spirit *(arthakauśalya)* and not conversant with the letter *(rutakauśalya).* To be conversant with the spirit is a view which is alien to the discussions of all the sectaries: it is not lapsing into it oneself and not making others lapse into it. In such conditions, there is a learning of the spirit. Such are those who should be approached by someone who seeks the spirit; the others, those who are attached to the literal interpretation, should be avoided by those who seek the truth.[26]

If scholars counseled the search for the spirit with so much insistence, it is because the meaning of the texts often lacks clarity and needs to be interpreted. This led to the imposition of the third rule.

III. *The sūtra of precise meaning (nītārtha) is the refuge, not (the sūtra) the meaning of which requires interpretation (neyārtha).* This distinction is not accepted by the Mahāsaṃghika school, which is of the opinion that "in all that the Blessed One expounded, there is nothing which does not conform to the meaning *(ayathārtha),* and that all the sūtras propounded by the Buddha are precise in meaning *(nītārtha).*"[27] However, that position is not easy to defend, since many sūtras contradict each other. Thus, to take just one example, the text of the *Bimbisārasūtra* states: "Foolish worldlings *(bālapṛthagjana)* who have not learned anything *(aśrutvat)* take the self for their self and are attached to the self. But there is no self *(ātman)* or anything pertaining to the self *(ātmīya);* the self is empty and anything pertaining to the self is empty."[28] This text, which denies the existence of a soul, is contradicted by another canonical passage, in the words of which: "An individual *(ekapudgala)* born in the world is born for the welfare of many."[29] If those two texts are taken literally, one is forced to conclude that the Buddha contradicted himself. For fear of maligning the omniscient one, the Sarvāstivādins, followed by the scholars of the Mahāyāna, preferred to accept that certain sūtras should be taken literally while others should be interpreted. According to Vasumitra and Bhavya, theses 49 and 50 of the Sarvāstivādins state that the Blessed One uttered words which were not in accordance with the meaning *(ayārtha),* that sūtras spoken by the Buddha were not all precise in meaning *(nītārtha)* and that the Buddha himself said that certain sūtras were indeterminate in meaning *(anītārtha).*[30]

The need for a fluid exegesis is admirably emphasized in the *Treatise* by Nāgārjuna: "The dharma of the Buddhas is immense, like the ocean. Depending on the aptitude of beings, it is expounded in various ways: sometimes it speaks of existence and sometimes of nonexistence, eternity or permanence, suffering or happiness, the self or the not-self; sometimes it teaches the diligent practice of the threefold activity [of body, speech and mind] which includes all good dharmas, and sometimes it teaches that all dharmas are intrinsically inactive. Such are the manifold and diverse teachings; an ignorant person who hears them considers them to be perversions, but the wise man who penetrates the threefold teaching of the dharma knows that all the words of the Buddha are the true dharma and do not contradict each other. The threefold teaching is the teaching of the [Sūtra]-piṭaka, the Abhidharma and Emptiness."[31] Having defined it, the *Treatise* continues: "The man who penetrates the threefold teaching knows that the Buddha's teachings do not contradict each other. To understand that is the power of the perfection of wisdom *(prajñāpāramitā)* which, when confronted with all the Buddha's teachings, does not encounter any impediment. Whoever has not grasped the rule of the *prajñāpāramitā* [will encounter numerous contradictions in the interpretation of the dharma]: if he takes up the teaching of the Abhidharma, he will lapse into nihilism; if he takes up the teaching of the Piṭaka, he will lapse [sometimes] into realism and [sometimes] into nihilism."[32]

It was in order to answer the requirements of exegesis that the distinction between sūtras of precise meaning and sūtras of indeterminate meaning was conceived. The *nītārtha* sūtra (Tib. *nges pa'i don,* Ch. *liao i*) is a sūtra the meaning of which is clear (*vibhaktārtha*; cf. *Kośa* III.75) and explicit (*kathattha*; cf. *Manorathapūraṇī* II.118); when taught without any ulterior motive *(niḥparyāyadeśita),* it can and should be taken literally. In contrast, the *neyārtha* sūtra (Tib. *drang ba'i don,* Ch. *pu liao i*) is one the meaning of which needs to be deduced (*yassa attho netabbo*; cf. *Manorathapūraṇī* II.118), because it is intentional *(ābhiprāyika)* and derives from a motivation *(paryāyadeśita).* The *neyārtha* sūtras constitute the *saṃdhāvacana,* the intentional teaching of the Buddha.

Three questions arise in connection with the *neyārtha* sūtras: Should they be accepted? How can they be distinguished from *nītārtha* sūtras? How should they be correctly interpreted?

1. The *neyārtha* sūtras are just as much the word of the Buddha as the *nītārtha* sūtras. They should therefore be accepted, and those who reject them by saying, "That is not the word of the Buddha but the word of Māra" commit a serious fault in repudiating the good doctrine *(saddharmapratikṣepakarmāvāraṇa).* The *Sarvadharmavaipulyasaṃgrahasūtra* says: "Subtle, O Manjuśrī, is the impediment which consists of repudiating the good doctrine. Whoever at times approves a text expounded by the Tathāgata and at others disapproves another one is repudiating the good doctrine. Whoever repudiates the good doctrine in that way maligns the Tathāgata, repudiates the doctrine and denies the community."[33]

2. With regard to the means of distinguishing between *nītārtha* and *neyārtha* sūtras, the authors turn out to be reticent, and we can only examine their method of procedure in each particular case. There is a very clear impression that the distinction is based on purely subjective criteria, which explains why, quite frequently, the scholars are not in agreement.

The *Treatise* by Nāgārjuna (I.539–540) considers sūtras to be of precise meaning when the allegations are obvious and easily understood, and sūtras the meaning of which needs to be determined are those which through skillful means *(upāya)* say things which at first sight seem to be incorrect and which demand an explanation. For example, the *sutta* in the *Aṅguttara* (III.41) on the five advantages of giving is a *nītārtha* sūtra because it is obvious that giving is meritorious; in contrast, another *sutta,* which attributes the same advantages of giving to teaching, is *neyārtha* because it is less clear that teaching, which cannot be translated by material giving, is as meritorious as almsgiving. However, after due reflection, the teacher has the same merit as the donor since, by praising almsgiving in all manner of ways, he is combatting his own avarice and that of others.

In general, it is considerations of a doctrinal type which enable a decision to be reached as to whether a sūtra is precise in meaning or with a meaning to be determined. The Hīnayāna and Mahāyāna are in agreement in rejecting the belief in the self *(ātmagraha)* and proclaim the nonexistence of the individual *(pudgalanairātmya).* However, we find texts in both vehicles in which the Buddha, in order to place himself within his listeners' range, speaks of a soul, a living being, a man, an individual, and so on. Scholars consider such texts to be *neyārtha* and requiring explanation, if not correction. Conversely, they regard as *nītārtha* and literal the Hīnayāna texts in which there is a question of impermanence *(anitya),* suffering *(duḥkha),* and impersonality *(anātman)* as well as Mahāyāna passages which deal with universal emptiness *(śūnyatā).* Here are some quotations which illustrate this statement:

For Buddhaghosa (in *Manorathapūraṇī* II.118), sūtras in which it is a matter of one or several individuals (cf. *Aṅguttara* I.22) are *neyārtha,* because "from the absolute point of view *(paramatthato)* no individual exists." In contrast, sūtras which deal with impermanence, suffering and the not-self (cf. *Aṅguttara* I.286) are *nītārtha,* since "whether or not the Tathāgatas appear in the world, that natural causality, that basic suchness of things remains."

The *Akṣayamatinirdeśasūtra* says: "Which are the doctrinal texts with a meaning to be determined *(neyārtha)* and which are the doctrinal texts of precise meaning *(nītārtha)*? The texts which have been expounded in order to teach the path of penetration *(mārgāvatārāya nirdiṣṭa)* are called *neyārtha;* those which have been expounded in order to teach the fruit of penetration *(phalāvatārāya nirdiṣṭa)* are called *nītārtha.* All texts which teach emptiness *(śūnyatā),* signlessness *(ānimitta),* wishlessness *(apraṇihita),* effortlessness *(anabhisaṃskāra),* nonbirth *(ajāta),* nonarising *(anutpāda),* nonexistence *(abhāva),* the not-self *(anātman),* the absence of a living being *(jīva),* of an individual *(pudgala)* and of a master *(svāmin),* such texts are called *nītārtha.*"[34]

Finally, the *Samādhirājasūtra* in turn declares: "Whoever knows the value of texts with a precise meaning knows the [precise] way in which emptiness has been taught by the Sugata; however, wherever there is a matter of an individual, being or man, he knows that all those texts are to be taken as having a provisional meaning."[35]

The subjective nature of this criterion is immediately apparent and explains the frequent disagreement between scholars: each school tends to take literally the doctrinal texts which conform to its theses and to consider those which cause dilemmas as being of provisional meaning. These are some of the texts which have been disputed over:

The Vaibhāṣikas considered *āvidya* (ignorance) and the other links of dependent origination as so many specific entities; the Sautrāntikas were of the opinion that *āvidya* is not a thing apart, but a modality of *prajñā* (wisdom). In order to support their thesis, the Sautrāntikas cited as their authority a sūtra in which it is said: "What is *āvidya?* Non-knowledge in relation to the past *(pūrvānte ajñānam)*"; that sūtra, they said, is clear and precise in meaning *(nītārtha);* you cannot therefore claim it is a sūtra with a meaning to be determined *(neyārtha).* The Vaibhāṣikas responded: "Nothing substantiates that that sūtra is clear in meaning; the fact that it is expressed in terms of definition proves nothing."[36]

The Vātsīputrīyas, who believed in the existence of an ineffable *pudgala,* based their authority on the *Bhārahārasūtra,* in which it is said: "The bearer of the burden [of existence] is such-and-such a venerable one, with such-and-such a name, from such-and-such a family, such-and-such a clan, etc.,"[37] and other similar sūtras which they took literally. The other Buddhist schools, while not rejecting such texts, only accepted that they have a provisional meaning and are not authoritative; they resorted to sūtras which are explicit in meaning and formally taught that, within that supposed *pudgala,* "there are merely things which are impermanent, conditioned, arisen from causes and conditions, and are created by action."[38]

In order to refute the existence of an external object, the Vijñānavādins took their authority from a passage in the *Daśabhūmika* (p. 49) which states that the triple world is mind only *(cittamātram idaṃ yad idaṃ traidhātukam).* However, the Mādhyamikas took them severely to task: "You are making yourselves ridiculous," they said, "the intention of the sūtra is nothing like it appears in your minds . . . ; that text only teaches the unimportance of visible things, but not the denial of their existence." However, the Vijñānavādins persisted and produced a passage from the *Laṅkāvatārasūtra* (p. 47) in which it says: "The external thing, however it may appear, does not exist; it is the mind which appears in various guises, such as a body *(deha),* objects of pleasure *(bhoga)* and a place *(sthāna).*" Nonetheless, the Mādhyamikas were determined to prove, in writing and by reasoning, that this quotation was provisional and not definitive.[39]

3. The Mahāyāna attached the greatest importance to sūtras of indeterminate and provisional meaning and which constitute the intentional teaching of the Buddha. The expression "intentional teaching" is rendered in Pali and Sanskrit by *saṃdhāya bhāṣita* (*Majjhima* I.503; *Bodhisattvabhūmi,* 174), *saṃdhāya bhaṇita* (*Dīpavaṃsa,* 5, 34), *saṃdhāya vāg bhāṣitā* (*Vajracchedikā,* 23), *saṃdhābhāṣita* (*Saddharmapuṇḍarīka,* 125, 199, 233), *saṃdhābhāṣya* (ibid., 29, 34, 60, 70, 273), *saṃdhāvacana* (ibid., 59), *saṃdhāya vacana* (*Bodhisattvabhūmi,* 56, 108). In Tibetan, we find *dgongs te bshad pa,* and in Chinese *mi i yu yen* 'the word of hidden thought'. The *saṃdhābhāṣya* has already been the subject of many studies,[40] so we will merely point out here the procedures which enable us to interpret and "discover the profound intentions of the Buddha" (*gambhīrārthasaṃdhinirmocanatā,* cf. *Bodhisattvabhūmi,* 303).

Sūtras of provisional meaning, which constitute the intentional teaching, should be understood in the light of sūtras the meaning of which is precise; the interpreter will then become determined to discover the point of view which the Buddha was taking as well as the motivation with which he was inspired.

Following the Council of Vaiśālī, certain dissident monks held separate meetings which were known as Mahāsaṃgītis. Among the reproaches with which the Sinhalese chronicle of the *Dīpavaṃsa* addressed those monks, the following complaint can be found: "Not knowing what should not be taken literally *(pariyāyadesita)* or what should be taken literally *(nippariyāyadesita),* not distinguishing the precise meaning *(nītattha)* from the meaning to be determined *(neyyattha),* those monks attribute to what is said with a particular intention *(sandhāya bhaṇita)* another meaning [than the true one] and hence, by respecting the letter *(byañjanacchāyāya),* they destroy a large part of the meaning *(bahu attham vināsayuṃ).*"[41]

The third refuge prescribes taking as one's guide the meaning and not the letter, *nītārtha* and not *neyārtha* sūtras: "The bodhisattva who resorts to the meaning and not to the letter penetrates all the enigmatic words of the Bhagavat Buddhas."[42] "The bodhisattva who has put his faith and confidence in the Tathāgata, trusting his word exclusively, resorts to the sūtra the meaning of which is precise, he cannot deviate from the Buddhist doctrine and discipline. Indeed, in the sūtra the meaning of which has to be determined, the interpretation of the meaning which is diffused in several directions is uncertain and causes hesitation and, if the bodhisattva does not adhere exclusively to the sūtra which is precise in meaning, he might deviate from the Buddhist doctrine and discipline."[43]

However, when the interpreter is certain of having grasped the meaning thanks to the *nītārtha* sūtras, it will profit him greatly to ponder over the enigmatic words of the Buddha which are also an integral part of the *saddharma* and constitute a method of teaching *(deśanānaya)* controlled by skillful means, but the end and aim *(svasiddhānta)* of which consist of a personal comprehension *(adhigama)* of the undefiled element *(anāsrava-dhātu)* which is superior to phrases and syllables.[44] In order to make use of this method of teaching and to understand the enigmatic words, it is important to discover the point of view which inspired the Buddha.

The *Treatise* by Nāgārjuna (I.26–46) lists four points of view *(siddhānta),* only the last of which is absolute *(paramārthika);* the other three pertain to relative or conventional *(saṃvṛti)* truth. The Buddha did not restrict himself to exactness of wording when expressing himself: (1) From the worldly point of view *(laukikasiddhānta),* he often adopted the current idiom and did not hesitate to speak in terms of beings *(sattva)* who die and go to be reborn in the five destinies (e.g. *Digha* I.82); he extolled the role of the single person *(ekapudgala)* who is born into the world for the joy, happiness and benefit of the many (*Aṅguttara* I.22). (2) From the personal point of view *(prātipauruṣikasiddhānta),* the Buddha often tried to adapt his teaching to the intellectual and moral dispositions *(āśaya)* of his listeners. To those who did not believe in the afterlife but believed everything disappears at death, he discoursed on immortality and predicted a fruition in different universes (*Aṅguttara* I.134); to Phalguna, who believed in the eternity of the self, he taught the nonexistence of a person as a thinking and fruition-incurring being (*Saṃyutta* II.13). This might be said to be a contradiction; it is, however, not the least so but merely skillful means *(upaya).* (3) From the remedial point of view *(prātipākṣikasiddhānta),* the Buddha who is the healer of universal suffering varied the remedies according to the diseases to be cured; to the sensuous *(rāgacarita),* he taught the contemplation of a decomposing corpse (*aśubhabhāvanā);* to vindictive and hate-filled men *(dveṣacarita),* he recommended thoughts of goodwill *(maitrīcitta)* regarding those close to one; to the deluded *(mohacarita),* he advised study on the subject of dependent origination *(pratītyasamutpāda).* We should never forget that the omniscient Buddha is less a teacher of philosophy and more a healer of universal suffering: he imparts to every person the teaching which suits them best.

Scholars have attempted to classify the intentions and motivations which guided the Buddha in his teaching.[45] They counted four intentions *(abhiprāya,* Tib. *dgongs pa,* Ch. *i ch'u)* and four motivations *(abhisaṃdhi,* Tib. *ldem por dgongs pa,* Ch. *pi mi).* However, since the two lists overlap, it is preferable, for ease of explanation, to review them together:

A person who might be tempted to feel some scorn for the Buddha *(buddhe 'vajñā)* is informed by the latter that, long ago, he was the Buddha Vipaśvin and fully enlightened *(aham eva sa tena kālena Vipaśvi samyaksaṃbuddho 'bhūvam)*. Obviously, the present Buddha Śākyamuni is not the Buddha Vipaśvin of the past, but he resembles him in all points because both Buddhas participate in the same body of the doctrine *(dharmakāya)*. By expressing himself in that way, the Buddha meant to point out the similarity *(samatābhiprayā)*.

The literal interpretation of the texts *(yathārutārthagrāha)* does not lead to a comprehension of the dharma but, in fact, is equal to scorning the doctrine *(dharme 'vajñā)*. The Buddha therefore teaches that one should have served Buddhas as numerous as the grains of sand in the Ganges in order to arrive at an understanding of the Mahāyāna *(iyato Gaṅganadīvalukāsamanābuddhān paryupāsya mahāyāne 'vabodha utpadyate)*. This is hyperbole since, in order to understand the Mahāyāna, it is not necessary to have served an infinite number of Buddhas; nevertheless, prolonged effort is required. Here, the intention of the Buddha is to speak of another thing *(arthāntarābhiprāya)*.

The lazy *(kusīda)* who do not resolutely practice the means of deliverance are told by the Buddha that those who make an aspiration with a view to the blissful abode will go to be reborn there *(ye sukhāvatyāṃ praṇidhānaṃ kariṣyanti te tatropapatsyante)*. In reality, matters are more complicated but every effort, however minimal, will have its recompense "later." Here, the Buddha is referring to another time *(kālāntarābhiprāya)*.

A virtuous action which is praiseworthy in a beginner appears insufficient on the part of an adherent who is more advanced in perfection. In order to combat satisfaction in mediocrity *(alpasaṃtuṣṭi)*, it happens that the Buddha scorns a virtue in one person which he has just praised in another *(yat tad eva kuśalamūlaṃ kasyacid praśaṃsate kasyacid vigarhate)*: here he is taking into account the dispositions of each individual *(pudgalāśayābhiprāya)*.

In order to cure the sensuous *(rāgacarita)*, the Buddha depicts the splendors of the Buddha-fields to them; so as to discomfit the proud *(mānacarita)*, he describes the supreme perfection of the Buddhas; he encourages those who are tortured by remorse *(kaukṛtya)* by telling them that those who have committed offenses against the Buddhas and bodhisattvas will indeed end by going to the heavens *(ye buddhabodhisattveṣvapakāraṃ kariṣyanti te sarve svargopagā bhaviṣyanti)*. Such declarations should obviously not be taken seriously, but interpreted as is appropriate in the light of sūtras of precise meaning.

Furthermore, and not necessarily intentionally, the Buddha sometimes cultivated paradox and plays on words: this is innocent amusement and not reason for complaint. Some extracts taken from the *Mahāyānasaṃgraha* (II.224–231) are sufficient to illustrate these stylistic methods:

"The bodhisattva," it says, "practices almsgiving extensively when he does not give anything." It should be understood that the bodhisattva does not give anything, because he identifies himself mentally with all those who give, because he has already given away everything he possessed and, finally, because he practices the triply pure giving, in which no distinction is made between the donor, beneficiary and thing given. "The bodhisattva," it says further, "is the supreme slayer of living beings *(prāṇātipātin).*" A fanciful etymology informs us that the bodhisattva is a *prāṇātipātin* insofar as *prāṇ[inaḥ saṃsārato] 'tipātayati,* that is, he "cuts beings off from the round of rebirths" by ensuring their nirvāṇa. Another śāstra dares to claim that the profound attributes of the Buddha correlate with craving *(rāga),* hatred *(dveṣa)* and delusion *(moha).* This is not blasphemy but a profound truth, since all beings, involved as they are with passion, are basically identical to the Buddha and destined to win supreme and perfect enlightenment.

IV. *Direct knowledge (jñāna) is the refuge and not discursive consciousness (vijñāna).* This last exegetical principle, which summarizes the previous three, shows that sound hermeneutics are based not on a literal though theoretical understanding of the noble truths, but on direct knowledge. Here again, the best commentary is supplied by the *Bodhisattvabhūmi:* "The bodhisattva attaches great importance to the knowledge of the direct comprehension [of the truths], and not to mere discursive consciousness of the letter of the meaning, which [consciousness] arises from listening and reflecting. Understanding that what should be known through knowledge arising from meditation cannot be recognized only through discursive consciousness arising from listening and reflecting, he abstains from rejecting or denying the teachings given by the Tathāgata, profound as they are."[46]

The Buddhist truths which the exegeticist seeks to penetrate can be the object of a threefold wisdom, or prajñā arising from listening *(śrutamayī),* reflecting *(cintāmayī)* or meditation *(bhāvanāmayī).*

The first two are worldly *(laukika)* and defiled *(sāsrava)* discursive consciousnesses *(vijñāna),* since, in their empiricism, they remain defiled by craving, hatred and delusion. *Śrutamayī* prajñā which is incurred by oral teaching accepts the truths on faith and is founded on confidence in the words of the Buddha; it is this which caused Siha (in *Aṅguttara* IV.82) to say: "That almsgiving bears fruit here below I do not believe, I know; but that the giver is reborn in heaven, I believe from the Buddha." The object of that wisdom is the word *(nāman)* or the letter, such as it was expounded by the Buddha. *Cintāmayī* prajñā, which follows the preceding, is a personal and reasoned understanding of the truths the meaning *(artha)* of which it grasps and not just the letter. Basing themselves on these, the monks which the *Majjhima* (I.265) presents can declare: "If we say this or that, it is not through respect for the master, but because we ourselves have recognized, seen and understood it."

These first two types of prajñā, which are dialectical in nature, remain blemished by delusion; they are practiced as a preparatory exercise *(prayoga)* by worldlings *(pṛthagjana)* who are not yet committed to the path of nirvāṇa. They are of only provisional value and are meant to be rejected after use. The *Mahāvibhāṣā* (*T* no. 1545, 42.217c–81.420a) and the *Abhidharmakośa* (VI.143) compare the first to a swimming aid which is constantly gripped by a man who does not know how to swim; the second, to the same aid which is sometimes used and at other times disregarded by a poor swimmer. Whoever possesses the third prajñā, wisdom arising from meditation *(bhāvanāmayī),* is like a strong swimmer who crosses the river without any point of support.

Bhāvanāmayī prajñā is no longer discursive consciousness *(vijñāna)* but authentic knowledge *(jñāna),* a direct comprehension of the truths *(satyābhisamaya);* being free from any hint of delusion, it is transcendental *(lokottara)* and undefiled *(anāsrava).* Its sudden acquisition marks the entry into the path of nirvāṇa and confers on the ascetic the quality of holy one *(ārya).* That holy one, during the stage of training *(śaikṣa)* which continues throughout the path of meditation *(bhāvanāmārga),* successively eliminates all the categories of passions which can still coexist with undefiled prajñā; however, it will finally lead him to arhatship where the holy one, having nothing more in which to train *(aśaikṣa),* enjoys nirvāṇa on earth because he knows that his impurities have been destroyed *(āsravakṣayajñāna)* and that they will not arise again *(anutpādajñāna).*

We can, as did L. de la Vallée Poussin,[47] take it as certain that Buddhist prajñā is not a gnosis, a vague apperception of a transcendental reality, as is, for the monists and pantheists of the Vedānta and Brāhminism, the knowledge of the absolute brahman and the consciousness of the identity of the "I" with the brahman. Prajñā has as its object the eternal laws of the dependent origination of phenomena *(pratītyasamutpāda),* and their general marks: impermanence, suffering, impersonality and emptiness; finally, the affirmation of nirvāṇa. Having been prepared through faith and reflection, undefiled prajñā transcends them with its sharpness *(paṭutva)* and attains its object directly. It constitutes the single and indispensable instrument of true exegesis.

From this brief survey, we derive the impression that the Buddhist scholars spared themselves no trouble in order to maintain intact and correctly interpret the extremely varied teachings of Śākyamuni. They were not content with memorizing their letter *(vyañjana),* and they were intent on grasping the meaning *(artha)* through a rational approach. The distinction which they established between texts with a precise meaning *(nītārtha)* and texts with a meaning to be determined *(neyārtha)* is, more often than not, perfectly justified. Even while allowing faith and reflection their due place, they accepted the priority of undefiled prajñā, that direct knowledge which attains its object in all lucidity. We cannot, therefore, accept, as does a certain critic, that as from the first Buddhist Council "a continual process of divergence from the original doctrine of the Teacher is evident";[48] on the contrary, we are of the opinion that the Buddhist doctrine evolved along the lines which its discoverer had unconsciously traced for it.

TRANSLATED BY SARA BOIN-WEBB

Notes

This article was first published as "La critique d'interprétation dans le bouddhisme" in *Annuaire de l'Institut de Philologie et d'Histoire Orientales et Slaves,* vol. 9 (Brussels, 1949), 341–361. Grateful acknowledgement is made to the editors of that journal for permission to publish this English translation by Sara Boin-Webb, which first appeared in *Buddhist Studies Review* 2, no. 1–2 (1985): 4–24.

1. *India Antiqua* (Leiden, 1947), 213–222; English translation in *Buddhist Studies Review* 1 (1): 4–15.

2. Cf. *Abhidharmakośavyākhyā,* 704: *catvārīmāni bhikṣavaḥ pratisaraṇāni. katamāni catvāri. dharmaḥ pratisaraṇaṃ na pudgalaḥ, arthaḥ pratisaraṇaṃ na vyañjanam, nītārthaṃ sūtraṃ pratisaraṇaṃ na neyārtham. jñānaṃ pratisaraṇaṃ na vijṇānam;* in other recensions, the order often differs.

3. Cf. *Majjhima* I.265: *nanu bhikkhave yad eva tumhākaṃ sāmaṃ ñātaṃ sāmaṃ diṭṭhaṃ sāmaṃ viditaṃ tad eva tumhe vadethā ti.*

4. *Bodhisattvabhūmi,* 257: *sa evaṃ yuktipratisarano na pudgalapratisaraṇas tattvārthān na vicalaty aparapratyayaś ca bhavati dharmeṣu.* Ibid., 108: *na parapratyayo bhavati teṣu yuktiparīkṣiteṣu dharmeṣu.*

5. Ibid., 108: *kiṃcit punar adhimucyamāno yeṣv asya dharmeṣu gambhīreṣu buddhir na gāhate, tathāgatagocarā ete dharmā nāsmadbuddhigocarā ity evam apratikṣipaṃs tān dharmān, ātmānam akṣataṃ cānupahataṃ ca pariharaty anavadyam.*

6. *Sūtrālaṃkāra,* 138: *ārṣadharmādhimuktito na praṇaśyati.*

7. *Saṃyutta* IV.281.

8. Ibid., 297.

9. *Saṃyutta* V.430: *idaṃ dukkhaṃ ti bhikkave tatham etam avitatham etam anaññatatham etam . . . tatha aparimāṇā vanna vyañjanā aparimāṇā saṃkāsanā itipidaṃ dukkhaṃ ariyasaccaṃ.*

10. *Sūtrālaṃkāra,* 82: *svarthaḥ saṃvṛtiparamārthasatyayogāt, suvyañjanaḥ pratītapadavyañjanatvāt.*

11. *Digha* III.129: *ayaṃ kho āyasmā atthaṃ ñeva sammā gaṇhāti, vyañjanāni sammā ropeti.*

12. Ibid.: *lābhā no āvuso, suladdhaṃ no āvuso, ye mayaṃ āyasmantaṃ tādisaṃ sabrahmacāriṃ passāma evaṃ atthūpetaṃ vyañjanūpetan ti.*

13. Ibid.: *imesaṃ nu kho āvuso vyañjanānaṃ ayaṃ vā attho eso vā attho, katama opāyikataro ti.*

14. Ibid.: *imassa nu kho āvuso atthassa imāni vā vyañjanāni etāni vā vyañjanāni, katamāni opāyikatarānī ti.*

15. *Aṅguttara* II.139: *n'ev' atthato no vyañjanato pariyādānaṃ gacchati.*
16. Ibid., 138: *dhammakathiko bahuñ ca bhāsati sahitañ ca, parisā ca kusalā hoti sahitāsahitassa.*
17. *Bodhisattvabhūmi,* 106: *yathākramaṃ padavyañjanam uddiśati, yathākramoddiṣaṃ ca padavyañjanaṃ yathākramam evārthato vibhajati.*
18. *Aṅguttara* II.381–383; IV.221–223: *anisaṃsā kālena dhammasavane kālena atthupaparikkhāya.*
19. Cf. *Milindapañha,* 18.
20. *Majjhima* I.133: *idha bhikkhave ekacce moghapurisā dhammaṃ pariyāpuṇanti, suttaṃ, geyyaṃ . . . ; te taṃ dhammaṃ pariyāpuṇitvā tesaṃ dhammānaṃ paññāya atthaṃ na upaparikkhanti, tesaṃ te dhammā paññāya atthaṃ anupaparikkhataṃ na nijjhānaṃ khamanti, te upārambhānisaṃsā c'eva dhammaṃ pariyāpuṇanti itivādappamokkhānisaṃsā ca, yassa c'atthāya dhammaṃ pariyāpuṇanti tañ c'assa atthaṃ nānubhonti, tesaṃ te dhammā duggahītā dīgharattaṃ ahitāya dukkhāya saṃvattanti. taṃ kissa hetu. duggahītittā bhikkhave dhammānam.*
21. *Aṅguttara* II.147; III.178: *duggahītaṃ suttantaṃ pariyāpuṇanti dunnikkhittehi padavyañjanehi.*
22. Ibid., III.178: *saddhammassa saṃmosaya antardhānāya saṃvattanti.*
23. *Nettipakaraṇa,* 21: *dunnikkhittassa padavyañjanassa attho pi dunnayo bhavati.*
24. Cf. *Vinaya* I.40.
25. Ibid.: *hotu āvuso, appaṃ vā bahuṃ vā bhāsassu, atthaṃ yeva me brūhi, atthen' eva me attho, kiṃ kāhasi vyañjanaṃ bahun ti.*
26. *Laṅkāvatāra,* 196.
27. Vasumitra in J. Masuda, "Origin and Doctrines of Indian Buddhist Schools," *Asia Major* 2 (1925): 19 and 28. See also M. Walleser, *Die Sekten des alten Buddhismus* (Heidelberg, 1927), 27.
28. Chung a han, *T* no. 26, 11.498b10.
29. *Aṅguttara* I.22.
30. Cf. Masuda, "Origin and Doctrines," 52; Walleser, *Die Sekten des alten Buddhismus,* 43
31. *Le Traité de la Grande Vertu de Sagesse,* vol. 2 (Louvain, 1949), 1074.
32. Ibid., 1095.
33. Quoted in *Śikṣāsamuccaya,* 95: *sūkṣmaṃ hi Mañjuśrīḥ saddharmapratikṣepakarmāvāraṇam. yo hi kaścin Mañjuśrīs tathāgatabhāṣite dharme kasmiṃścic chobanasaṃjñaṃ karoti kvacid aśobhanasaṃjñāṃ sa saddharmaṃ pratikṣipati tena saddharmaṃ pratikṣipata tathāgato 'bhyākhyāto bhavati dharmaḥ pratikṣipto bhavati saṃgho 'pa vadito bhavati.*
34. Quoted in *Madhyamakavṛtti,* 43
35. *Samādhirājasūtra,* ed. N. Dutt, *Gilgit Manuscripts,* II.78; also quoted in *Madhyamakavṛtti,* 44, 276: *nītārthasūtrāntaviśeṣa jānati yathopadiṣṭā sugatena śūnyatā, yasmin punaḥ pudgalasattvapuruṣa neyārthato jānati sarvadharmān.*
36. Cf. *Kosa* III.75.
37. On the *Bhārahārasūtra,* see *Saṃyutta* III.25–26; *Kośavyākhyā,* 706; *Sūtrālaṃkāra,* 159.
38. Cf. *Kośa* IX.256.
39. Cf. *Madhyamakāvatāra,* 181–194.
40. V. Bhattacharya, "Sandhābhāṣā," *Indian Historical Quarterly* 4 (1928): 287–296; P. C. Bagchi, "The Sandhābhāṣā and Sandhāvacana," *Indian Historical Quarterly* 6 (1930): 389–396; P. Pelliot, in *Toung Pao* (1932): 147; P. C. Bagchi, "Some Aspects of Buddhist Mysticism in the Caryāpadas," *Calcutta Oriental Series* 1, no. 5 (1934); J. R. Ware, *Journal of the American Oriental Society* 57: 123; F. Edgerton, *Journal of the American Oriental Society* 57: 185–188; L. de la Vallée Poussin, "Buddhica," *Harvard Journal of Asian Studies* 3: 137–139.

41. *Dīpavaṃsa* V.30–35.

42. *Bodhisattvabhūmi,* 108: *arthaṃ pratisaran bodhisattvo na vyañjanaṃ buddhānāṃ bhagavatāṃ sarvasaṃdhāyavacanāny anupraviśati.*

43. *Bodhisattvabhūmi,* 257: *bodhisattvas tathāgate niviṣṭaśraddho niviṣṭaprasāda ekāntiko vacasy abhiprasannas tathāgatanītārthaṃ sūtraṃ pratisarati na neyārthaṃ. nītārthaṃ sūtraṃ pratisarann asaṃhāryo bhavaty asmād dharmavinayāt. tathā hi neyārthasya sūtrasya nānāmukhaprakṛtārthavibhāgo 'niścitaḥ saṃdehakāro bhavati. sacet punar bodhisattvaḥ nītārthe 'pi sūtre 'naikāntikaḥ syād evam asau saṃhāryaḥ syād asmād dharmavinayāt.*

44. On the contrast between *deśanānaya* and *siddhāntanaya,* see *Laṅkāvatāra,* 148, 172, etc.

45. Cf. *Mahāvyutpatti,* nos. 1666–1675; *Sūtrālaṃkāra,* 82–84; *La Somme du Grand Véhicule,* 2:129–132.

46. *Bodhisattvabhūmi,* 257: *Punar bodhisattvaḥ adhigamajñāne sāradarśī bhavati na śrutacintādharmārthavijñānamātrake. sa yad bhāvanāmayena jñānena jñātavyaṃ na tac chakyaṃ śrutacintājñānamātrakeṇa vijñātum iti viditvā paramagambhīrān api tathāgatabhāṣitān dharmān śrutvā na pratikṣipati nāpavadati.*

47. L. de la Vallée Poussin, *La Morale bouddhique* (Paris, 1927), 302.

48. J. C. Jennings, *The Vedantic Buddhism of the Buddha* (Oxford, 1947).

The Gradual Path as a Hermeneutical Approach to the *Dhamma*

George D. Bond

Theravāda Buddhism, from an early period, placed the *Tipiṭaka* at the center of the tradition, regarding it as "the word of the Buddha" *(buddha-vacanaṃ)* and even as the dharmakāya.[1] With the *Tipiṭaka* occupying the central place, hermeneutical questions concerning the interpretation of the canon took on great importance for Theravāda, and as a result, many of the distinctive doctrines and ideas of Theravāda developed in the commentaries and subcommentaries to the *Tipiṭaka*. As I have noted elsewhere,[2] the commentarial writings represented Theravāda's second and final solution to the problem of how to interpret and understand the *Tipiṭaka*. Theravāda's first solution to the problem of interpretation is found, however, in two postcanonical texts, the *Netti Pakaraṇa* and the *Peṭakopadesa*. These two works set forth an approach to the interpretation of the *Tipiṭaka,* a hermeneutical method and viewpoint that shaped Theravāda's thinking on these matters and profoundly influenced the commentarial tradition. Traditionally attributed to Mahākaccāna, both the *Netti* and the *Peṭakopadesa* represent complex, highly technical manuals of interpretation. Although these two works are not identical, they present the same views and the same method of interpretation.[3]

Both the *Netti* and the *Peṭakopadesa* develop the notion of the gradual path to *nibbāna* and employ it as a hermeneutical strategy for explaining the *dhamma*. Although the notion of a gradual path became common in later Buddhism, both in Theravāda and Mahāyāna, and came to represent the hallmark of the Theravāda tradition through works such as the *Visuddhimagga,* the idea does not seem to have been explicitly worked out in Theravāda texts prior to the *Netti* and *Peṭakopadesa*. How then did these texts come to state it so forcefully and in such detail? Could the context in which these two texts arose have shaped and necessitated this hermeneutical viewpoint? We shall begin by considering this second question for it will enable us to see both the significance and the meaning of the hermeneutical strategy of these texts.

In his recent book, *Selfless Persons,* Steven Collins has endorsed the notion that Theravāda texts should be understood against the backdrop of their context. He writes, "Theravāda thinking has arisen from the historical and cultural context," and it embodies certain "constructions and hypotheses which are addressed to quite specific (and socially derived) concerns. . . ."[4] The texts can be understood, he argues, in Durkheim's sense as "social facts."[5] Collins' views regarding the relation between Theravāda texts and their contexts bear out the opinions of other scholars on the question of the relation between a text and its context.

Without digressing too far into this broader subject, we can summarize this research by saying that context seems to function on at least two levels to shape the process of text production and interpretation in a cumulative religious tradition. First, contexts generate texts. This truth has been long accepted in Biblical studies where it represents the basis for form criticism and other approaches to understanding the text. Other scholars such as Mary Douglas have also shown that the beliefs and values that constitute a person or group's cosmology both are shaped by and reciprocally reshape the context.[6] A social context establishes a cost structure and a pattern of rewards and punishments; it permits or requires certain value systems and interpretations of the meaning of existence and, at the same time, it renders implausible other values and interpretations. By its constraining influence upon belief, each context generates a particular cultural or cosmological bias, "a collective moral consciousness about man and his place in the universe."[7] Since texts represent "frozen cosmologies," we can see that texts also arise subject to the constraints of a context and represent that context.

The second point to note is that just as the context permits certain cosmologies as plausible and prevents others as implausible, so the context also permits certain interpretations of texts and prevents others. As W. Cantwell Smith has shown, religious texts, as part of the cumulative tradition that comes down from the past, confront the individual of faith, but the individual has to interpret the text in a way that gives it meaning and plausibility in his context.[8] The context strongly influences the decisions people make about how to understand a text—which ideas should a people take up and emphasize, and which ideas should they leave aside?

The *Netti* and the *Peṭakopadesa* seem both to have arisen in and to reflect a specific historical context that shaped their understanding of the *dhamma.* Both texts seem to represent what Collins calls "social facts" in this sense. The danger, of course, in speculating about the social context behind Buddhist texts is that since we can never be entirely sure, the project remains somewhat speculative. We cannot be certain about all the details of the ancient Indian context in which the *Netti* and the *Peṭakopadesa* emerged. There is, however, a general scholarly consensus about the nature of the Indian context and the place of religion in it, and the picture painted by this consensus sheds important light on the backgrounds and intentions of our texts.

Louis Dumont has described the Indian context as having had two kinds of people: "those that live in the world and those that have renounced it."[9] Those who lived according to the norms of the caste system and the village he describes as "men of the world," and those who went to the forest he styles "renouncers."[10] This basic depiction of ancient Indian society agrees with Weber's view of the dichotomy between ordinary people and "virtuosos."[11] Dumont goes on to argue that the religious thought of this period must be understood in relation to these two types of persons.[12] The renouncer has an individualistic religion, while the men in the world do not see themselves individualistically and thus have group-oriented religious ideas.

Louis de la Vallée Poussin also depicted the Indian context in this way and explained how Indian religions expressed this context.[13] Ancient India, he observed, generated two kinds of religious traditions, one kind suited for the renouncer, the individuals, and another kind suited for the men in the world. The former kind he termed "disciplines of salvation" and the latter kind "religions." The religions "properly so called" were characterized by the provisions they made to meet the needs of the people living in society. Religions provided prayers, rituals, sacrifices, deities, and sacraments that addressed both the immediate and ultimate needs of these people. By setting forth moral guidelines, the religions adjusted the sacred to the secular, thereby sanctioning life in the world. By holding funeral rituals, they provided for the "welfare of the dead" and the afterlife.[14] The religions supplied the kind of hierarchical cosmology needed by people living in a group-dominated society.

The "disciplines of salvation," however, had none of these group-cosmology characteristics. "Disciplines of salvation" were neither philosophies nor religions, but paths *(mārga)* leading to liberation *(mokṣa)* or nirvāna. Supramundane rather than mundane ends represented the focus of the disciplines of salvation. No provisions were made for marriage, funerals, or even for social interaction, since the disciplines were intended for those who had renounced secular life and society. It was as such a discipline of salvation that early Buddhism began, Poussin explained.

Poussin's view of the ancient Indian context and the place of Buddhism in it also resembles that of Max Weber. Weber described early Buddhism as an asocial system of "radical salvation striving" that set out a path for those ascetics who had fled the world, but had little to offer to people who remained in the world.[15] He compared the role of the laity in Buddhism to that of the "tolerated infidels in Islam" who "existed only for the purpose of sustaining by alms" those who sought the true goal of the religion.[16]

That early Buddhism represented a "discipline of salvation" seems fairly probable.[17] The Buddha and his early disciples were part of a wider movement of *samaṇas* or world renouncers in ancient India. Many Buddhist suttas and teachings reflect the individualistic cosmology and liberation-seeking characteristic of Poussin's "disciplines of salvation." If, as Poussin believed, early Buddhism began as a discipline for renouncers, it seems clear that it soon had to come to terms with the needs of men in the world. As Buddhism developed, it necessarily began to establish relations with the society in which the men in the world lived. Dumont has commented on this process of development in Indian religions, saying that "the secret of Hinduism may be found in the dialogue between the renouncer and the man in the world."[18] Change occurred and the Hindu religious tradition evolved because the renouncers, who were "the agent(s) of development in Indian religion and speculation, the 'creators of values,' " had to address themselves to the larger society.[19] Again Dumont writes, "The true historical development of Hinduism is in the sannyasic developments on the one hand and their aggregation to worldly religion on the other."[20]

For Buddhism, also, the interaction between these two contexts and two cosmologies served as the catalyst for developments that shaped the religion. One of the major problems that Buddhism faced as it spread in India and elsewhere was the necessity of validating the role of the man in the world, of meeting the social or religious needs of nonrenouncers.

This clash of contexts appears to have been the setting in which both the *Netti* and the *Peṭakopadesa* originated. More clearly, perhaps, than any other early Theravāda texts, these two texts reflect this process of development in the Theravāda tradition and the formulation of Theravāda's distinctive viewpoint. Both the *Netti* and the *Peṭakopadesa* acknowledge the two ideal types, the renouncers and the men in the world, and attempt to explain the *dhamma* in relation to them. The method of interpretation and the hermeneutical viewpoint of these texts appear to have been developed in response to the problem of finding a way of addressing the religious concerns of people with quite different needs and yet retaining the central notion that the *dhamma* had one truth and led to one goal, *nibbāna*. The *Netti* and the *Peṭakopadesa* responded to this contextual dilemma by positing the gradual path to *nibbāna* as a hermeneutical device that enabled them to reconcile the differing cosmologies and ideals under the umbrella of the unitary truth of the *dhamma*.

The notion of the gradual path to *nibbāna* allowed the *Netti* and the *Peṭakopadesa* to subsume mundane goals under the supramundane goal and to explain how the truth of the *dhamma* relates to all people. In developing the gradual path as a hermeneutical strategy, Theravāda followed the same pattern that Dumont perceives in Hinduism. The doctrine of transmigration, Dumont observes, "establishes the relation between the renouncer as an individual man, and the phantom-like men who have remained in the world and support him."[21] "Transmigration appears as a bold design lending to the men in the world some reality taken from that which the renouncer has found for himself."[22] The *Netti* and the *Peṭakopadesa* employ the gradual path similarly; they use it as a way of viewing transmigration as what Collins terms a "soteriological strategy"[23] with which the doctrines of Buddhism relate to the two major contexts and all shades of contexts in between. Collins explains that in correlating these two contexts Theravāda developed "an intermediate range of thought and practice, such that certain symbols from the 'disciplines' came to be used for goals usually associated with the religions."[24]

As manuals of interpretation, the *Netti* and the *Peṭakopadesa* present the gradual path as a key that unlocks the meaning of the Buddha's *dhamma*. The *Netti* describes the nature of the *dhamma* by citing a saying attributed to the Buddha. "O Bhikkhus, I shall teach you a *dhamma* that is good in the beginning, good in the middle, and good in the end, with its own meaning and phrasing" (N. 5; *Majjhima Nikāya* III.280). The complexity of this *dhamma* was increased, the *Netti* maintains, by the fact that the Buddha's teaching was "unbounded" or "immeasurable" *(aparimāṇa)* (N. 8). These descriptions point up the uniqueness of the *dhamma:* as the Buddha set it forth, it was supreme, unbounded truth with its own inherent structure and logic. To comprehend the *dhamma,* an interpreter must penetrate this logic and grasp the meaning and phrasing of the *dhamma* properly. As the *Aṅguttara Nikāya* points out, incorrectly interpreting the meaning and phrasing of the *dhamma* leads to the breakup and destruction of the *dhamma* (II.147).

Both the *Netti* and the *Peṭakopadesa* assume that the internal logic and structure of the *dhamma* derive from the gradual path. The gradual path expresses the *dhamma*'s goodness in the beginning, middle, and end. It is through the concept of a gradual path, these manuals say, that the Buddha related the ultimate end to all people. All the elements of the *Netti* and the *Peṭakopadesa*'s method, including the meaning and phrasing elements, function within the framework of this gradual path. By superimposing the pattern of the gradual path onto the *dhamma,* these two texts find the hierarchy of means and ends necessary to relate the *dhamma* to a variety of people and yet to maintain the belief in one ultimate goal and one ultimate meaning of the *dhamma.*

To delineate the logic and structure of the gradual path and the integral nature of this path to the Buddha's *dhamma,* the *Netti* and the *Peṭakopadesa* set forth classifications of types of persons to whom the Buddha addressed his teachings and types of suttas that the Buddha employed to reach these persons. These typologies are presented in the chapter in each text entitled "The foundation of the *sāsana,*" which indicates the central importance that the *Netti* and the *Peṭakopadesa* assigned to them. An interpreter who approached the *dhamma* without being aware of these distinctions could not comprehend the *dhamma,* and would be in danger, the *Peṭakopadesa* declares, of "mixing up the suttas" (P. 80).

In classifying the various types of persons to whom the Buddha directed his teaching, our texts posit the two basic contextual types that parallel those Dumont has suggested; however, these texts present a somewhat more complex description of those types. The basic classification given divides persons into three types: the ordinary person *(puthujjana),* the learner or initiate *(sekha),* and the adept *(asekha)* (P. 42; N. 49). These classifications represent levels on the path, from beginner to *arahant.* The first two types clearly represent men in the world and renouncers, respectively. The third type elaborates on the category of renouncers by adding to those who are on the way *(sekhas)* those who have reached the goal *(asekhas);* these two groups can be called those who are being purified and those who have reached purification (N. 20).

In addition to these levels of persons, the texts also classify persons according to their nature or temperament *(carita)* and their abilities. Reflecting the Buddhist doctrines of karma and saṃsāra, this classification scheme assumes that persons at each level of the path may have varying needs, propensities, and abilities. Although the texts suggest several classifications of temperaments, the basic one employed divides people into two groups: persons of desire-temperament *(taṇhācarita)* and persons of view-temperament *(diṭṭhicarita)* (N. 109). A person's temperament determines what kind of defilements the person will have. For example, the view-temperament person will have ignorance as a defilement while the desire-temperament person will be defiled by craving (N. 109). Temperament also determines how people seek release unsuccessfully—for example, by asceticism in the case of the view-temperament person, and by the pursuit of sensual pleasures in the case of a person of desire-temperament (P. 242).

Other temperament classifications are suggested at various points in the manuals, but all classifications are said to be reducible to the view-temperament and desire-temperament types (N. 126). Another classification posits the three types of lusting-temperament *(rāgacarita),* hating-temperament *(dosacarita),* and deluded-temperament *(moharcarita)* (N. 190). Employing a different criterion, still another classification divides persons into the three types of those who gain knowledge from a condensed or brief teaching *(ugghaṭitaññū),* those who gain knowledge from a teaching that is expanded *(vipañcitaññū),* and those who are merely or barely guidable *(neyya)* (N. 7). These classifications of persons are at times multiplied by qualifying the basic types with adjectives such as dull-facultied or bright-facultied.

Correlated with these types of persons, the *Netti* and the *Peṭakopadesa* identify various types of suttas. These typologies of suttas also indicate the nature of the gradual path in the *dhamma.* Both texts posit four basic types of suttas that represent the "foundation of the *sāsana.*" The four types include suttas dealing with defilement *(saṃkilesa),* suttas dealing with moral living *(vāsanā),* suttas dealing with penetration *(nibbedha),* and suttas dealing with the adept *(asekha).* This classification of suttas is said to be increased from four to eight (in the *Netti*) and to sixteen (in the *Peṭakopadesa*) because of various combinations of these four basic types.

These sutta types clearly reflect the two major contexts suggested by Dumont and also the two types of religion described by Poussin. The two primary types of suttas are those dealing with morality and those dealing with penetration, which correspond to the religion of the man in the world and the discipline of the renouncers, respectively. At one point the *Netti* suggests that these two types of suttas are the only two kinds (N. 48) and the *Peṭakopadesa* defines the two primary types of suttas as those dealing with "previous devotion" and those dealing with penetration (P. 42).

By expanding these two basic types to four, these manuals indicate the outlines of the gradual path. The type of sutta dealing with defilement *(saṃkilesa)* describes the sufferings persons endure from life to life because of wrong desires and wrong actions. In the "Foundation of the sāsana" section, the *Netti* illustrates this type of sutta with short quotations such as the first verse of the *Dhammapada:* "If a person speaks or acts with an impure mind, suffering follows him just as the wheel follows the hoof [of the ox]" (N. 129). Other examples show that suttas of this type have as their subject the predicament of the unenlightened person. Ignorance and desire lead astray the people described or admonished by this type of sutta. This is the negative side of the life of the man in the world.

The positive side of the life of the man in the world is covered by the type of sutta dealing with the morality appropriate to one living in the world *(vāsanā).* The *Netti* explains that these suttas concern merit *(puññaṃ)* and the way to earn a favorable rebirth (N. 48f.). Under this category of sutta, the *Netti* lists the traditional components of the merit-making ritual system in Theravāda: giving *(dāna),* virtue *(sīla),* and heaven as a goal for rebirth *(sagga)* (N. 49). Suttas dealing with morality do not provide instruction about the higher stages of the path but have to do with virtue as restraint and the rewards of good karma (N. 49, 159). The examples given of this type of sutta describe the progress that people made toward the goal as a result of virtuous acts and favorable rebirths. One such example cites the story of a man who gave a flower-garland to the Buddha and, as a consequence, the Buddha told Ānanda that the man would have good rebirths for eighty-four thousand aeons, whence, after fulfilling roles as a king and a deva, he would go forth as a monk to find the truth (N. 138f.). Other examples of suttas of this type mention similar meritorious acts, such as giving four flowers or a measure of rice, that resulted in thousands of delightful rebirths. One sutta declares, "Today these thirty eons have passed (after my meritorious act) and since then I have not been to a bad destination" (N. 141). Clearly, this classification of suttas sanctions rebirth as an acceptable goal for people in the world. By doing meritorious deeds a person is assured of a "good destination." Favorable rebirths are seen not as ends in themselves, however, but as stages on the path, stepping stones to a birth in which a person is able to strive for the ultimate goal. The sutta passages cited in the *Netti,* many of which cannot be traced in the canon, make it clear that rebirth in good destinations represents a penultimate, not an ultimate goal. One passage, for instance, tells of a man who gave a gift of robes to a *Paccekabuddha* and was reborn in various heavenly realms until finally being reborn as the son of a wealthy banker in Varanasi. In that lifetime, he encountered the Buddha and went forth to find enlightenment. Fortunate births neither represent nor replace the supreme goal, but they constitute a hierarchy of subgoals of the kind needed by persons in the world. Far from being irrelevant or unnecessary for the attainment of *nibbāna,* these births represent necessary stages on the path of purification and development (N. 143). In this way, the suttas on morality provide for the kind of active, devotional religion that Poussin attributes to the village dweller.

Sharply contrasted with the suttas on morality are the suttas on penetration. Where morality suttas deal with merit, penetration suttas deal with the fruit of the noble path, or the supreme goal of *nibbāna* (N. 48). Where morality suttas describe virtue as restraint, penetration suttas describe virtue as abandoning. Where morality suttas have no reference to wisdom, the noble path, and the noble fruit, these subjects are central in penetration suttas (N. 49). Although suttas on morality that set forth the ideal of merit-making are said to present the first kind of "striving" *(padhāna),* the suttas on penetration present the higher "striving" of going forth from home to homelessness (N. 159f.).

In the examples of this kind of sutta given by the *Netti,* penetration clearly represents a discipline of salvation for renouncers. These suttas teach a path for "forest dwellers" and "rag-robe wearers" who have abandoned worldly matters (N. 145). Although the *Netti* and the *Peṭakopadesa* are not adamant on the point, they represent the renouncers in the penetration-type as bhikkhus. They do not say that no lay persons can pursue this path, but at the same time they do not cite any examples of this type of sutta that refer to lay persons. The *Peṭakopadesa* refers to the path of these suttas as "the four noble planes and four noble fruits of the bhikkhu's state" (P. 130). The authors appear to have understood the tasks of penetration to be monastic tasks, whereas the tasks of morality were primarily tasks of the laity. The suttas that the *Netti* cites to exemplify this type do not concern the kind of legalistic monastic discipline such as is given in the *Vinaya Piṭaka* with its minor rules of conduct, but instead these suttas have to do with the higher monastic discipline of conquering the ego and the emotions in order to progress in meditation. Penetration suttas refer, for example, to "a mindful bhikkhu (who) abandons lust for sensual desires" (N. 146) and to bhikkhus who are liberated. Suttas that describe how one eliminates desire, hatred, and other defilements are suttas of the penetration type (N. 145). In the penetration suttas, beings are described and instructed regarding "crossing the flood" and attaining liberation from becoming.

The fourth type of sutta, that dealing with the adept, completes the progression from ordinary persons to liberated individuals by describing the fully enlightened *arahant.* Suttas in this category deal with the saints who have conquered defilements and live in mindfulness and self-control (N. 150). The goal of Buddhism constitutes the subject of these suttas. The *Netti* illustrates this type of sutta by citing passages from the *Udāna* that describe one who is a brahmin in the Buddhist sense of a holy person (N. 150; Ud. 6). Such persons have attained equanimity and transcended rebirth in form or formlessness, as well as both pain and pleasure. The *Netti* shows that adepts such as Mogharaja have exhausted the *āsavas,* display the threefold wisdom *(tevijja)* and miraculous powers, and "bear their last body" (N. 152).

In addition to this fourfold classification of suttas, the *Netti* and the *Peṭakopadesa* both offer further classifications of suttas. They explain that the fourfold scheme can be expanded to five by dividing the penetration type into two: suttas on seeing *(dassana)* and suttas on developing *(bhāvanā)* (P. 39; N. 168). Suttas on "seeing" are shown to describe the stream-enterer's path, whereas suttas on developing deal with the other three noble paths. Our texts also propose a second classification scheme that revolves around two basic types, which are mundane suttas *(lokika)* and supramundane suttas *(lokuttara)* (P. 23; N. 162). This scheme, however, is put forward not to identify other different types of suttas but as an alternate way of classifying the four basic types. Suttas dealing with corruption and with morality are classified as mundane while suttas on penetration and the adept come under the supramundane category. The other types in the *Netti*'s second list of classifications function similarly as alternate ways of categorizing the basic sutta types, for example, as suttas on beings *(sattā)* or suttas on ideas *(dhammas),* suttas on knowledge, and suttas on the profitable *(kusala)* or the unprofitable *(akusala)* (N. 161).[25]

The *Peṭakopadesa* offers two additional schemes for classifying suttas, comprising some thirteen and twenty-eight types, respectively. Although these schemes present different perspectives on the suttas, such as suttas on karma and suttas on results *(vipaka),* or suttas on gratification *(assāda)* and suttas on disadvantage *(ādīnava),* the *Peṭakopadesa* explains that all these types also represent only variations or expressions of the four, now five, basic types (P. 42).

Having explained these four or five types of suttas and their variations, the *Netti* and the *Peṭakopadesa* indicate another sense in which the stages represented by the different types constitute a gradual path: each type of sutta is said to counteract the stage that precedes it. Suttas on morality counteract suttas on defilement, suttas on seeing counteract suttas on morality, suttas on developing counteract suttas on seeing, and suttas on the adept counteract suttas on developing (N. 189). The types of suttas are said to represent a definite progression from defilement to enlightenment.

The most comprehensive picture of the progression of stages on the gradual path emerges, however, when the manuals indicate how these various types of suttas apply to the different levels and types of persons. By multiplying suttas by the levels and personality types, the manuals present an elaborately elongated gradual path. The basic correlation, of course, is that between the five sutta types and the three levels of beings: ordinary persons, learners, and adepts. The defilement and morality type of suttas apply to ordinary persons, the seeing and developing types to the learners, and suttas on the adept have their obvious application. This process of correlation becomes more complex in the *Netti* when the sutta types are applied to personality types (N. 189f.). There, the mundane suttas, which comprise the defilement and morality types, are demonstrated by nineteen types of temperaments, all derivations of the lusting, hating, and deluded types. Similarly, the supramundane suttas are demonstrated by twenty-six types of learners and adepts (N. 189f.).

The *Peṭakopadesa*'s equation of suttas and persons, however, goes even beyond the *Netti*'s calculations to display the complete gradual path. This path begins with the defilement suttas that have reference to persons defiled by craving-temperament, view-temperament, or misconduct (P. 29). In the morality suttas, instructions are given that indicate how persons of these types overcome their defilements. The trances or *jhānas* of samādhi meditation can be employed by these persons to overcome defilements such as lusting, hating, and delusion (P. 144). When, through making merit and through *jhānas,* these persons gain a foothold in the *dhamma* and enter the path, the supramundane stage, they lose their defilements but retain their distinctive characters. The person of desire-temperament becomes a follower by faith *(saddhānusāri)* and the view-temperament person becomes a follower by *dhammas (dhammānusāri)* (P. 243; N. 112). These attainments shape their further incarnations on the path.

At the penetration sutta stage, the follower by *dhammas* becomes one who gains knowledge by a condensed teaching *(ugghaṭitaññū),* and the follower by faith becomes one who is merely guidable *(neyyo).* The third epistemological type, the one who learns from an expanded teaching *(vipancitaññū),* results when the two previous knowledge types are divided further according to whether they possess dull or keen faculties. The ones who learn from a condensed teaching and have dull faculties and those who are guidable with keen faculties constitute the third or "expanded" teaching type (P. 30).

From this point on, these three knowledge types dominate the *Peṭakopadesa*'s explanation of the path. In suttas describing the plane of seeing, these three types attain different levels of stream entry. The condensed-teaching person becomes a "single-seeder" *(ekabījin),* the most advanced kind of stream-enterer. The guidable person becomes a "clan to clan" *(kolaṅkola),* and the learner by expanded teaching becomes a "seven times at most," a stream-enterer who requires the maximum time to complete the path.

At the higher levels, these variations in attainments continue. The "single-seeder" becomes either a nonreturner who attains release early or a nonreturner who attains release only after reducing the time of rebirth. The expanded-teaching type also takes one of two different forms of nonreturner, while the guidable person becomes a nonreturner who goes upstream to the Akaniṭṭha gods. Finally, at the level of the *arahant,* these three knowledge types evolve into nine kinds of *arahants.* The evolution of these is described below:

Condensed with keen faculties becomes two kinds:
(1) Both ways liberated *(ubhato bhāgavimutto)*
(2) Liberated by wisdom *(paññāvimutto)*

Condensed with dull faculties becomes two:
(3) Waiting for an eon *(ṭhitakappī)*
(4) Penetrator *(paṭivedhana bhāva)*
Expanded with keen faculties becomes two:
(5) Able by choice *(cetanābhabba)*
(6) Able by guarding *(rakkhaṇābhabba)*
Expanded with dull faculties becomes two:
(7) No-liberation attainer if he seeks it, liberation attainer if he does not seek it
(8) No-liberation attainer if he guards it, liberation attainer if he does not guard it
Guidable becomes
(9) One liable to fall away or an Even-headed[26]

Thus, by illustrating the various combinations of suttas, levels, and personality types, the *Peṭakopadesa* is able to depict the length and diversity of the gradual path. This formulation of the path has lengthened it significantly from the earlier notion of the four noble persons as the only higher stages.

This understanding of the gradual path as the basic structure of the Buddha's *dhamma* also provides the rationale for the other elements in the method of interpretation presented by the *Netti* and the *Peṭakopadesa*.[27] The *Netti* identifies the two concerns of interpretation as meaning *(attha)* and phrasing *(byañjana)* (N. 5). To deal with these two concerns, the other two main sections of the *Netti* and the *Peṭakopadesa* (in addition to the "Foundation of the sāsana") present specific guidelines for interpreting the suttas.[28] The *nayā* or meaning guidelines demonstrate three ways that suttas counteract defilements with profitable states and move people toward the meaning or goal *(attha)* of the *dhamma*. These meaning guidelines are intended to show interpreters how the eighteen root terms[29] encode the meaning of the *dhamma* and relate it to specific types of persons. This interpretive task can also be seen as another explanation of the way that the suttas address and counteract the defilements of persons at the lower levels of the path. The types of persons that are the subjects of the guidelines are those that we have seen on the level of ordinary persons and in mundane suttas.

The first meaning guideline, conversion of relishing *(nandiyāvatta)*, concerns the desire-temperament and the view-temperament types of persons. This guideline demonstrates how desire and ignorance, the two unprofitable root terms at work in these types, are counteracted in the suttas by two profitable root terms, concentration *(samātha)* and insight *(vipassanā)* (N. 110f.). The *Netti* intends to teach the interpreter to recognize the dynamic at work here in order to understand and apply the *dhamma* properly. The second meaning guideline, lion's play *(sīha-vikkīlitaṃ),* correlates four unprofitable and profitable root terms with four temperament types: lusting, hating, dull view-temperament, and intelligent view-temperament (N. 118). The final meaning guideline reintroduces the three knowledge types of persons (see above) and indicates how the suttas relate profitable root terms to counteract the unprofitable ones associated with these types. These profitable and unprofitable root terms in all three guidelines represent the essence of the *dhamma* and the guidelines provide further explanations of how this essence is expressed in the suttas in various ways to fit various persons.

The remaining major element in the method of interpretation of the *Netti* and the *Peṭakopadesa* takes the phrasing of the suttas and demonstrates the unity beneath the diversity. The *hārā* or phrasing categories are sixteen different ways of analyzing suttas in order to recognize that their "meaning is one and only the phrasing is different." The purpose of these categories is to teach the interpreter how to analyze suttas in order to reduce them to their "prime factors." The manuals establish an outline of these prime factors or ideas that constitute the heart of the *dhamma.* Among the ideas included in this outline are the four noble truths, dependent origination, aggregates, elements, bases, and faculties (N. 21f, 63f; P. 98f.). Regarding this outline, the *Peṭakopadesa* explains that there is no sutta of any kind that is not in accord with these ideas (P. 98).

Thus the *hārā* interpret the logic of the suttas by providing an understanding of the basic presuppositions and intentions of the *dhamma.* These *hārā* also reveal how the Buddha applied various teachings to various types of persons. The primary function of the *hārā,* however, is to identify the essential ideas within various kinds of suttas. Having identified the type of sutta and its application to persons, the interpreter would employ these categories to penetrate to the essence of the sutta by correlating the sutta's phraseology with the central concepts of the *dhamma.*

Conclusion

To conclude, we can summarize the main points in our analysis of the *Netti* and the *Peṭakopadesa.* These two texts represent manuals of interpretation which present methods for the correct understanding of the *dhamma.* Central to these methods is the concept of the gradual path to *nibbāna* as a hermeneutical device or strategy to explain the logic and the structure of the *dhamma.* The gradual path provides a framework that permits the *dhamma* to have both great diversity and an underlying unity. The *Netti* and the *Peṭakopadesa* demonstrate the diversity of the *dhamma* by identifying various types of suttas that have relevance to various types of persons on various levels. With almost infinite variations, these combinations of types of suttas and types of persons constitute an immensely long gradual path to the goal of *nibbāna.* This notion of the path links all the diverse persons, stages, and goals. Although these manuals define some suttas as mundane and others as supramundane, and though they identify some suttas as applying to ordinary persons and others as applying to adepts, the manuals do not regard these as distinct religious paths; they do not separate the *kammic* from the *nibbānic* path. Though the path has many levels and applications, the *dhamma* is one and the path is one. This, the *Netti* shows, is the secret to understanding the logic and meaning of the Buddha's teachings.

The manuals demonstrate the unity underlying the diversity in many ways. The diverse types of suttas can be reduced to two types, seen either as mundane and supramundane, or as dealing with morality or penetration. All suttas represent parallel expressions of the truth of the *dhamma,* while their diversity reflects the diverse needs and contexts of persons. Similarly the almost countless stages or levels of the path can all be reduced to three levels: ordinary person, learner, and adept. The two main interpretive categories of the *Netti* and the *Peṭakopadesa,* the *nayā* and the *hārā,* serve to indicate how the interpreter can find the unity of essential truth in the diversity of the *dhamma.* This implicit unity is such that if a person understands one sutta well, he understands the whole truth of the *dhamma.* This principle applies both to the interpreters of the *dhamma* whom these manuals intend to instruct and to the persons striving at the various levels of the path.

The *Netti* and the *Peṭakopadesa* attribute the dividing of the *dhamma* into these diverse levels and the arranging of them along the gradual path to *nibbāna* to the Buddha himself. The *Peṭakopadesa* states that the suttas were "broken up" according to meaning and phrasing and divided according to application by the Buddha, and it is the interpreter's task to restore their original unity (P. 80). If, however, contexts generate texts so that texts represent "social facts," as we have noted above, then it seems probable that this elaborate division of the *dhamma* and the structuring of it along a gradual path grew out of the context in which the *Netti* and the *Peṭakopadesa* were written—that is, the later Theravāda tradition in India. To be sure, as an enlightened teacher the Buddha doubtless adjusted his teachings to suit the needs of the various people he met. The Pali suttas, for example, contain a great variety of teachings on various levels. It remained, however, for followers of the Buddha such as the author(s) of the *Netti* and the *Peṭakopadesa* to arrange and categorize these various *dhamma* teachings according to the logic of development. In the clash of religious contexts that Dumont and Poussin describe, these texts had to clarify the nature of the path and the roles of the renouncers and the men in the world, here identified as learners/adepts and ordinary persons. These manuals accept all these forms of religious practice and spiritual development and link them together via the gradual path. The gradual path provides for the kind of hierarchical religion needed in the context of the man in the world while also providing for the individualistic discipline and cosmology required by the adept. Thus, although the *Netti* and the *Peṭakopadesa* attempt to recontextualize this understanding of the gradual path by attributing it to the Buddha, the conception of the *dhamma* and its interpretation they present seem to reveal, in large part, a later context in which Theravāda was wrestling with the question of how to give the *dhamma* an inclusive interpretation without sacrificing its true intention.

Finally, finding this inclusive interpretation of the path spelled out in these early Theravāda works is significant because it documents both the antiquity and the legitimacy of the lay person's role in the Theravāda tradition. Although it might seem that "merit-making" represented a later development among Theravādins in Sri Lanka or Burma, these texts indicate that the tradition has long regarded the gradual path to be central and has understood "merit-making" to be an integral stage of that path. Contrary to Weber's views, early Theravāda, according to the *Netti* and the *Peṭakopadesa,* did have something to offer to the householders who remained in the world.

Notes

1. See George Coedes, "Dhammakāya," *Adyar Library Bulletin* 20 (1956): 248–286. Also see Frank Reynolds, "The Two Wheels of Dhamma: A Study of Early Buddhism," in *The Two Wheels of Dhamma: Essays on the Theravada Tradition in India and Ceylon,* ed. Bardwell L. Smith, AAR Studies in Religion, no. 3 (Chambersburg, Penn.: American Academy of Religion, 1972).

2. George D. Bond, *The Word of the Buddha: The Tipiṭaka and Its Interpretation in Theravāda Buddhism* (Colombo: M. D. Gunasena & Co. Publishers, 1982). In this article, my purpose is to add a new dimension to the analysis of the *Netti* in my book.

3. It is beyond the scope of this article to discuss the question of the relation of these two texts. For the most insightful explanation of their relation, see Venerable Ñāṇamoli, "Translator's Introduction," *The Guide* (London: Pali Text Society, 1962).

4. Steven Collins, *Selfless Persons: Imagery and Thought in Theravāda Buddhism* (London: Cambridge University Press, 1982), 3.

5. Ibid., 20.

6. Among her works related to this topic are *Cultural Bias,* Occasional Paper no. 35 of the Royal Anthropological Institute of Great Britain and Ireland, 1978; *Natural Symbols: Explorations in Cosmology* (London: Barrie and Rockcliff, 1970); and *Purity and Danger* (London: Routledge and Kegan Paul, 1966).

7. *Cultural Bias,* 14.

8. Wilfred Cantwell Smith, *The Meaning and End of Religion* (New York: New American Library, 1964).

9. Louis Dumont, "World Renunciation in Indian Religions," Appendix B in *Homo Hierarchicus: The Caste System and Its Implications,* trans. M. Sainsbury, L. Dumont, and B. Gulati (Chicago: University of Chicago Press, 1980), 270.

10. Ibid.

11. Max Weber, *The Religion of India,* trans. H. Gerth and D. Martindale (New York: The Free Press, 1958), 204ff.

12. Dumont, "World Renunciation," 275.

13. Louis de la Vallée Poussin, *The Way to Nirvana: Six Lectures on Ancient Buddhism as a Discipline of Salvation* (Cambridge: Cambridge University Press, 1917).

14. Ibid., 2f.

15. Weber, *Religion of India,* 206, 214.

16. Ibid., 214.

17. This theory seems to represent the scholarly consensus, although Edward Conze seems to have doubted it. See his "Recent Progress in Buddhist Studies," in *Thirty Years of Buddhist Studies: Selected Essays* (Columbia, S.C.: University of South Carolina Press, 1968), 11.

18. Dumont, "World Renunciation," 270.

19. Ibid., 275f.

20. Ibid., 434 n. 21.

21. Ibid., 276.

22. Ibid.

23. Collins, *Selfless Persons,* 12.

24. Ibid., 16.

25. The types of suttas in this second classification are:
    1. (a) mundane, (b) supramundane, (c) both
    2. (a) expressed in terms of creatures, (b) expressed in terms of ideas, (c) expressed in terms of creatures and in terms of ideas
    3. (a) knowledge, (b) the knowable, (c) knowledge and the knowable
    4. (a) seeing, (b) developing, (c) seeing and developing
    5. (a) our own statement, (b) someone else's statement, (c) our own statement and someone else's statement
    6. (a) the answerable, (b) the unanswerable, (c) the answerable and the unanswerable
    7. (a) action, (b) ripening, (c) action and ripening
    8. (a) the profitable, (b) the unprofitable, (c) the profitable and unprofitable
    9. (a) the agreed, (b) the refused, (c) the agreed and refused
    10. eulogy

26. Note that these appear to amount to ten types, since the ninth type has two meanings.

27. The basic elements are the *hārā* or interpretive categories, the *nayā* or guidelines, the root terms, and the "foundation of the sāsana."

28. In the *Netti,* the two sections are called the "Hāravibhaṅga" and the "Nayasamuṭṭhāna."

29. The root terms are divided into two groups, the profitable *(kusala)* and the unprofitable *(akusala).* The unprofitable root terms are desire *(taṇhā),* ignorance *(avijjā),* greed *(lobha),* anger *(dosa),* confusion *(moha),* perception of beauty

(subhasaññā), perception of pleasure *(sukhasaññā),* perception of permanence *(niccasaññā),* and perception of self *(attasaññā).* The profitable root terms are calmness *(samatha),* insight *(vipassanā),* non-greed *(alobha),* non-anger *(adosa),* non-confusion *(amoha),* perception of foulness *(asubhasaññā),* perception of pain *(dukkasaññā),* perception of impermanence *(aniccasaññā),* and perception of no-self *(anattasaññā).*

On the Interpretation of the Mahāyāna Sūtras

DONALD S. LOPEZ, JR.

> We are of the opinion that the Buddhist doctrine evolved along the lines which its discoverer had unconsciously traced for it.
>
> É. LAMOTTE

In his story "Tlön, Uqbar, and Orbus Tertius" Borges tells of the fantastic planet of Tlön, where the metaphysicians seek not truth but rather a kind of amazement and where, in literary matters, "the dominant notion is that everything is the work of one single author. Books are rarely signed. The concept of plagiarism does not exist; it has been established that all books are the work of a single writer, who is timeless and anonymous."[1] Such are the sūtras of the Mahāyāna, composed over the course of centuries in a wide array of languages but attributed to a single author, all considered *buddhavacana.* It is a vast canon.[2] The Peking edition of the Tibetan tripiṭaka contains 326 sūtras (some of which, like the *Ratnakūṭa,* include scores of autonomous works) in 34 volumes. Approximately 150 volumes would be required to translate these works into English. The longest of the sūtras is the *Śatasāhasrikā-prajñāpāramitā,* the *Perfection of Wisdom in 100,000 Stanzas,* which fills 6 of the 34 volumes of sūtras. The shortest is the *Ekākṣarīprajñāpāramitā*, the *Perfection of Wisdom in One Letter,* translated here in its entirety:

> Thus did I hear at one time. The Bhagavan was sitting on Vulture Peak with a great assembly of 1,250 monks and many billions of bodhisattvas. At that time, the Bhagavan said this to the venerable Ānanda, "Ānanda, keep this perfection of wisdom in one letter for the benefit and happiness of sentient beings. It is thus, *a.*" So said the Bhagavan and everyone—Ānanda, the monks, and the bodhisattva mahāsattvas—having understood and admired the perfection of wisdom, praised what the Bhagavan had said.[3]

Here the perfection of wisdom is radically contracted to a single letter, the letter *a,* the first letter of the Sanskrit alphabet, inherent in each consonant, the symbol of emptiness *(śūnyatā).* This is, clearly, an attempt to synthesize and condense the vaster scriptures, to proclaim their essence most succinctly. It can also be seen as an attempt at interpretation, simultaneously eliminating all that is not essential, while implying that that which has been eliminated is entailed by and derived from an essence, both infinite and indeterminate.[4]

There is, of course, something even more succinct than a single letter. Nāgārjuna states at *Mūlamadhyamakakārikā* XXV.24:

> The cessation of all objects,
> The cessation of all elaborations is auspicious.
> The Buddha did not teach any doctrine
> Anywhere to anyone.[5]

And in commentary, Candrakīrti cites several sūtras that tell of the Buddha's supreme economy of expression. Playing on the famous statement, called the "Sūtra of the Two Nights" *(dharmarātridvayasūtra),* that the Buddha constantly taught the doctrine from the night he achieved enlightenment to the night he passed into nirvāṇa,[6] Vajrapāṇi proclaims in the *Sūtra Setting Forth the Inconceivable Secrets of the Tathāgata (Tathāgatācintyaguhyanirdeśasūtra):*

> Śāntamati, from the night when the Tathāgata fully awakened into unsurpassed, perfect, complete enlightenment, until the night when he passed without remainder into final nirvāṇa, the Tathāgata did not declare or speak even a single syllable, nor will he speak. Then how does the Bhagavan teach the doctrine to the various beings who are to be instructed—the gods, demigods, humans, *kiṃnaras* [half-human, half-horse], adepts *(siddha), vidyādharas,* and serpents? Through giving voice for one instant, there is a great light of autumn gold that removes the darkness from beings' minds, opens the many varieties of awareness like a cluster of lotuses, evaporates the rivers and oceans of birth and death, and shames the multitude of rays of the seven suns that shine at the end of an age.[7]

The same sūtra compares the word of the Buddha to the sound of a wind chime, which, without being played by anyone, produces music when stirred by the wind. So does the word of the Buddha arise when stirred by the minds of sentient beings, although he has no thought; it is due to his fulfillment of the bodhisattva deeds in the past that his speech conforms to the diverse needs of all sentient beings.[8] Candrakīrti also cites the *Samādhirājasūtra:*

> When the Buddha, the king of doctrine, the proclaimer of all doctrines, a subduer, appears
> The refrain that phenomena do not exist arises from the grass, bushes, trees, plants, stones, and mountains.[9]

The passage from the *Tathāgatācintyaguhya* is quoted by Candrakīrti as a Mādhyamika proclamation of the final nature of the word of the Buddha; all of the speech of the Buddha is no speech because his words, like all other phenomena, are empty of any substantial nature *(svabhāva)*. But Candrakīrti cites the passage out of context. Vajrapāṇi makes his declaration in explaining to Śāntamati the secret of the Buddha's speech, indicating not so much an ontology of the Buddha's words but rather a wondrous Buddhology in which the Buddha as speaker and author disappears. It is not merely that words spoken by the Buddha did not ultimately exist; Vajrapāṇi explains that the Buddha was actually silent throughout his life, remaining constantly absorbed in samādhi, without speech, without thought, without breath. The Tathāgata is thus like a speaking prism; perfect, impassive, with no color of its own, it is touched by the faith, the development, the questions, the intentions of sentient beings and refracts the teaching that is appropriate to each.

But our concern is not so much the magical mechanism by which the Buddha spoke or his miraculous pedagogical powers, but his words. The question here is not whether the Buddha expatiated the perfection of wisdom in one hundred stanzas, or spoke one syllable, or made no sound at all; the question rather is how to account for the apparent inconsistencies in what was "heard." It is the question of the conflict of interpretation in the Mahāyāna sūtras. Hence, it is Candrakīrti's reading of the passage out of context to which we must return.

Upāya and Intention

As noted above, Candrakīrti cites the passage from the *Tathāgatācintyaguhya* that the Buddha never spoke to support Nāgārjuna's statement that because all objects and elaborations cease in the understanding of the emptiness of self, there is nothing for the Buddha to teach. Ultimately, the Buddha never taught anything to anyone; hence his silence from the night of his enlightenment to the night of his passage into nirvāṇa. But having fulfilled his commentator's role of providing sūtra support for Nāgārjuna's statement, Candrakīrti seems compelled to go farther. The statement from the *Tathāgatācintyaguhya* evokes other passages that proclaim rather different, and contradictory, characteristics of the word of the Buddha. Thus, he was not silent but spoke for a single instant and thereby cleared away the darkness that obscures the minds of beings. Or, he did not speak for a single instant but spoke repeatedly when moved by the thoughts of sentient beings, like music from a wind chime moved by the wind. Or, Indra and the storm gods, the *maruts,* beat drums that declare that all things are like illusions and mirages and moons reflected in water. Or, the teaching that phenomena do not exist was heard from the grass, trees, and mountains. Or, the Buddha, with one sound, teaches what is beneficial in accordance with the diverse aspirations of his audience.[10]

The variety of characterizations of the word of the Buddha, a variety that Candrakīrti makes no attempt to account for, citing the diverse sūtra passages without comment, points up a tension that moves through the exegesis of the Mahāyāna sūtras, a tension between what the Buddha taught and what he intended, between upāya and doctrine, between method and truth. Simply stated, the problem is this: the Buddha taught many things to many people, in accordance with their aspirations, capacities, and needs. How is one to choose among these myriad teachings, each "true" for its listener, to determine the final view of the teacher?

Because many of his disciples were emotionally and intellectually unable to comprehend his true teaching, it is said that the Buddha often taught what was ultimately false but provisionally true in order compassionately to lead all, eventually, to the final truth of enlightenment. The theory of the Buddha's expediency or skillful methods *(upāya)* is delineated most fully in the *Lotus Sūtra (Saddharmapuṇḍarīka),* where through a series of parables the Buddha explains how his teaching of three vehicles effectively leads to his disciples' mounting of the one vehicle *(ekayāna),* the Buddhayāna.[11]

The case of the *Lotus Sūtra* is a fairly straightforward one in that the Buddha repeatedly explains what he meant by a certain teaching. But what of cases of contradictory statements where no such gloss is provided by the speaker? Here it is the task of the exegete to determine the intention of the Buddha. Yet, while the question of the possibility of determining the author's intention and the usefulness of having identified that intention in the interpretation of a text has been very much at issue in literary theory, beginning with "The Intentional Fallacy" and subsequent verbal icons of the New Criticism,[12] the task of the Buddhist exegete is not simply "the modest, and in the old-fashioned sense, philological effort to find out what the author meant."[13] This is because the Buddha apparently meant what he said, for example, when he told the *śrāvakas* that theirs was a path to enlightenment; that is, that is what he meant for them to understand because they were incapable of understanding that they must eventually enter the Mahāyāna. Rather, the task of the Buddhist hermeneutician appears more akin to Schleiermacher's divinatory method in which the interpreter seeks "to transform himself, so to speak, into the author" in order to understand the meaning of the text.[14] But again, the Buddhist exegetes are not dealing with the mental processes of an ordinary author. The author is the Buddha, the Awakened One, endowed with the knowledge of all aspects *(sarvāka-*

rajñāna), fully aware in each instant of the modes and varieties of all phenomena in the universe, and possessed of superknowledges *(abhijñā)* such as clairvoyance, clairaudience, telepathy, and knowledge of the past lives of himself and all other beings. Nor is the Buddhist exegete to discern the unconscious intentions of the Buddha, for he has none. It is impossible, then, for the Buddhist interpreter to follow Schleiermacher's dictum, "to understand the text at first as well as and then even better than its author."[15] How is the unenlightened exegete to know the enlightened mind of the Buddha? One option is to rely on instructions provided by the Buddha on the problem of interpretation; two such instructions will be considered in detail below. However, before moving further, some observations concerning the relationship of the Buddhist exegete to the text will be instructive.

First, in dealing with the hermeneutical strategies devised by the Mahāyāna exegetes, there seems to be little value in questioning the sincerity of their belief that the Mahāyāna sūtras are the word of the Buddha. Modern studies have concluded that these sūtras were composed over a period of a millennium, from the second century B.C.E. to the seventh or eighth centuries of the common era. That such figures as Nāgārjuna, Asaṅga, Bhāvaviveka, and Candrakīrti should have been unaware of the composition of these texts during their lifetimes seems far-fetched, yet we find them arguing for the authenticity of the Mahāyāna sūtras as the word of the Buddha.[16] These savants of the Mahāyāna were aware of the charges of fabrication and went to some lengths to rebut them. The authors of the sūtras were also aware of such charges, as is evident from devices such as that employed in the thirteenth chapter of the *Pratyutpanna-Buddha-Saṃmukhāvasthita-Samādhi,* where the Buddha predicts that the sūtra will be preserved in a cave[17] and the retrospective predictions that occur in works like the *Laṅkāvatāra* and the *Mañjuśrīmūlatantra,* where the Buddha is endowed with the presbyopia to forecast the appearance of Nāgārjuna and Asaṅga, four hundred years and nine hundred years after his passage into nirvāṇa respectively.[18]

However, it is not possible to bracket entirely the questions of authorship of the Mahāyāna sūtras and the intentions of the authors of the sūtras to speak as the Buddha; the relationship between the authors of the texts and the Yogācāra and Mādhyamika interpreters of those texts is highly ambiguous. Even with the assumption that the Mahāyāna interpreters believed the sūtras to be the word of the Buddha, there remains a complex dialectic between the sūtras and the schools that interpret them, in that the sūtras themselves provide the scriptural bases for the formulations of the doctrinal schools, such as Yogācāra and Mādhyamika; the ideas set forth in the sūtras were subsequently systematized by thinkers such as Asaṅga and Candrakīrti. What, then, was the nature of the preunderstanding that the exegetes brought to their interpretation of the sūtras? We cannot assume that the texts, or at least the positions delineated in the texts, were wholly unknown to the interpreter prior to his encounter with the text. The exegete was faced with a twin commitment, one to the presuppositions of his own philosophical school and the other to the teachings of the Buddha contained in the sūtras, commitments that potentially entail conflict. The situation is further complicated by the fact that sūtras continued to be composed during the period of the exegetes, sūtras that presumably were not immune from the influence of śāstras.

There is, thus, a compounding of the traditional problem of the hermeneutical circle as described by Heidegger in *Being and Time:*

> Any interpretation which is to contribute understanding, must already have understood what it is to be interpreted. . . . But if interpretation must in any case already operate in that which is understood, and if it must draw its nurture from this, how is it to bring any scientific results to maturity without moving in a circle, especially if, moreover, the understanding which is presupposed still operates within our common information about man and the world?[19]

Stated in other terms, if preunderstanding operates in every act of understanding, how can there be new understanding? For the Buddhist exegete, original understanding is not the issue; the goal is the communication and eventual replication of the content of the Buddha's enlightenment. Nonetheless, the question remains as to the nature of the "conversation" that takes place between the interpreter and the sūtra. Rather than a circle, it is perhaps more useful to visualize a symbiotic process along a Moebius strip, where the sūtra provides the discourse that is interpreted into philosophical doctrine, that doctrine turning back upon the sūtra as the standard of interpretation of the sūtra and, in some cases, stimulating the generation of new sūtras. Consequently, the interpretation of a sūtra is significantly determined by the affiliations of the interpreter, as is evident from considering a Mādhyamika exegesis of passages often cited in support of the Yogācāra view of mind-only.

Although it is always suspect to allow one opponent to present the position of another, Candrakīrti's summary of Yogācāra epistemology in his *Madhyamakāvatāra* (VI.45–46) provides a useful starting point.

> Because no object exists, no apprehension is seen.
> Therefore, understanding that the three realms are mere
> consciousness,
> The bodhisattva who abides in wisdom
> Comes to understand that reality is mere consciousness.

Just as waves arise on a great ocean
Stirred by the wind,
So does consciousness arise through its potency
From the basis of all seeds, called the foundation
consciousness.[20]

The Yogācāra position as summarized by Candrakīrti is that there are no objects of a substance other than mind. Because no external objects exist, none are apprehended by consciousness. Rather, everything in the universe is of the nature of consciousness, and this realization constitutes the bodhisattva's vision of reality. The Yogācāra accounts for the appearance of objects by positing the existence of seeds which exist in a foundation consciousness, the *ālayavijñāna.* These seeds, or karmic potencies, fructify as the experience of subject and object but are in fact consciousness alone.

Candrakīrti goes on to cite two well-known sūtra passages that seem to support the Yogācāra position that no external objects exist apart from consciousness. The first is from the *Daśabhūmika:* "The three realms are mind only." The other, from the *Laṅkāvatāra,* is the Buddha's statement "I teach mind only."[21] Both Bhāvaviveka and Candrakīrti argue that it is evident from the context of the passage that it is not the intention of the statement "the three realms are mind only" to indicate that there are no external objects. The sūtra itself says:

> A bodhisattva on the sixth bodhisattva level *(bhūmi)* views dependent arising in forward and reverse order and thinks, "These aggregates of suffering, devoid of agent or subject, arise from the twelve branches of ignorance, etc., and the tree of suffering is established." O children of the Conqueror, because this is certain, it is thus: the three realms are mind only, they are completely composed and inscribed by mind; there is no agent or subject whatsoever other than mind.[22]

Thus, according to Candrakīrti, the point of the Buddha's instruction is that the world is created by the mind; there is no permanent self *(ātman)* that acts as creator. The statement in the sūtra that the three realms are mind only is an abbreviated way of saying that only mind is primary—nothing else, including form, is as important as mind. This does not entail, however, that form does not exist.[23] He goes on to argue that if the Buddha had intended to deny external objects and uphold the pristine status of mind in the *Daśabhūmikasūtra,* he would not have declared that the mind arises from obscuration *(moha)* and karma. He says at *Madhyamakāvatāra* VI.88–90:

If he meant to refute form
With the knowledge that "these [three realms] are mind only,"

Why did the Mahātman go on to state
That mind is produced from obscuration and karma?

Mind alone establishes the world of sentient beings
And the myriad worlds that they inhabit.
It is taught that all the realms [of rebirth] are produced from karma.
But without mind, there is no karma.

Although form exists,
It is not an agent, as is mind.
Thus, an agent other than mind is denied,
But form is not refuted.[24]

Candrakīrti also denies that the statement from the *Laṅkāvatāra* means that external objects do not exist. The passage from the sūtra is:

The person, the continuum, the aggregates,
Likewise causes, atoms,
The *pradhāna,* Iśvara, and agents,
I explain to be mind only.[25]

Candrakīrti argues that this passage is intended to refute the various kinds of permanent agents propounded by the various heretical *(tīrthika)* schools, such as the *pradhāna* of the Sāṃkhyas and a creator deity. All of these are false; only mind creates the world.[26]

Candrakīrti concedes later, however, that there are statements in the sūtras that do indeed teach that externally appearing objects do not exist. For example, he cites the *Laṅkāvatāra*:

External objects do not exist, although they so appear;
It is the mind that appears as various [objects],
In the image of bodies, resources, and abodes.
I explain [everything] as mind only.[27]

In the case of the earlier passages that ostensibly taught mind-only, Candrakīrti relied on the context of the passage to argue that this was not the Buddha's intention. In this case, however, Candrakīrti says that the Buddha's statement was intentional (*abhiprāyika,* Tib. *dgongs pa can*) —that is, it does not represent the Buddha's final position but is directed to those beings who are greatly attached to form and who, consequently, are powerlessly drawn into sins such as anger and pride. With the purpose of putting an end to the afflictions *(kleśa)* that are related to form, the Buddha denied the existence of form, although this is an interpretable *(neyārtha)* teaching because, in fact, form exists.[28]

And to crown his argument that, although the Buddha intended to teach mind-only here, his purpose was expedient, Candrakīrti is able to cite a passage from the same sūtra that suggests this:

> Just as a physician provides
> Medicine for the sick,
> So the Buddha teaches
> Mind-only to sentient beings.[29]

Later, Candrakīrti explains the Buddha's method.

> The Bhagavat Buddhas cause disciples to enter into [the knowledge] of no inherent existence *(niḥsvabhāva)* gradually. Initially, they instruct them in such things as giving because it is a method for entering reality; the meritorious enter reality easily. In the same way, because the refutation of objects of knowledge is a method for penetrating selflessness, the Bhagavan at first sets forth only the refutation of objects of consciousness; those who understand the selflessness of objects of consciousness easily enter the selflessness of consciousness.[30]

Thus, the Yogācāra doctrine of mind-only is identified as one of the many skillful methods of the Buddha, a propaedeutic whereby he gradually leads those who are initially unable to comprehend the truth exactly as it is. Other Mādhyamika thinkers saw the Yogācāra in the same way.[31] Upāya does not, then, simply provide the basis for a hermeneutics of accommodation, but also establishes one of appropriation and control, for to declare a teaching to be expedient is to declare knowledge of the Buddha's intention and, hence, his final view.

Tibetan exegetes refined the process of determining whether a statement was of interpretable meaning through the delineation of four criteria:

1. The intended meaning *(dgongs pa)*
2. The foundation of the intention *(dgongs gzhi)*
3. The motive *(dgos pa)*
4. The contradiction if taken literally *(dngos la gnod byed)*[32]

Each of these requires discussion. The intended meaning *(dgongs pa, abhiprāya)* is what the Buddha says—that is, what he intends his audience to understand. This intended meaning is multiple and hence difficult to determine, especially when "with one sound your voice, beneficial to the world, comes forth in accordance with diverse aspirations."[33] In any case, the intended meaning must differ from the Buddha's own knowledge of reality in order for the statement to be interpretable *(neyārtha)*. This knowledge of reality is the foundation of the intention *(dgongs gzhi)*, the truth or fact that the Buddha has in mind when he says what is not ultimately true. The motivation *(dgos pa, prayojana)* is the Buddha's purpose, based on his knowledge of the capacities and needs of his disciples, in teaching what is not actually the case. The last criterion, the contradiction if taken literally *(dngos la gnod byed, mukhyārthabādha),* refers to the contradiction by reasoning and by definitive scriptures if the statement were accepted without interpretation.

Although Candrakīrti does not discuss the passage from the *Laṅkāvatāra* cited below in terms of this fourfold system, his position can be inferred from his arguments discussed above.

> External objects do not exist, although they so appear;
> It is the mind that appears as various [objects],
> In the image of bodies, resources, and abodes.
> I explain [everything] as mind only.[34]

The intended meaning is what the sūtra says: external objects do not exist; only mind exists. The foundation of the intention, that is, the deep meaning or fact, which the Buddha will eventually lead the auditors of this statement to understand, is that all phenomena, both form and consciousness, are empty of any intrinsic nature *(svabhāva).* However, both objects and the mind exist conventionally. Neither holds ontological precedence over the other. The Buddha's motivation in denying the existence of form is to cause his disciples who are excessively attached to form to overcome that attachment. Once that attachment has been destroyed, they will be able to understand that consciousness also does not exist in and of itself, and will, thereby, come to enter into the knowledge of reality, the emptiness of all phenomena in the universe. The contradiction if the statement is accepted as being literally true would include Candrakīrti's arguments against the mind-only position and statements from sūtras to the effect that external objects exist.

This theory of interpretation again raises the question of how the interpreter is to discern the intention of the Buddha—in these terms, the intended meaning, the foundation of the intention, and the motivation. Since the interpreter is not enlightened, what are the standards by which the boundaries of the interpretable and the definitive are traced? It should not be surprising at this juncture to discover that the sūtras, the supposed objects of interpretation, take up this question themselves.

The *Saṃdhinirmocana* and the Supplement

At the beginning of the seventh chapter of the *Saṃdhinirmocanasūtra,* the bodhisattva Paramārthasamudgata is puzzled by the apparent contradiction in the Buddha's teaching. He points out that on numerous occasions the Buddha has taught that the aggregates *(skandha),* the truths *(satya),* and the constituents *(dhātu)* exist by their own character *(svalakṣaṇa),* yet on other occasions he has said that all phenomena lack entityness *(svabhāva),* that all phenomena are unproduced, unceased, originally quiescent, and naturally passed beyond sorrow.[35] The Buddha responds:

> Listen, Paramārthasamudgata, and I will explain to you what I intended when I said that all phenomena are without entityness, all phenomena are unproduced, unceased, originally quiescent, and naturally passed beyond sorrow. Paramārthasamudgata, I was thinking of these three aspects of the nonentityness *(niḥsvabhāva)* of phenomena when I taught that all phenomena are without entityness: the nonentityness of character, the nonentityness of production, and the ultimate nonentityness.[36]

The Buddha's answer, briefly stated, is that his teaching that all phenomena lack entityness should be taken as a qualified apophasis. He had in mind three different types of nonentityness which qualify the three natures *(trilakṣaṇa),* the imaginary *(parikalpita),* the dependent *(paratantra),* and the consummate *(pariniṣpanna).* The meaning and implications of the doctrine of the three natures are topics of considerable controversy among the Yogācāra, Svātantrika, and Prāsaṅgika philosophers. According to the sūtra, imaginary natures are the entities and qualities that thought imputes to conditioned phenomena. These imputations are merely mental designations and thus do not exist by their own character. Dependent natures are the conditioned phenomena which are the objects of thought's operation and which serve as the bases of imputation by thought and terminology. These impermanent phenomena arise in dependence on causes and cannot produce themselves, and thus are said to lack entityness of production. The consummate nature is the fact that the imaginary nature is not established in conditioned phenomena. It is the selflessness of phenomena *(dharmanairātmya),* according to the sūtra.[37]

The Buddha concedes Paramārthasamudgata's observation that in some sūtras he taught that all phenomena are established by their own character and that in other sūtras he taught that no phenomenon is established by way of its own character. But here, in the *Saṃdhinirmocana,* he explains that, in fact, some phenomena are established by their own character, namely dependent and consummate natures, and some are not so established, namely imaginary natures.

Having understood this, Paramārthasamudgata offers a chronology of the Buddha's teaching. The Buddha's first sermon is renowned as the turning of the wheel of doctrine. In the *Aṣṭasāhasrikāprajñāpāramitā,* the gods declare that teaching of the four truths at Sarnath to be the first turning of the wheel, which has been superseded by the new dispensation, the second turning of the wheel of doctrine of the perfection of wisdom. Here, in the seventh chapter of the *Saṃdhinirmocana,* a third wheel is proclaimed:

> First, in the Deer Park at Ṛṣivadana in Vārāṇāsī, the Bhagavan turned a wheel of doctrine, wondrous and amazing, the likes of which had never been turned in the world by gods or humans, teaching the aspects of the four truths of Superiors *(ārya)* to those who had correctly entered the vehicles of *śrāvakas*. Yet even this wheel of doctrine turned by the Bhagavan is surpassable, provisional, of interpretable meaning *(neyārtha),* and subject to disputation.
>
> The Bhagavan turned a second wheel of doctrine, wondrous and amazing, through proclaiming emptiness to those who had correctly entered the Mahāyāna, dealing with the lack of entityness of phenomena, that they are unproduced, unceased, originally quiescent, and naturally passed beyond sorrow. Yet even this wheel of doctrine turned by the Bhagavan is surpassable, provisional, of interpretable meaning, and subject to disputation.
>
> The Bhagavan turned the third wheel of doctrine, very wondrous and amazing, possessing good differentiations for those who have correctly entered all vehicles, dealing with the lack of entityness of phenomena, that they are unproduced, unceased, originally quiescent, and naturally passed beyond sorrow. This wheel of doctrine turned by the Bhagavan is unsurpassed, not provisional, of definitive meaning *(nītārtha);* it is indisputable.[38]

The first wheel comprises the teaching of the four truths for disciples of the Hīnayāna. This is the wheel, presumably, in which Paramārthasamudgata recalls that the Buddha does not deny but upholds the reality or own-character *(svalakṣaṇa)* of the various constituents of the person, such as the five aggregates. The second wheel includes the Perfection of Wisdom sūtras, where the emptiness, the lack of entityness, of all phenomena is indiscriminately proclaimed. Both of these wheels are declared here to be provisional and subject to interpretation; that is, neither is literally acceptable because neither is wholly accurate in its characterization of the nature of phenomena. It is the third, and final, wheel which is "unsurpassed, not provisional, and of definitive meaning" because it is here that the Buddha interprets what he means by "no entityness" with his delineation of the three natures. It is this teaching of the third wheel, contained in the *Saṃdhinirmocana* itself, that is proclaimed as the Buddha's final view.

Thus, in the *Saṃdhinirmocana,* as its very title indicates, the Buddha explains what "I was thinking of." Here the Buddha provides a retrospective reading of his teachings, complete with chronology; he provides his own hermeneutic. The term *saṃdhi* in this context means "intention" with the sense of a deep or underlying meaning—hence

Lamotte's rendering as "mystère." *Nirmocana,* often translated as "explanation" or "interpretation," is derived from *nirmuc* 'loosen, untie, unravel, cast off, free'. This, then, is the sūtra in which the Buddha's intention, his underlying meaning, is freed from the illusory knots of contradiction that appear when all his statements are read literally. The key that unlocks this meaning is the knowledge of the Buddha's intention, the importance of which is indicated by Asvābhava in his *Mahāyānasaṃgrahopanibandhana:*

> Up until now, explanations of the meaning [of the sūtras] have not taken into account the intention of the author. But it is in taking into account that intention that one should explain the meaning of what has been declared [in the sūtras].[39]

With the knowledge of the Buddha's intention, the interpreter's task is a fairly simple one. If the statement is what the Buddha meant, it is definitive *(nītārtha).* If it is not, it is interpretable *(neyārtha).* In other words, that which is literal is definitive, that which is not literal requires interpretation. However, a simple hermeneutic may also be problematical, for, according to the *Saṃdhinirmocana,* it itself is the sūtra which is unsurpassed, not provisional, and of definitive meaning. This self-proclamation of authority immediately draws the exegetical system of the sūtra into questions of self-verification and subjectivism.

Perhaps of greater interest, however, are the implications entailed by the repeated addition of wheels of doctrine, each of which is claimed to outdistance those that have gone before. These implications can be considered in light of Jacques Derrida's notion of the supplement.[40] He writes that what is supplementary is "the operation of differing which at one and the same time both fissures and retards presence, submitting it simultaneously to primordial division and delay."[41] The supplement is both an addition and a compensation for a deficiency, compensating for nonself-presence. The dilemma of the interpreter of the sūtra is that he is dealing with a text that pretends to be a record of speech, an account of the discourse of the enlightened teacher. Even if we bracket the question of the authorship of the Mahāyāna sūtras, the Mahāyāna exegete is still faced with a double absence, the absence of the Buddha and the absence of the audience to whom and for whom he speaks. So long as intention and upāya remain the keys to interpretation, these twin deficiencies lure the supplement. The commentator, who claims to be able to see beyond the exigencies of the always already absent audience, is compelled to attempt to provide presence, to provide the text that is present elsewhere, that is, in the mind of the always already absent Buddha. The "present" which the sūtra attempts to capture must then be continually reconstituted. Derrida writes:

> Everything begins with reproduction. Always already: repositories of a meaning which was never present, whose signified presence is always reconstituted as deferral, *nachträglich,* belatedly, *supplementarily:* for the *nachträglich* also means *supplementary.* The call of the supplement is primary, here, and it hollows out that which will be reconstituted by deferral as the present. The supplement, which seems to be added as a plenitude, is equally that which compensates for a lack *(qui supplée).*[42]

With the addition of each new wheel, the previous one is not simply augmented but is also displaced; the supplement takes and keeps the place of the other. The supplement does not simply enrich presence; it "adds only to replace. It intervenes or insinuates itself *in-the-place-of;* it fills, it is as if one fills a void."[43] And because the presence sought by the interpreter can never be reclaimed, the supplements are multiplied one upon the other, thereby creating "the mirage of the thing itself, of immediate presence."[44]

One need only turn again to Candrakīrti to see the multiplication of the supplement. After explaining how the passage from the *Laṅkāvatāra* which sets forth the nonexistence of external objects is a statement requiring interpretation, he remarks that that passage makes it clear that other such sūtras also require interpretation. "What are 'other such sūtras'? The *Saṃdhinirmocanasūtra,* in setting forth the three natures —the imaginary, dependent, and consummate—[teaches] that the imaginary does not exist and the dependent exists."[45] Thus, the third wheel of the *Saṃdhinirmocana,* which was declared to be "unsurpassed, not provisional, of definitive meaning, indisputable" is here surpassed, disputed, declared provisional and interpretable; the third wheel is supplemented. Candrakīrti both adds to and displaces the third wheel with his implication that it indeed was not the Buddha's final view, but rather is yet another example of the skillful methods whereby he taught those disposed toward the Yogācāra position that some phenomena have their own character while others do not. This position, however, is ultimately false, for the Mādhyamika view of Candrakīrti is that all phenomena equally lack their own character.

From Intention to Emptiness

In the *Saṃdhinirmocana,* the Buddha explains to Paramārthasamudgata that he was compelled to turn the third wheel because the second wheel had been misunderstood by some. These disciples took the Buddha at his word when he said that all phenomena lack entityness. As a consequence, they fall to the nihilistic view that phenomena do not exist. The third wheel was provided, then, as a corrective.[46] Once the *Saṃdhinirmocana* establishes such a progression, complete with the chronology of the three wheels, the possibility of endless correctives arises. A very different, perhaps ahistorical hermeneutic, is provided by the *Akṣayamatinirdeśasūtra,* which says:

> If it is asked, "What is a sūtra of definitive meaning? What is a sūtra whose meaning requires interpretation?" Sūtras that teach the establishment of the conventional are called [sūtras] whose meaning requires interpretation. Those sūtras that teach the establishment of the ultimate are called [sūtras] of definitive meaning. Sūtras which teach with various words and letters are called [sūtras] whose meaning requires interpretation. Those sūtras that teach the profound—difficult to see and difficult to understand—are called [sūtras] of definitive meaning. Sūtras that teach, for instance, an owner where there is no owner, with [the owner] being described with a variety of terms [such as] self, sentient being, life, nourisher, being, person, born of Manu, child of Manu, agent, and experiencer, are called [sūtras] whose meaning requires interpretation. Those sūtras that teach the doors of liberation *(vimokṣamukha)*—the emptiness of things, no signs, no wishes, no composition, no production, no birth, no sentient beings, no living beings, no persons, no owner—are called [sūtras] of definitive meaning. This is called relying on sūtras of definitive meaning and not relying on sūtras whose meaning requires interpretation.[47]

This passage addresses a specific problem that arises in the interpretation of the pronouncements of the Buddha, but also has implications for the problem of supplementation that appears to be systemic to Buddhist hermeneutics. Let us consider the specific context of the passage first.

Perhaps the most commonly cited examples of an apparent contradiction in the Buddha's teachings are his statements in which he makes reference to the self *(ātman)* or the person *(pudgala).* Although the doctrine of selflessness *(anātman)* is renowned as the very heart of Buddhist philosophy, there are numerous statements that ostensibly uphold the existence of the self. For example, the *Dhammapada* (XII.4/160) says:

> The self is protector of the self.
> What other protector could there be?
> Through subduing the self,
> One gains protection difficult to gain.[48]

In order to avoid the inconvenience of expunging all nouns such as "I," "myself," "oneself," and "person" from common parlance, Buddhist commentators have traditionally accommodated the provisional use of such terms by the Buddha by classifying them as teachings that require interpretation, while assigning the statements that there is no self to the more exalted category of the definitive. As Lamotte has noted,[49] the

Therāvadin exegete Buddhaghosa consigns references to the person to the *neyārtha* class while preserving the class of the *nītārtha* for the transtemporal truths of impermanence, suffering, and selflessness. Candrakīrti makes a similar point at *Madhyamakāvatāra* VI.44:

> Even though the Buddha is free from the view of self *(satkayadṛṣṭi),*
> He teaches [using the terms] "I" and "mine."
> In the same way, although things lack intrinsic nature,
> He teaches that they exist as an interpretable meaning.[50]

The statement cited above from the *Akṣayamatinirdeśa* appears to be addressing the same problem, while defining the definitive in even more exclusive terms than does Buddhaghosa. It provides a long list of synonyms for the person and says that sūtras which teach in such terms require interpretation. Those sūtras that teach that there are no persons *(pudgala),* no sentient beings *(sattva),* no living beings *(puruṣa)* are definitive. The categories of the interpretable and the definitive are hence similar to those outlined by Buddhaghosa, as is the resolution of the contradictions between those statements in which the Buddha speaks of the person and those in which he speaks of the nonexistence of the person. The latter statements are afforded prepotency. However, the *Akṣayamatinirdeśa* goes further.

First, it equates the interpretable with the conventional *(saṃvṛti);* sūtras that set forth conventional truths require interpretation. Consequently, the *Akṣayamatinirdeśa* does not equate the interpretable with that which is not literally acceptable. Although it is the case that suffering and impermanence are facts of mundane existence, the expositions of suffering and impermanence that occur in the Buddha's first sermon, for example, would, according to the *Akṣayamatinirdeśa,* be classed as teachings requiring interpretation because suffering and impermanence are conventionalities; suffering and impermanence, which according to Buddhaghosa are definitive, here require interpretation. For the *Akṣayamatinirdeśa,* "sūtras that teach the profound—difficult to see and difficult to understand—are called [sūtras] of definitive meaning." That is, sūtras teaching emptiness, the ultimate truth *(paramārthasatya),* are definitive. This same distinction occurs in the *Samādhirājasūtra*:

> Instances of definitive sūtras are known
> To accord with the Sugata's teaching of emptiness.
> All doctrines teaching sentient being, person, or being
> Are to be known to require interpretation.[51]

As emptiness is the definitive, final nature of phenomena, sūtras that set forth this final nature are definitive; all others require interpretation.

This method of categorizing scripture radically centers the hermeneutic endeavor on the ontological question, excluding from consideration questions of authorial intention, contextual circumstance, expediency, and literal acceptability. Sūtras whose referent is emptiness are definitive, those whose referent is not emptiness require interpretation. One can thus provide examples of literal statements that are interpretable, such as the common ethical axiom that the practice of giving brings about the karmic effect of wealth in the future. Although it is indeed the case that giving causes wealth for the donor such that it can be said that the creation of wealth is a quality of giving, the creation of wealth is not the final quality or mode of being of giving. This final mode of being is the emptiness of giving, which is not to be inferred from the statement that giving causes wealth. Thus, the statement requires interpretation.[52]

The *Akṣayamatinirdeśa* defines the definitive and the interpretable strictly in terms of the subject matter, the signified of the passage, without consideration of the time, place, audience, or mode of expression of the text in question. This provides an element of distanciation which the *Saṃdhinirmocana,* identifying itself as the final and only definitive wheel, lacks. The *Akṣayamatinirdeśa* provides a universal and disinterested approach by which texts can be distinguished as definitive and interpretable, without making dogmatic claims about its own priority. Indeed, the statement in the *Akṣayamatinirdeśa* that sūtras which teach emptiness are definitive is itself interpretable, because it does not set forth the final mode of being, the emptiness, of those sūtras. By aligning the interpretable with conventional truths and the definitive with ultimate truths, however, the *Akṣayamatinirdeśa* in no way relegates the interpretable to a class of provisional teachings to be superseded. As Nāgārjuna says at *Madhyamakakārikās* XXIV.10:

> Without relying on conventions
> The ultimate cannot be taught.
> Without understanding the ultimate
> Nirvāṇa cannot be attained.[53]

Thus, the *Akṣayamatinirdeśa*'s hermeneutical program seeks to point beyond the literal meaning of the text; it is not concerned with establishing what the author intended. The text is allowed to speak, as it is restricted from doing under the constraints of establishing intention and upāya. At the same time, the hermeneutic of the sūtra provides a constant reminder of the need to seek the ultimate in all cases where the ultimate is not explicitly set forth; the attention of the reader of sūtras requiring interpretation is constantly displaced from both the signifier and signified of the text to emptiness, although emptiness is not manifestly present. Indeed, the *Akṣayamatinirdeśa* seems to transcend strictly textual concerns by classifying not merely sūtras but all phenomena as either interpretable or definitive. Emptiness is definitive, everything else requires interpretation; it is only by extension that texts which discuss the ultimate are definitive and those which discuss the conventional are interpretable.

The appeal of the *Akṣayamatinirdeśa* to Candrakīrti is not difficult to appreciate; he echoes its formula at *Madhyamakāvatāra* VI.97:

> Interpretation is undertaken upon knowing the application of scripture
> And understanding that sūtras which teach what is not reality
> Are said to require interpretation.
> Know [that sūtras] having the meaning of emptiness are definitive.[54]

Here the question of interpretation is, at least for the moment, freed from questions of intention and upāya, of fathoming the Buddha's profound techniques for leading diverse disciples in diverse situations. The hermeneutic of the *Akṣayamatinirdeśa* prefers not to engage such questions, but to point always to the emptiness, the lack of any own-being or intrinsic nature of the words of the sūtras, the emptiness that is the object of Nāgārjuna's reasoning, accessible to those still on the path, yet also the constant content of the Buddha's mind. Hence, Candrakīrti can claim that the purpose of Nāgārjuna's composition of the *Madhyamakakārikās* was to prove with reasoning what the *Akṣayamatinirdeśa* proclaims in scripture: that emptiness is the definitive nature of reality, all else requires interpretation.

> Some have the doubt: "What is the teaching that has the meaning of reality? Which [teachings] are intentional?" Some, because of their feeble minds, think that teachings of interpretable meaning are of definitive meaning. In order to clear away the doubt and mistaken ideas of both [of these] through reasoning and scripture, the master composed this [text].[55]

But is the hermeneutic of the *Akṣayamatinirdeśa* free from the dangerous supplement? It is a hermeneutic that seeks closure with a single supplement, allowing texts dealing with the conventional to stand as literal while undermining them by pointing beyond to their final nature, their self-absence, their emptiness, their unsupplemented nature. And texts that take the definitive as their subject require no supplement, no addition, no compensation; their subject is the absence which need not be promoted by the supplement.

Conclusions

In her work entitled *Intention,* G. E. M. Anscombe notes that "to explain one's actions by an account indicating a motive is to put them in a certain light."[56] This observation pertains in the case of the problem of intention in the interpretation of the Mahāyāna sūtras, where it is not the actor, but another who explains the motives of the actor. So long as intention remains central to the process of interpretation, it is the exegete's present description of a past intention that constitutes the goal of that process. The commentator must be able to reproduce the circumstances of the discourse in order to know its meaning. It is such an agenda that Gadamer terms romantic, arguing at length in *Truth and Method* that it is inadequate, in part because it does not take into account the significance of temporal distance for understanding.

Before taking up this question in the Buddhist context, let us examine briefly Gadamer's notion of understanding—and, by extension, commentary—as projection. He writes:

> A person who is trying to understand a text is always performing an act of projecting. He projects before himself a meaning for the text as a whole as soon as some initial meaning emerges in the text. Again, the latter emerges only because he is reading the text with particular expectations in regard to a certain meaning. The working out of this fore-project, which is constantly revised in terms of what emerges as he penetrates into the meaning, is understanding what is there.[57]

What appears to be the case with the Buddhist exegete, however, is that the foreknowledge or prejudice remains determinative; understanding is not modified through a conversation with the text, but rather "meaning" is imposed upon it. The concept of upāya suggests the fluid nature of meaning, adapted by the Buddha for each of his listeners. The goal of the interpreter, however, is to freeze that nature for all time, declaring what the Buddha really meant. The interpreter, ironically, participates in a hermeneutics of suspicion, in the case of interpretable scriptures, allowing the Buddha's statement its illocutionary function but denying its perlocutionary effect; acknowledging his words but being unpersuaded by them.

"Every encounter with tradition that takes place within historical consciousness involves the experience of the tension between the text and the present,"[58] writes Gadamer. The question, however, is whether the interpretation of the Mahāyāna sūtras takes place within such historical consciousness. For the Buddhist interpreter, the discovery of the true meaning of the text is not the infinite process that Gadamer envisions; the horizons of the Buddha and the interpreter are not even imagined to exist separately. There is no need for their fusion. It is essential for the Buddhist interpreter to believe that the genius of the creator of the discourse can ultimately be matched by the genius of the interpreter, for it is the intention of the Buddha, the duplication of his enlightenment, that is the interpreter's goal. Meaning must be determinate.

But what is that meaning? How is the intention of the Buddha in a specific instance to be determined except by what the Buddha retrospectively declares it to have been? If the categories of the interpretable and the definitive are based on what a particular sūtra says they are, how can the vicious circle of textual claims to authority be broken? This problem was not one of which Buddhist thinkers were unaware. For example, Tsong-kha-pa writes at the beginning of his *Legs bshad snying po:*

> Seeing that the reality of phenomena is most difficult to understand and that, if it is not understood, there can be no liberation from saṃsāra, the Compassionate Teacher is said to have guided [beings] to penetrate that [reality] through many methods *(upāya)* and doors of reasoning. Therefore, the discriminating must strive for a method to understand what reality is like, which, in turn, depends on distinguishing the interpretable meaning and the definitive meaning in the pronouncements of the Conqueror.
>
> It is not possible to differentiate those two merely through [citing] scriptures that say, "This is the interpretable meaning. This is the definitive meaning." Otherwise, it would have been purposeless for the great charioteers [such as Nāgārjuna and Asaṅga] to compose commentaries that differentiate the interpretable and the definitive. There are also many conflicting modes of positing the interpretable and the definitive set forth in the scriptures. . . .
>
> Therefore, one must seek the intention [of the Buddha] by following the great charioteers, prophesied [by the Buddha] to differentiate [his] interpretable and definitive pronouncements. They commented on the [Buddha's] intention concerning the interpretable and definitive and employed reasoning to delineate well the faults of interpreting the meaning of definitive pronouncements in some other way and [gave] proofs that [those scriptures] are definitive, it being unsuitable to interpret them otherwise. Thus, in the end, one must distinguish [the interpretable and the definitive] using stainless reasoning.[59]

An analysis of the autonomy of reasoning in Buddhism must for the moment be deferred. However, it seems clear that there is no escape from the text, for the great formulators of the reasonings employed in the interpretation of scripture appear to gain authority for Tsong-kha-pa, at least in part, from the fact that they are prophesied by the Buddha himself in the scriptures.

Hence, interpretation is projection of prejudice, of preunderstanding, "an allegorical act, which consists in rewriting a given text in terms of a particular master code."[60] Commentary becomes the endless search for a meaning that can be discerned once and for all, free from sectarian concerns, such as those of Yogācāra and Mādhyamika. And what text better receives these projections than the letter *a*, or perhaps, that from the night of his enlightenment until the night of his passage into nirvāṇa the Tathāgata uttered not a sound. Here the interpreter becomes the arbiter of meaning, the interpreter becomes the author as the author sits in silence. A unity of thought is thus imposed upon diverse texts, as the commentators "reconstitute another discourse, rediscover the silent murmuring, the inexhaustible speech that animates from within the voice that one hears, re-establish the tiny, invisible text that runs between and sometimes collides with them."[61] The silence of the Buddha or the letter *a* stands for the original unsupplemented nature which does not exist without commentary, supplementation seeking endlessly to constitute that mythic, unsupplemented entity.

In undertaking this task, the commentator must recall Borges' cautionary "Parable of the Palace," in which the Yellow Emperor showed the poet through his palace.

> It was at the foot of the penultimate tower that the poet (who seemed remote from the wonders that were a marvel to all) recited the brief composition that today we link indissolubly to his name and that, as the most elegant historians repeat, presented him with immortality and death. The text has been lost; there are those who believe that it consisted of a line of verse; others, of a single word. What is certain, and incredible, is that all the enormous palace was, in its most minute details, there in the poem, with each illustrious porcelain and each design on each porcelain and the penumbrae and light of each dawn and twilight, and each unfortunate and happy instant in the glorious dynasties of the mortals, of gods and dragons that had inhabited it from the unfathomable past. Everyone was silent, but the Emperor exclaimed: *You have robbed me of my palace!* And the executioner's iron sword cut the poet down.[62]

Notes

1. Jorge Luis Borges, *Ficciones* (New York: Grove Press, 1962), 28.
2. Because of the lack of any definitive list of texts in India and because of the lack of consistency among Tibetan and Chinese sources as to which sūtras are to be considered authentic, one cannot speak of a single Mahāyāna canon.
3. P 741, vol. 21, 257.4.3–8.
4. Compare the view of Rabbi Mendel of Rymadov that the revelation of the law on Mount Sinai consisted only of the *aleph,* the consonant in the Hebrew alphabet which represents the position of the larynx when a word begins with a vowel. See Gershom G. Scholem, *On the Kabbalah and Its Symbolism* (New York: Schocken Books, 1969), 30.
5. For the Sanskrit, see Louis de la Vallée Poussin, ed., *Mūlamadhyamakakāri-*

kās de Nāgārjuna avec la Commentaire Prasannapadā de Candrakīrti (Osnabruck: Biblio Verlag, 1970), 364.

6. For references to this statement in the Pali canon, see É. Lamotte, trans., *L'Enseignement de Vimalakīrti (Vimalakīrtinirdeśa)* (Louvain: Université de Louvain Institut Orientaliste, 1962), 109 n. 52.

7. See la Vallée Poussin, *Mūlamadhyamakakārikās,* 366. For the Tibetan translation of the passage in the *Tathāgatācintyaguhya,* see P 760.3, vol. 50, 62.5.4–5, where the first part of the passage appears but the second is absent. See also Lamotte, *L'Enseignement de Vimalakīrti,* 110 n. 52.

8. See la Vallée Poussin, *Mūlamadhyamakakarikas,* 366–367. See also P 760.3, vol. 50, 63.5.6–64.1.2 and 66.2.2–3.

9. See la Vallée Poussin, *Mūlamadhyamakakārikās,* 367.

10. See ibid., 366–368.

11. For a useful analysis of the theory of upāya in the *Lotus* and other Mahāyāna sūtras, see Michael Pye, *Skillful Means* (London: Duckworth, 1978). Pye argues, primarily on the basis of East Asian sources, that all of the Buddha's teachings are upāya. This does not appear to be the view of Candrakīrti, who suggests that only teachings of interpretable meaning *(neyārtha)* are upāya, that is, methods by which the Buddha leads beings to the final truth.

12. See David Newton-De Molina, ed., *On Literary Intention* (Edinburgh: Edinburgh University Press, 1976). Especially useful is the essay by Quentin Skinner, "Motives, Intentions, and the Interpretation of Texts," 210–221.

13. E. D. Hirsch, Jr., *Validity in Interpretation* (New Haven: Yale University Press, 1967), 57.

14. Schleiermacher's various writings on hermeneutics, collected by Heinz Kimmerle, have been translated by James Duke and Jack Forstman in F. D. E. Schleiermacher, *Hermeneutics: The Handwritten Manuscripts* (Missoula, Montana: Scholars Press, 1977). The phrase cited here appears on p. 150.

15. Ibid., 112.

16. See, for example, Nāgārjuna's argument in *Ratnāvalī* IV.67–100 and Bhāvaviveka's long defense in the fourth chapter of the *Tarkajvālā.*

17. See Paul Harrison, "The *Pratyutpanna-Buddha-Saṃmukhāvasthita-Samādhi-Sūtra*" (Ph.D. diss., Australian National University, 1979), 86–90.

18. For these and other prophecies, see E. Obermiller, trans., *History of Buddhism by Bu-ston,* Part II (Heidelberg: Heft, 1932), 108–122.

19. Martin Heidegger, *Being and Time,* trans. J. Macquarrie and E. Robinson (New York: Harper and Row, 1962), 194.

20. See Louis de la Vallée Poussin, ed., *Madhyamakāvatāra par Candrakīrti* (Osnabruck: Biblio Verlag, 1970), 135–137.

21. Cited by Candrakīrti in ibid., 181 and 183, respectively.

22. Cited by lCang-skya-rol-pa'i-rdo-rje, *Grub pa'i mtha'i rnam par bzhag pa gsal bar bshad pa thub bstan lhun po'i mdzes rgyan* (Sarnath: Pleasure of Elegant Sayings Press, 1970), 340–341. See also la Vallée Poussin, *Madhyamakāvatāra,* 182.

23. See *Madhyamakāvatāra,* VI.84, 87, in la Vallée Poussin, *Madhyamakāvatāra,* 182, 185.

24. Ibid., 186–191.

25. Cited by Candrakīrti in commentary on VI.85; see ibid., 183.

26. *Madhyamakāvatāra* VI.86; see ibid., 183–185.

27. Cited by Candrakīrti in commentary on *Madhyamakāvatāra* VI.23; see ibid., 194.

28. These points are made at *Madhyamakāvatāra* VI.94–95 and their autocommentary; see ibid., 194–196.

29. Cited by Candrakīrti in commentary on *Madhyamakāvatāra* VI.95; see ibid., 196.

30. Autocommentary to *Madhyamakāvatāra* VI.96; see ibid., 199.

31. For example, Jñānagarbha writes in his *Satyadvayavibhaṅgavṛtti* (Toh. 3882, folio 13a3-4.):

> The Bhagavan himself, the knower of actions and their effects, whose body is the nature of compassion, sees transmigrators bound by the chains of misconception in the prison of saṃsāra and completely destroys the conception of true existence by setting forth in stages the aggregates, constituents *(dhātu),* sources *(āyatana),* mind-only, and the selflessness of phenomena.

Śāntarakṣita in his *Madhyamakālaṃkāra* (P 5284, vol. 101, 2.3.4.):

> The nonexistence of external objects should be known
> Through relying on mind-only.
> [Then] relying on this [Mādhyamika] mode, it should be known
> That this [mind] as well is completely without self.

Kamalaśīla says in his *Madhyamakāloka:*

> Some sections [of sūtras] such as the *Saṃdhinirmocana,* the *Laṅkāvatāra,* and the *Ghanavyuha* establish the Cittamātra system [through] refuting external objects and not refuting the inherent existence of the mind. This teaching accords with the thoughts of those who are unable to realize that all phenomena are simultaneously without intrinsic nature [and thus] must be led in stages.

This passage is cited by Tsong-kha-pa in his *Drang nges legs bshad snying po* (Sarnath: Pleasure of Elegant Sayings Press, 1973), 129-130.

32. This list is derived from Pan-chen bSod-nam-grags-pa (1478-1554) who employs it in *Drang nges utpala'i 'phreng pa,* his commentary on Tsong-kha-pa's *Legs bshad snying po.* Earlier Tibetan scholars, such as bSod nam rtse mo, Sa skya Pandita, and Bu-ston speak only of the last three criteria. See the excellent study by D. Seyfort Ruegg, "Purport, Implicature, and Presupposition: Sanskrit *abhiprāya* and Tibetan *dgons pa/dgons gzhi* as Hermeneutical Concepts," *Journal of Indian Philosophy* 13 (1985): 311. Pan-chen bSod-nam-grags-pa probably derives the first criteria, *dgongs pa,* from Tsong-kha-pa's uses of the terms *gsung ba po'i dgongs pa* (intention of the speaker) and *gsung rab kyi dgongs pa* (intention of the scripture). On *abhiprāya,* see also Michael Broido, "Abhiprāya and Intention in Tibetan Linguistics," *Journal of Indian Philosophy* 12 (1984): 1-33.

33. See la Vallée Poussin, *Mūlamadhyamakakārikās,* 368.

34. Cited by Candrakīrti in commentary on *Madhyamakāvatāra,* VI.23; see la Vallée Poussin, *Madhyamakāvatāra,* 194.

35. For an edition of the Tibetan translation of the sūtra, see Étienne Lamotte, ed., *Saṃdhinirmocana Sūtra: L'Explication des Mystères* (Paris: Adrien Maisonneuve, 1935). The passage translated here occurs on pp. 65-66.

36. See ibid., 67.

37. See ibid., 67-69.

38. See ibid., 85.

39. Cited by Lamotte, *La Somme du Grand Véhicule d'Asaṅga,* Tome II (Louvain: Institut Orientaliste, 1973), 134 n. 3. Thanks to John Keenan for pointing out this passage.

40. Derrida deals with the supplement in the seventh chapter of *Speech and*

Phenomena, trans. David B. Allison (Evanston, Ill.: Northwestern University Press, 1973). It also figures in his essay "Freud and the Scene of Writing," in *Writing and Difference,* trans. Alan Bass (Chicago: University of Chicago Press, 1978), 196–231. The most extensive treatment is in the second half of *Of Grammatology,* trans. Gayatri Chakravorty Spivak (Baltimore: Johns Hopkins University Press, 1976).

41. *Speech and Phenomena,* 88.

42. "Freud and the Scene of Writing," *Writing and Difference,* 211–212.

43. *Of Grammatology,* 145.

44. Ibid., 157.

45. la Vallée Poussin, *Madhyamakāvatāra,* 195–196.

46. See Lamotte, *Saṃdhinirmocana Sūtra,* 77.

47. Cited by Candrakīrti in the *Prasannapadā;* see la Vallée Poussin, *Mūlamadhyamakakārikās,* 43. For the Tibetan, see Tsong-kha-pa, *Drang nges legs bshad snying po,* 89–90.

48. Translated from the Pali edition of S. Radhakrishnan in *The Dhammapada* (London: Oxford University Press, 1966), 112. A series of similar statements occurs in the *Udānavarga* XXIII.10–22. For English translations of this text, see W. W. Rockhill, *Udānavarga: A Collection of Verse from the Buddhist Canon* (Calcutta: Trubner's Oriental Series, 1892), and Gareth Sparham, *The Tibetan Dhammapada* (New Delhi: Mahayana Publications, 1983).

49. See p. 18.

50. la Vallée Poussin, *Madhyamakāvatāra,* 133.

51. This passage is cited by Candrakīrti in both the *Madhyamakāvatāra* and the *Prasannapadā;* the former is in la Vallée Poussin, *Madhyamakāvatāra,* 200, the latter in la Vallée Poussin, *Mūlamadhyamakakārikās,* 44.

52. This example is drawn from lCang-skya-rol-pa'i-rdo-rje's exegesis of the passage from the *Akṣayamatinirdeśa.* See his *Grub mtha'i rnam par bzhag pa* (Sarnath: Pleasure of Elegant Sayings Press, 1970), 317. For an English translation, see Donald S. Lopez, Jr., *A Study of Svātantrika* (Ithaca: Snow Lion Publications, 1987), 285.

53. la Vallée Poussin, *Mūlamadhyamakakārikās,* 494.

54. Ibid., 199.

55. Ibid., 42.

56. G. E. M. Anscombe, *Intention* (Ithaca: Cornell University Press, 1957), 21.

57. Hans-Georg Gadamer, *Truth and Method* (London: Sheed and Ward, 1975), 236.

58. Ibid., 273.

59. Tsong-kha-pa, *Drang nges legs bshad snying po,* 2–3. This work has been translated by Robert A. F. Thurman as *Tsong Khapa's Speech of Gold in the Essence of True Eloquence* (Princeton: Princeton University Press, 1984). The passage cited above is translated by Thurman on p. 189.

60. Frederic Jameson, *The Political Unconscious* (Ithaca: Cornell University Press, 1981), 10.

61. Michel Foucault, *The Archaeology of Knowledge,* trans. A. M. Sheridan Smith (New York: Pantheon Books, 1972), 27.

62. Jorge Luis Borges, *A Personal Anthology* (New York: Grove Press, 1967), 88.

Killing, Lying, Stealing, and Adultery: A Problem of Interpretation in the Tantras

MICHAEL M. BROIDO

Part I: Killing, Lying, Stealing, and Adultery in the *Kālacakratantra*

1. *Introduction*

Buddhism of all kinds has stressed the connection between cause and effect, especially in the ethical sphere. In the *Abhidharmakośa* (IV.68–74) we find a list of ten *karmapathas,* ten kinds of action which are not only unethical in themselves but will surely lead to undesirable results. The first four are killing *(prāṇātipātaḥ),* stealing *(adattādana),* illicit love *(kāmamithya),* and lying *(mṛṣavāca).* Yet in the tantras there are many passages which if taken literally tell us to do just these or very similar things. Clearly, then, we have a pressing problem of interpretation: is it a hermeneutical problem?

In the *Kālacakratantra,* for instance, we find a list of six apparently recommended actions or activities, linked with the six families[1] into which the adepts are divided. The correspondence may be set out thus:

Table 1

Activity		Family *(kula, rigs)*
Killing	*(prāṇātipātaḥ, srog-gcod)*	vajra (krodha, kuliśa)
Lying	*(asatya vākyaṃ, brdzun-tshig smra-ba)*	khaḍga
Stealing	*(hāryam parasvam, gzhan-nor 'phrog-pa)*	ratna
Adultery	*(hāryā parastrī, gzhan-gyi bud-med 'phrog-pa)*	padma (kamala)
Drinking wine	*(madyaṃ, chang)*	cakra
Loving women of low caste	*(ḍombyādyāḥ vanitā)*	karttikā

Obviously such passages present problems of interpretation: obviously we cannot just take them literally. Appropriate interpretations are found in the many commentaries available especially in Tibetan. For our *Kālacakra* passage we will rely on the *Vimalaprabhā* of King Puṇḍarīka. This commentary is detailed and yet written in a straightforward style, and it is available in Sanskrit mss.; by using the Sanskrit text we may hope to gain an understanding of tantric commentary in India, independently of the vastly greater quantity of commentaries available only in Tibetan. However, in comparing the *Kālacakra* treatment of killing, lying, etc. with that in other tantras (*Hevajra,*[2] *Guhyasamāja,*[3] and the like), it will be necessary to use the Tibetan translations of Indian works. (This chapter is not about *Tibetan* hermeneutics, and so will not use indigenous Tibetan works except on quite peripheral points.) The *Vimalaprabhā* is a very important work, perhaps the most distinguished tantric commentary to have come down to us, and it carries enormous authority in Tibet, where it is the only commentatorial work to have been included in the canonical collection of the Buddha's own utterances, the *bka-'gyur.* The Sanskrit and Tibetan texts of the *Kālacakra* passage and of the *Vimalaprabhā* on it are given in Appendices A and B.

In order to systematize the process of interpretation, our *Vimalaprabhā* passage uses two main technical terms, *neyārtha* and *nītārtha.* These terms are well known in the sūtra literature, where they mean roughly "provisional" and "final"; there they apply to *texts,* in the sense that a passage is either provisional or final but not both. Here in the tantras the two terms are normally applied to *one and the same passage,* and clearly their meaning has changed; they are properties not of texts, but of *interpretations* of texts. Though *artha* can of course mean "meaning," it also commonly means "intention," and here it refers to the intentions attributed to the text (or to the speaker) in the various interpretations. We will see that this is a common idea in Indian theories of meaning, and in Buddhist logic.

The idea of this chapter is to rely on the texts alone and not to assume vaguely that we already know what the technical terms mean from other tantras or from Tibetan texts. In the second half of the chapter we will sketch the way such passages on killing, lying, etc. are treated in other tantras, and we will be able to see the differences in the approaches. Again, when one looks at Tibetan commentaries on the *Kālacakra* (such as that of Mi-pham) it is obvious that the techniques of interpretation are different from those in the *Vimalaprabhā.* For example Mi-pham uses techniques taken from the *Guhyasamāja* literature; this does not seem to have been the practice in India.

Perhaps one of the reasons for the weakness of current western work on the tantras is the almost complete neglect of the methods of interpretation which were used by the commentators and teachers who interpreted them. We may not have access to the methods used in oral instruction, but there is no good reason for this neglect of the methods used in the available commentaries.

In Tibet, the theory of interpreting the tantras corresponds roughly to the topic called "method of explanation" *(bshad-thabs).*[4] The normal practice of many Tibetan authors was to apply a single system of *bshad-thabs* uniformly to all the principal tantras of the highest class, the *anuttarayogatantras* such as *Guhyasamāja, Hevajra, Cakrasaṃvara,* and *Kālacakra.* The most popular system of explanation used seven groups of technical terms called "ornaments" *(alaṃkāra, rgyan)* which come from the *Guhyasamāja* literature. The Sa-skya school used a different and in some ways better system called the "six instructions" *(gdams-ngag drug).* I have discussed these systems carefully elsewhere.[5] The most important of these methods are linguistic (broadly speaking), but there were in addition important nonlinguistic methods within *bshad-thabs,* such as the "three tantras" of ground, path, and goal, also derived from the *Guhyasamāja* cycle.[6] In India, however, it is necessary to look separately at the strategies used for each tantra.

In the *Vimalaprabhā,* each of the activities mentioned in the *Kālacakra* verses (see table 1) is given two interpretations: one *neyārtha* and one *nītārtha.* A crude summary of these interpretations for each activity is this:

KILLING

neyārtha: A Buddha may kill those who are really committing the five immediacies, who break their vows, and who damage the teaching. But a mantrin who has not attained the five special knowledges *(abhijñā, mngon-shes)* should not perform such fearful actions (C–G, J).

nītārtha: Holding the semen *(retas, khu-ba)* at the top of the head (R, U).

LYING

neyārtha: One may tell untruths not for one's own benefit, but in order to raise up those who have fallen from the path (K).

nītārtha: The dharma is taught in an instant by causing the unstruck sound *(anāhatadhvani, gzhom-du med-pa'i sgra)* to resound in the heart center (V, W).

STEALING

neyārtha: One may take what is not given, not for one's own benefit but to prevent the avaricious from taking rebirth as *pretas* (L).

nītārtha: One attains the eighth bodhisattva stage by retaining the semen in the throat center (X).

ADULTERY
neyārtha: One commits adultery not for one's own purposes, but so that others will not be reborn as animals (M).
nītārtha: One attains the tenth bodhisattva stage by retaining the semen at the forehead center (Y).

WINE-DRINKING, etc.
neyārtha: Relying on the vows connected with the five nectars and so forth, one destroys attachment to one's tantric family (*kula,* table 1) (N).
nītārtha: Relying on the lotus in the navel, one retains feces, urine, and semen (Z, AA).

LOW-CASTE WOMEN, etc.
neyārtha: In order to accumulate merit one does not denigrate women of low caste, and so attains the siddhi of *karmamudrā (las-kyi phyag-rgya)* (O).
nītārtha: None (but see BB–CC).

These interpretations may themselves appear pretty bizarre, and for a western audience may well call for further interpretation. That, however, is not a problem of *Buddhist* interpretation and will not be considered here.[7]

The remainder of Part I of this chapter contains an English rendering of the *Vimalaprabhā* passage just summarized (sec. 2), some comments on the passage (sec. 3), and a preliminary attempt to work out the senses of the terms *nītārtha* and *neyārtha* as used here (sec. 4). Part II relates the extract to the wider field of Indian Buddhist hermeneutics.

2. *The* Vimalaprabhā *on Killing, Lying, Stealing, and Adultery*

This section contains an interpretation in English of the Sanskrit text of the *Vimalaprabhā* on *Kālacakra* III.97cd and 98. My notes relate purely to questions of interpretation; notes on textual questions are found in the appendices. On those few occasions when I have followed the Tibetan in preference to the Sanskrit, it is indicated in the notes to this section. Otherwise the Sanskrit text will stand up by itself. Since there are disputes among orientalists over the notion of translation, I will not claim to be providing one; my aim is to make sense of the text taken in its context, insofar as I am familiar with it.[8] Subject to this overriding constraint, there is no reason why those Sanskrit sentences capable of literal rendering consistent with their content, such as A, F, N, should not be so rendered. But in many cases it will not be possible, because of the vocabulary or because of the state of the texts (e.g. W), or because of my own limitations.

The terms *nītārtha* and *neyārtha* are left untranslated, since part of our objective is to find out (if possible) just how these terms are being used. Certain other technical terms are unsuitable for accurate translation, and are either left untranslated *(samādhi, karmamudrā, mahāmudrā)* or are translated in what one might call a nominal way, not intended to convey their full sense (*cakra* 'center'; *kula* 'family'; *ānantarya* 'immediacy'). Such terms as *retas, khu-ba* 'semen' present special problems because they may well have been taken literally in India but not in Tibet. On the whole I render these literally (*viṭ* 'feces'; *mūtra* 'urine', etc.).

THE VERSES

Surely in the Diamond family you should kill living beings, and in the Sword family you should tell lies (97c)
In the Jewel family you should take the wealth of others, and in the great Lotus family the wives of others (97d)
In the Wheel family you should rely completely on wine, lights, and other objects of the Buddhas and of the good (98a)
And in the Dagger family you should love women of low caste without reservation, not despising the sky-lotus. (98b)
For the benefit of beings you should sacrifice the body with all its wealth, and not look after them. (98c)
Son of noble a family! Thus you will become a Buddha, and otherwise not in countless ages, the Jina has said. (98d)

THE COMMENTARY

A And now the instruction on pure dharma[9] is expressed by the verse "killing living beings," etc.,

B expressing two kinds of vows[10] as *neyārtha* and *nītārtha*, as outer and inner respectively.

C So in the outer method, speaking of the Buddha killing living beings means carrying out the five immediacies, or breaking vows,

D the five immediacies being known before and after,[11]

E as one who first performs the five immediacies and later creates merit, like the wicked king Aśoka[12] and the dharma-king[13] Aśoka.

F So the mantrin who does harm will go to hell, because he does not fully understand virtuous and nonvirtuous action.

G And so if he does not have the five special knowledges, the mantrin should not perform fearful actions[14] other than peaceful, prosperity-, power and attraction-rites.

H Thus, speaking misleadingly for the benefit of others, taking what has not been given, committing adultery, and enjoying intercourse with persons of caste and with outcastes while adhering to one's vows, one makes the ultimate gift of one's own body and does not act for one's own benefit.

J Here, whoever performs the five immediacies continually until death, that one, if he has previously fully practiced the mantra in the anger-family *(krodha-kula),* may commit murder by means of another Akṣobhya-samādhi (?), the Buddha says: this is *neyārtha.*

K Similarly one speaks misleading words not for one's own purposes but in order to raise up *(abhyuddharaṇāya,* but Tib. *mngon-par gnod-pa'i slad-du)* those who have fallen out of the way.

L Similarly one takes what is not given, not for one's own purposes, but to prevent others from descending into the preta-realms.

M Similarly one takes the wife of another not for one's own purposes, but to prevent him from taking rebirth as an animal,

N and one adheres to the vows of the five nectars *(amṛta, bdud-rtsi),* etc. in order to destroy attachment to the five families.

O And for the sake of the attainments *(prasiddhi, dngos-grub)* of *karma-mudrā* one must not despise women such as Ḍombi; and to accumulate merit, one gives great gifts.

P Thus in the khaḍga, ratna, padma, cakra and karttikā families, a yogin who has fully practiced the mantras and obtained power may do anything.

Q Thus there will be no laughter in the world: all this is *neyārtha.*

R And now we shall speak of *nītārtha.* Here, since it opposes[15] the life *(prāṇa, srog)* in one's own body, *prāṇātipātaḥ* is killing, and in the Diamond family this brings about the stopping [of prāṇa] at the top of the head.[16]

U Thus through stopping the prāṇa the yogin's semen stays up.

V *Misleading speech in the Sword (khaḍga, ral-gri) family:* "misleading" here means that the words have no fixed sense;[17] this is *neyārtha.*

W *Nītārtha* here is that when the unstruck sound resounds in the heart center, in an instant the dharma is taught to all sentient beings, each in his own language.[18]

X *In the Jewel family one takes what belongs to others:* "others" here means Vajrasattva, and what belongs to them is a jewel, the wish-fulfilling gem. "Taking it away" means that in the Jewel family the eighth bodhisattva stage occurs at the throat [center].

Y *In the excellent Lotus family one takes the wife of another:* here "wife of another" is the mahāmudrā, and taking her away is called adultery. This taking away is said to occur in the Lotus family when the semen is retained at the forehead [center], the place of the tenth bodhisattva stage.

Z *In the Wheel family you should rely completely on wine, lights, and other objects*[19] *of the Buddhas:* here wine is *sahajānanda*,[20] the lights, *goku*[21] and so forth are the five inner senses, and the Buddhas are the five nectars;

AA one should rely on them in the lotus at the navel, in the Wheel [family] they are to be enjoyed. Feces and urine and semen are not to be released *(aśrāvaḥ karttavya, mi-'dzag-par bya'o)* externally: this is *nītārtha.*

BB In the Dagger family, you should not look down upon such women as Ḍombi, etc. in the secret lotus,

CC *in the sky-lotus* meaning that when the vulva is rubbed(?) it is said to be a life of virtue *(brahmacarya)* [provided that] no semen falls externally.[22]

DD *For the benefit of beings you should give wealth,* sons, wives, etc. and at the same time you should give your own body in order to accumulate merit.

EE Similarly in order to accumulate propriety you should not look down upon the sky-lotus of women. Thus the accumulations of merit and propriety [yield] the accumulation of awareness.

FF And from these three accumulations there is perfect Buddhahood. Thus the verse says *Son of a noble family! Thus you will become a Buddha, and otherwise not in countless ages, the Jina has said.* This is the teaching on pure dharma as taught in all the tantras.

3. *Comments on the* Vimalaprabhā *Text*

Mi-pham sets the scene thus:[23] the preliminary seven empowerments *(seka)* have been completed. The pupil has received a name[24] for the duration of this whole series of empowerments. The first of the four main stages of empowerment[25] is about to begin. This is the "teacher's empowerment" *(ācārya-abhiṣeka).* In most *anuttarayogatantras* this is in five stages correlated with the five families and with the five Tathāgatas (Akṣobhya, etc.). In the *Kālacakratantra,* however, though the teacher's empowerment still has five stages[26] the correlation cannot be set up since there are now six families. The *Vimalaprabhā* starts the commentary on III.97cd by saying that the five stages do not correspond to the five Tathāgata-purifications as is often said in respect of other tantras. For instance, in the crown *(makuṭa)* section the pupil's own Tathāgata is placed at the top of the crown, and not necessarily Ratnasambhāva.[27] Mi-pham suggests that the section on pure dharmas is relevant only to the person who is going to be empowered to give abhiṣeka himself; in view of the interpretations given in the *Vimalaprabhā,* this seems quite plausible.[28]

The *Kālacakra* verse mentions briefly each of the six families. The *Vimalaprabhā* starts out by saying (B) that these remarks can be taken in the sense of *neyārtha* or *nītārtha,* an "outer" or an "inner"[29] interpretation. It then gives (C–Q) the outer interpretations for the six families. They are "outer" in the sense of activity visible in the world. They are also "outer" in the sense of taking the phrases in the verses fairly literally; they explain away the literal sense (rather than just ignoring it, say). This section is summed up (P) by saying that it is the accomplished yogin, one who has attained power, who may do the things mentioned in the verses. This is the *neyārtha* (J, Q) interpretation of the verses. The *Vimalaprabhā* commentary takes all these *neyārtha* interpretations together without quoting individually the relevant pieces of the verses. Then follows the *nītārtha* section (R–CC). Here, relevant phrases from the verses are quoted, but little attempt is made to explain (or explain away) their literal senses.[30] Rather, another "symbolic" sense is associated with various phrases. Some examples:

killing: stopping at the *uṣṇīṣa*
taking away: in the jewel family, stopping at the throat; in the lotus family, stopping at the forehead
what belongs to others: the wish-fulfilling gem of Vajrasattva
another's wife: mahāmudrā
wine: sahajānanda
(five) lights: the five senses

Of course the text contains a mass of such correspondences. If one looks at all of them, it seems obvious that there is no systematic correlation between the phrases and their "interpretations." The arbitrariness of the correspondence reminds one of the "code" used in the *Hevajratantra* and elsewhere.[31] There is no reason to suppose that a code is being set out here; but it does seem clear that what is being offered is not some kind of *translation* of the verses (they are not being treated as part of some other language). And it is obvious that these interpretations are concerned with the stage of completion *(sampannakrama, rdzogs-rim).*

Elsewhere[32] it has been shown in detail that the use of the terms *neyārtha* and *nītārtha,* at least in Tibet, was different, in the tantras, from its use in the sūtras. The tantric use was for less and more advanced interpretations *of one and the same passage,* such as we indeed find here in the *Vimalaprabhā.* "Advanced" relates to the person to whom the interpretation was addressed (e.g. to his level of practice of meditation, etc.) and not to the complexity and so forth of the linguistic process of interpretation. (Both terms can be used of *literal* interpretations—of course not of the same passage.) Did Puṇḍarīka use these terms in the same way as the Tibetans?

We may perhaps start by asking ourselves whether, in the terms *neyārtha, nītārtha,* the word *artha* concerns the purpose of the utterances in a general sense (cf. *prayojana*), or whether it concerns some kind of speaker's intention (cf. *śabdasyābhiprāya,* etc.), or whether the two terms here involve some distinction between literal and nonliteral uses of the words. (The latter idea is not at all implausible. The words are not to be taken strictly literally, but the *neyārtha* interpretations are surely *connected* with the literal sense of the words, in a way which the *nītārtha* ones are not.) It may help us to see what might be involved in these distinctions if we briefly anticipate Part II of this chapter and glance at some of the vocabulary of the *Guhyasamāja* system.

The hermeneutic vocabulary of the *Guhyasamāja* literature is considerably richer than that of the *Vimalaprabhā.* At a rather primitive level of *Guhyasamāja* interpretation, that of the *Jñānavajrasamuccayatantra,* we do find *neyārtha/nītārtha* used for the literal/nonliteral distinction.[33] But from the *Pradīpoddyotana* on, this distinction is the province of the terms *yathāruta* and *nayathāruta,* and perhaps also of *dgongs-pas bshad-pa,*[34] terms not found in our *Vimalaprabhā* passage. Nor do we find here the quite different term *sandhābhāṣa* (*dgongs-skad, gsang-skad;* see note 31). With a few exceptions, the *Vimalaprabhā* interpretations bear little resemblance to the *sandhābhāṣa* of the *Hevajra* and *Guhyasamāja* cycles.[35]

The Tibetan literature on our *Kālacakra* verses uses terms additional to those of the *Vimalaprabhā.* Let us consider Mi-pham's vocabulary, for example. First of all, he says explicitly that the *nītārtha* interpretations are concerned with the completion stage.[36] This is only implied and perhaps not uniform in the *Vimalaprabhā.* He also says that these "inner" interpretations are the "hidden meaning" *(sbas-don).*[37] This is a typical term of the *Guhyasamāja* system, not found in Indian texts of the *Hevajra* or *Kālacakra* cycles, so far as I know; and it is specifically concerned with mudrā practices and the like. Whereas in the "seven ornaments" of *Guhyasamāja* interpretation, *neyārtha* and *nītārtha* are found among the "ornament of the six alternatives" *(ṣaṭkoṭi-alaṅkāra, mtha-drug-gi rgyan), sbas-don (garbhī)* is found among the "four methods of explanation" *(bshad-tshul bzhi).* These four methods are indeed concerned with different levels of practice, providing quite a different kind of distinction from anything in the "six alternatives."

As mentioned in the Introduction, similar verses on killing living beings, etc. are found in both the *Hevajra* and *Guhyasamāja* tantras. The *Vimalaprabhā* claims that the basic idea of the explanation is the same in all tantras (FF), and perhaps this is true at a certain level; but this very truth throws light on the interpretive apparatus. We will give a brief comparison with the treatment in these other tantras in Part II of this chapter; though this treatment will have to be based mainly on Tibetan translations, we will still be able to say something there about the differences between Indian and Tibetan views of the problem.

4. Nītārtha *and* Neyārtha *in the* Vimalaprabhā *Passage*

We now come to the core of our enquiry. We have a good grasp of the structure and content of the *Vimalaprabhā* passage on killing, stealing, lying, adultery, etc., and we are to ask exactly what *nītārtha* and *neyārtha* mean here, that is, what they are used for or how they are used. We are to treat this as a problem in what might be called quasi-radical interpretation, that is, we suppose that we know sufficiently well what the rest of the passage is saying and we want to draw what conclusions we can about the contributions made by these two words.

As so often when pressing hard on the notion of meaning, it will be convenient to maintain some feeling for the distinction between sense and reference. Now it is notoriously difficult to explain these terms clearly (let alone to produce a reductive analysis of them), but this much at least seems unproblematic: on the side of reference falls whatever the word points to or applies to *on the separate occasions when it is used,* while on the side of sense fall the conventions governing the use of the word *in general.* We may note an ambiguity about this "in general": does it mean "in all uses (whatever)" or "as used in the present context"? We want to remain open to the possibility that the sense may be different in the present context from others.[38] So it may be best just to live with the ambiguity.

Let us remind ourselves of some of the conventions governing the use of tantric commentaries such as the *Vimalaprabhā.* The *Kālacakratantra* was uttered by the Buddha to a certain audience. Puṇḍarīka interprets certain of the Buddha's utterances twice. In doing so, he ascribes two different intentions *(artha)* to the Buddha. What, then, is the point of having two different intentions connected with a single passage?

In Tibet, this double interpretation was always taken to correspond to a division in the audience (in Vajrayāna contexts, of course). At a more elementary level of understanding are those who are ready for the *neyārtha* interpretations; those at a more advanced level are ready for the *nītārtha* interpretations. These two levels are often, but by no means universally, correlated with the two *satyas (paramārtha* and *saṃvṛti).* There is no general correlation with the terms "outer" and "inner" *(bāhya, ādhyātmika).*[39] All this is a perfect example of what Nathan Katz[40] has called "adept-based hermeneutics." According to this Tibetan view, in relation say to the Buddha's utterance of *asatya vākyaṃ ca khaḍge* ("and misleading speech in the Sword family"), the reference of *neyārtha* would be the intention of communicating to the appropriate audience what is spelled out in sentence K, while the reference of *nītārtha* would be the intention of communicating to another audience (or another part of the same audience) what is spelled out in sentence W. The senses of *neyārtha* and *nītārtha* would be just that where two interpretations are given for one passage of the Buddha-word, the corresponding intentions should be in the relation described: *neyārtha* for the intention relating to the less advanced audience, *nītārtha* to the more advanced one.

Given the vast authority of the *Vimalaprabhā* in Tibet, it would be very surprising if we were to find that the uses of *neyārtha* and *nītārtha* in that work were actually inconsistent with the usual Tibetan usage. Yet it seems quite plain that the weight of Puṇḍarīka's intention in using these words was not where the Tibetan usage would have us place it. First of all, it seems obvious that Puṇḍarīka intends us to take seriously the distinction between "outer" and "inner," even though we may say (partly because of the ambiguity of "sense" mentioned above) that it is not clear whether this is a part of the *sense* of the words, or an extra circumstance, related perhaps to the subject matter of the first two chapters of the tantra. Second, there seems to be no independent reason to think that the *neyārtha* interpretations are particularly elementary, or the *nītārtha* ones particularly advanced. It is true that the latter concern fairly sophisticated meditation techniques. Now the *neyārtha* interpretations themselves seem to apply to two kinds of people. A mantrin (F) who does not have the five special insights *(abhijñā)* merely goes to hell; this is a warning to ordinary people to stick to ordinary morality and ordinary accumulation of merit, contrary to what the *Kālacakra* verses say. But a mantrin who has the insights and who has obtained power through practicing the mantras may do whatever he pleases (P), even murder (J), since it is all for the benefit of others (H, K–O). This second aspect of the *neyārtha* interpretations, then, seems to be for people who may possibly be *more* advanced than the audience for the *nītārtha* interpretations. Nor is there any reason for thinking that the distinction is correlated with the two *satyas*. In particular, the *neyārtha* interpretations do not seem to be correlated with means *(upāya),* nor the *nītārtha* ones with insight *(prajñā);* rather, both seem to involve both (cf. note 39). Finally, though the elementary *neyārtha* interpretation does not seem to be for the same audience as the *nītārtha* one, the more advanced *neyārtha* and the *nītārtha* one could perhaps represent the "outer" *(bāhya)* and "inner" *(adhyātmika)* behavior to which the vows commit *one and the same person.*

Can we conclude that the use of the terms *nītārtha* and *neyārtha* in the *Vimalaprabhā* is specifically intended to be different from the *Guhyasamāja* usage adopted in Tibet? I think that while there is not a sharp contradiction, enough has been done to show that there are significant differences of emphasis. If this is confirmed by further work on the *Vimalaprabhā,* we should not be too surprised; for we know that the Tibetans tended to harmonize the usage of the different tantras in a manner which does not seem to have been practiced in India. On the other hand it has sometimes been suggested that in the *Kālacakra* the *neyārtha* level is the deeper while the *nītārtha* level, though perhaps more advanced, is also closer to the surface form of the tantra; such a suggestion would be consistent with the frequent assertion that the mother-tantras are more literal than the father-tantras. But this suggestion is difficult to reconcile with what we find here.

In Part I of this chapter, the treatment has focused on a very short piece of the *Kālacakra* and on the most obvious features of the explanation provided by the *Vimalaprabhā.* Many things have been left unexplained, especially the status of the *particular* interpretation-claims made by the *Vimalaprabhā,* and the claim that the hermeneutic vocabulary is based on notions related to intention. On the other hand, verses on killing, lying, stealing, and adultery are found in other tantras, such as *Hevajra* and *Guhyasamāja.* Part II of this chapter represents a more broadly based, but also more sketchy, attempt to "place" what we have seen up till now in the general framework of Indian Buddhist interpretation, especially that of the tantras. Though Sanskrit texts will be used where possible, we will have to make some use of Tibetan translations of Indian works in order to draw this more general picture.

Part II: Killing, Lying, Stealing, and Adultery as a Problem in Buddhist Hermeneutics

1. *Hermeneutics and Buddhist Hermeneutics*

Following Steinkellner,[41] we may consider taking hermeneutics to be the study of the methodological principles which guide the interpretation of revelatory texts. Now "hermeneutics" is not a colloquial English word, and "interpretation," if colloquial, is not very clear; so it is of some interest to clarify what might be meant by the remark. It would seem that the emphasis must be placed on the *principles* of interpretation. For instance, in our *Vimalaprabhā* passage, the principle lying behind the two styles or forms of interpretation is indicated by the use of the words *nītārtha, neyārtha.* It is true that the *Vimalaprabhā* takes the entire *Kālacakra* passage to be about vows (B, C, etc.), but this can hardly be described as a *principle* of interpretation. Indeed, we will later see some evidence for the following proposition: when a tantra passage on killing living beings is taken to be about vows, it is interpreted (as in the *Vimalaprabhā*) by the general method of *nītārtha* and *neyārtha* interpretations; but when it is not about vows (but say about ultimacy), it is interpreted by another method (say *dgongs-bshad*). Now here it is the *general method* alone which deserves to be called hermeneutic, according to Steinkellner's remark, and not the highly *specific* question of whether the passage is taken to be about vows or not. This last question is part of the general subject matter of Buddhism, of course, but is not hermeneutic. This important distinction cannot perhaps be made completely hard-and-fast, but it is essential that we nevertheless try to keep it in mind; for otherwise there will be nothing to prevent the study of Buddhist hermeneutics from becoming the study of absolutely anything within Buddhism. It is not difficult to see that this confusion is rampant in much work on Buddhist hermeneutics.

The confusion has been compounded by the use of the phrase "hermeneutic strategy." In the case of the *Vimalaprabhā,* we may reasonably describe the claim that *Kālacakra* III.97–98 is about vows as an *interpretative* strategy, but for the reason just given there is nothing *hermeneutic* about it. The notions of *neyārtha* and *nītārtha* are of course hermeneutic, but somehow the attraction of the word "strategy" seems less here; they are simply hermeneutic principles, principles guiding the interpretation of the *Kālacakra* verses, according to the *Vimalaprabhā.*

Now let us try and see how we might put some content into Steinkellner's remark as connecting hermeneutics with *interpretation.* What can we say about the general notion of interpretation? Western thinking seems to have provided us with three streams of theory which may help us to understand the activities of Buddhists interpreting Buddhist texts. These three derive, broadly speaking, from literary criticism, from the study of the Bible, and from the philosophy of language.

Since the relevance of the philosophy of language may not be obvious to all readers of this volume, let me sketch it briefly. According to speech-act theory, such an act as the utterance or the writing of words cannot even be *recognized* as a linguistic act unless we are prepared to ascribe to its author the intention to communicate information or knowledge, to issue a command, to ask a question, or to influence his audience in some way; and these ascriptions are to be related to further ascriptions of beliefs and other propositional attitudes to the author. Upon the ascription of these attitudes is imposed the requirement that they make the author's utterances on different occasions intelligible, and that his linguistic behavior be seen as consistent with his nonlinguistic behavior. Those who work in this framework take meaning as closely related to understanding. They would agree that in speaking of the meanings of words and sentences, one must distinguish carefully between the general rules or conventions governing the use of an utterance-type on all the occasions when it is used, and the particular purpose or intention with which tokens of that type are uttered, or their particular semantic functions, on distinct particular occasions of use. When Frege's sense/reference distinction is adapted to take into account the way a name may have a different bearer on different occasions of use, it falls in this general area. There is indeed a difference among theorists working in this area as to whether (very roughly) it is the particular (intention, reference) aspect of meaning or the general (convention, sense) aspect which has the logical priority. Those who give intention the priority have included Grice, Austin, the later Wittgenstein, and Strawson;[42] those who gave sense the priority have included Frege and Tarski. Among modern representatives of the latter tradition of *formal semantics* we find those with proof-theoretic leanings, such as Davidson and McDowell, and those with model-theoretic leanings, such as Montague. But in spite of those logical differences all would agree[43] that intention and related notions must play a key role in anything which is to count as an analysis of speech-acts or as a theory of meaning (even if that key role is to be the subject of a reduction).[44] It is this general attitude toward language which leads to the notion of interpretation as propositional-attitude ascription.

Some of the best descriptions of what this notion comes to are found in the work of John McDowell; for example:

> Actions are made intelligible by finding descriptions under which one can see how they might have seemed reasonable; on the conception sketched here, this applies, as it ought, to linguistic actions just as much as others. Understanding linguistic behavior, and hence understanding languages, involves no more than a special case of understanding what behavior, in general, involves. Understanding a language consists in the ability to know, when speakers produce utterances in it, what propositional acts, with what contents, they are performing. . . .[45]

It is important to be clear that the propositional-attitude-ascription notion of interpretation is a *minimalist* notion; in a sense, it is the most austere notion of interpretation which enables us to make sense of linguistic acts. There is nothing in this notion which prevents us from *adding* further components to it, drawn perhaps from literary theory or from the various theories of interpretation advanced in religious studies.

How can these various ideas be fitted in with the situation actually available to us in dealing with Buddhist hermeneutics? Consider the most normal situation, of which Part I of this chapter is an example: we have a root-text (the *Kālacakra*) and a commentary on it (the *Vimalapra-*

bhā). We want to say what we can in English about their relationship. Clearly we have *two* interpretation-situations: that of King Puṇḍarīka, author of the *Vimalaprabhā,* in respect of the root-text, the *Kālacakra*; and our own situation in respect of both *Kālacakra* and *Vimalaprabhā* together.

How might these two situations relate, say, to Gadamer's model of interpretation as conversation? Clearly we might think of *ourselves* as having a conversation with the two texts; but just as clearly, such a conversation does not constitute a model of *Buddhist* hermeneutics. On the other hand, King Puṇḍarīka may perhaps have experienced nearly one thousand years ago something like a conversation with the *Kālacakra,* but there seems no way we can retrieve such a conversation *from the two texts,* which are almost the only evidence available to us, no way therefore that the conversational model can help us to formulate a notion of *Buddhist* hermeneutics in this situation.

Sometimes the situation will not be so clear. We may consider a case in which the root-text T is subject successively to commentary by texts T_1, T_2, T_3 . . . We can perhaps think of this series as a conversation in which text T_n represents a reply by its author to the accumulated tradition of texts T, T_1, . . . T_{n-1}. This succession of exchanges does have something of a conversational character. Later I shall give an example of such a succession in relation to "killing living beings" as found in the *Guhyasamāja* and its literature.

Nevertheless, I feel that the analogy is a distant one. It seems to me that the psychological point of Gadamer's notion—the intimacy and ease of the conversational relationship, the possibility of as many exchanges as you will issuing in just one interpretation—is not found at all in the case of successive commentaries.

The proposed example also shows up a general weakness in the ascription to the Indian interpretive process of such *a priori* western models. The conversational model has no descriptive or explanatory power. It can be applied only when we have *already* done all the work needed to understand the texts; we might indeed do just as well without the model.

It might be objected that the same argument can be applied to the use of propositional-attitude ascriptions. But the claim about them is not that *Indians* made such ascriptions. On the other hand, Indians did interpret texts on the basis of the related method of intention-ascription; evidence for this will be presented later, both in general and for the case of "killing living beings."

Nothing has been said so far about the stream of theory deriving from the interpretation of Christian religious texts in the West. One might naively think that this must impinge in some way on the property of the Buddhist sūtras and tantras as "revelatory texts," as Steinkellner puts it. But what is here the cash value of *revelatory?* Of course *we* can interpret these texts however we wish, can read whatever "religious" and other values into them which we can find; but this process has nothing to do with *Buddhist* hermeneutics. Here it might be objected that the texts in question surely have some kind of characteristic content, and that even if the points made in earlier paragraphs about not taking the whole of the subject matter of Buddhism to fall within hermeneutics are accepted, surely there must be some principles of interpretation which relate directly to the *content* of the texts.

This point is correct, but it should not be overdrawn. The texts on interpretation distinguish between methods of interpretation concerned with the text *(abhidhāna),* and those concerned with the content *(abhidheya).* Some of the methods, such as the "three tantras" method discussed in chap. 18 of the *Guhyasamāja* itself, are concerned purely with content, others with the text, according to the texts themselves. So it is certain that in India, interpretation is concerned with the content as well as the text.

Nothing follows from this about any connection with "revelatory." It may be that there exists some Sanskrit word whose linguistic meaning is similar to that of "revelatory" and which is used in a similar way in hermeneutic texts. But really there is no evidence that anything like all the Buddhist texts to which (broadly) hermeneutic methods were applied in India were treated as revelatory (in such a sense). So even if we do have the odd revelatory text, nothing follows about the character of Buddhist interpretation in general; to presuppose the contrary is merely to project our own prejudices onto Indian thought.

2. *An Indian Framework for Buddhist Hermeneutics*

There seems, then, to be no other possibility than to go back and look at what Indian texts themselves have to say about the process of interpretation. Of course they say different things. One thing which is common to many commentaries is their suggestion that the root-text upon which they are commenting is a śāstra. Now not just anything can count as a śāstra; in order so to count, a work must possess a text *(abhidhāna, rjod-byed),* a content or topic or subject matter *(abhidheya, brjod-bya),* a purpose or motive *(prayojana, dgos-pa),* and a connection *(sambandha, 'brel-ba)* between these. Often a more distant purpose *(prayojanasya prayojana, dgos-pa'i dgos-pa* or *nying-dgos)* is included as well. For instance, in the case of the *Nyāyabindu,* Dharmottara says that the topic of the text is right knowledge *(samyagjñāna),* and that the purpose of the text is indicated as fulfilling people's needs by providing an analysis of right knowledge.[46] Vinītadeva distinguishes also a distant purpose, related to the fact that right knowledge is necessary for *any* purposive activity.[47]

Similarly, Candrakīrti's *Prasannapadā* says[48] that the *Madhyamakakārikā* have as their subject matter eight special topics, *pratītyasamutpāda,* etc., and that their purpose is that all *prapañcas* should come to rest in nirvāṇa. Now obviously in both cases these brief remarks do not *themselves* constitute a purpose- or intention-based hermeneutic, but equally obviously they invite one; and similar suggestions are found throughout the Buddhist scholarly literature. For this reason alone, it seems wholly plausible that we shall be able to make sense of the Buddhist hermeneutic enterprise by seeing it as founded upon intention-ascription.

But why should this apply to the tantras? Surely the tantras are just the opposite of a work of scholarship, a śāstra? It seems that the Indian commentators anticipated this kind of *a priori* objection, for many of their commentaries, including what are perhaps the three most important which have come down to us, set out elaborately and in detail just those features required to show that the tantra upon which they are commenting is indeed a śāstra. For instance the *Vimalaprabhā* says:

> Here the topic is the blessed *Kālacakra* founded on the essence of the five chapters [of the tantra] taken in order. The text which sets out [this topic] is the collection of chapters [forming this] king of tantras. This text and its topic being mutually in the relationship of speech and that which is to be spoken of, that mark is their connection. . . . Accordingly the purpose *(prayojana)* is to act so as to accumulate merit once one has been granted the worldly abhiṣeka and entered the maṇḍala. The distant purpose *(prayojanaprayojana)* is to accumulate both merit and awareness once one has attained the [causally] unconnected *(niranvaya)* attainments of mahāmudrā by having been granted the transworldly fourth abhiṣeka of great wisdom.[49]

The treatment of this topic is basically the same in the principal Indian commentary on the *Hevajratantra,* that of Vajragarbha.[50] The text is here the *Hevajratantra* in seven hundred verses; its topic is *Hevajra* together with *Nairātmyā;* the connection is again just the mutual relationship of the text and its topic; the purpose is to give the abhiṣeka which brings the candidate into the maṇḍala, and the distant purpose is to make suchness clear [to him], following on abhiṣeka.[51]

The situation is only slightly different in the main Indian commentary on the *Guhyasamāja,* the *Pradīpoddyotana* of Candrakīrti. As is well known,[52] the introduction to this work sets out the hermeneutic system known as the "seven ornaments" *(saptālaṅkārāḥ).* Here we have to do with the first of the seven, the "introduction" *(upodghātaḥ, gleng bslang-ba).* This contains five items: the name and type of the tantra; the kind of person for whom it is intended; its originator; its length; and its purpose *(prayojana).* The connection of this list with the requirements for the text under commentary (the *Guhyasamāja*) to be a śāstra has been noted by Steinkellner.[53] The *Pradīpoddyotana* explains the purpose of the *Guhyasamāja* as being:

> [to explain] the procedure to attain peace *(śamatha)* and so forth; [to accomplish] the eight [worldly] siddhis and [to attain] the best [siddhi of] Buddhahood.[54]

This *prayojana* corresponds to the *prayojanaprayojana* of the two commentaries discussed above, and is clearly less interesting as having nothing to do with the *specific* purposes of the *Guhyasamāja*.

We have just shown that the most distinguished commentators on three of the principal tantras held (at the very least, as a matter of convention) that those tantras were composed by definite people, with a definite purpose; and in this way they satisfy the classical criteria for being śāstras. Now Indian theorists of meaning held, quite generally, that a speaker's intention is a fundamental part of what has to be taken into account in explaining speech-acts.[55] It is perhaps not as well known as it ought to be that this holds just as much for Buddhist theorists of meaning such as Dharmottara and Vinītadeva as for the orthodox traditions. Dharmottara makes it clear that ordinary assertoric utterances are to be regarded as caused or motivated by intentions *(abhiprāya),* such as the intention to draw attention to some state of affairs in the external world:[56]

> Others have said that when knowledge arises from words by the action of intention, that knowledge has that intention *(abhiprāya)* as its object *(ālambanaṃ)*. An utterance is intended *(icchataḥ)* [to communicate] a real state of affairs.[57] The proposition that inference is not a *pramaṇa* contradicts this [intention, and so is untenable].
>
> [Dharmottara replies:] This view is mistaken. The theory [of Dharmakīrti] holds that it is only discursively *(kalpitaṃ)* that our ideas are the *svabhāvahetu* and our speech the *kāryahetu* [of communication]. The intention does not really act, does not really belong to the words, does not grasp them. If someone says that there is no inference *(anumāṇa),* he will not be able to infer fire from smoke, and similarly will not be able to infer intention from words. Now speech is used in order to communicate [information about] external things. So an utterance does not express a previous understanding of an invariable connection with the speaker's intention. We utter words, not in order to communicate our intentions *(na svābhiprāya nivedanāya),* but in order to communicate the external state of affairs. Thus an utterance expresses a previous understanding of an invariable connection with an external state of affairs.

As Stcherbatsky pointed out, it is noteworthy that Dharmottara and his opponent (perhaps Vinītadeva) simply take it for granted that purposes or intentions play a vital role in the explanation of speech-acts. Stcherbatsky gave a remarkably good account of this passage without certain of the modern developments in philosophical logic which make Dharmottara's point[58] seem especially natural. We might perhaps say that his point is that of a Davidsonian theorist of meaning, who discusses meaning directly in relation to truth, as against a communication-intention theorist of a somewhat excessively Gricean persuasion who confuses the intention to communicate with the communication of intentions.

We find just the same thing in the *Sandhivyākaraṇa,* which is the main explanatory tantra of the *Guhyasamāja* cycle, and this is important because the actual *interpretations* provided by the *Sandhivyākaraṇa* are authoritative for the whole of the subsequent *Guhyasamāja* tradition. In the title of the *Sandhivyākarana, sandhi* means "intention" quite generally. *Vyākaraṇa* means "analysis," and so the title means "the analysis of intention(s)." What this boils down to, as a method of explanation, has been clearly explained in the *Yogaratnamālā* on *Hevajra* II.iii.53, where *sandhi* is said to mean:

> intention *(abhiprāya),* that is, explanation mainly in terms of intention, and not mainly in terms of the literal sense.[59]

In fact the *Sandhivyākaraṇa* corresponds just to the level of explanation where the speaker's intention is spelled out explicitly (though often, in this case, not very clearly). The work contains almost no other hermeneutics in the sense of *principles* of interpretation. What is important for our present purposes is simply that it is the speaker's intention which is held to be the basis for the explanations offered.

To this line of description of the *Sandhivyākaraṇa* it might be objected that *sandhi* can also mean "special intention," that is, an intention radically different from that associated (e.g. in the way discussed by Dharmottara) with the words uttered. (On this view the *Yogaratnamālā* passage would be irrelevant, perhaps because the mother-tantras, such as *Hevajra,* are generally more literal than the father-tantras, such as *Guhyasamāja.*) This objection will not survive any critical examination of the actual contents of the *Sandhivyākaraṇa;* but perhaps more important, it would bring the *Sandhivyākaraṇa* into sharp conflict with the whole subsequent tradition of interpretation of the *Guhyasamāja,* including the *Pradīpoddyotana.* Surely this is unacceptable, given the generally accepted view that the *Sandhivyākaraṇa* is the foundation of this tradition.

Accordingly the *Sandhivyākaraṇa* is not a hermeneutic text, except in the straightforward sense of setting out the Buddha-intention *(sangs-rgyas-kyi dgongs-pa, *buddhābhiprāya)* behind the words of the *Guhyasamāja.* The authority of the *Sandhivyākaraṇa* rests on the fact (or claim) that it is itself the Buddha-word, and not on the validity of any general principles which might have lain behind the particular interpretations of the *Guhyasamāja* which it offers.[60] The elucidation of such principles belongs to the hermeneutic tradition proper of the *Guhyasamāja*, which will be dealt with in the following section.

3. *Killing Living Beings and the Hermeneutics of the* Hevajra *and* Guhyasamāja *Tantras*

Having sketched the general basis of Buddhist hermeneutics and demonstrated its relevance to the *Kālacakra, Hevajra,* and *Guhyasamāja* tantras, we are now in a position to consider various tantric commentators' explanations of "you should kill living beings" and similar remarks, with good general reasons for taking at their face value the commentators' claim to explain on the basis of intentions (*artha, don; prayojana, dgos-pa; abhiprāya, dgongs-pa; sandhi, dgongs-pa,* etc.), ascribed to the Buddha (Vajradhara, etc.) who is regarded as the author of the tantra in question. The word *artha* has indeed a great measure of the vagueness of the English "meaning," but that does not mean that its sense is not restricted, in particular cases, by the context and the demands of consistency. There seems no need to add anything to what was said previously about the use of *nītārtha* and *neyārtha* in interpreting the passage from the *Vimalaprabhā;* but it will be of help if we compare this with what is done with similar passages in the *Hevajra* and *Guhyasamāja.* Both these tantras contain the verse:

> *prāṇinaśca tvayā ghātyā vaktavyaṃ ca mṛṣāvacaḥ/*
> *adattañ ca tvayā grāhyaṃ sevanam parayoṣitaḥ//* [61]

> "You should harm living beings, you should tell lies, you should take what belongs to others, and you should rely on an external[62] woman."

Vajragarbha expands this verse into four verses, yielding explanations of the four injunctions. These explanations he describes as *nītārtha,* and they are broadly similar in character to the *nītārtha* explanations in the *Vimalaprabhā* (R–AA). He gives no *neyārtha* explanations, though one wonders whether there is not a lacuna in the text. The *Hevajra* contains another similar verse[63] but the commentaries which I have studied do not yield anything of obvious hermeneutic interest.

The treatment in the *Guhyasamāja* is very much more complex than that in the *Hevajra.* Not only are there several passages of verses on "killing living beings," etc., variously explained in the commentaries, but the hermeneutic principles themselves evolved a good deal over the course of time. This introduces a number of different layers of commentary, and for those to whom Gadamer's metaphor appeals, the resulting sequence of treatments in the commentaries may perhaps be compared with a conversation.

The general hermeneutic stance of the *Sandhivyākaraṇa* was mentioned in the previous section: it just says what intention is to be associated with each passage of the *Guhyasamāja,* without attempting any hermeneutic analysis. But since the *Sandhivyākaraṇa'*s interpretations are authoritative and are quoted at length by the later commentaries, we will return to some of them later, discussing what later commentaries claimed about the hermeneutic attitudes underlying them.

The next stage in the development of *Guhyasamāja* hermeneutics seems to be that of the *Jñānavajrasamuccayatantra.* If this is genuine[64]—as was certainly thought in Tibet—it is the original source of the hermeneutic scheme of the seven ornaments. However, the definitions given in the *Jñānavajrasamuccayatantra* are not very clear and on the whole the later commentators have used the definitions of the *Pradīpoddyotana.*[65]

The *Jñānavajrasamuccayatantra*[66] takes *neyārtha* and *nītārtha* to be literal and figurative modes of explanation. It also introduces[67] the hermeneutic technique called "explanation by *intention" *(dgongs-pas bshad-pa),* itself explained thus:

> Whatever is explained as relating to the ultimate *(mthar-thug-pa)* is explained *intentionally. For instance, such passages as "There is no desire, there is no nondesire, and no third alternative is seen."

However, the *Jñānavajrasamuccayatantra* does not discuss "killing living beings," etc.

The next layer of explanation is that of the *Pradīpoddyotana.* This work makes use of the "seven ornaments" introduced in the *Jñānavajrasamuccayatantra,* but it emphasizes a particular ornament called "six alternatives," setting out in its introduction just what passages of the *Guhyasamāja* are to be explained in terms of each of the six. This claim that the "six alternatives" are the hermeneutic foundation of the *Pradīpoddyotana* is repeated frequently and is found for instance in the colophon of each chapter. The six are *neyārtha* and *nītārtha* (taken here as something like a provisional and an ultimate interpretation); literal and nonliteral use of words *(yathāruta/nayathāruta);* and explanation with and without *intention as just mentioned. For the definitions discussed below (as also for those in the *Jñānavajrasamuccayatantra*) it is quite certain that the *intention here is a special intention, and not just intention *tout court* as in the *Sandhivyākaraṇa.*[68] It is helpful here to think of all three pairs of distinctions as based on one fundamental logical distinction, one indeed which we have mentioned several times already: that between the *general* rules governing the use of a word or a sentence on every occasion when it is used, and the *particular* intentions, etc. with which it is used on different occasions. While this distinction had already been known in India for a long time, as pointed out by Raja,[69] so was perhaps presupposed by Candrakīrti, it did not emerge explicitly in the *Guhyasamāja* literature until a later period. Yet the *Pradīpoddyotana* itself (like the *Jñānavajrasamuccayatantra*) is hardly intelligible unless we suppose that this general logical distinction implicitly underlies the three distinctions specifically made in the "six alternatives."[70] (Needless to say, it underlies them in three different ways. The three distinctions are very far from being merely variations on one single distinction.)

Now let us consider a passage of the *Guhyasamāja* in which killing, lying, etc. are enjoined, and which is interpreted by the *Pradīpoddyotana* in terms of *neyārtha/nītārtha;* such a passage is, for example, IX.3–22. This passage (like the *Vimalaprabhā* one) is about the different vows of all six families. The verse on the Diamond family tells us to kill living beings so that they will be reborn in the Buddha-field of Akṣobhya as sons of the Buddha. The *neyārtha* interpretation given by the *Pradīpoddyotana*[71] runs:

> By this secret vajra all living beings are to be killed [the verse says], that is, by making them void they are to be destroyed. If they are killed by means of this special samādhi, they will become Buddha-sons in the Buddha-field of Akṣobhya. The vow of the anger-family is precisely that they will be reborn as bodhisattvas [in this way]. As it is said: only in this secret place many people may go to nirvāṇa, and a great heap of merit will pile up; otherwise there is much defilement. This is *neyārtha.*[72]

The *nītārtha* interpretation[73] is difficult to follow, but according to Buston[74] it is concerned with the completion stage, and the vow is not to go beyond the cultivation of *yuganaddha.* It seems clear that there is a considerable parallelism with the *Vimalaprabhā* treatment.

Now let us go back to the verse, viz. *Guhyasamāja* XVI.59c–60b, which is also found in the *Hevajra* discussed above as such. The *Pradīpoddyotana* does say that this verse is connected with vows; but in all other matters we are merely referred back to another verse, viz. *Guhyasamāja* V.5c–6b, which does *not* seem to be connected with vows, and which treats "killing living beings," etc. not by the *neyārtha/nītārtha* distinction, but by "explanation by *intention." The explanation itself, according to the *Pradīpoddyotana* (35b5) is that found in the *Sandhivyākaraṇa.* This runs:

> What establishes one in the best vehicle [the Vajrayāna?] is killing living beings; for this is whatever demonstrates that the skandhas, etc. are substanceless, and are created by the mind out of the state of tranquility. Joy in telling untruths is showing outer and inner objects to be conditionally dependent. . . . The object *(viṣaya)* of ignorance, which is fear of the void

> (?) is called "ordure"; the senses are called "urine," and bringing these [objects and senses] to rest is called "eating."[75]

This has little in common with the *Vimalaprabhā* explanations. It has in common with the *Vimalaprabhā*'s *nītārtha* explanations the almost complete lack of interest in the literal meanings of the words, but the explanations offered here in the *Sandhivyākaraṇa* and *Pradīpoddyotana* do not seem to have anything to do with the completion stage. This is not surprising, since in *Guhyasamāja* exegesis (at least descending from the *Pradīpoddyotana*) explanation by *intention is concerned mainly with the radiant light and with ultimacy, these concerns being *contrasted* with concern with the details of the practices of the completion stage. (This contrast falls under the *bshad-tshul bzhi.*) But we see here a tension between two styles of explanation, or rather between a style of explanation and a purpose of explanation. For the remark "What establishes one in the best vehicle is killing living beings" might perhaps be a live word pointing beyond itself to the ultimate, as seems to be suggested by the *Jñānavajrasamuccayatantra* explanation of the hermeneutic technique *dgongs-bshad;* but going on to talk about the skandhas being substanceless surely turns this live word into a dead one.[76]

On this same verse, viz. *Guhyasamāja* V.5c–6b, the *Pradīpoddyotana* adds:

> Having established [in the preceding verses] that this king of tantras is special, and with the intention of [bringing about] the thought that there can be no entry [into the maṇḍala] without an ācārya, since special actions are set forth by means of words which *contradict the world ('jig-rten-dang-'gal-ba'i tshig-gis, *lokaviruddhālāpena),* the tantra says "killing living beings," etc. This is explained as in the *ākhyā-tantra* . . . which *explains it *intentionally.*[77]

The dots are filled in with just the quotation from the *Sandhivyākaraṇa* which was given in the last paragraph. In neither case does there seem to be any connection with vows.

So far we have had three passages interpreted as connected with vows: *Kālacakra* III.97–98, *Hevajra* II.iii.29–30,[78] and *Guhyasamāja* IX. 3–22, all of which are explained by *neyārtha* and *nītārtha.* The present passage is explained by *intention and does not seem to be connected with vows at all. Unfortunately this picture is confused by the *Pradīpoddyotana*'s remark[79] on *Guhyasamāja* XVI.59–60 that this passage, otherwise parallel to *Guhyasamāja* V. 5–6 and dissimilar to the three just listed, nevertheless *is* about vows. This passage is not covered by the *Sandhivyākaraṇa,* which goes only as far as *Guhyasamāja,* chap. XII. Further work will be needed to determine whether the supposed picture is merely an illusion, or whether the remark on XVI.59–60 is mistaken.

Let us continue the "conversation" on *Guhyasamāja* V.5c–6b by considering the development, in India, of the general explanation of the term "explanation by *intention" *(dgongs-bshad)*. Candrakīrti gives the following definition:

viśiṣṭa-ruci-sattvānāṃ dharma-tattva-prakāśanaṃ/
viruddha-ālāpa-yogena yat tat sandhyābhāṣitaṃ// [80]

One problem here is that it has not been clear to everybody that the first line of this verse really belongs to explanation by *intention rather than to *nītārtha;*[81] but it seems most natural to follow Bu-ston and suppose that it does. The word *yoga* here is awkward and might perhaps be better read *prayoga,* consistently with Tib. *sbyor-ba* 'formulation, formula'. In any case we get something like:

> Demonstrating the nature of things to beings who wish for the highest *by means of contradictory discourse* is explained *intentionally *(sandhyābhāṣitaṃ).*

Here *bhāṣitaṃ* is to be translated by "expressed" if the speaker is the Buddha, but by "explained" if the speaker is the commentator. On *Guhyasamāja* V.5–6, the *Pradīpoddyotana* itself glosses "contradictory" by "contradicting the world." This idea is taken up by a number of later commentators,[82] but other interpretations have also been offered.[83]

The *Pradīpoddyotana* itself shows signs of an attempt to fit the "six alternatives" together with some of the other ornaments into an interlocking *system* of hermeneutic terms. Some of these attempts are quite informal; others are explicitly based on general linguistic and other principles. This systematizing tendency is important both in the Indian subcommentaries and in Tibetan works.[84] Our understanding of the historical development in India is limited because we are not certain when the various commentators worked, but the order Āryadeva–Bhavyakīrti–Kumāra–Karuṇaśrīpāda is at least plausible.[85] I will conclude this chapter by sketching some of the views of these four commentators on the *Pradīpoddyotana,* both on general questions of interpretation and on the passages on killing, lying, stealing, and adultery.

On the notion of an ornament in general, the question arises whether it is taken from *alaṃkāraśāstra* (poetics). Āryadeva's notion of an ornament exhibits this connection only in a rather vague way. He mentions the well-known distinction between a natural *(rang-bzhin)* ornament and a beautifying *(gsal-ba'i)* one, and the parallel with a woman's own beauty and the jewels which beautify her.[86] His treatment of the six alternatives is based on the old Buddhist idea of *koṭi* as a fixed view. He says[87] that by proposing *alternative* koṭis of *artha* (viz. *nīta-* and *neya-*), the *Pradīpoddyotana* works against the idea that the Buddha-word has a single, fixed *artha;* by proposing alternative koṭis of *śabda* (viz. *yathāruta* and *nayathāruta*) it works against the idea of a fixed *śabda;* and by proposing alternative koṭis of both *śabda* and *artha,* viz. *dgongs-bshad* and *dgongs-min,* it works against the idea of a dharma with fixed *śabda* and *artha.* This scheme has obvious weaknesses, some of which were recognized by Bu-ston (who reorganized it).

On the lines *viśiṣṭaruci* . . . , Āryadeva gives two explanations,[88] but they seem to form part of the same line of argument. On *dgongs-bshad* he stresses that not every teaching *(nirdeśa)* is addressed to everybody.[89] Several of these points are illustrated by his treatment of stealing *(adattādānam):*

> How is the suchness of things demonstrated? By means of contradictory discourse. It contradicts the śāstras, for instance, by saying that one should steal what belongs to others. Here, giving up stealing and carrying on stealing are both fixed positions *(koṭi)* which are to be renounced. So the saying "By the power of stealing what belongs to others one will become a Buddha" contradicts the śāstras, and suchness is demonstrated by such contradictory discourse. Words which act in this way are called *dgongs-pas bshad-pa.* And to what is the intention *(sandhi)* in question directed? This is to be known from the *Sandhi-vyākaraṇa-tantra.*[90]

What we possess of the *Pradīpoddyotana-nāma-ṭīkā,* by Āryadeva, is only the introduction of a very long work, now mainly lost. Though it is prolix and written in an archaic style, it makes interesting points.

Bhavyakīrti's *Pradīpoddyotana-abhisandhi-prakāśikā-nāma vyākhyā-ṭīkā* is a long work in nearly two volumes[91] and is complete. On the general notion of an ornament, he shows two separate forms of influence stemming from poetics. He introduces the general distinction between *śabdālaṅkāra* and *arthālaṅkāra*[92] in a way which reminds us of ancient *alaṅkāraśāstra* (before Ānandavardhana). But he does not explain the distinction; evidently he thought it too familiar. Further, an ornament adorns in two ways:[93] by expressing a definite idea *(vastu),*[94] and by its (suggestive) functioning *(vyāpāra);*[95] but these two are not to be separated. So the connection between this idea and the *śabdārthālankārāḥ* distinction remains obscure. In any case, *neyārtha, nītārtha,* and *dgongs-min* are *arthālaṅkāras,* while *yathāruta, nayathāruta,* and *dgongs-bshad* are *śabdālaṅkāras.* The discussion of these points is very poor and it is not surprising that later writers did not use the scheme.[96]

Bhavyakīrti uses a further distinction of great linguistic importance, that between what is directly expressed *(vācya, brjod-bya)* and what is suggested or implied *(vyaṅgya, gsal-bar bya-ba).* Though he introduces these notions as a method of working out the *vastu/vyāpāra* distinction just mentioned, it is clear from the detailed development of the new notion that it comes from the first *uddyota* of Ānandavardhana's *Dhvany-*

āloka. In particular, Bhavyakīrti takes from the *Dhvanyāloka* a well-known verse about a lion killing a dog on the bank of the river Godāvarī:[97]

> There are two kinds of *śabdārtha:* the expressed and the implied. Here the expressed one is the literal meaning *(akṣarārtha),* as when one says that the lower part of a jar is wide like a belly. The implied one, though not distinct from what is expressed, is suggested *(lakṣya)* by various verbal formulations. For instance: "In the country *(yul)* of Godāvarī on the bank of the river a dog was killed by a lion." This is like the Buddha saying: "Bhikṣus, you should go over into bliss," where *you should go* has "to go" as its main *śabdārtha (song-zhig sgra'i don 'gro-ba gtso-bo ste),* but what is implied is the opposite of what is suggested. [According to the *Dhvanyāloka* this is just the point of the lion/dog verse.] Following the functional approach *(byed-pa sgrub-pa'i phyogs-su, *vyāpārasiddhipakṣe),* there is no [rigid] distinction, the expressed and the implied content are inseparable. This is like the beauty of a handsome man or woman, inseparably associated [with the person, and not like a jewel which, though separable, also adorns].

Of course the last idea (cf. *Dhvanyāloka* I.4) is much older, and we have seen a crude variant of it already in Āryadeva. But it is most strange that, after introducing the *vācya/vyaṅgya* distinction which is so central in Indian poetics (and hardly found anywhere else in the Vajrayāna), Bhavyakīrti does nothing with it. He promises[98] that later it will be used to clarify the *śabda/artha* distinction, but this is not done.[99] One would think that the *vācya/vyaṅgya* distinction would be just what is needed to explain *dgongs-bshad* clearly, and we will later see Karuṇa trying to use it in this way; but he (unlike Bhavyakīrti) does not seem to have the necessary clear grasp of the basic distinction.

Earlier we mentioned that the verses *Guhyasamāja* IX.3–22, associating killing, etc. with vows, are taken in the *neyārtha/nītārtha* senses by the *Pradīpoddyotana,* but that it is difficult to see what the *Pradīpoddyotana* means by its *nītārtha* explanation. Bhavyakīrti deals very well with this point. In general, *nītārtha* is the sense *(artha)* to be expressed with certainty.[100] *Neyārtha* is a provisional sense for those persons of low merit from whom the *nītārtha* is hidden.[101] Generally,[102] and specifically in chap. IX,[103] they are respectively concerned with the stages of generation and completion. On the difficult *nītārtha* passage in the *Pradīpoddyotana,* Bhavyakīrti says:

> "Explained by scripture" *(lung)* means the *nītārtha* indicated by a proper source of knowledge, viz. the Sandhivyākaraṇa. "Only the intention" *(dgongs-pa gcig-pu)* means that these words have a deep sense which is explained in a secret manner. The vows are those explained before; and "their sense" means the *nītārtha;* "expressed the hidden sense" means that Vajradhara spoke words which express such a sense. *"Nītārtha"* means that the completion stage is indicated.[104]

In the Tibetan translation, the first of these remarks depends on a play of words between *lung (āgama)* and *lung-ston (vyākaraṇa);* it is impossible to see exactly how it worked in Sanskrit. Unfortunately Bhavyakīrti's explanations of the other alternatives are not very convincing; they cry out to be supplemented with the Dhvanyāloka-like considerations which he introduced earlier but now ignores.[105] He makes few comparisons between the different "alternatives,"[106] but gives a good account of the relationships between them and the "four methods of explanation" (i.e. the *tshul-bzhi, akṣarārtha* [*yig-don*], etc.),[107] pointing out clearly why no simple correlation is possible (on this he is much better than Kumāra). Generally speaking, Bhavyakīrti's account derives most of its strength from connections between the different ornaments, rather than from anything he has to say about each one separately.

Kumāra's *Pradīpadīpa-ṭippaṇī-hṛdayādarśa-nāma* is a short work, conceived as a set of notes *(ṭippaṇī)* on the *Pradīpoddyotana.* He pays little attention to his predecessors' complex attempts at systematization but makes many useful observations of a more modest kind. For instance, the *Pradīpoddyotana* says that the six alternatives bring about certainty by means of words *(tshig-gis nges byas-pa).* Kumāra notes that even so, words are merely what indicates *(mtshon-pa-tsam);* the certainty itself is one of *artha.*[108] The six alternatives explain the *yogatantras,*[109] and there is no reason why this should not be taken to include the *yogīnītantras.*[110] Kumāra takes *viśiṣṭaruci . . .*[111] as applying to both *nītārtha*[112] and *dgongs-bshad,* and as referring to the completion stage. (If this hermeneutic strategy is accepted, though the styles of explanation still differ as between the passages on killing, etc. in chaps. V and IX, there no longer remains any difference in the general purpose of the explanations.) *dGongs-bshad* contradicts the world by being contrary to logic *(nyāyaviruddha),* as for instance a word with an analysis similar to that of "cloth" making reference to a pot.[113]

He is especially good on *nayathārutaśabda,* giving a clear explanation without using the word *brda* (usually *saṅketa,* but here surely *chomā*) which gives everybody so much trouble:[114]

> The words *koṭākhya,* etc. are said to be *nayathāruta* since they are not found in the world or in śāstras [*Pradīpoddyotana*]. There are two kinds of word: colloquial and technical. Colloquial words are, for example, cow, horse, man, . . . elephant, Brahmin, etc. Technical terms are, for example, *tattva, bhūtakoṭi, . . . triratna,* etc. *Koṭākhya,* etc. being neither technical nor colloquial have no *artha.* So why did the Buddhas utter them? They belong to the Tathāgatas. The point is this: they stand for the marks of the five Tathāgatas, for the sake of that *buddhārtha* which is so difficult for logicians and grammarians to understand. Even so, Āryadeva has taken them differently in his *Cāryamelāpakapradīpa,*[115] and has associated them with the five *vāyus,* prāṇa, etc.

Kumāra also gives very useful comparisons between various pairs of alternatives other than the obvious ones:[116]

> What is the difference between explanation by *intention *(dgongs-bshad)* and by *neyārtha?*
> They rest on distinctions of convention and of intention, respectively.
> What is the difference between explanation by *intention and by *nayathārutaśabda?*
> It is the difference between contradiction and unknown symbols.[117]
> What is the difference between explanation by *intention and by *yathārutaśabda?*
> It is the difference between contradiction and noncontradiction.
> What is the difference between *nītārtha* and an *artha* lacking in *intention?
> It is the difference between [explanation for] a person of sharp senses and a person of dull senses.

(Here the last remark is of some technical interest: *dgongs-pa ma-yin-pa'i don* means "an intention [*artha*] without an *intention" [*abhiprāya,* necessarily used in its "special" sense].)

Though Kumāra's observations are a bit unsystematic, in the first one he gives us hope of distinguishing clearly between the two kinds of explanation of the passages on killing living beings. The rendering of *śabda* by "convention" and *artha* by "intention" is doubtless an anachronism, but it is difficult to find anything wholly satisfactory. Indian linguists were aware of the aspect of the *śabda/artha* distinction reflected (as we might say) in de Saussure's *signifiant/signifié,* but this French distinction does not have the needed explanatory power. (Needless to say, the rendering by *word/meaning* is quite useless.) The idea seems to have been that in the *intention explanation there is opposition *(viruddha)* between the linguistic conventions for using the words and the ethical conventions which form part of their contextual framework, as mentioned in the opening paragraphs of this chapter. That is, there is an opposition or tension just in the area of convention, i.e. between the linguistic and nonlinguistic conventions in use. It is this tension which (on the proposed line of explanation) gives rise to the sense of shock which one experiences when one hears the verses. None of this is taken into account in the alternative type of explanation of killing, lying, etc., namely that in terms of *nītārtha* and *neyārtha;* for these explanations simply supply two alternative interpretations, ascribing different intentions to the same words *(śabda),* here regarded as associated with their normal linguistic conventions. (The *neyārtha/nītārtha* style of explanation does not rest on *nonlinguistic* conventions at all. It seems to have been a moot point whether or not *śabda* should be held to include these.)

In the first part of this chapter we mentioned the difference between the *Vimalaprabhā* and the *Pradīpddyotana* uses of *neyārtha* and *nītārtha.* In spite of these differences, the *śabda/artha* distinction, as handled here by Kumāra, does seem to have the explanatory power needed to distinguish clearly between *both* these styles of *neyārtha/nītārtha* explanation on the one hand, in contrast with the *intention explanation *(dgongs-bshad)* which is offered in the *Guhyasamāja* literature as a distinct method of explaining some of the passages on killing, lying, stealing, and adultery.

Karuṇaśrīpāda abandons any attempt to bring the six ornaments under a comprehensive scheme. He says[118] that when the *Pradīpoddyotana* says that the six alternatives are words of six kinds, it means that they indicate the *artha,* establish concepts, and bring about understanding; and in so doing they adorn whatever understanding there may be of the *nītārtha.* "Explanation according to the methods of the *yogatantras*" means according to three (specified) methods of yoga, this being the *buddhamantras.* Though the *Vajrapañjara* says that the essence of a *yogatantra* is *prajñopāya,* there is no contradiction; for what is expressed explicitly *(abhihita)* in the *yogīnītantras* is also really expressed in the *Guhyasamāja.*[119] The ms. which Bu-ston translated seems[120] to have had a verse */dgongs-pa'i skad dang dgongs-min dang/* in the summary of the six alternatives; Karuṇa takes this as meaning that the six kinds of words (of those six alternatives) are themselves to be taken literally[121] and that they indicate the *abhisandhi*[122] expressed by the Buddha. This point is taken under *neyārtha/nītārtha.* There are numerous other indications that Karuṇa was working with a form of the *Pradīpoddyotana* verses rather different from that transmitted by Rin-chen bZang-po (of whom Bu-ston says that he rearranged them himself).

On *nītārtha,* Karuṇa says that it is the *artha* of śūnyatā and, though it is expressed, yet it is inconceivable.[123] (Of course it is perfectly intelligible that we can *refer* to something without being able to *say what it is.*) Accordingly the doctrine that *abhisandhi* in reference to the three *svabhāvas* is *nītārtha* is unintelligible, since certainty as it is can only be suggested *(vyakta, gsal-bar-byas-pa)* by the word-meanings *(tshig-gi don, akṣarārtha).*[124] Under *viśiṣṭaruci* . . . he says that if by means of verbal forms contradicting worldly usage such as "killing living beings" the Buddha suggests[125] the essence of the *dharmatattva,* then those who are vessels of the profound dharma and who delight in killing living beings will be induced to do so, and there will be great benefit for beings. For, whatever may be the wish of such people, it is for the sake of (this) *intention that the Buddhas have spoken. The phrase *viruddhālāpa* means *upalakṣaṇa.*[126] Now the passages on living beings are not *viruddhālāpa* in this sense, yet in the various commentaries such partial senses are assigned to them and in this way *dgongs-pas bshad-pa* is introduced. (The account *is* unclear.) By contrast, *dgongs-min* is straightforward, clear[127] explanation for the sake of people who are not very sharp, but who are in the process of becoming vessels for the profound dharma. Just as with *neyārtha,* what is hidden is not explained.[128] Perhaps Karuṇa's account (like Bhavyakīrti's) is best understood in terms of the two styles of explanation (*tshogs-bshad* and *slob-bshad,* the fifth ornament). He seems to see each of the six alternatives as part of one or other of the explanatory procedures associated with one of these styles of explanation and the corresponding audience.

Kālacakratantra III.97–98 apparently enjoins the reader to kill, lie, steal, and commit adultery, and in Part I of this chapter we showed how the *Vimalaprabhā* tried to explain these verses. Its explanatory technique revolves around the notions of *nītārtha* and *neyārtha.* Here in Part II we have shown that the *Guhyasamājatantra* contains several passages of this type; some of these (and some similar passages of the *Hevajratantra*) are also taken under *neyārtha/nītārtha.* However, other *Guhyasamāja* passages are taken under explanation by *intention, *dgongs-bshad,* a method of explanation which does not seem to be used in the *Hevajra* or the *Kālacakra.* We have traced the commentatorial literature on the *Guhyasamāja* through a number of different stages, in the course of which these two strategies of explanation, and the differences between them, have gradually become clearer and perhaps more explicit. The most important commentary on the *Guhyasamāja* is the *Pradīpoddyotana,* and here, while there seems to be an effort to distinguish the two styles, its point is not yet apparent. Some of the subcommentaries on the *Pradīpoddyotana* partly amalgamate them, while others vary considerably on how the interpretations offered by the *Pradīpoddyotana* itself are to be taken. While none of the treatments of killing, lying, stealing, and adultery found in the *Guhyasamāja* literature is exactly the same as that in the *Vimalaprabhā,* yet some of them show important similarities.

Thus, even in the very limited confines of this study, we have shown that Indian commentaries on the tantras offer a variety of interpretations, drawing their techniques of interpretation from different sources. We have also shown the importance of certain general principles of interpretation used in India, especially the great importance attached to the intention of the speaker (here, the Buddha), and the role played by suggestion or implication. To some extent this story is one of a gradually unfolding historical development; and in this sense the story continues in Tibet. That continuation has been dealt with elsewhere.

To state these general conclusions is to say little more than that in India, the interpretation of the tantras[129] is subject to the same general principles as the interpretation of texts of almost any other kind. Maybe this conclusion is trivial, but it is certainly not what one would suspect from other western writings on the tantras. If this chapter has succeeded, however slightly, in contributing toward the demystification of the tantras, that triviality is perhaps not a bad thing.

We have thrown some light on one aspect of Buddhist *theories of interpretation.* Does this constitute a contribution to the elucidation of a Buddhist conception of *hermeneutics?* My belief is that if it does, it does so trivially, as a matter of definition. I leave it to wiser and more learned men to decide whether all this has anything to do with hermeneutics, as that word is currently understood in the West.

Abbreviations

Tibetan Editions

D: sDe-dge
N: sNar-thang
P: Peking

Indian Works

ADK: *Abhidharmakośa* of Vasubandhu (with the Vyākhyā of Yaśomitra), ed. Shastri
Dhv.: *Dhvanyāloka* of Ānandavardhana, ed. Shastri (Kashi Skt. Ser. 135)
GST: *Guhyasamājatantra,* ed. Bagchi (and Tib.: P)
HBT: *Hetubinduṭīkā* of Arcaṭa, ed. Sanghavi (Baroda 1949)
HT: *Hevajratantra,* ed. Snellgrove
JVS: *Jñānavajrasamuccayatantra,* P
KT: *Kālacakratantra*
KTS: Skt. text of KT, ed. Lokesh Chandra
KTT: Tib. text of KT, see KTS
NB: *Nyāyabindu* of Dharmakīrti, see NBT
NBT: *Nyāyabinduṭīkā* of Dharmottara, ed. Malvania
NBTV: *Nyāyabinduṭīkā* of Vinītadeva, ed. Poussin
PDPAP: *Pradīpoddyotana-abhisandhi-prakāśikā-nāma vyākhyā-ṭīkā* of Bhavyakīrti (see note 91)
PDPU: *Pradīpoddyotanodyota* of Karuṇaśrīpāda, P
PPD: *Pradīpoddyotana* of Candrakīrti, D
PPDT: *Pradīpoddyotana-nāma-ṭīkā* by Āryadeva, P
PSP: *Prasannapadā* of Candrakīrti, ed. Poussin
PTH: *Pradīpadīpa-ṭippaṇī-hṛdayādarśa-nāma* by Kumāra, P

ST: *Sekoddeśaṭīkā* of Nāropa, ed. Carelli
SV: *Sandhivyākarana,* P
V: *Vajragarbhaṭīkā,* N
VP: *Vimalaprabhā* of Puṇḍarīka
VPS: Skt. text of VP, Nepalese ms., see Appendix A
VPT: Tib. text of VP, D

Tibetan Works

B: Bu-ston, *dpal gsang-ba 'dus-pa'i ṭīkkā sgron-ma rab-tu gsal-ba* (gsung-'bum, vol. ta)
D: Tsong-kha-pa: *ye-shes rdo-rje kun-las-btus-pa'i rgya-cher 'grel-pa* (P, vol. tsa)
E: sGam-po-pa bKra-shis rNam-rgyal, *kye'i rdo-rje'i 'grel-pa legs-bshad nyi-ma'i od-zer*
F: Padma dKar-po: *gsang-ba 'dus-pa'i rgyan zhes-bya-ba mar-lugs thun-mong ma-yin-pa'i bshad-pa*
K: Kong-sprul: *rgyud-kyi rgyal-po dpal brtag-pa gnyis-pa'i tshig-don rnam-par 'grel-pa gzhom-med rdo-rje'i gsang-ba 'byed-pa*
M: Mi-pham, *dpal dus-kyi 'khor-lo rgyud-kyi tshig-don rab-gsal rdo-rje nyi-ma'i snang-ba,* Vol. 2

Notes

1. *kula, rigs;* really these are personality types dominated by particular emotions—for example, anger for the *vajra-kula* (hence often *krodha-kula*), etc.
2. HT II.iii.20–30; cf. also HT II.ii.13.
3. GST V.5–6, IX.3–22, XVI.59c–60b (the latter almost identical to HT II.iii.29; see Part II).
4. For a review of Tibetan methods of explaining the tantras *(bshad-thabs),* see my "*bshad-thabs:* Some Tibetan Methods of Explaining the Tantras," in Ernst Steinkellner and H. Tauscher, eds., *Proceedings of the 1981 Csoma de Körös Symposium* (Vienna: Wiener Studien zur Tibetologie u. Buddhismuskunde, 1983). Specific methods and their applications are dealt with in my "Padma dKar-po on Tantra as Ground, Path and Goal," *Journal of the Tibet Society* 4 (1984): 5–46; "Does Tibetan Hermeneutics Throw Any Light on *Sandhābhāṣa?*" *Journal of the Tibet Society* 2 (1982): 5–39; and "*Abhiprāya* and Implication in Tibetan Linguistics," *Journal of Indian Philosophy* 12 (1984): 1–33. For the "seven ornaments" of the GST cycle (mainly in India) see also Ernst Steinkellner, "Remarks on Tantristic Hermeneutics," in L. Ligeti, ed., *Proceedings of the 1976 Csoma de Körös Symposium,* Biblioteca Orientalia Hungarica, no. 23 (Budapest, 1978), 445–458.
5. See note 4.
6. The "three tantras" are reviewed at length in my "Padma dKar-po on Tantra as Ground, Path and Goal."
7. The *nītārtha* interpretations are all concerned with the completion stage *(sampannakrama, rdzogs-rim)* and can be recognized as such by anyone familiar

with the material. See also the *sampannakrama* section of the *sādhana-paṭala* of KT, say IV.115 ff. Mi-pham is explicit on the point, 142.5: *srog-gcod-la-sogs rdzogs-rim nges-don-la sbyar-ba.* No good account of these practices is yet available in any Western language, but the reader is recommended to the critical study of H. V. Guenther's *Life and Teaching of Nāropa* (Oxford: Clarendon Press, 1963). The translation of Nāropa's hagiography is generally accurate, and Guenther's comments contain some penetrating observations, in spite of his idiosyncracies of interpretation and even though nothing can be accepted at its face value.

8. The notion of interpretation in use here is that of propositional-attitude ascription: my English sentences are claims about the beliefs, injunctions, etc. expressed by King Puṇḍarīka in writing his Sanskrit text. They are not mirror-images of the Sanskrit sentences (no such mirror exists): see Donald Davidson, *Radical Interpretation* (*Dialectica,* 1973), and Richard Rorty, *Philosophy and the Mirror of Nature* (Princeton: Princeton University Press, 1979). The idea is familiar enough in contemporary analytic philosophy, both in the Anglo-Saxon world and on the Continent. Though this does not, of course, commit the Indians to such a view of interpretation, I show in Part II of this chapter that Indian interpreters of the tantras were committed to a rather similar view of interpretation, viz. as intention-ascription. For the application of these notions to the problem of *sandhābhāṣa* in the *Hevajra-tantra,* see my "Does Tibetan Hermeneutics Throw Any Light on *Sandhābhāṣa?*"

9. *viśuddhadharma, rnam-par-dag-pa'i chos.* It is not clear whether *dharma* here means "teaching" or "thing, element of existence"; I incline to the first (A, FF).

10. *samaya, dam-tshig.* Though the Skt. can mean "convention," by comparing with [C, N] and with similar passages in HT and GST commentaries I am inclined to go for "vow," in agreement with Tib.

11. *pūrvāparaṃ, sngon-dang-phyi-mar.* The idea seems to be that so as to understand the consequences of one's acts, one must know past and future; Mi-pham, 141.2,7.

12. *Caṇḍāśoka, gtum-po Mya-ngan-med-pa,* lit. "terrible Aśoka."

13. Tib. *chos-rgyal Mya-ngan-med-pa,* but Skt. only *dharmāśoka.*

14. The reference is to the standard list of mantra-rites found, for example, at HT I.ii.

15. *atipātāt;* Tib. *bkag-pa* takes some account of the ambiguity of *prāṇa* (life, breath). The whole passage plays on the ambiguity of *prāṇātipātaḥ* = killing and *prāṇātipātaḥ* = opposing the breath. The Tibetan cannot translate this play on words except by using the different phrases *srog gcod-pa* 'killing' and *srog bkag-pa* 'stopping the breath'.

16. *uṣṇīṣa* means the top of the head (not the topknot); the reference is to the center *(cakra)* there.

17. *apratiṣṭhitavacanam, rab-tu mi-gnas-pa'i tshig,* lit. "words which do not stand upon anything" (cf. *apratiṣṭhitanirvāna*). This does not seem to be a technical term, in contrast to *nayathāruta.*

18. The texts do not seem to make sense. Tib. lit. something like "by *nītārtha,* demonstrating the dharma to all beings in a moment to the utterance *(vakyam, tshig)* of the words *(ruta, skad)* of all beings, and the unstruck sound in their hearts." My version is based partly on Mi-pham, who apparently takes *skad* as "language" (even though this seems unlikely for *ruta*). Skt. seems hopelessly confused.

19. *viṣayāḥ, yul-rnams.* Mi-pham takes these as the five sense-objects (*yul dbang-yul-rnams-te,* 142.7), but since VP does not interpret them separately it

would be better to take *viṣayāḥ* in opposition to *madyaṃ, dīpa* and *buddhāḥ* as in VPT. Mi-pham also does not make sense of *sakala, mtha-dag* (fully, completely).

20. "Together-born bliss," cf. HT I.viii.32–33 and Kāṇha on it.

21. Meaning unknown to me (and probably also to Tib., who just transcribes: *go-ku*). Mi-pham drops this word (142.7).

22. Note that BB–CC (relating to the Dagger family) is not said to be *nītārtha,* probably because it is part of the same topic as the *neyārtha* remark at [O]. This example suggests that Puṇḍarīka did not simply assume a mechanical correlation between *nītārtha* and the completion stage, as Mi-pham seems to do.

23. 140.6.

24. Here the name is *Amukhavajra, rdo-rje che-ge-mo.*

25. The four stages are called *ācārya-* or *kalaśa-abhiṣeka, (slob-dpon-gyi dbang, bum-dbang), guhya-a. (gsang-dbang), prajñājñāna-a. (shes-rab ye-shes-kyi dbang)* and *caturtha-a.* (*dbang bzhi-pa,* often *tshig-dbang*). Of their various correlations, perhaps the most important is the one with the division of sādhana practice into the generation stage, *karmamudrā,* the *ṣaḍaṅgayoga,* and *mahāmudrā.*

26. They are the usual water *(toya, chu),* crown *(makuṭa, cod-pan),* etc.

27. This remark, differing from what is accepted in other tantras, throws into relief the remark [FF] that the treatment of pure dharma is the same in all the tantras (that is, presumably, in its general structure).

28. This point is unclear in ST (22.22 ff.). Mi-pham's heading is *rdo-rje slob-dpon-du dbang-bskur-ba.*

29. *bāhya* and *adhyātmika.* These are the names of the first two chapters of KT; and in contrast to other *anuttarayogatantras,* KT takes these two worlds *themselves* to be the bases for purification by sādhana, etc. See Geshe Lhundrup Sopa, "An Excursus on the Subtle Body in Tantric Buddhism," *Journal of the International Association of Buddhist Studies* 6 (1983): 48–66, esp. 56. It is difficult to be clear whether these terms "outer" and "inner" should count as hermeneutic or not.

30. Some attempt at using the literal sense is made in the case of killing living beings, by the play on the two senses of *prāṇa (srog);* see note 15. There is no need to take seriously the claim that different *senses* are being associated with the word *unless such a double association occurs in a variety of contexts.* If the texts appear to be claiming this, our interpretation needs revision (by the charity principle).

31. HT II.iii.29 ff.; see my "Does Tibetan Hermeneutics Throw Any Light on *Sandhabhāṣa?*" and references given there. Much nonsense has been written about *sandhābhāṣa.* Though I am certainly not saying that this word means "code," *what it refers to* is like a code, and the Tibetans have recognized this by the use of the term *brda-skad* with this reference (again, not sense!).

32. See note 4.

33. In the JVS, the literal use of *vajra* and *padma* counts as *neyārtha;* the *nītārtha* is non-literal. This point is taken up in Part II.

34. The Skt. for *dgongs-bshad* is not known with certainty, perhaps *sandhyābhāṣita;* see Alex Wayman, "Concerning saṃdhā-bhāṣa / saṃdhi-bhāṣa / saṃdhyā bhāṣa," in *Mélanges d'Indianisme a la Mémoire de Louis Renou* (Paris: de Boccard, 1968), 789–796; idem, "Twilight Language and a Tantric Song," in his *The Buddhist Tantras* (New York: Samuel Weiser, 1973), chap. 11. The vast difference between the apparently similar *dgongs-bshad* and *dgongs-skad* (or *gsang-skad*), as these terms were used in Tibet, is the main theme of my "Does Tibetan Hermeneutics Throw Any Light on *Sandhabhāṣa?*"

35. At first sight, the VP's *madyaṃ sahajānandaṃ* is somewhat similar to the

HT's *madanaṃ madyaṃ,* but the resemblance, superficial even in this isolated case, extends little further.

36. Mi-pham 142.5; see note 7.

37. Mi-pham 143.3: *'di-dag-la . . . nang-du sbas-don gyi tshul . . . rtogs-par-bya'o.*

38. For example, the sense in the VP might be different from that in the GST cycle. (Of course there is a problem about saying *what it means* to claim that an expression has several different senses; but that does not seem to be the issue here.)

39. However Mi-pham does mention this (143.3): *de-ltar 'di-dag-la phyi-ltar thabs-shes-kyi dgongs spyod khyad-par-can-gyis zin-pa'i sgo-nas spyod-tshul dang/ nang-du sbas-don-gyi tshul gnyis-kyis rtogs-par-bya'o/*

40. See Nathan Katz, "*Prasaṅga* and Deconstruction: Tibetan Hermeneutics and the *Yāna* Controversy," *Philosophy East and West* 34 (1984): 185.

41. "Remarks on Tantristic Hermeneutics," in L. Ligeti, *Proceedings of the 1976 Csoma de Körös Symposium.*

42. See, for example, P. F. Strawson, "Meaning and Truth," in his *Logico-Linguistic Papers* (London: Methuen, 1969).

43. See John McDowell, "Meaning, Communication and Knowledge," in Zak van Straaten, ed., *Philosophical Subjects: Essays Presented to P. F. Strawson* (Oxford: Clarendon Press, 1980). McDowell attempts to find common ground between the communication-intention theorists and (some) theorists of formal semantics. See also Strawson's "Reply to McDowell" in the same volume.

44. Alfred Tarski, in "The Concept of Truth in the Deductive Sciences" (in his *Logic, Semantics, and Metamathematics* [Oxford: Clarendon Press, 1956]), held that a satisfactory theory would reduce all semantic notions to non-semantic ones; this requirement forms part of his physicalism. As Field points out in "Tarski's Theory of Truth" (in Mark Platts, ed., *Reference, Truth and Reality: Essays in the Philosophy of Language* [London: Routledge & Kegan Paul, 1980]), Tarski himself did not achieve such a reduction. It is now widely held to be impossible—see, for example, John McDowell, "Physicalism and Primitive Denotion: Field on Tarski," in Platts, *Reference, Truth and Reality.*

45. See, for example, John McDowell, "Bivalence and Verificationism," in Evans and McDowell, eds., *Truth and Meaning: Essays in Semantics* (Oxford: Clarendon Press, 1976). Another useful account of this topic is found in McDowell's "On the Sense and Reference of a Proper Name," in Platts, *Reference, Truth and Reality;* the latter account is diccussed more fully and applied to various questions of Buddhist hermeneutics in my "Does Tibetan Hermeneutics Throw Any Light on *Sandhabhāṣa?*"

46. For example, NBT I.1: *atra ca prakaraṇābhideyasya samyagjñānasya sarvapuruṣārthasiddhihetutvam prayojanamuktam/,* etc. (The word *sarvapuruṣārthasiddhi* occurs in the sūtra; and it is noteworthy that in commenting on it, Vinītadeva remarks that here *artha* means *prayojana.*)

47. NBTV on NB I.1 (see also T. Stcherbatski, *Buddhist Logic* 2 [New York: Dover, 1972], p 1, n. 3).

48. For example, PSP, p 2: *tasya kāni sambandhābhideyaprayojanāni iti,* etc.; but the Tibetan reads 2a1: */de'i 'brel-ba dang brjod-par-bya-ba dang/ dgos-pa'i dgos-pa-dag gang yin zhes,* etc.

49. For this passage in Skt. and Tib. see Appendix A of my "Note on *dgos-'brel,*" *Journal of the Tibet Society* 3: 5–19 (1983). The Tibetan is incomprehensible, because *vācya* and *abhidheya* are both translated by *brjod-bya.* It seems that *abhidheya* stands for what the speaker intends to talk about (hence my "topic";

but "content" sometimes works better). In contrast, the *vācya* is the literal sense of the words, independent of the speaker's intention. Thus there can be no enquiry into whether *vācaka* and *vācya* are appropriately related *(sambaddha),* but there can be an enquiry as to whether *abhidhāna* and *abhidheya* are thus related—as the VP puts it, whether their relation *(sambandha)* is that of *vācaka* and *vācya.* Relevant issues of intensionality (with-an-s) are discussed in Appendix B of this reference.

50. V. 7a3.

51. Vajragarbha supplies some interesting literary and exegetic details which take his treatment well beyond that offered in the VP, but there is no space for all this here.

52. Concerning the *Guhyasamāja* system of seven ornaments, some philological observations may be found in Steinkellner, "Remarks on Tantristic Hermeneutics"; this useful paper has the advantage of being based partly on the Skt. ms. of PPD found at Zha-lu by Sāṅkṛtyāyana, whose photographs are kept at Patna (see its n. 6.). Steinkellner notes the Skt. terms for the five introductory topics as *samjñā, nimitta, kartā, pramā,* and *prayojana.* Unfortunately his attempts to analyze the content of the ornaments are not easy to follow. My "*bshad-thabs:* Some Tibetan Methods of Explaining the Tantras" contains an independent attempt to describe that content, as seen by various Tibetan authors. On various current mistranslations of the technical terms, see also the final section of my "Does Tibetan Hermeneutics Throw Any Light on *Sandhabhāṣa?*"

53. Steinkellner, "Remarks on Tantristic Hermeneutics," note 12.

54. PPD 2b2:

/dgos-pa yang ni bshad-bya ste/
/zhi-sogs bya-ba'i cho-ga dang/
/de-bzhin grub-pa brgyad dang ni/
/sangs-rgyas kyang ni mchog yin-no/

55. See, for example, K. Kunjunni Raja, *Indian Theories of Meaning* (Madras: Adyar Library, 1969).

56. NBT III.54. In the translated passage, which occurs toward the end of the commentary on this sūtra, Dharmottara repeatedly uses *śabdasya-abhiprāya* as we might use "speaker's intention" (cf. Arcaṭa's *vaktur abhiprāya* below). The opponent claims that knowledge resulting from words is the *direct* result of such intentions *(abhiprāya-kārya-śabdājjātaṃ jñānam).* Dharmottara does not so much reject this view as distinguish sharply between the (speaker's) intention *(śabdasya-abhiprāya)* and the *content* of what is thereby to be communicated *(nivedanāya).* The utterance (*śabdaprayoga,* cf. note 58) expresses the content, not the intention:

na śabdasya-abhiprāya avinābhāvitva-abhyupagama-pūrvakaḥ śabdaprayogaḥ/ . . .
bahya-vastv-avinābhāvitva-abhyupagama-pūrvakaḥ śabdaprayogaḥ/

Arcaṭa has very clearly expressed the idea that the function *(vṛtti)* of a word conforms with the intention *(abhiprāya)* of the speaker *(vaktṛ)* at HBT, p 3:

vaktur abhiprāya-anuvidhyāyitayā śabdavṛtteḥ.

57. *bāhya-vastu,* lit. an external thing (cf. note 56).

58. Stcherbatsky supplies both a literal and a more polished translation of this passage (*Buddhist Logic* 2, 168 n. 7 and text, respectively). Here it has been completely retranslated, but considerable use has been made of his literal translation. However I have one mild criticism: *śabdaprayoga* does not seem to mean

"language" or "words" in a general sense, but rather "use of words" or "verbal formulation" in relation to specific occasions; hence my "utterance."

59. *sandhir abhiprāyaḥ abhiprāyapradhānam bhāṣaṇaṃ nākṣarapradhānam ity arthaḥ/* This passage has been discussed in my "*Abhiprāya* and Implication in Tibetan Linguistics."

60. The Christian Fathers wrote of a literal and a spiritual sense (see, for example, the first chapter of Beryl Smalley's *The Study of the Bible in the Middle Ages* [Oxford: Clarendon Press, 1941]); the SV implicitly contrasts the literal sense of the GST with the buddha-intention *(*buddhābhisandhi).* In my view there is virtually no parallel between these two pairs of contrasting modes of interpretation. Inasmuch as the Fathers *supplied* the spiritual sense, they were not doing hermeneutics (any more than was the SV in spelling out the buddha-intention). Now the Fathers of course tried to explain and justify their conception of the spiritual sense. The SV does not do this for the **buddhābhisandhi;* and when it is done at a later stage in GST exegesis, it soon becomes clear that **buddhābhisandhi* has almost nothing to do with the Fathers' "spiritual sense." But more important than this lack of parallelism is the fact that we cannot even *investigate* whether Buddhist and Christian hermeneutics are related until we have some independent understanding of Buddhist hermeneutics. For this vital methodological reason, Christian hermeneutical terms are not used in this paper.

61. HT II.iii.29 = GST XVI 59c–60b. The texts are identical except for the last word, which in GST reads *yoṣitāmapi.* Tib. in both cases is *pha-rol bud-med,* which is not only consistent with HT, but clarifies it. However Vajragarbha gives both "external" and "other":

/pha-rol bud-med bsten-par-bya/
/rdo-rje sems sogs gzhan bud-med/

(only the first of these lines appears in the *laghu-Hevajra,* 29d). The Skt. of GST is surely corrupt here. The Tib. in HT perhaps reflects a Tibetan wish to get away from talk about real women and adultery. (VP is too explicit for this.)

62. *para* (HT only) would permit "of another," but *pha-rol* (HT and GST) means "external" (n. 61).

63. HT II.ii.13a–14b. Snellgrove's translation is not wholly clear. The point is perhaps this: those who commit the five immediacies, who delight in taking life, who have a low birth, who are confused, and who do wrong (i.e. those who perform terrible acts, *krūra-karmiṇāḥ* as in the VP passage G) and those who have evil forms and ugly limbs, *even they* will attain siddhi by means of reflection *(cintayā).* But this hardly needs interpretation, since it is clear as it stands (cf. E, 178a4; K, 187b6).

64. Matsunaga Yūkei has raised "A Doubt as to the Authority of the *Guyhasamāja-ākhyā-tantras*" in *Indogaku bukkyōgaku kenkyū* 12 (1964): 840ff. (cf. Steinkellner, "Remarks on Tantristic Hermeneutics," n. 8). The doubts can surely not be about the SV or the *Vajramālā;* they concern the JVS. As Steinkellner remarks, the JVS was accepted as the main canonical source for GST hermeneutics by Bu-ston and especially by Tsong-kha-pa, who wrote a commentary on it (P Tsa 171b). But against Steinkellner's note 9, we *do* find references to the JVS in such Indian commentaries as that of Bhavyakīrti (PPDAP, N vol. A, e.g., 80a2). The issue needs more detailed work.

65. Apart from the unclarity of the definitions in the JVS, there are some plain inconsistencies between it and PPD (see my "*bshad-thabs:* Some Tibetan

Methods of Explaining the Tantras"). Now such inconsistencies do raise doubts about the *authority* of the JVS, but they serve if anything to corroborate its *authenticity.*

66. JVS 293a2–4, excerpts: *ga-bur dang khrag chen-po . . . rdo-rje'i tshig-rnams ni drang-ba'i don-te/ ga-bur khu-ba dang khrag chen-po ni zla-mtshan-gyi khrag . . . rdo-rje'i tshig-rnams ni nges-pa'i don-to/:* The words "camphor" and "great blood" [themselves] are *neyārtha,* but taking "camphor" to stand for "semen" and "great blood" to stand for "menstrual blood" is *nītārtha.*

If we want to take the JVS account seriously in its own right, it is best not to approach it through the PPD. See my "*bshad-thabs:* Some Tibetan Methods of Explaining the Tantras" for a very clear Tibetan discussion.

67. JVS 292b8. Tsong-kha-pa's gloss on this (D 209b7) is discussed in my "*bshad-thabs:* Some Tibetan Methods of Explaining the Tantras," p. 35 and n. 81.

68. *Intention here is not intention in general (as in the SV), but more like Edgerton's "specially intended" (see *Buddhist Hybrid Sanskrit Dictionary* s.v. *abhiprāya, sandhyā*). An alternative translation would be "explanation by implication"; this exploits the "special" senses of *sandhi* and *ābhiprāyika.* See my "*Abhiprāya* and Implication in Tibetan Linguistics."

69. Raja, *Indian Theories of Meaning.*

70. While the general hermeneutic stance of the SV might with some sense of strain be compared with something in Biblical exegesis (see note 60 above), not even this seems true of the PPD. The reason, in the end, is that the tantras are *not* claimed to be revelatory in anything like the same sense. *Nītārtha, nayathāruta,* and *sandhyābhāṣita* explanations do not claim to reveal a world other than the one in which we live already. The Buddha is an "image of human perfection," to use Nathan Katz's helpful phrase; and, especially as "embodying cognition" *(pramāṇabhūtam)* he represents the cognitive capacities which we, as human beings, have possessed all along. These are simply the capacities to see the same world in which we have always lived as it is and always was.

71. PPD 64a1.

72. On the ascription as *neyārtha,* see also PPD, P 6a4 and 66b6.

73. PPD, 66b6 ff.

74. B 140b3.

75. SV 255b5. This passage is quoted in full in PPD (D 35b6, P 41b1). SV also says that this is *dgongs-pas bshad-pa* but for the general reasons mentioned already this only means explanation by intention in general, and not by a special *intention.

76. Terms translatable by "live word" and "dead word" are used in the Chinese and Korean Ch'an traditions, as discussed by Robert Buswell in this volume. The view that live words (or words effectively pointing to the ultimate) should not be *explained* was widely held in Tibet and is much emphasized in the writings of Padma dKar-po. In the *Guyhasamāja* system, the interpretative category *mthar-thug-don (kolikaṃ)* is reserved particularly for such "live words," but the connection between this mode of using language and *dgongs-bshad* was not made clear before PPD, in spite of the passage JVS 292b8 (cf. note 67).

77. PPD, D 35b5: */rgyud-kyi rgyal-po khyad-par-du gyur-pa bstan-nas/ slob-dpon med-par 'jug-par mi-gyur-cig snyam-du dgongs-nas/* 'jig-rten-dang-'gal-ba'i *tshig-gis spyod-pa'i khyad-par bstan-pa'i phyir/* srog-gcod-pa-yi *zhes-bya-ba-la-sogs gsungs-te/ 'di'i don ni bshad-pa'i rgyud-las gsungs-te/. . . . 'di ni* dgongs-pas bshad-pa'o/

78. V. 105a1: *. . . nges-pa'i don-gyi sdom-pa bstan-to/*

79. PPD, D 165b4: khyod-kyis srog-chags gsad-par-bya/ */zhes-bya-ba-la-sogs-*

pa'i dam-tshig bzhi ni/ le'u lnga-pa-las gsungs-pa'i dgongs-pas bshad-pa bzhin-du shes-par-bya'o/

80. The Sanskrit is as given (and modified somewhat) by Wayman, "Concerning saṃdhā-bhāṣa." The Tibetan is the last four lines of the quotation in note 81.

81. In PPD (D 2b6) the definitions of *nītārtha* and *dgongs-bshad* are run together:

> */yang-dag don ni rab-ston-phyir/*
> */nges-pa'i don yang gsungs-pa yin/*
> */mchod 'dod sems-can-rnams-kyi phyir/*
> */chos-kyi de-nyid rab-ston-pa/*
> */gal-ba'i tshig-gi sbyor-ba-yis/*
> */gsungs-pa gang yin dgongs-bshad-de/*

The two middle lines are taken by Bhavyakīrti, Karuṇa and Bu-ston as belonging to *dgongs-bshad* only, and by Āryadeva and Kumāra as belonging to both *nītārtha* and *dgongs-bshad.* This is connected with the complex question of whether *nītārtha* is concerned with a "real" *(niṣparyāya)* ultimate, or merely a "provisional" *(paryāya)* one. All the texts on vows discussed in this paper seem to associate *nītārtha* with a "provisional" ultimate. Of the writers I have studied, only Padma dKar-po has tried to put */mchog-'dod . . .* = *viśiṣṭaruci . . .* exclusively with *nītārtha* (in F, 36a6). In doing this, he seems to have been influenced by Kumāra's confused attempt (which he quotes, *ibid.;* cf. PTH, 208b5) to connect *dgongs-bshad* with *sbas-don.* Padma dKar-po abandoned the attempt in his later works, such as the *dbu-ma'i gzhung-lugs-gsum gsal-bar byed-pa'i nges-don grub-pa'i shing-rta* (see my "*Abhiprāya* and Implication in Tibetan Linguistics").

82. See note 77.

83. Bhavyakīrti, Bu-ston, and Padma dKar-po stress that it contradicts the world; Āryadeva, that it contradicts the śāstras; Kumāra, that it contradicts logic. Karuṇa refuses to take *viruddha* literally. Tsong-kha-pa and bKra-shis rNam-rgyal stress contradictions between convention and intention *(śabda* and *artha).* For the Indians, see below; for the Tibetans, see my articles "Does Tibetan Hermeneutics Throw Any Light on *Sandhabhāṣa?*" and "*Abhiprāya* and Implication in Tibetan Linguistics." These various lines of explanation are certainly not independent.

84. The obvious idea that the six alternatives form three contrasting *pairs* was important in Tibet (see my articles "*bshad-thabs:* Some Tibetan Methods of Explaining the Tantras" and "*Abhiprāya* and Implication in Tibetan Linguistics"). In India only Āryadeva takes it seriously, and he uses another version. Bhavyakīrti uses two sets of three (i.e. three *śabdālaṅkāras* and three *arthālaṅkāras* —see below). Kumāra and Karuṇa make less use of this type of systemization.

85. Since Kumāra is the translator of Bhavyakīrti, he is the later. Kumāra mentions a remark of Āryadeva on *nayathārutaśabda;* the reference is to the *Cāryamelāpakapradīpa,* but the same observation is found in the PPDT (see below). If these works are by the same Āryadeva, the PPDT is certainly earlier than the PTH. Āryadeva does not seem to know the Dhv., while Bhavyakīrti certainly knows it, and so should be the later. The style of the PPDT also suggests that it is an early work; and of course tradition stresses that Āryadeva was (like Candrakīrti) the pupil of Nāgārjuna, author of the *Pañcakrama.* Karuṇa was perhaps a contemporary of Atīśa; his PDPU was certainly translated by Bu-ston. I have no clear grounds for placing him last, but the order of the other three does seem fairly certain.

86. PPDT, P 17b2.
87. Ibid. 19a6.
88. Ibid. 20b1–4 (under *nītārtha*) and 20b6–8 (under *dgongs-bshad*). These two passages have to be taken together, especially since *nītārtha* is discussed in both.
89. Ibid. 21a6.
90. Ibid. 21a1.
91. The catalogue entries in vols. 60 and 61 of the Otani reprint of P are wrong (about PDPAP and PPDT), but the errors are corrected in the catalogue volume. The sNar-thang catalogue is also confused.
92. PDPAP, P vol. A, 106b5, 107a1, a3, a6, b3, b5 (scattered among other materials).
93. Ibid. 101b4.
94. *dngos-po sgrub-par byed-pa;* for example, ibid., 101b6. Of course the word *dngos-po, vastu* takes the sense usual in poetics (a fixed, definite idea), and not the one usual in logic (thing, substance; for the same reason *bhāva* is impossible).
95. *byed-pa sgrub-par byed-pa,* ibid. (The correspondence *vyāpāra* = *byed-pa* is well known both in logic and linguistics.)
96. Bhavyakīrti says, perfectly sensibly, that *nītārtha* and *neyārtha* are called *arthālaṅkāra* because they associate different *arthas* with a single *śabda;* ibid., 106b7. But his explanation is that one *vācaka* can have the capacity to express two *arthas,* "just as one word may have several meanings *(gzhan-sel, apoha),* for instance as *gauḥ* may mean 'speech,' 'the earth,' 'light-ray,' 'arrow,' etc."; this is hopeless, since the *nītārtha/neyārtha* distinction precisely does *not* rest on this kind of ambiguity of linguistic meaning. (This is clear from all the examples.) Further, on the *yathāruta/nayathāruta* distinction, he says (107a6) that an *artha* which is expressed by *nayathāruta* utterances such as *brda* [*chomā:* HT I.vii.1] is not similar to the *śabda,* yet that we have a *śabdālaṅkāra* since *brda is a* [*variety of*] *śabda;* this tells us nothing about *how* or *why* brda is different from *yathārutaśabda.* Since *dgongs-min* is an *arthālaṅkāra* while *dgongs-bshad* is a *śabdālaṅkāra,* the difference between the two rests upon the unexplained difference between these two kinds of *alaṅkāra;* this scarcely seems enough.
97. PDPAP, P 102a1. The verse about the lion and the dog was originally in Prakrit; the Sanskrit version runs (Dhv., p. 50, quoted by Krishnamoorthy in his *Dhavanyāloka and Its Critics* [Mysore: Kāvyālaya, 1968], 103):

> *bhrama dhārmika visrabdhaḥ sa śunako'dya māritastena/*
> *godāvarīnadīkūlalatāgahanavāsinā dṛptasiṃhena//*

The verse is very well known and goes back to before the Dhv. The idea of Ānanda's explanation is that the expressed sense *(vācyārtha)* is that since the dangerous dog has been killed, the hermit may now wander safely along the riverbank; the implied sense *(vyaṅgyārtha)* is just the opposite, viz. that since there is a lion wandering around, the situation is even more dangerous. The idea of Bhavyakīrti's example *(bde-bar song-zhig)* is perhaps that in the Mahāyāna there is really no coming or going or any bliss, so that even though the Buddha says "Go!" the implied sense is the opposite.
98. PDPAP, P 102a4.
99. At least not in the section of the PDPAP dealing with the seven ornaments, where it is most obviously needed.
100. PDPAP, P 106b4.
101. Ibid. 106b2.

102. Ibid. 109a2–5.
103. PDPAP, N vol. Ki, 68b3.
104. Ibid., and 71a5.
105. For instance on *dgongs-bshad* he says (P vol. A, 106b8) that *viruddhālāpa-[pra]yoga* means words which contradict worldly usage, and that *"dgongs-bshad"* itself is synonymous with *"dgongs-pa-dang-bcas-pa'i sgra'i sbyor-ba"* (**ābhiprāyika-śabdaprayoga,* cf. note 129); since this is mainly a matter of words *(śabda)* we have a *śabdālaṅkāra.* The second remark seems quite arbitrary; cf. note 96. Yet could Bhavyakīrti have been relying on Vasubandhu? Cf. note 129.
106. PDPAP, P vol. A, 107b4.
107. Ibid. 109a1.
108. PTH 206b1; for */mtha-drug tshig-gis nges byas-pa/,* PPD, D 2b5.
109. PTH 206b2; for */rnal-'byor rgyud-tshul-las bshad-pa/,* PPD, D 2b5.
110. PTH 206b7.
111. Ibid. 206b8: *gdon mi-za-ba'i don* (quoted by Padma dKar-po, F 35b5).
112. PTH 207a1.
113. Ibid. 207a3.
114. Ibid. 207a7.
115. Also in PPDT, 21b8.
116. PTH 207b7.
117. *grags-pa ma-yin-pa'i brda.* See my articles "Does Tibetan Hermeneutics Throw Any Light on *Sandhabhāṣa?*" and "*Abhiprāya* and Implication in Tibetan Linguistics" for the importance of *brda (chomā)* in exegesis of the *Hevajra-tantra.* But the term is also used a good deal in the GST literature (Skt. uncertain) for symbols without standard rules for using them; for example, the words *koṭākhya,* etc. just mentioned under *nayathāruta,* and other adventitious symbols. "Adventitious" stands for *glo-bur (āgantuka),* frequently used of such symbols by Bu-ston and Tsong-kha-pa. The Skt. *āgantuka* is well known, but only in other contexts. Padma dKar-po has given several careful discussions of *brda* just in the present context (see my two articles cited above in this note).
118. PDPU 22b8.
119. Ibid. 23a5: *'di zhes-pa 'dis rnal-'byor-ma'i rgyud-du mngon-par-brjod-pa yang 'dus-pa'i brjod-par bya'o zhes-pa 'gal-ba ma-yin-no/*
120. Ibid.: */dgongs-pa'i skad dang* zhes-bya-ba-sogs-te/ . . . */dgons-min dang* zhes-pa-na/ (On the whole these translations do not distinguish consistently between quotation [*zhes-pa*] and disquotation [*zhes-bya-ba*].)
121. Ibid.: *tshig-gi don drug-gis smra-bar-byed-pa'i. . . .*
122. Ibid. *mngon-par dgongs-pa* is unusual; *abhisandhi* is usually translated by *ldem-por dgongs-pa* or just plain *dgongs-pa;* but since *sandhi* is also usually translated by *dgongs-pa, mngon-par dgongs-pa* for *abhisandhi* is "literal."
123. Ibid. 23b7.
124. Ibid. 24a2: *rang-bzhin gsum-la mngon-par dgongs-nas bstan-pa ni/ nges-pa'i don-no, zhes-pa ni 'gal-ba'i tshig-go/ /nges-pa ji-lta-ba kho-nar tshig-gi don de-lta-bu kho-nar gsal-bar-byas-pa'i don ni/ nges-pa'i don-no/* This confirms the conjecture (note 122) that *mngon-par dgongs-pa* here is *abhisandhi;* there is a plain reference here to the topic of *abhisandhi* as developed, for example, in *Mahayānasūtrālaṅkāra* XII.16–18 and Vasubandhu and Sthiramati on them; see my "*Abhiprāya* and Implication in Tibetan Linguistics," which discusses these sources at length.
125. PDPU 24a4: *rab-tu gsal-bar byed-de.* It is only from the context that one can tell whether such a phrase means "makes very clear" or "suggests"; both of course being senses of Skt. *vyañj-.* My rendering is based on the apparent contrast with the description of *dgongs-min* at 24b2, which quotes the

standard phrase *mchog-tu gsal-ba* from the PPD, where it certainly means "very clearly."

126. PDPU 24a6: *'gal-ba'i tshig ni nye-bar mtshon-pa ste.* The word *upalakṣaṇa* can mean "metaphor" or "implication." It has several other meanings; for example,

(a) "accidental qualifier," in contrast to "essential qualifier" *(viśeṣana);* see B. K. Matilal, *Nāvya-Nyāya Doctrine of Negation* (Cambridge, Mass.: Harvard University Press, 1968), 118.

(b) "Upalakṣaṇa is the act of implying any analogous object where only one is specified"; see Raja, *Indian Theories of Meaning,* 261. (He gives a case where *kāka* 'crow' stands for any animal which might eat curd.)

But it seems unlikely that Karuṇa intended either of these more specialized senses.

127. PDPU 24b2. On *mchog-tu gsal-ba,* see note 125.

128. Ibid. 24b3. Strictly speaking, the text says that what is not hidden is explained here, as with *neyārtha: drang-ba'i don-bzhin, sbas-pa ma-yin-par bshad-pa'o/*

129. No attempt has been made in this paper to compare the interpretation of the tantras to that of the sūtras. While *nītārtha* and *neyārtha* are certainly quite different in the sūtras, it seems that the phrase *sandhāya . . . bhāṣitaṃ* (*dgongs-te gsungs-pa,* etc.) is very similar to the *dgongs-pas bshad-pa* of the tantras. X *sandhāya* Y *bhāṣitaṃ* Z (a common schema) means "*implying* X, Y said Z." One example will have to suffice. *Samyutta Nikāya* iv.216 contains a remark that everything which may be sensed is *dukkha;* the Buddha himself comments that this remark is only suggestive. (Remark and explanation are given in Pali by Louis de la Vallée Poussin, *L'Abhidharmakośa de Vasubandhu* [Bruxelles: Institut Belge des Hautes Études Chinoises, 1971], 4:131); our phrase in Pali is *sandhāya bhāsitam.*) Vasubandhu makes use of this explanation in commenting on ADK VI.3, according to which there are three kinds of *vedanā,* of which only one is *duḥkha;* the Buddha's own explanation resolves the apparent contradiction:

> Indeed, the final *artha (nītārtha)* of the Buddha's remark "Everything which can be sensed is *duḥkha*" has been explained by the Buddha himself. He has said, "Implying the momentariness and the changeability of *saṃskāras,* Ānanda, I have said that everything which can be sensed is *duḥkha.*" This remark [of the Buddha] shows that it was *not* implied that [everything which can be sensed] is *duḥkha-duḥkha* [etc.].

Vasubandhu's Sanskrit runs thus:

> *yattu bhagavatoktaṃ "yat kiñcitveditam idam atra duḥkhasya" iti tad bhagavataiva nītārthaṃ "saṃskārānityatām Ānanda mayā sandhāya bhāṣitaṃ saṃskāravipariṇāmatāṃ ca, yat kiñcitveditam idam atra duḥkhasya" iti/ ato na duḥkhaduḥkhatām sandhāyaitad uktam iti siddham bhavati/*

Vasubandhu's own explanation of such sūtra passages as "Whatever can be sensed is *duḥkha*" is that they are suggestive or *intentional *(ābhiprāyika).* We noted exactly the same line of explanation with Bhavyakīrti in note 105. Padma dKar-po develops and deepens this line of explanation of *dgongs-bshad.*

Vasubandhu's analysis is the most careful I have seen; but even without it, one can show that *sandhāya* here is a verbal form (a gerundive) and not a noun (instr. of *sandhi*), and that it means "implying" or "suggesting" and not "intending." On the last point, *sandhāya* reports (part of) a speech *act,* while intention can only be *intention to perform* an act, not the act itself; also the object of *sandhāya* is not the act that would be needed if *sandhāya* meant "intending"—it is a quality (momentariness, etc.). One can well *suggest* or *imply* momentariness, but talk of *intending* momentariness is impossible except at a level of sloppiness which cannot do justice to Vasubandhu. In general, Poussin's translation is a splendid achievement and impressively reliable, but he is less careful over these important details. I deal with this properly elsewhere: "Intention and Suggestion in the *Abhidharma Kośa: Sandhābhāsā* Revisited," *Journal of Indian Philosophy* 13 (1985): 327–381.

Appendix A: The Sanskrit Texts

The Verses

Verses III.97c–98d of the Kālacakratantra are taken from the Carelli ed. (C) of ST, apart from certain emendations based on KTS; in this case the rejected C version is given in a note. VPS does not display the verses separately from the commentary, but most of them are found in the commentary. All the variants (from C) are supported by VPS and by the Tibetan.

kuryāt prāṇātipatāṃ khalu kuliśa-kule'satya-vākyaṃ ca khaḍge (97c)
ratne hāryaṃ parasvaṃ vara-kamala-kule 'pyeva hāryā parastrī // (97d)
madyaṃ dīpaśca buddhāḥ su[a]*-sakala viṣayā*[b] *sevanīyāśca cakre*[c] (98a)
Ḍombyādyāḥ karttikāyām su[a]*-sakala-vanitā na-avamanyāḥ*[d] *kha*[e]*-padme /* (98b)
deyā sattvārthahetoḥ sa[f]*-dhana tanuriyaṃ na tvayā rakṣaṇīyā* (98c)
buddhatvaṃ nānyathā vai bhavati kulaputra[g]*-ananta-kalpair-jinoktam //* (98d)

Notes: **a.** C: sva-; **b.** -āḥ C & LC note; **c.** C: sevanīyāḥ svacakre; **d.** C: -ā; **e.** C: svapadme; **f.** VPS: saha; **g.** Thus VP; KTT and VPT rigs-kyi bu; C: kulasuta; KTS: kuśalata.

The Commentary

VPS on KT III.97c–98d is transcribed from a microfilm of text E 13746 as filmed by the Nepal-German Ms. Preservation Project. (I am grateful to Mr. Alexis Sanderson for lending me his copy of this microfilm.) The text is a recent Nepalese ms. in a modified devanāgari (see below). The first four chapters seem to be roughly complete; the *jñānapaṭala* is missing. In the ms. the sections relating to successive verses are numbered separately, and are sometimes broken up into "paragraphs" separated by a gap of about 1½ cm. starting and finishing with a double //. The transcribed material is found at 234b5–235b4 and contains no such breaks other than that at the end of the commentary on 97d. The scribe's / and occasional // are reproduced, even though they often seem inappropriate. I have undone the *sandhi* in a few places to help the reader with less specialized knowledge; all these places are indicated by hyphens, which have also been used in a few other places to break up long phrases. Where undoing the *sandhi* has required a decision on meaning, I have followed the Tibetan; this is indicated in the notes.

On the whole I have not corrected misspellings, with a few exceptions again recorded in the notes. Since it is not clear to me what principles should govern such corrections, I have preferred to reproduce what is found. (In saying this, I do not wish to claim to have read the individual letters without any reference to their being grouped together in words.) There are numerous cases of systematic ambiguity, e.g., dv/dhv/ddh; ṇṭ/ṇṭh; ṣṭ/ṣṭh; bh/h; ty/bhy/hy; s/ṣ/ś; u/ū (both initial and medial); p/y. They have not been noted except where there is special difficulty, when the Tibetan has been followed.

These methods of editing are appropriate for a short section of a clearly written ms. where the availability of a Tibetan translation is a subsidiary consideration. It has seemed pointless to note the many places where the ms. diverges from the Tibetan but makes perfectly good sense on its own (cf. Appendix B).

A *idānīṃ viśuddha-dharma-deśanām*[h]*-āha //* kuryāt prāṇātipātam *ity-ādinā //*

B *iha prāṇātipātyādyāḥ*[k] *// samayā dvidhā neyārthena nītārthena bāhya-adhyātmikāśceti*[l] *//*

C *tatra bāhye prāṇātipātaṃ bhagavān yat kuryāt // tat pañca-ānantarya kāriṇāṃ*[m] *samaya-bhedinām iti niyamaḥ //*

D *tadeva pañcānantaryaṃ pūrvāparaṃ jñātvā //*

E *iha kaścit pūrvaṃ pañcānantarya kārī paścāt puṇya karttā bhavati, caṇḍāśoko dharmāśokavat //*

F *tasmāt tasya-apakārato narakaṃ bhavati mantriṇaḥ // śubhāśubha karma*[n] *aparijñānāt //*

G *tena yāvat pañcābhijñā na bhavanti // tāvan mantriṇā krūra-karma na karttavyam // śānti-puṣṭi-vaśya-ākṛṣṭibhir-vinā //*

H *evaṃ mṛṣā-vādaḥ // para-upakārataḥ // adatta-ādānamapi // parastrī grahaṇamapi // samaya-sevā varṇṇāvarṇṇa-abhigamanaṃ svaśarīra*[o] *paryantaṃ dānamapi na svārthataḥ iti //*

J *idānīṃ yadā āmaraṇāntaṃ pañcānantaryaṃ karoti // tadā pūrva sādhitaṃ mantram krodha kule Akṣobhya samādhinā'nena māraṇaṃ kuryāt // bhagavāniti neyārthaḥ //*

K *evam*[p] *amārge pātitānām abhyuddharaṇāya mṛṣavākyaṃ vaktavyaṃ na svārthataḥ //*

L *evam adattādanaṃ // preta-gati-gamana nivāraṇāya na svārthataḥ //*

M *tatha parastrī-grahaṇaṃ tiryag-gati-gamana nivāraṇāya na svārthataḥ //*

N *samayān pañcāmṛtādyān sevayet // kula-graha-vināśāya //*

O *evaṃ karmamudrā prasiddhyarthaṃ Ḍombyādyāḥ striyo na-avamanyeta // puṇya-sambhārāya mahā dānam dādati //*

P *evam*[q] *khaḍga kule / ratna kule / padma kule / cakra kule / karttikā kule / mantrān sādhayitvā sāmarthya-yuktaḥ san yogī sarvaṃ kuryāt //*

Q *yathā loke hāsyaṃ na bhavati-iti neyārthaḥ //*

R *idānīṃ nītārtha ucyate // iha svaśarīre prāṇasya-atipātāt, prāṇātipātaḥ kuliśa kule uṣṇīṣe*[r] *nirodham kuryāt //*

U *tena prāṇātipātena yogī ūrdhva*[s] *retā bhavatīti niyamaḥ //*

V asatya vākyam ca khaḍge *iha asatyaṃ nāma-apratiṣṭhita-vacanaṃ neyārthena //*

W *nītārthena sarva satva ruta*[t] *vākyam yaugapadyena satvānāṃ dharma-deśakaṃ tadeva hṛdaye'nāhata*[u] *dhvanir-iti niyamaḥ //*

X ratne hāryam parasvaṃ */ parasvamiti / iha paro Vajrasatvaḥ // tasya svaṃ ratnaṃ cintamaṇiḥ // tasya-apaharaṇaṃ / ratna kule kaṇṭhe*[v] *aṣṭama-bhūmi sthāne iti niyamaḥ //*

Y vara kamala kule'pyeva hāryā parastrī-*iti // parastrī mahāmudrā, tasya-apaharaṇaṃ parastrī haraṇaṃ / sāhāryā / kamalakule lalāṭe daśama bhūmi sthāne ūrdhva*[w] *retaśeti niyamaḥ //*

Z madyaṃ dīpaśca buddhāḥ susakala viṣayāḥ śevanīyāśca cakre *iti // iha madyaṃ sahajānandaṃ dīpo gokkvādikāni pañcendriyāṇi // adhyāt-mani buddhāḥ // pancāmṛtaś*

AA *cakre nābhi-kamale sevanīyā bhajaṇīyāḥ // bāhye viṭ-mūtra-śukrāśrāvaḥ*[x] *karttavya iti nītārthaḥ //*

BB *Ḍombyādyāḥ striyaḥ karttikāyāṃ guhya-kamale nāvamanyāḥ*

CC khapadme *yonau manth*[y]*āne brahmacaryeṇeti // bāhye śukra*[z] *acyavanena-iti-niyamaḥ //*

DD deyā sattvārthahetoḥ sa*hadhan*ena *putra-kalatrādibhiḥ sārddhaṃ sva-*tanuḥ *// pradeyā puṇyasambhārārthaṃ /*

EE *evaṃ śīlasambhārārthaṃ / striyo nāvamanyāḥ khapadme ataḥ puṇya-śīla-sambhārābhyāṃ jñānasambhāraḥ /*

FF *evam sambhāra-trayeṇa samyaksam*buddhatvaṃ *te* bhavati he kulaputra // nānyathā // anantaṃ kalpair-*yad*-jina*ir*-uktam-*iti viśuddha-dharma-deśanā niyamaḥ // iha sarvatantreṣu // //*

Textual notes to the Sanskrit commentary

h. S deśenām, T bstan-pa; **k.** S -ādāyaḥ, T sogs-pa; **l.** T nang-gi bdag-nyid;

m. T includes *sangs-rgyas-kyi bstan-pa-la gnod-pa byed-pa-rnams* (those who harm the teaching of the Buddha).
n. S karmīparijñānāt, T las yongs-su mi-shes-pa; **o.** S śerīra, T lus;
p. S evaṃmārge, T de-bzhin-du lam ma-yin-par; **q.** S omits *vaṃ;* T de-ltar;
r. -ṣṇ- unclear, T gtsug-tor-du; **s.** S ūrdva, T steng-du (cf. note **w**);
t. T skad-kyi, S rūta? For *ruta/artha,* see BHSD s.v. *ruta.*
u. T snying-khar gzhom-du med-pa; **v.** T mgrin-par;
w. S urdva, T steng-du (cf. note **s**);
x. The sandhi must be *śukra-aśrāvaḥ* (T khu-ba . . . mi-'dzag-pa);
y. -nth- uncertain, but T bsrubs-pa; **z.** T khu-ba mi-'pho-ba (cf. note **x**).

Appendix B: The Tibetan Texts

The verses are transcribed from KTT, the commentary from VPT (322a7 ff.). There seems to be no need to edit or alter either.

The Verses

KT III.97c–98d

/nges-par rdo-rje'i rigs-dag-la ni srog-gcod-bya ste, ral-gri-la yang bden-par min-pa'i tshig/
/rin-chen-la ni gzhan-nor dprog-bya, mchog-gi padma'i rigs-nyid-la yang gzhan-gyi bud-med dprog/
/chang dang sgron-ma sangs-rgyas-rnams dang bzang-po'i yul-rnams mtha-dag 'khor-lo-la ni bsten-par-bya/
/g.yung-mo-la-sogs mtha-dag bud-med-rnams ni gri-gug-la yang mkha-yi padmar smad mi-bya/
/sems-can don-gyi slad-du nor-dang-bcas-pa'i lus 'di sbyin-par-bya-ste khyod-kyis bsrung-mi-bya/
/rigs-kyi bu kye sangs-rgyas-nyid-du 'gyur-pa gzhan-du mtha-yas skal-pas min-par rgyal-bas gsungs/

The Commentary

A /da ni *nges-par rdo-rje* zhes-pa-la-sogs-pas, rnam-par-dag-pa'i chos bstan-pa gsungs-pa
B 'dir srog-gcod-pa-la-sogs-pa'i dam-tshig ni rnam-par gnyis-te/ drang-ba'i don dang nges-pa'i don-gyis phyi-rol dang nang-gi bdag-nyid-do/

C de-la phyi-rol-du, bcom-ldan-'das-kyis srog-gcod-pa bya-ba gang yin-pa de ni mtshams-med-pa lnga byed-pa-rnams dang sangs-rgyas-kyi bstan-pa-la gnod-pa-byed-pa-rnams dang dam-tshig 'dral-ba-rnams-so, zhes-so nges-pa ste/

D mtshams-med-pa lnga-po de-nyid sngon-dang-phyi-mar shes-nas-so/

E /'dir 'ga-zhig sngar mtshams-med-pa-lnga byed-pa-po phyis bsod-nams byed-pa-por 'gyur-te/ gtum-po Mya-ngan-med-pa dang chos-rgyal Mya-ngan-med-pa bzhin-no/

F /de'i phyir de-la gnod-pa-byas-na dmyal-bar 'gyur-te/ sngags-pas dge-ba dang mi-dge-ba'i las yongs-su mi-shes-pa'i phyir-ro/

G /des-na ji-srid-du mngon-par-shes-pa lnga-dang-ldan-par ma-gyur-pa, de-srid-du sngags-pas zhi-ba dang rgyas-pa dang dbang dang dgug-pa ma-gtogs-pa drag-po'i las mi-bya'o/

H /de-bzhin-du, brdzun-du-smra-ba dang ma-byin-par len-pa dang gzhan-gyi bud-med 'phrog-pa dang dam-tshig bsten-pa dang rigs dang rigs-ma-yin-pa-la mngon-par 'gro-ba dang rang-gi lus-kyi mthar-thug-pa sbyin-pa yang gzhan-la 'phan-pa'i phyir-te/ rang-gi don-du ni ma-yin-no, zhes-pa nges-pa'o/

J /'dir gang-gi tshe 'chi-ba'i mtha'i bar-du mtshams-med-pa lnga byed-pa, de'i tshe khro-bo'i rigs-las sngar bsgrubs-pa'i sngags dang Mi-bskyod-pa'i ting-nge-'dzin-gyis gsad-par-bya'o zhes-pa ni, bcom-ldan-'das-kyi drang-ba'i don-to/

K /de-bzhin-du, lam ma-yin-par ltung-ba-rnams mngon-par gnod-pa'i slad-du brdzun-pa'i tshig smra-bar-bya ste, rang-gi don-du ni ma-yin-no/

L /de-bzhin-du, ma-byin-par len-pa ni yi-dwags-kyi 'gro-bar 'gro-ba bzlog-pa'i don-du ste, rang-gi don-du ni ma-yin-no/

M /de-bzhin-du, gzhan-gyi bud-med 'phrog-pa ni dud-'gro'i skye-gnas-su 'gro-ba bzlog-pa'i don-du ste, rang-gi don-du ni ma-yin-no/

N /rigs-su 'dzin-pa rnam-par-gzhig-pa'i slad-du bdud-rtsi-lnga-la-sogs-pa'i dam-tshig-rnams bsten-par-bya'o/

O /de-bzhin-du, las-kyi phyag-rgya'i dngos-grub-kyi don-du, g.Yung-mo-la-sogs-pa'i bud-med-rnams-la smad-par mi-bya'o // bsod-nams-kyi tshogs-kyi slad-du sbyin-pa-chen-po sbyin-par-bya'o/

P /de-ltar ral-gri'i rigs dang rin-po-che'i rigs dang padma'i rigs dang/ 'khor-lo'i rigs dang gri-gug-gi rigs-la, sngags-rnams bsgrubs-nas nus-pa-dang-ldan-par gyur-pa-na, rnal-'byor-pas thams-cad bya-ste

Q ji-ltar 'jig-rten-pa'i bzhad gang-du mi-'gyur-pa'o, zhes-pa ni drang-ba'i don-to/

R /da ni nges-pa'i don brjod-par-bya-ste, 'dir rang-gi lus-la srog bkag-pa ni, srog gcod-pa ste/ *rdo-rje'i rigs-dag-la ni* zhes-pa gtsug-tor-du dgag-par-bya'o/

U /*srog-gcod*-pa des rnal-'byor-pa'i khu-ba steng-du 'gyur-ro, zhes-pa'o/

V /*ral-gri-la yang bden-par min-pa'i tshig* ni, 'dir bden-pa min-pa zhes-bya-ba rab-tu mi-gnas-pa'i tshig-ste/ drang-ba'i don dang

W nges-pa'i don-gyis sems-can thams-cad-kyi skad-kyi tshig-tu cig-car sems-can-rnams-la chos ston-pa dang de-nyid snying-khar gzhom-du med-pa'i sgra'o, zhes-pa ni nges-pa'o/

X /*rin-chen-la ni gzhan-nor dprog-bya* zhes-pa-la 'dir gzhan ni rDo-rje Sems-dpa'o/ /de'i nor ni rin-po-che ste, yid-bzhin-nor-bu'o/ de 'phrog-pa ni, rin-chen rigs-la ste, mgrin-par sa brgyad-pa'i gnas-su'o, zhes-pa nges-pa'o/

Y /*mchog-gi padma'i rigs-nyid-la yang gzhan-gyi bud-med dprog* ces-pa-la, gzhan-gyi bud-med ni phyag-rgya chen-mo ste, de 'phrog-pa ni gzhan-gyi bud-med 'phrog-pa'o/ /dprog-pa de ni mchog-gi padma'i rigs-la ste, dpral-bar sa-bcu-pa'i gnas-su steng-du khu-ba'o, zhes-pa'o/

Z /*chang dang sgron-ma sangs-rgyas-rnams dang bzang-po'i yul-rnams mtha-dag 'khor-lo-la ni bsten-par-bya* zhes-pa-la 'dir chang ni, lhan-cig-skyes-pa'i dga-ba'o/ /sgron-ma ni, go-ku-la-sogs-pa ste, nang-du dbang-po lnga'o/ /sangs-rgyas-rnams ni, bdud-rtsi lnga'o/

AA /'khor-lo-la ni ste, lte-ba'i padmar bsten-par-bya-ba ni, bza-bar-bya'o/ /bshang-ba dang gci-ba dang khu-ba phyi-rol-du mi-'dzag-par-bya'o, zhes-pa ni, nges-pa'i don-to/

BB /*g. Yung-mo-la-sogs*-pa'i *bud-med-rnams ni gri-gug-la* ste, gsang-ba'i padmar *smad*-par *mi-bya'*o/

CC /*mkha-yi padmar* te, skye-gnas-su bsrubs-pa-la phyi-rol-du khu-ba mi-'pho-ba'i tshangs-par spyod-pa nges-pa'o/

DD /*sems-can don-gyi slad-du* sbyin-par-bya ste, *nor-dang-bcas-pa* bu dang chung-ma-la-sogs-pa dang lhan-cig-tu rang-gi *lus* bsod-nams-kyi tshogs-kyi don-du rab-tu *sbyin-par-bya'o*/

EE /de-bzhin-du tshul-khrims-kyi tshogs-kyi don-du bud-med-rnams-kyi mkha-yi padmar smad-par mi-bya'o/ /de'i phyir bsod-nams dang tshul-khrims-kyi tshogs-dag-las ye-shes-kyi tshogs-so/

FF /de-ltar tshogs-gsum-gyis *kye rigs-kyi bu* khyod yang-dag-par rdzogs-pa'i *sangs-rgyas-nyid-du 'gyur*-ro/ /*gzhan-du mtha-yas bskal-pas min-par* gang *rgyal-bas gsungs*-pa'o zhes-pa-ste, rgyud thams-cad-las rnam-par-dag-pa'i chos bstan-pa'i nges-pa'o// //

Vajra Hermeneutics

ROBERT A. F. THURMAN

Background

Since the publication of my essay "Buddhist Hermeneutics" in 1978,[1] I have turned my attention to the tantras, especially the unexcelled yoga tantras *(anuttarayoga tantra),* and particularly the *Guhyasamāja,* or, as I like to translate it, the *Esoteric Communion.*

The major thesis of my previous essay was that "critical reason" is the major authority in Buddhist hermeneutics, in virtually all its systems or schools. In this I followed the formulations of the great Tibetan lama Tsong-kha-pa (1357–1419) as stated in his *Essence of True Eloquence (Legs bshad snying po).* I also followed Tsong-kha-pa in arguing that the *most reasonable* hermeneutical use of critical reason had been made by the Dialecticist Centrist *(Prāsaṅgika-Mādhyamika)* tradition. I departed from him in discerning the essence of the Dialecticist method pulsing in the veins of the East Asian Ch'an/Zen tradition as well.

Some have challenged my enthusiasm for the Dialecticist tradition,[2] arguing that there is another "more reasonable use of reason" in some other school of Buddhism, especially the East Asian schools. Unfortunately, such arguments have created the sense of a great divide between the Indo-Tibetan and the East Asian traditions, a divide based on the following error of reasoning. "You say the Buddhists employ reason in the service of hermeneutics, and that the Indo-Tibetans do it best. We say they do not. And there are other approaches to hermeneutics than the rational or rationalistic. In East Asia, 'scripture' or 'faith' or 'experience' was often more important than 'reason.' " Thus, instead of arguing for other more reasonable uses of reason, my critics slip over in mid-argument into an argument for something other than reason.

But if the point is to elevate something other than reason, then there is *no reason* to argue. "Argument" presupposes the usefulness of reason. And this was the main point of the original thesis: all the Buddhists use rational argument to interpret their experience and the teachings of the Buddhas. They may say that one or another of Buddha's teachings was the supreme one. They may say that argument and the understanding it can generate may not be the supreme understanding. But they invariably use reasons to persuade others of their view. Therefore the tradition as a whole honors *reason* in teaching, interpreting, arguing, and composing.

Let me give an example from traditional Buddhist epistemology. There are said to be three kinds of objects of knowledge: the manifest, the obscure, and the extremely obscure. The manifest is known by intuition *(pratyakṣa),* the obscure by reason *(anumāna),* and the extremely obscure by authoritative statement *(āgama).*[3] Of these three, intuition or direct experience is considered most effective. Reason is always based on some experienced or manifest sign, moving from some previously manifest object to a presently obscure one, with a view to eventually gaining a direct intuition of that object. Thus one reasons from smoke to fire based on previous experience of fire and with a view to reaching the manifest fire effectively. And one trusts authoritative statement about a very obscure object because it comes from one who is judged to have obtained direct intuition of that object, and with a view to taking effective action aimed at ultimately gaining direct intuitive experience of that extremely obscure object.

Thus one accepts on faith a Buddha's statement that generosity brings wealth, morality human life, and tolerance beauty in future lives, because one's future lives are temporarily obscured. One accepts it *because* a Buddha has proven reliable about verifiable things, such as selflessness, and because he has proven himself benevolent and truthful. One cannot verify it right away, but one can in principle verify it eventually. Therefore, even such faith in authority is clearly a kind of *reasonable* faith, and is often distinguished from blind faith.

Therefore, even the Buddhist hermeneutics that base themselves on scriptural statements, such as the Idealist hermeneutic based on the *Saṃdhinirmocana* (Elucidation of the Intention), Chih I's system based on the *Lotus,* Fa Tsang's based on the *Avataṃsaka* (Garland), Honen's based on the *Sukhāvatīvyūha* (Pure Land), and so forth, do so because it seems to them the reasonable thing to do. Furthermore, they present their reasons to their fellow Buddhists and followers. Among their reasons they may give the enlightenment of the Buddha, the historical sanctity of the scripture, even the power of their personal experience. But all this is presented as evidence in a rational, persuasive hermeneutical program that becomes the basis of the new movement or school. The bottom line is that almost none of the founders of lasting Buddhist movements demanded blind allegiance to their dogmatic authority.

Once that point is clarified, then of course there should be no end to the hermeneutical differences over which of the many hermeneutics is in fact the most reasonable.

For example, there are some real differences between the hermeneutical principles of the tantric literatures and those of the philosophical schools, even though the "realistic view" *(saṃyagdṛṣṭi)* of emptiness is said to be the same for exoteric and esoteric schools, at least by the great Tibetan masters such as Sa-pan, Bu-ston, Tsong-kha-pa, and others. The principle of the use of reason would seem to be shared; the tantric literature is rational and persuasive in its commentaries, at least. But reason is harnessed to different ends, it seems to me. To put it very bluntly, if you can say that the aim in the exoteric Centrist and Idealist schools is *clarity,* then the aim in the esoteric tantric traditions is, "clearly," *obscurity.*

Context

This exploration of the hermeneutics of the unexcelled yoga tantras involves the poetic as well as the philosophic, synthesis as well as analysis, and a tolerance of obscurity as well as a striving for clarity. So it seems fitting to proceed with these reflections within the atmosphere of the second case of the *Blue Cliff Record,* which runs as follows:

> Chao Chou, teaching the assembly, said: "The Ultimate Path is without difficulty; just avoid picking and choosing. As soon as there are words spoken, 'this is picking and choosing,' 'this is clarity.' This old monk does not abide within clarity; do you still preserve anything or not?"
>
> At that time a certain monk asked, "Since you do not abide within clarity, what do you preserve?"
>
> Chao Chou replied, "I don't know either."
>
> The monk said, "Since you don't know, Teacher, why do you nevertheless say that you do not abide within clarity?"
>
> Chao Chou said, "It is enough to ask about the matter; bow and withdraw."[4]

On the brink of the plunge into the realm of vajra hermeneutics, it would be delightful if one could merely "bow and withdraw" at the outset, just after having asked about the matter!

Why does it seem such a forbidding territory? The realm of the tantras, of the Vajrayāna, is an exquisite realm, the aesthetic realm par excellence. It is the vehicle of *beauty,* wherein the dharmakāya manifests its saṃbhoga beatitude as the irresistible beauty of emanation, drawing all living beings through its field of bliss into their own evolutionary perfection as Buddhas. It would seem that the hermeneutics of the "interior science" of the tantras would be the most delightful of all.

Why then does one hesitate? Is it the secrecy? Perhaps, partially. The Taoist rule was never more aptly applied than to the modern writers on tantra: "He who knows does not speak. He who speaks does not know." Or is it the fact that here we go *beyond clarity,* hence beyond elucidation, and yet we scholars tend to "abide within clarity"? If, in the quest of truth, the goal of hermeneutics is self-relinquishment and revelation, as Ricoeur and Tracy have suggested, is it then that, *beyond truth,* its goal can only be self-resurrection and emanation? If the quest of truth is primarily for one's own sake, as one is driven by the inexorable need to know for oneself, is not then the way beyond truth, we speak here of ultimate truth, primarily for the sake of others, driven only by compassion for the need of others?

Once pushed to such reflections, it is perhaps not surprising that one becomes reluctant to plunge into this realm analytically; surely mystification is quite as proper here as elucidation! But let me elucidate anyway, up to a point.

What do I mean by the appropriateness of mystification in the context of the apocalyptic vehicle of the tantras?[5] What do I mean by "beyond truth"? What is "self-resurrection" and "emanation"? The apocalyptic vehicle in an important sense has to be understood to *begin from* enlightenment, rather than to *lead to* enlightenment. It is of course employed as the most refined technique of achieving enlightenment, but in principle it goes beyond enlightenment. The Vajrayāna apocalyptic vehicle is considered by most of its practitioners to be the esoteric part of the Mahāyāna universal vehicle.

It is said not to be differentiated from the exoteric universal vehicle from the point of view of wisdom. *Prajñāpāramitā,* transcendent wisdom, is still its goal. She, the goddess Wisdom, is the patroness of the Vajrayāna. In the exoteric vehicle, she is the mother of all Buddhas, as their father is liberative art *(upāya).* In the esoteric vehicle she is the consort of all Buddhas, Wisdom united with Art in bliss, giving embodiment to limitless Buddhas. She remains herself, whether she is giving body to her children, or embracing the body of her consort.

The main thrust of the Vajrayāna is the achievement of the Buddha body, not primarily the Buddha mind. When we think of the goal of Buddhism as enlightenment, we think of it mainly as an attainment of some kind of higher understanding. But Buddhahood is a physical transformation as much as a mental transcendence. The bodhisattva goes through a long physical evolution, developing his mind through wisdom and contemplation, and developing his body through compassion and liberative art. The Vajrayāna is primarily intended to accelerate the cultivation of compassion.

Of course within that process there is an immeasurable deepening of understanding. To be precise, you could say that the Vajrayāna approaches the changeless objective, the "kind old Mother Emptiness,"[6] with a different subjectivity, a subtle subjectivity instead of the coarse subjectivity of the ordinary mind. That subtle subjectivity is known as "great bliss" *(mahāsukha)*. It is mobilized as a subatomic subjectivity which is focused upon emptiness. And that "bliss-void-indivisible intuition" intensifies immeasurably the development of wisdom. But the main point is that the apocalyptic vehicle teaches the art of the creation of the Buddha body.

To fit this theory in a more general Buddhological scheme, there are two lines of development in classical Mahāyāna: wisdom develops to achieve the dharmakāya body of truth, and compassion develops to achieve the rūpakāya body of form. The body of form divides into the saṃbhogakāya body of beatitude and the nirmāṇakāya body of emanation. In the ordinary Mahāyāna, the bodhisattva, from the time of conceiving of the spirit of enlightenment, is said to pass through incalculable eons to develop the body of Buddha, the body actually able to deliver other beings from suffering, and to create a Buddha-land. The following figure helps to remember the alignment of these categories.

ultimate level	= wisdom	- self-interest	- store of knowledge		- body of truth
relative level	= compassion	- other-interest	- store of merit	- *three eons*	- body of form
			or		
relative level	= bliss	- other-interest	- merit	- *one or a few lives*	- body of form

The Tantrayāna as the "quick and easy path" is only understandable within this world view—within this "preunderstanding"—that there are three immeasurable eons of lifetimes. The bodhisattva has to go through three evolutions, "up from pre-Cambrian slime," so to speak, and not as a race or a species but individually. Life after life, the bodhisattva has to evolve up to humanity and then become a Buddha. As a metaphysical or biological world view, this is utterly fantastic to the "modern" or materialistic preunderstanding. It is, however, the metaphysical preunderstanding within which Tantrayāna has meaning and the expression "easy path" has meaning. It is only quick and easy compared to three incalculable evolutions. In the Zen tradition, there is the image of three planetfuls of bones of skeletons of bodies that one has recently inhabited. One jumps over such a graveyard of evolution in a single instant of enlightenment.

The unexcelled yoga tantra claims that Buddhahood is possible within a single lifetime—and even that has to be interpreted as meaning "within a single coarse body lifetime." For the Buddha body cannot be attained without death, without at least what Zen calls "the great death," without many deaths and resurrections. The unexcelled yoga is a yoga of dying and resurrecting. It is very precise, very technically analyzed and practically laid out. It has the yoga of the death-dissolutions, the yoga of arresting the breath, the yoga of venturing out from the coarse body into the dream state and then being reborn back into that same coarse body. This is the realm of the subtle acceleration of evolution of the Vajrayāna.

This metaphysical background is too often taken for granted because one wants to talk about the hermeneutical issues, the elegant technicalities of textual interpretation. But understanding the Buddhist world view is essential to the discussion. Otherwise, one hears about the five stages of the perfection stage, the creation stage, the four kinds of tantras, and all such wonderful typologies, and one thinks they are just different ideas, different puzzles or *kōans.* But in fact, in the tantric multiverse, the different stages are really different universes. The person who is on each different stage is an utterly different subjectivity, a different form of life. So to say that different texts can be interpreted simultaneously on different levels is not to say that someone with a slightly different attitude or concept interprets them a different way. It is rather that someone whose subjectivity, whose very self is quite different, perceives things quite differently.

For example, a creation-stage person is inhabiting a "vajra identity," a "vajra self," a Buddha self, a self born of the realization of the emptiness of the self perceived as a Buddha or "Buddhess." Such a person completely reenvisions him/herself in that sort of identity, from which the world is seen quite differently. Imagination has totally transformed the world. In the perfection stage, a person may identify himself or herself as a set of wheels radiating seventy-two thousand nerve fibers collected around energy channels, points of awareness being endocrine drops of what is usually called "blood" and "semen" but is actually like endocrine subtle substances circulating around these wheels (like Don Juan's famous "cluster of luminous fibers").[7] At other levels there are other vajra identities of different bodies such as being a person with three faces and six arms, completely united with a consort, emanating light rays all around in different directions, and so forth. The yogin or yoginī practices inhabiting such a dreamlike illusory body.

Therefore, the tantric teachings are said to be multiply interpretable, intending that they resonate within those completely different subjectivities of persons. We must be aware of this evolutionary stratification of yogins in the creation and perfection stages in order to understand the purpose of the vajra hermeneutic, with its systematic structuring of multivalence of meaning. Again, it is utterly fantastic in the context of western, materialistic preunderstanding—this world of the tantra.

Mystification

In my previous essay, my survey of hermeneutical methods, methods of interpretation of the interpretation of sacred texts, was exclusively concerned with exoteric Buddhist teachings. In that realm, the usual aim of the teacher is enlightenment as the awakening of understanding. Thus, interpretation is for the sake of *clarity,* by means of the removal of *obscurity.* The goal of most exoteric philosophical teaching is rhetorical, elucidative, persuasive—it presents pathways of thought to the conceptual mind that enable it to see more clearly, more comprehensively, and more penetratingly. But *esoteric* teaching is by definition secret, occult, mysterious. It is purposely to be hidden from most eyes. It has no rhetorical or persuasive function, hence its communicative or elucidative function is of a different kind. It also might seek to move the conceptual mind, but not necessarily to understanding, perhaps sometimes to confusion, to feeling, to action, to creation, growth, compassion, or bliss. It might seek sometimes to generate *obscurity,* by means of the mystification of *clarity.* This is perhaps why one feels reluctant to write in the essay form about "vajra hermeneutics."

There is a form of use of language that seems to mediate this apparent dichotomy, namely that of poetry. The poet seeks not to clarify or persuade, but to intrigue and to evoke. The "inconceivable liberation" teachings of exoteric Buddhism found in the *Avataṃsaka Sūtra* (Garland Scripture) are similar in this respect. One cannot be *persuaded* to comprehend the mystery of Mount Sumeru in a mustard seed, or to behold the splendor of the jewel net of Indra. One must become involved in the former and the latter must be evoked in the imagination. Engagement, evocation, embodiment are the life of the poetic. This seems to apply to tantra as well, and there is much poetry in the tantric texts.

But poetry is not esoteric, at least not in the same sense. True, the poet does not seek to persuade the audience, to compel it with reasons; he invites, attracts, draws them into the subject by losing himself within it first. Yet the poet communicates with an audience, a general audience. The tantric tradition, however, hides itself from the world. According to its own legend, it was taught by Śākyamuni himself in different emanations in different regions and even on different planes. It was brought into the human plane by Saraha, Nāgārjuna, Indrabhūti, and others, with the help of angelic bodhisattvas such as Vajrapāṇi, Mañjuśrī, and Avalokiteśvara. From this time, around 100 B.C.E., when the universal vehicle itself began, it remained completely esoteric for seven hundred years, *with no written texts during all that time.* Or rather, since there are divine texts of tantric scripture incorporated in the architecture of the maṇḍala-palaces, there were no written elucidations of these scriptures that would enable anyone to decipher their meaning.

The tradition was kept in the confines of person-to-person succession, with individual masters initiating and teaching individual disciples. And even in this context, clarity was not necessarily the main thing. The disciple did not always require persuasion or rational compulsion. Sometimes a disciple would need his clarity shattered, his intellectual control of reality shaken by the deliberate introduction of obscurity. And often the vajra guru spoke in riddles or symbolically, cultivating a special type of discourse known (controversially) as "twilight language," a greyish transparent language suitable for directing one to the pre-dawn twilight translucency of clear light.[8]

We might be less surprised at the cultivation of obscurity and mystery if we reflect that this esoteric vehicle was an advanced vehicle, its aspirants usually already realized in a philosophical sense and determined to use their human lives in the quest of self-transformation. They already had a high degree of wisdom. They sought the guru and his personal precept to deepen that wisdom and to develop the actual transformed embodiment of the higher powers compassion needs to actually accomplish the benefit of other living beings. Sometimes the deepening of wisdom does not involve renewed inferential insight, already conceptually on target, but only continuous focus on that insight through single-minded concentration or through symbolic ritual contemplations. And the transformation of embodiment on the path of compassion and liberative art must involve relinquishment of control on shallower levels of conceptuality to release the deeper, subtler powers of the mind; hence clarity must often be sacrificed, or at least balanced with creative obscurity.

This would all be fine and *clear* and would let us demarcate an esoteric realm of studied obscurity, outside the clarity-oriented realm of exoteric hermeneutics, in which we could leave the adepts in their joyous twilights. The problem returns, however, with the fact that eventually, after the mythic seven centuries, the adepts themselves do begin to codify their tradition and technology in written texts. They begin to interpret, develop varieties of interpretations, and begin the systematization of methods of interpretation that is hermeneutics.

Why do they do this? Is it a process of degeneration? Or is it an evolutionary progress? This becomes important to us nowadays as the answer affects vitally our continuing study and elucidation of this literature. For example, His Holiness the Dalai Lama has begun to write very explicitly about perfection-stage practices of unexcelled yoga tantras such as *Guhyasamāja* and *Kālacakra.* The older Tibetan lamas are quite concerned about this and would be critical if it were anyone else but His Holiness. They worry more about such elucidation of these practices than they do about the practice of lamas of the older schools giving initiations widely to people who lack the understanding that would qualify them to receive them. Clearly, they feel a process of degeneration is taking place with the commercialization of the ancient mysteries. And the Dalai Lama himself seems to agree when he writes that he is attempting to clarify the tradition because so many writers have already written publicly and have given a warped idea of the tantras. The issue then becomes, how far beyond merely refuting the warped ideas do you have to go before you are adding to the degeneration rather than checking it?

If there is indeed a process of degeneration going on nowadays, it seems also to have been a danger during the emergence of the tantric literature in the seventh and eighth centuries. It is reflected in the words of Buddha Guhyasamāja quoted by Candrakīrti in his *Pradīpoddyotana* (Brilliant Lamp) from the explanatory tantra *Saṃdhivyākaraṇa* (Revelation of the Ulterior Intent):[9]

> Having not discovered this great way of sealed import, O Lord of Secrets (Vajrapāṇi), but grasping the literal meaning, they find they will always enter evil paths in their pride of intellect. They rejoice saying, "We are the yogis." They are deceived by doctrines. Such persons do not understand the *Guhyasamāja,* the great Communion, they do not preserve the secret as is required to maintain their vows, and they show off to all beings. They despise their guru, who is clearly like the Buddha, and they do not honor him. They become furious in an instant and also lustful in an instant. They have intercourse with unsuitable persons such as mother, sister, and daughter. They kill father and mother and also kill other animals. Likewise, they tell lies and especially they commit thefts. They consort with the wives of others and commit other sorts of atrocities. They do not know the vows which are the source of wisdom. For just a little fault they immediately engage in killing. Though they apply themselves to the yoga, they will not even achieve the lowest mantras. They will always like the heterodox sciences, will be skilled in their youth, and abandoning their own vows, will behave like elephants who know no goad. They will achieve those mantras and mudrās to make a living wherever they can get some profit. They will teach the dharma for personal profit. In order to protect them, the esoteric teaching is declared with ulterior intentions.

Candrakīrti in the seventh century considered these words worthy of quoting at length. Here the mystification process is explained as aiming to protect people from such abuses; public demystification by the writers of commentaries might only contribute to the degenerate activities of such people.

On the other hand, the systematic "elucidation of the mysteries" could also be a response by the vajra gurus to a positive development, to evolutionary progress. Not only degeneration, but the actual improvement of the population of disciples could create the need for more accessible teaching and thus lead to the de-esotericization of the tradition, or at least of certain of its aspects. This seems discernible in Tibetan religious history, wherein the great syntheses of the Nyingmas, Sakyapas, Karmapas, and finally of Tsong-kha-pa himself, each represents an improvement over preceding versions of teaching. These improvements came from integrating the tantric meditative techniques and philosophical insights with the exoteric teachings. If this was the case in seventh to eighth-century India and in fourteenth-century Tibet, it might just be the case now in modern times, and things may not be as bad as they admittedly appear in our "ordinary" perception.

Elucidations

Let us see what light can be thrown or shadow can be restored by going over the opening section of Candrakīrti's *Pradīpoddyotana,* giving some of Tsong-kha-pa's comments on the verses, and adding a modern "hermeneutical" commentary of my own. I will let reflections emerge in the order they are given in Candrakīrti at first. Then, in a concluding section, I will reflect on what deepening of our idea of Buddhist hermeneutics occurs as a result of this excursion.[10]

> Having discovered, thanks to Nāgārjuna,
> That glorious king of tantras,
> Elucidated with brilliant precision
> (By Buddha himself) in the yogī tantras;
> Concentrate of Victors, domain of bodhisattvas,
> Sealed in by all the Buddhas,
> Secured with bonds of the six parameters,
> And localized with reference to the two stages;—
> Having bowed to Vajrasattva, glorious lord,
> (I) Candrakīrti explain it accordingly.

Before giving the gist of Tsong-kha-pa's comments on this verse, we must notice certain things he does not point out, taking them as given for his audience. The Buddha himself, in his quintessential embodiment as Vajradhara, is the original interpreter of the *Guhyasamāja.* He himself "elucidates" its meaning with "brilliant precision" in the "yogī tantras"—the six "explanatory tantras," *Saṃdhivyākaraṇa, Caturdevīpariprcchā, Vajramāla, Jñānavajrasamuccaya, Devendraparipṛcchā,* and the *Uttaratantra,* or *Eighteenth Chapter,* of the *Guhyasamāja* itself.[11] Thus, the Buddha does not teach the meaning of the tantra openly and directly, but scatters the meaning throughout the explanatory tantras. This is the only tantra in which the elucidations are given by the Buddha himself, not by later masters; this is the first of its distinctive excellences, according to Candrakīrti.

This poses our opening paradox very starkly, as the Buddha himself is presented as being simultaneously mystifying and clarifying. His *root tantra* texts are hard to understand, encoded purposely to be obscure. His *explanatory tantra* texts clarify the mystery, but in an enigmatic manner. Even with such help, though, it was only "thanks to Nāgārjuna" that Candrakīrti could discover the "glorious king of tantras"; that is, it takes the guru's personal teaching to unravel the code and reconnect root and explanatory.

The meaning of the tantra, its revelatory power, is bound up by the "bonds of the six parameters," and this bound bundle is again "sealed in" by the "four programs," which refer to "place on" the levels of "the two stages." These are the hermeneutical strategies that are our main concern. This is the second distinctive excellence of the *Guhyasamāja,* that its meaning is sealed in code in terms of these possibilities, making it the domain of the accomplished bodhisattvas and the jewel-like persons. And its third distinctive excellence is that it always refers back to a specific disciple on a specific level of the creation and perfection stages.

Candrakīrti concludes this opening verse by saluting Vajrasattva, and by "accordingly" refers back to his guru, Nāgārjuna, according to whose teaching he is able to explain. Tsong-kha-pa here comments that the guru Nāgārjuna helped Candrakīrti in three ways, implying that the hermeneutical teaching about tantric interpretation functions in the same way: (1) he taught how to connect root and explanatory tantras; (2) he released the pattern sealed in by the six parameters by identifying which parameters pertain to which passages, unlocking the code, so to speak; and (3) he compressed the elucidated meanings into the stages of the path of practice.

This brings up the question of the hermeneutical circle in vajra hermeneutics. The interesting thing about these texts is that they seem to have emerged from the beginning as totally bound up in the hermeneutical circle. They are texts, promulgated as part of the experiential, personal, sacramental transmission. It is puzzling that texts are needed at all, as there is person-to-person "mind-seal transmission." And yet they are there. In other words, the hermeneutical circle does not just consist of an author and a text and a distant reader. It consists of a teacher and a disciple and then some form of codification in text. Later that text is brought out and unpacked again by a later teacher and disciple. So it is fourfold: there are four persons involved in the hermeneutical circle of the appropriation, the realization, and the employment of this text in their living tradition. And Candrakīrti—even though he is making a secondary or tertiary level of explanatory treatise in his writing of the *Pradīpoddyotana*—states very clearly that it is only by the kindness of his guru Nāgārjuna that he is able to do that. We would think that he could himself ferret out interconnections between the explanatory tantras and the root tantra. But he is saying that without the guru's precept, this is impossible—which is fascinating. It means that this particular textual tradition ranges at least four persons around a text.

Before we can circle back to the six parameters and the four programs, we must give some sense of the layout of the stages of gross and subtle body and mind understood in the tantric metaphysics, to which the four programs explicitly, and the six parameters implicitly, refer. Candrakīrti himself provides the framework, and Tsong-kha-pa's pointer adds an important dimension.[12] That is, the polysemic nature of tantric language, which makes vajra hermeneutics such a unique enterprise, arises due to the multilayered nature of the universe—in a real sense, it is different according to the level one is on. The main levels are enumerated as five.

> First is the stage of creation,
> Means of accomplishing the mantra body.
> The second stage is called
> Just "the mind-objective."
> The fascinating third stage
> Relies on the superficial reality.
> The fourth stage is called
> "Purification of the superficial."
> The union of the two realities
> Is called "the stage of integration."
>
> These (five) are the supreme way of achievement,
> Compressing the import of all tantra.
> Whoever knows that all the many kinds
> Of fabricated stages (of the various tantras),
> Are but types of these stages, compressed in them,
> That one understands the tantras.
> And, knowing the concise import
> Of the five stages—mantra, mind,

Body, purity, and integration—
He should employ the six parameters.

This is not the usual enumeration of the "five stages," into which Nāgārjuna's work of that name divides the perfection stage itself, placing the vajra recitation *(vajrajāpa)* as the first stage. Candrakīrti uses this system here, however, because the creation stage must be included in the levels taken into account in the hermeneutic of the "four programs," explained below. So, before I continue commenting on his hermeneutic, I shall give a brief summary of the five stages as he lists them.

First, the creation stage is basically the stage of the imaginative visualization of the universe. The physical universe is reenvisioned as a pure land, a different, purified universe that is the Buddha-dimension of this universe. All the other beings are envisioned as male and female Buddhas and bodhisattvas, dwelling in the play of illusions, pretending to be ignorant, pretending to suffer, pretending to need deliverance. But actually, they are already liberated and it is only the practitioner who is not. They are acting out the drama of the world for one's benefit.

But having reenvisioned others that way, one then reenvisions oneself as having the purified identity of Buddhahood, the "vajra self of selflessness," as they call it. One is perfect in a perfect *maṇḍala* environment, the diamond palace of the vajra hero. Emptiness is not reified as a lifeless void, but as the soft, jeweled womb of compassionate embodiment, life expanding to give freedom and bliss to others, boundless life. The creation-stage imagination uses the *Avataṃsaka Sūtra* principle of interpenetration to cultivate the bliss and security of the Buddha-land reality in every atom, every fiber.

Timewise, it transforms the life process in its three elements of death, the between-state, and birth (one of the English senses of "life") into the three bodies of Buddhahood. Death, along with sleep, is experienced as the body of truth. The between-state, along with dream, becomes the body of beatitude. And the living state, along with waking consciousness, becomes the body of emanation. Every part of the body and mind becomes a Buddha or Buddhess, even confused, passionate, or angry mental functions. This transformed universe is systematically cultivated (like a controlled psychosis, so to speak), using samādhi, ritual performance, fasting, and solitude. And that is the coarse level of the creation stage. It is said to reach a certain point where even the atoms of the coarse body and environment are perceived as full of Buddhas, as in the famous visionary practice of Samantabhadra so important in the Hua-yen school of East Asia. The universe is perceived so that every hair tip contains millions of Buddhas, and there are micromaṇḍalas within maṇḍalas, and it becomes like the mystery of the inconceivable liberation, the placing of the axial Mount Sumeru in a mustard seed, as Vimalakīrti taught.[13]

From such a vision the creation stage concludes by opening into the perfection stage, its early stages known as "body isolation" and "speech isolation." "Isolation" here means that body and speech are isolated from ordinary perception and ordinary conception; ordinary perception of the world of ordinary appearance, ordinary conception of self and other as ordinary deluded beings. Now, this isolation is not just an escapist, psychotic retreat into a world of fantasized perfection. With the stable self-identification with Buddhahood, one gains the confidence to begin the process of dissolution of the coarse identities of body and mind. One enters the vajra yoga of the subtle body and mind and begins to rehearse the eight-step dissolution process of death, called earth to water, water to fire, fire to wind, wind to space, space to moonlike luminance, luminance to sunlike radiance, radiance to dark-like imminence, and imminence to dawn-twilight-like translucency or clear light.[14]

When the yogin or yoginī reaches the fifth, sixth, seventh, and eighth dissolutions, one has dissolved the five sense faculties and their objective realms, and the whole subjectivity is pure mental consciousness. The coarse self no longer functions and the body has become cataleptic. One cannot see, one cannot hear, one cannot move, one has no more motor control, one does not even breathe. Therefore, one has actually simulated death. One has died as a coarse body and mind, and one has entered an internalized realm of the subtle body and mind, a "microverse" where one perceives pure patterns of interconnection of all beings and things, patterns of pure light and energy.

Once one reaches the first taste of clear light, one has reached Candrakīrti's second stage, "mind-objective," wherein ordinary death is transcended and the body of truth is experienced as the be-all and end-all. One then practices the arisal of a subtle between-state beatific body, and then various stages of resurrection back into coarse embodiment, henceforth perceived as emanation bodies. Candrakīrti's third, fourth, and fifth stages are realms along the way of perfecting this Buddha-state of simultaneous, indivisible presence in death, between, and life, the three bodies of enlightenment.

The diamond womb of the maṇḍala palace now becomes a gymnasium wherein one practices the arts of dying and creative resurrecting. All the tantric deity forms with many faces and arms and legs, with and without consorts, with and without retinues—all these are artistic techniques assisting the process of resurrecting, their forms symbolizing the spiritual DNA of the Buddha wisdoms and powers required to liberate all beings. Finally, since the perfection-stage yoga can be understood as a practice of many dyings, one sees how the tantra fulfills its claim to compress the evolution to Buddhahood in a single coarse lifetime—thousands of lives are concentrated in the one by a kind of psychic miniaturization on the subtle level. But there is no space here to discuss the details of these stages, for which I must refer you to other works.[15]

What is important here is that the disciples on different levels are really in quite different situations. Hence the meanings of a given statement apply specifically to each of them; and we have the basis for a systematic multivocality of meaning. This reminds us of the "exclusive quality" of a Buddha, that he can say one word and be understood by each of an unlimited number of persons appropriately. Our vajra hermeneutic here begins to systematize at least some of the possible ambiguities.

Another interesting point these lines bring up is that the knowledge of the five stages enables a tantric scholar and/or yogin to understand any unexcelled yoga tantra, not just the *Guhyasamāja*. Tsong-kha-pa himself remarks in his commentary on the *Jñānavajrasamuccaya*[16] that the hermeneutical system of the seven ornaments is applicable not just to the *Guhyasamāja* but also to all other unexcelled tantras. This is in fact a reason why the *Guhyasamāja* is a "king of tantras"; it is the only one that has explanatory tantras that are themselves Buddha-revelations, hence it provides the rules of interpretation of the other root tantras and serves as a key to open up their innermost treasuries of meaning.

Having mentioned first the six parameters as the most important hermeneutical framework, Candrakīrti moves toward the enumeration of the seven ornaments themselves:

> Those (tantras) ending with *ya, ra, la, ha,*
> With *ka, kha, gha,* with *na* and *ja,*
> With *da,* and *dha,* and with the *ma* group,
> The root of all is three syllables
> *(sa ma ja* or *om ah hum).*[17]
> The great muni taught exoteric doctrines
> To the number of eighty-four thousand,
> This glorious *Samāja* is their vessel.
> And so, it is the summit of all tantra.

The first verse indicates all tantras from all categories, and asserts that the *Guhyasamāja* contains the ultimate technical quintessence of all of them. Thus, once one understands the layouts of death, between, and birth states converted to the three bodies of Buddhahood, of the coarse, subtle, and extremely subtle minds and bodies, and of the five stages, one can understand the essential import of all other tantras, no matter how different the forms of visualization or practice. The second verse mentions that this *Guhyasamāja* is like a precious casket or vessel of treasures, in that it radiates all the many teachings of the sūtras inexhaustibly. Therefore, it is supreme of tantras, which implies that it is supreme of all Buddha's teachings, the summit of the mountain.

> A short text with manifold meanings,
> This *Guhyasamāja Tantra* is hard to discover,
> Its seven ornaments hard to understand,
> And so people constantly wander (in error).
> Therefore, through the kindness of the guru,
> One should strive to come to understand,
> And distinguish those (seven ornaments),
> If one wants to look after living beings.

Candrakīrti turns to the issue of interpretation of the tantra, emphasizing the need for a hermeneutic by the fact of the multivocality of the text, hence of its recondite nature, hard to discover. In regard to the ornaments themselves, they also are confusing and difficult, and so most interpreters flounder about, wandering astray (a fact certainly attestable in present circles of tantric scholarship). So difficult is this hermeneutical system, a guru is required to explain it, and show the student how to apply the ornaments, which must be understood if one wants to be able to take responsibility for living beings.

> There are five preliminaries,
> Four kinds of procedures,
> Six parameters in elucidation,
> And four kinds of interpretation.
> The fifth (ornament) has two types,
> The sixth has five types,
> And the seventh has two types—
> This is the summary of ornaments.

The *locus classicus* of these seven ornaments is the explanatory tantra, the *Jñānavajrasamuccaya,* whose main subject is the "seven ornaments," glossed by Tsong-kha-pa as the "personal instruction in tantric hermeneutics."[18] Tsong-kha-pa gives a rough summary of the function of the seven in his commentary:

> Such and such a tantra is to be elucidated, its meanings to be interpreted by such and such hermeneutical procedures *(dgongs pa 'grel tshul),* and to be concentrated into such and such a stage of progress on the path. Then, to

> such and such a disciple, one makes use of two such types of elucidation, and when there is certainty of the meaning of such and such major insights, then the import of the root tantra is unerringly explained. This is what the seven ornaments establish.[19]

We can see here how the entire hermeneutical context is established in the seven ornaments. The dimensions of historical origin, hermeneutical method, level of application in practice, type and stage of development of recipient, programs of understanding relating to main experiential goals—all are taken into account. But some major differences immediately leap to mind when comparing this context to that of modern philosophical hermeneutics. The understanding that the "hearer" (reader) is engaged in a program of practice to which the text is vitally relevant; the attention to the stage of enlightenment (ability, purity, understanding) of the "hearer" (reader); the assumption that there are a number of equally valid interpretations depending on the stage of development; and the implication that there are certain major insights that are universally desirable as the successful outcome of the encounter with the text/teaching—all these aspects make up quite a different "hermeneutical circle."

There is no "romantic" attempt to reconstitute the subjectivity or intention of the teacher via elaborate historical interpolation. Nor is there any idea of the nihilistically relativistic use of the text to constitute an entirely new personal meaning locked away in the subjectivity of the hearer. There is an acknowledgment of the horizon of the work, in the first ornament, and of the horizon of the hearer in the sixth. There is attention to the process of interpretation in the third and fourth and fifth, and to the process of appropriation in the second and seventh. There are always more than two "horizons" in the context here; at least those of the text/teacher, of the subject/hearer, and of the realm of enlightenment to which the text is but a doorway, its meanings but ladders leading to the referents which are the enlightened reality in its various aspects.

Finally, there is always the awareness of the teaching as a direct personal process. Thus, considered important are not only the original author, but the original audience, and not only the current "hearer" (reader), but also the current teacher who is using the text in teaching. Thus, the hermeneutic is given not just out of concern for how one reads a text for oneself, a secondary enterprise, but out of concern for how to *explain* the text to a disciple, the primary purpose of learning the ornaments, which one does when one wants "to look after other beings." Thus, as I mentioned above, in thinking of the hermeneutical circle, there is a fourfold process to take into account; original author/

original audience//current teacher/current audience. But these considerations jump ahead of our exposition.

As for the meaning of "ornament," Tsong-kha-pa gives the example of a person who is himself an ornament due to natural beauty, yet can appear even more pleasing when adorned by a jewel diadem; so the root tantra itself has its natural beauty, yet is even more pleasing to the wise when adorned by the seven ornaments of its own hermeneutic.[20]

The first ornament, called "preliminaries," is fivefold, and establishes the text's original context. It is constituted by (1) the name of the tantra, (2) identification of its original audience, (3) identity of its author, (4) its size, and (5) its purpose. The author is significant here, claimed to be Vajrasattva Buddha himself, thus the "horizon of the work" is the realm of Buddha-emanation. And the purpose is threefold: at least success in the four types of operations for the benefit of beings (peaceful, prosperous, powerful, and terrific); better, attainment of the eight supernormal powers, for the benefit of beings; and best, attainment of the supreme accomplishment of Buddhahood with its three bodies. These are significant hermeneutically for us because they precisely locate the process of interpretation and appropriation of the text. The text itself is an avenue to Buddhahood, is indeed a revelation of the heart of Buddhahood. The hearer/reader must appropriate the work finally by relinquishing himself into the world of the work, to use the marvelous language of Ricoeur.[21] But the release into the world of this work is none other than the attainment of Buddhahood. It is an attainment, a practice, only for the benefit of beings on any of its three possible levels.[22] The other three preliminaries are not generally crucial to our discussion.

Next we come to the practice dimension in the second ornament, the four procedures: continuum, ground, definition, and means. Of interest here is the fact that there are two sets of these procedures, one set for the dispassionate disciple, another for the passionate. As the first ornament (second part) already mentioned that the audience of this tantra consists of the passionate ones, the first set of four, modeled on Buddha's life, are mentioned in order to show the greatness of the tantric procedures,[23] which otherwise might not be recognized as capable of leading to perfect Buddhahood in a single lifetime.

Now we come to the six parameters of elucidation, one of the two ornaments directly concerned with hermeneutics.

> The third ornament (elucidation) itself ascertained
> By the expression of the six parameters
> Given in the interpretations by the yogī tantras,
> One should realize the meaning sealed within (the root tantra).

This third ornament, elucidation *(rgyas bshad)* as the extensive unfolding of the multiple meanings of each text, can only be understood by observing how the explanatory (yogī) tantras employ the six parameters *(koṭi)*[24] in unpacking the root tantra. Then one can open the various seals set upon the root tantra and experience its multiple revelations oneself.

> "Interpretable meaning" and "definitive meaning,"
> "Ulterior statement" and "ingenuous statement,"
> "Literal speech" and "symbolic speech,"
> These should be known as the six parameters.

Here we have a hermeneutic prescription[25] for the *disclosive* explanation *(rgyas-bshad)* of any tantric texts, the first pair operating at the level of the sentence, the second at the level of the statement, the third at the level of the word, primarily.[26] The first pair is said to be dependent on a semantic parameter, the second dependent on a linguistic parameter, and the third to be dependent on both semantic and linguistic parameters. In regard to the interpretable/definitive parameters, these are quite different from the same terms in the exoteric philosophic literature, where they are pivotal in scriptural hermeneutics. In the exoteric, one text, statement or whole work (at least in overall thrust) can be either interpretable *(neyārtha)* or definitive *(nītārtha)*, according to criteria which different schools establish somewhat differently, though the Dialecticist Centrists (Prāsaṅgika-Mādhyamikas), whose philosophy Tsong-kha-pa, for example, advocates, posit "interpretable" as teachings having relative concerns and "definitive" as teachings having ultimate concerns.[27] One statement cannot, however, be *both* interpretable and definitive at the same time, according to interpretive capacity of the hearer or teacher. In vajra hermeneutics a single statement can be both interpretable and definitive according to level of hearer.

This is extremely significant for our general appreciation of the depth of vajra hermeneutics—exoteric texts are themselves interpretable or definitive, as if objectively, ahistorically. Esoteric texts on the other hand are not themselves objectively one way or the other. They invite a more active interpretive participation of teacher and hearer, and provide a hermeneutic in the six parameters that is aware of the subjectivity of the hearer, hence of the process of appropriation of the meaning in the reliving of the text in its reading or teaching. It is thus clearly more sophisticated than the exoteric hermeneutic. Tsong-kha-pa makes the startling assertion that there are *no* statements of vajra definitive meaning—referring to clear light translucency *(prabhāvara)* or to integration *(yuganaddha)*—in any exoteric discourse, or even in the lower categories of tantras.[28]

Candrakīrti further describes interpretable and definitive:

> The unfortunate ones, the Champion teaches mysteriously,
> Providing them with the interpretable meaning.
> And to manifest the true reality,
> He also declares definitive meaning.

Tsong-kha-pa comments here[29] that Buddhas do not teach mysteriously only the inferior disciples, as otherwise there would be a totally definitive-style root tantra, and the explanatory tantras would be pointless. He teaches mysteriously to all, sealing in the definitive meaning behind a symbolic veil of interpretable meaning, so that the guru can bring forth the true reality by connecting explanatory and root, so that no one can enter the vajra practice without a proper reliance on a vajra guru. This is not out of selfishness or tight-fistedness of tantric teachers, but because success in such a practice depends on proper service, transference, and understanding of the guru. A point that comes to mind here ahead of time is that in the root tantra, the Buddha would of course hide the definitive within the interpretable, because the root tantra, as potential *text,* beyond *discourse, written,* and *fixed,* is what is later called "public teaching," as opposed to "private teaching"; hence mysterious teaching is more suitable.

Candrakīrti gives two verses on ulterior and ingenuous statement:

> Teaching the actuality of things
> For those wishing the supreme,
> Using a paradoxical expression;
> That is "ulterior teaching."
>
> Teaching the actuality certainly,
> To make beings of lesser faculties
> Understand with superior clarity;
> That is "non-ulterior teaching."

Both these types of teaching "intend" to communicate the ultimate realities of translucency or integration, so "intentional" is inappropriate to translate the former. What is fascinating here is the reversal of the usual valuation of clarity over mystery. The sharper disciple is taught via paradoxical expressions, the duller one is taught with full explication. Why is it preferable to teach mysteriously, even paradoxically? It can only be that the disciple's need to break free from his dependency on the guru's authority is better fulfilled by his breaking free from the deadened dependency on literal language. A second reason is that the unexcelled yoga tantras deal with disciples in advanced stages, where the experience of the "great death" and other terrifying realms are necessarily confronted. The yogins or yoginīs must always be aware that they act voluntarily, must not feel pushed, must keep their fears controlled by staying mindful that they are delusory, and must overcome their habitual addiction to ordinariness of conception and perception. They must go beyond the ordinariness of the conventionally described world. So "the Victor" accelerates their breakthrough by speaking paradoxically *with ulterior intention,* leaving them free to understand on whichever level they feel capable.

Another interesting point is that there seems to be some access to the higher levels of perfection-stage practice for the duller disciples. They need a more straightforward teaching, and probably proceed more slowly. Nevertheless, sharpness of intelligence is not the only quality opening up the perfection stage. (Of course, the "duller" here is probably quite a bit sharper than what we might think of as a dullard.)

Again, Tsong-kha-pa remarks that exoteric scriptures and lower tantras have indirect and paradoxical speech, but they have neither of the ulterior or non-ulterior statements indicated here, as the Victor in those contexts *refrains from intending* the higher referents of unexcelled yoga tantra, namely translucency and so on.[30]

Candrakīrti describes literal and symbolic teachings:

> Detailed explanation of meaning,
> Describing activities as prescribed,
> Such as making maṇḍalas, and various rites;
> These are literal teachings.
>
> The special communications of Buddha,
> Using (coined) words such as *koṭākhyā,*
> Not found in the mundane sciences;
> These are symbolic teachings.

Here the literal expression is common to exoteric language as well, but the symbolic expression is peculiar to the esoteric. Nonexplicit *(nayathāruṭā)* expressions exist in the esoteric realm (indeed are a definition of interpretable expressions in some systems). But the nonliteral or symbolic expressions of the tantras are special jargon words, a secret code, completely unknown in the world, although also used in the lower tantras.

There are helpful ways of looking at the overlapping and exclusions of these categories. But first it may be best to push on to the next ornament, that of the four programs of interpretation. Candrakīrti continues:

> Having analyzed the six parameters,
> Let us analyze the four interpretations;
> Linguistic meaning, common meaning,
> Mystic meaning, and ultimate meaning.
> The first has but one type,
> Common meaning has two types,
> The mystic has three types,
> And there are two types of ultimate.

Candrakīrti goes on to define each:

> Linguistic meaning is said to be
> That controlled by what is established
> By experts in the exterior sciences,
> Obsessed with just the words alone.

This is very similar to literal statement among the six parameters, and is indeed equated.

> Common meaning is what is taught
> To dispel remorse, (doubt, and contempt,)
> In those devoted to the scriptures and so on,
> And in those in the creation stages.

These meanings are those in the tantra that can be understood as common to other Buddhist teachings. They thus can reassure the exoteric Buddhists that the tantra is a part of the Buddha-dharma in general, helping them over their aversion to the tantras' subconscious-stirring aspects. They can also reassure the practitioners of the lower tantras that the yogas of the unexcelled yoga tantra are connected to their vehicles, and even can reassure those on the creation stage of unexcelled yoga not to fear the perfection-stage yogas.

> The mystic has an inner essence,
> Either manifesting the passion-practice,
> Or realizing relative reality,
> Or discerning the three intuitions.
>
> The ultimate is explained to be twofold;
> Either showing clear light translucency,

Or affording realization of integration;
"Ultimate" means here "reaching the limit."

These final two programs of interpretation refer to the five stages of the perfection stage. In fact, the four programs as a whole refer to a structure of levels of being from ordinary human in society to integration-body Vajradharahood. This can be shown by a table:[31]

1. Linguistic meaning		for mundane scientists
2. Common meaning	(a)	for exoteric Buddhists
	(b)	for lower tantra practitioners
	(c)	for creation-stage practitioners
3. Mystic meaning	(a)	concealing passion practice, thus significant for those on the vajra-recitation stage
	(b)	concealing discernment of three intuitions, thus significant for those on the mind-isolation or mind-purification stages of the perfection stage
	(c)	concealing realization of superficial reality, hence significant for those at the stage of self-consecration, where the impure illusion body is realized
4. Ultimate meaning	(a)	teaching the translucency which is the fourth stage of the perfection stage
	(b)	teaching the supreme fifth stage of the perfection stage, the stage of integration

Tsong-kha-pa points out[32] that the parameters of interpretable and definitive can be used to generate a precise multivocality related to those levels. He takes a verse of the *Guhyasamāja* root tantra, chapter 8: "Always diligently contemplate a five-colored jewel the size of a mustard seed staying on the tip of your nose!" He explains how Candrakīrti unpacks the five levels indicated by the interpretable and definitive meanings of this statement: (1) One interpretable meaning teaches a creation-stage samādhi used to develop the basis for passion-practice in the perfection stage. (2) A second interpretable meaning teaches the creation-stage subtle yoga wherein the five-colored jewel would contain the entire maṇḍala palace with its thirty-two deities in all details. (3) The first definitive meaning refers to the vajra recitation perfection-stage practice, wherein the five main neural winds, *prāṇa, udāna, samāna, apāna,* and *vyāna,* are brought into stable focus within the rainbow jewel the size of a mustard seed, so that the yogin's or yoginī's ordinary time sense and respiration cease and the process of dissolution toward the clear light begins. (4) The second definitive meaning refers to the *māyā*-body practice wherein the five main neural winds are moved down from the tip of the nose and gather in the heart center in what is known as the "indestructible drop." And as these five root winds gathered there in their blue, red, green, yellow, and white gemlike reality suddenly as one arise out of clear light, dark light, sunlight, and moonlight, instead of going back into the coarse body (by reattaching to the coarse elements of wind, fire, water, and earth), one rises as the *māyā* body. It is said to be just like a small fish jumping out of a clear mountain stream. It is like awakening from deep sleep into inhabiting a particular embodiment in a dream; one suddenly is a being in a dream, conscious of being resurrected from unconsciousness in a dream body. That is how the *māyā* body arises. (5) Finally, a third definitive meaning refers to the "purity of divine Thatness," wherein all dimensions and realities have become perfectly integrated, where the *māyā* body and the coarse body have coalesced in the inconceivability of the body of Buddhahood, and the five colors have become the five Buddha-wisdoms, the omnipervasive energy pattern of all things, the bliss-radiation infused in every atom and filling every space.

However, Tsong-kha-pa continues, there is no certainty that any passage will have a fixed number of meanings; sometimes interpretable meaning will correlate with linguistic and common-meaning programs of interpretation, and sometimes not; sometimes definitive meaning will correlate with mystic and ultimate-meaning programs, and sometimes not. The maximum valid unpacking of a passage is attributed by Tsong-kha-pa to Candrakīrti, on a verse in the sixth chapter of the root tantra, where he finds seven meanings: all four programs and interpretable, definitive, and ulterior explanations. (He rejects a fourteenfold interpretation of a passage by a certain Ratnamāla, on the grounds that no passage can be both ulterior and ingenuous, or literal and symbolic.)

In the next ornament, the two types of teaching and the relationship between the six parameters and the four programs are illustrated;

> There are two types of teaching
> For those who wish to study;
> Teaching by expounding in public,
> And teaching in private to a disciple.
> Public teaching should consist
> Of literal, ingenuous, and interpretable
> (Meanings among the six parameters),

And of linguistic and common meanings
(Among the four programs).
Private instruction should consist
Of symbolic, definitive, and ulterior,
(Among the six types of meaning),
And of mystic and ultimate meanings
(Among the four programs).

He goes on to equate further these two types of teaching with the two stages of the unexcelled yoga tantra, public teaching being appropriate for creation-stage disciples, but perfection-stage disciples requiring private instruction.[33]

The sixth ornament is the five types of disciple, the jewel-like being superior, and the sandalwood-like being inferior, with disciples comparable to various kinds of lotuses in between. The seventh ornament is the goal of the whole process, and is the two realities in the perfection-stage context of translucency and integration.

Conclusion

How to conclude, other than just to "ask about the question, bow and withdraw," as Chao Chou said? It is difficult to enter these realms of thought without going on to elucidate the exquisite world of the subtle and extremely subtle, and the stages of subatomic and genetic transformation. But one must recover and return to the hermeneutical focus, to reflect upon what we have learned from this tantric hermeneutic in connection with the tantric literature, and what that teaches us about the hermeneutical enterprise in general.

Hermes might be the patron of hermeneutics, Hermes the god of messages, of communication. His counterpart in the Buddhist world must be Mañjuśrī, the Buddha/bodhisattva who patronizes wisdom, and so language, the Word, which is its vehicle. Hermeneutics grew in the West out of the attempt to understand sacred scripture. This sacred text was not just any sort of reading material but was believed to represent the trace of divine reality—a communication from ultimate reality to alienated humans. Hence, the understanding of that communication was a way to join the divine mind, a pathway to re-connection to reality. So hermeneutics, as the attempt to map that pathway, was not at all a sterile, academic pursuit.

In the Buddhist context, although there may be a different view of the mode of operation of divine reality, the situation is otherwise very similar. The Buddha mind *is* the realm of divine reality. The Buddha's speech is thus the bridge between that transcendent wholeness and the dancing fragmentation of life. Hermeneutics thus is not at all a merely scholastic enterprise, but is the "physics" of that Buddha-bridge.

And this brings out an important difference between the divine operations, West and East. Buddhahood is not only a state apart from life. It is both transcendent and immanent. Śākyamuni Buddha repeatedly points out that he was both human and divine in previous lives, and has become something different from either yet encompassing both. So the Buddha's speech does not only proceed from there to here. It is here as much as there. And so the exegesis of the utterance is also part of the utterance. And the hermeneutic of the exegesis, too. Exegesis and hermeneutic are not only concerned with the journey from alienation into connectedness, from the human into the divine, by the tracking of the pathway of speech into reality. They have another facet that concerns the return from oneness into alienation realized as integrated individuation, the emanation of the divine into the realm of humanity and all beings.

Thus, to repeat the refrain of this essay, while the usual Buddhist hermeneutic seeks to travel from darkness into light, cultivating *clarity* above all, there is a Buddhist hermeneutic that comprehends also the movement back from light into the darkness. If wisdom seeks the light, then compassion must embrace the darkness. And so this hermeneutic of compassion, this vajra hermeneutic, encompasses the uses of *obscurity* in the art of liberating beings. And I will be happy if this essay has touched the surface of the ocean of this vajra hermeneutic, tested the water with a toe to encourage others to dive deep and explore it for themselves.

Finally, I want to close by honoring the bright and shadowed world of Chao Chou's *kōan,* as it seems this whole study is a process of learning his "ultimate path is without difficulty!" I think he wants to make it easier for us by challenging our way of "preserving things." I have "asked about the matter." But I do not feel happy just to "bow and withdraw" without rejoicing in his clear insistence that he does "not abide within clarity," and thanking him for his kind acknowledgment that he *does* "preserve" his balance, his calm and good humor, and his concern for his people and all beings. It is said that the time between clarity and obscurity is the pre-dawn twilight, the time of transparency, of the clear light.

Notes

1. In *Journal of the American Academy of Religion* 46 (1978); it also appeared as part of my introduction to *Tsong-kha-pa's Speech of Gold in the Essence of True Eloquence* (Princeton: Princeton University Press, 1984).

2. Peter Gregory's essay, "Chinese Buddhist Hermeneutics: The Case of Hua-yen," appeared in *Journal of the American Academy of Religion* 51 (1983). Allan Andrews' essay "Pure Land Buddhist Hermeneutics: Honen's Interpretation of *Nembutsu*" will appear in the *Journal of the International Association of Buddhist Studies* 10, no. 2 (1987).

3. Of course, the great Dignāga (fifth century) and Dharmakīrti (seventh century) developed a formalized logic that allowed only two validating cognitions, intuition and inferential reason, subsuming authority under the latter. Nevertheless, the threefold system remained in general use.

4. Thomas and J. C. Cleary, trans., *The Blue Cliff Record,* Volume 1 (Boulder: Shambala, 1977), p 10.

5. I call the three vehicles (Hīnayāna-Mahāyāna-Tantrayāna) the monastic, messianic, and apocalyptic vehicles.

6. lCang-kya-rol-ba'i-rdo-rje (eighteenth century) personified emptiness in this charming way in his astonishing poem "Philosophical Song of Mother Emptiness"; see my translation in the journal *Vajra Bodhi Sea* (1976), special issue.

7. I refer here to the physiology of the yogins and yoginīs of the world of Carlos Castañeda's works, such as *Journey to Ixtlan* (New York: Simon and Schuster, 1972).

8. This traditional account finds no favor with modern historical scholars, who insist that there can have been no Buddhist tantrism in India until there was evidence of Buddhist tantric texts, which appeared in the eighth century or a bit earlier. This is not the place to dispute their notions of reality. Only one can register a small complaint. The tradition records many tantric works written by Nāgārjuna, Āryadeva, Nāgabodhi, Candrakīrti, Dharmakīrti, Kamalaśīla, and so forth. All these figures are considered earlier than the tantras by western scholars. So there are at least two of each of them. Nāgārjuna, whom the outrageous myth credits with having lived six hundred years, presents the most complicated case. If there were indeed two of each, why would not the Indian historians, later writers in the tradition, the writers themselves, have mentioned the fact? It is insulting to Indian intellectuals and contrary to common sense to assume that the whole tradition would have happily conflated such major works of such major figures. So, historical scholars must keep working until they find a more suitable explanation.

9. One of the five main *vyākhyā* tantras of the *Guhyasamāja,* the *Saṃdhivyākaraṇa.* This translation and all the passages below from Candrakīrti's *Pradīpoddyotana* come from my own translation from the Tibetan, following Tsong-kha-pa's *mChan 'grel Chen mo* (*Collected Works,* vol. nga). The edition used is *rJe yab sras gsung 'bum,* bKra-shis Lhun-po edition (Delhi: Ngawang Gelek Demo, 1980).

10. At the time of this symposium I was aware of one useful article on the seven *alaṃkāra* as defined by Candrakīrti: E. Steinkellner's essay "Remarks on Tantristic Hermeneutics," in L. Ligeti, ed., *Proceedings of the 1976 Csoma de Körös Symposium,* Biblioteca Orientalia Hungarica, no. 23 (Budapest, 1978). Since then, I have profited by the study of M. Broido's interesting article "*bshad thabs:* Some Tibetan Methods of Explaining the Tantras," in E. Steinkellner and H. Tauscher, eds., *Proceedings of the 1981 Csoma de Körös Symposium,* Wiener Studien zur Tibetologie u. Buddhismuskunde, vol. 2 (Vienna, 1983). Steinkellner's work gives a useful analysis of the Sanskrit basis of the terminology of the *Guhyasamāja.* Broido gives a thought-provoking treatment of the "linguistic"

basis of the hermeneutical or explanatory methods. In the present essay, I touch on both issues somewhat, but my main interest is to explore how the hermeneutical strategies actually worked in the study and transmission of the tantra. The three papers may therefore, to repeat Broido's pleasant phrase (n. 33), "complement each other in a very fortunate way."

11. Tsong-kha-pa mentions (in his *Extremely Brilliant Lamp,* f. 16b5) that Nāgārjuna's *Pañcakrama* refers to the first three, Āryadeva's *Cāryāmelāpaka-pradīpa* refers to the fourth, and the *Pradīpoddyotana* itself refers to the fifth. All these writers use the *Uttaratantra* as the foremost explanatory tantra.

12. This is a key point for the *obscurity;* ambiguity, mentioned above, is not to be removed in Tantric hermeneutics, contrary to ordinary hermeneutics, which analytically reduces ambiguity by making a rational choice of alternatives to reach univocality of meaning, hence clarity.

13. See Thurman, *Holy Teaching of Vimalakīrti* (University Park: Penn State University Press, 1977), chap. 6.

14. See Lati Rimpochay and Jeffrey Hopkins, *Death, Intermediate State, and Rebirth in Tibetan Buddhism* (Valois: Snow Lion Press, 1979), for a detailed description of the tantric understanding of the death process.

15. I refer here to my essay "The Practice of Unexcelled Yoga Tantra, According to Tsong-kha-pa," in S. Park, ed., *Practice in Buddhism* (Albany, N.Y.: SUNY Press, forthcoming). Another useful source on the perfection stage is Kelsang Gyatso, *Clear Light of Bliss* (London: Wisdom Publications, 1982).

16. *Man gsal, Tsong-kha-pa Collected Works,* vol. ca, fol. 451ff.

17. According to Tsong-kha-pa's *mChan 'grel.*

18. Tib. *rgyud bshad thabs kyi man ngag rgyan bdun.* Tsong-kha-pa's *Man gsal (Ye rdor 'grel pa), Collected Works,* vol. ca, fol. 4a ff.

19. *Ye rdor man gsal, Collected Works,* vol. ca, fol. 5a.

20. *Man gsal,* fol. 56b. This same metaphor is given as underlying the textual notion of *alaṃkāra* in the *Mahāyānasūtrālaṃkāra,* in the prologue, though there it is about a jewel set off in a setting or viewed in a polished mirror, rather than a person wearing a crown. Here I am not altogether happy with Steinkellner's suggestion to translate the seven as "preparations," by returning to an earlier meaning of *alaṃkāra,* granted that it is a trifle obscure how these serve as "ornaments." See Steinkellner, "Remarks on Tantristic Hermeneutics," 445–458.

Alaṃkāra "prepares" a sacred offering by setting off its beauty and desirability and making it thus pleasing to a deity. Then, in works of art *alaṃkāra* makes the main content accessible and appealing to the audience. In Indian music, they are trills, entry and exit notes, syncopations, and so on. In poetry, they are figures of speech, ways of conveying sense and meaning through metaphor, hyperbole, synechdoche, and the like. Eventually, the word itself came to stand for the entire critical, interpretive enterprise, as in *Alaṃkāraśāstra,* the "Science of Ornament." In Buddhism, I would contend, it came to mean *belle lettres* or "literature" in general, as in *Sūtrālaṃkāra* and *Abhisamayālaṃkāra,* which could be rendered "Scriptures Literature" and "Realization Literature," indicating that the contents of these subjects had been ordered into works of literature for a cultivated audience. Thus, the "seven ornaments" in our context are merely seven sets of critical, interpretive apparati, not only making meaning mechanically available, but bringing out the beauty of the text at the same time—a hermeneutic terminology based on esthetic, rather than mechanical, metaphor.

A final fancy here is that these texts were originally sensed as manifestations of the goddess Speech, *Vāk,* in Buddhism the goddess Sarasvati/Prajñāpāramitā, and the "ornaments" were those critical apparati that were to render the vision of her more accessible, were offerings of homage.

21. I am referring here to the pattern of language in Ricoeur's *Hermeneutics and the Human Sciences* (Cambridge: Cambridge University Press, 1981), especially pt. 2. I frequently refer to his language on interpretation—approaching some of the questions in the tantric tradition within the "horizon" of his analytic sensibility, which I find extremely helpful.

22. So much otherwise excellent exposition of tantra has missed this fundamentally bodhisattvic drive essential to it, and thus becomes over-fascinated by the ritualistic concerns, or by the magical, manipulative power elements of the tantras, here clearly relegated to the inferior and the mediocre levels of appropriation of the text. The recent works of A. Wayman, who sees only rites (see *The Yoga of the Guhya Samāja* [Delhi: Motilal Banarsidass, 1978]), and S. Beyer, who sees only magic and powers (see the *Cult of Tara* [Berkeley: University of California Press, 1976]), are recent examples of these distortions of the Buddhist tantras.

23. The dispassionate procedures are (1) human birth, (2) renunciation of the retinue of wives, (3) reliance on the vows of the discipline, and (4) practice of the dharma. The passionate procedures are (1) birth through the five Buddha-clans, (2) identification with a single family, (3) upholding the tantric vows, and (4) practice of erotic movements and so on.

24. I use "parameter" in preference to the usual "alternative" for *koṭi* following Tsong-kha-pa's remark in the *mChan 'grel* (TLSB, vol. nga, fol. 9a) that "*koṭi* could mean 'peak' or 'door' and is here better understood as a 'door of specific explanation.' " "Alternative" by itself is also adequate if understood not in the sense of mutually exclusive, but as complementary and coexisting. My intuitive preference for "parameter" was reinforced by the OED definition: "A quantity which is constant in a particular case considered, but which varies in different cases; a constant occurring in the equation of a curve or surface, by the variation of which the equation is made to represent a family of such curves or surfaces."

Thus, while in the exoteric hermeneutic the terms *neyārtha/nītārtha* and so forth are mutually exclusive alternatives, here in the esoteric hermeneutic of polysemy and creative multivalence they serve as "parameters," constants whose variation enables the same structures, equations of meaning, to generate various values and configurations.

25. Steinkellner in his "Remarks on Tantristic Hermeneutics" seems to think this ornament is not truly hermeneutic—"prescriptural for an interpretation"—but I do not understand his argument. I think he thinks these are ways in which the tantras explain their meanings, as also in the case of the four programs below. In fact, the explanatory tantras use these hermeneutical categories to unpack the multiple meanings of the root tantra—that is, to understand the exclusive quality of Buddha-multivocality in a precise range of meanings. He also seems to think that these parameters cannot be used to refer to the five stages' ontological levels, as can the four programs, whereas Tsong-kha-pa shows that definitive meaning and ulterior statements *by definition* refer to the highest stages.

26. I draw this distinction inspired by Ricoeur's work on metaphor, *The Rule of Metaphor* (Toronto: Toronto University Press, 1977), and in a playful way, not trying all at once for an exact fit, so to speak.

27. See my translation of Tsong-kha-pa's *Essence of True Eloquence,* in Thur-

man, *Tsong-kha-pa's Speech of Gold,* for an extensive treatment of these terms in their exoteric usages; see also my essay "Buddhist Hermeneutics."

28. *Man gsal,* fol. 43b–44a. He does allow that such reference can be *read into* exoteric scriptural statements by an adept of the Vajrayāna, or into lower tantra teaching by an adept of the unexcelled yoga tantra.

29. *mChan 'grel,* fol. 9b.

30. *Man gsal,* fol. 44b.

31. See Steinkellner, "Remarks on Tantristic Hermeneutics," for a similar table. I reverse the order of the second and third levels of the mystic meaning to conform with the order of presentation of the stages given in *Jñānavajrasamuccaya,* and Tsong-kha-pa's commentary *Man gsal.*

32. *Man gsal,* fol. 45a.

33. For perfection-stage yoga, see Kelsang Gyatso, *Clear Light of Bliss,* and S. Beyer, *Cult of Tāra.* On the *Guhyasamāja* in particular, see A. Wayman, *The Yoga of the Guhya Samāja,* and Thurman, "The Practice of Unexcelled Yoga Tantra."

Mi-pham's Theory of Interpretation

MATTHEW KAPSTEIN

Introduction

This chapter takes for its subject matter the theory of interpretation explicitly advanced by the late Tibetan scholastic philosopher 'Jam-mgon 'Ju Mi-pham rgya-mtsho (1846–1912).[1] We will not be concerned with Mi-pham's actual application of this theory in his commentarial writing: his tremendous output (traditionally said to amount to thirty-two large Tibetan volumes) precludes our undertaking here a critical study, or even a perfunctory sketch, of his practice of interpretation.

The scriptural corpus representing the transmitted doctrine (Skt. *āgama,* Tib. *lung*) of the Buddha, the enlightening teaching of the enlightened sage, is, by virtue of its extent and heterogeneous composition, a source of bewilderment no less than of illumination for those who have not fully realized the founder's intention. In the face of apparent contradiction and obscurity systematic interpretation is required, and, so that this does not become merely the arbitrary reformulation of the doctrine according to erroneous preconception or pure fancy, interpretive guidelines have been elaborated within the Buddhist tradition. We must thus distinguish carefully at the outset between Buddhist *interpretations* and *rules for interpretation,* the latter being those directives whereby the former, representing the actual content of the teaching, may be established. Rules of thumb, however, if not grounded in reasonable extrasystemic foundations, may support the construction of fantastic theories (if unreasonable) or conduce to circularity (if purely intrasystemic).[2] A complete *theory of interpretation* should, therefore, be more than a miscellany of such rules; it must ground its rules and indicate their proper application. Read with this in mind, the śāstraic lists of rules for interpretation, so familiar to students of Buddhism, seem not to resolve satisfactorily the problem for whose solution they were drawn up.

We must distinguish, too, between *implicit* and *explicit* rules for or theories of interpretation. In our study of a given interpretation of the doctrine we may arrive at the conclusion that the interpreter is guided in his thinking by certain principles which, however, he never actually sets forth. For strictly formal reasons such a conclusion can never be more than probabilistic, though the particulars in any given case may strongly suggest our determination of the interpretive principles in question to be appropriate.[3] Nonetheless, it is only when an explicit statement of such principles is available to us that we can speak authoritatively of an actual theory of interpretation. This does not mean, of course, that explicit theoretical statements allow us to assume without further evidence that their author ever actually employed his theory in practice. Indeed, the examination of his actual interpretive work may lead us to discover that his explicit theory could not have supported his own avowed conclusions. We may infer that our author misapplied his own theory, or that there are further implicit principles he assumed but did not set forth—in other words, that his theory was deficient even with respect to his own interpretive work. This problem need concern us no longer, for only the fundamental distinction made here is relevant to the present investigation.

These remarks may help to clarify the manner in which the central concerns of this chapter are to be related to the multifarious body of thought we in the West call hermeneutics. As a point of departure, at least, our problematic lies within the domain of scriptural interpretation. Specifically, it centers on the theory of the interpretation of Buddhist scriptures. As we proceed, however, it will become apparent that Mi-pham's theory addresses basic philosophical concerns, and that our understanding of just what, in Mi-pham's case, it is that can be termed "Buddhist hermeneutics" will have to be broadened accordingly.

The Scholastic Background

Mi-pham did not create his theory *ex nihilo*. Its ingredients, one and all, were derived from traditions of scholastic exegesis that can be traced back to India, to sūtras such as the *Saṃdhinirmocana,* and to such towering interpreters of the Buddha's doctrine as Asaṅga and Vasubandhu, Dharmakīrti and Candrakīrti. The historical evolution of all the many relevant themes cannot be surveyed here. What is most useful for our present purposes is some knowledge of the tradition on which Mi-pham immediately drew. We are fortunate that this tradition is represented to some extent in the work of Mi-pham's senior contemporary 'Jam-mgon Kong-sprul Blo-gros mtha'-yas (1813–1899/1900).[4]

Kong-sprul's *The All-Embracing Treasury of Knowledge (Shes bya kun khyab mdzod)* was the last great Tibetan encyclopedia.[5] Its three volumes survey all branches of Tibetan scholastic learning with erudition and clarity, if not often with great originality. Of its ten books, the seventh is devoted to "the progressive disclosure of the lesson of superior discernment" *(lhag pa shes rab kyi bslab pa rim par phye ba).* The methods and objects of Buddhist scriptural interpretation are the subject matter of the first two chapters of this book: (1) the ascertainment of the interpretive keys *('jal byed kyi lde'u mig rnam par nges pa,* viz. that open up the treasure-house of the genuine doctrine, which is the object of interpretation, *gzhal bya'i dam chos rin chen mdzod khang);* and (2) the ascertainment of provisional and definitive meaning in connection with the three wheels, and of the two truths and dependent origination *('khor lo gsum gyi drang nges dang bden gnyis rten 'brel rnam par nges pa).* As the second of these treats the Buddha's teaching *qua* object of interpretation in particular, its contents would have to be surveyed in any thorough treatment of Tibetan hermeneutics.[6] It is the first, however, that encompasses the relevant background for Mi-pham's work, and so only its contents will be described here.

In his general introduction to "the ascertainment of the interpretive keys," Kong-sprul proposes that study *(thos pa)* alone is productive only of rough understanding *(rags par go ba)* of its objects and leaves us still subject to doubts. The demand for certainty *(nges shes)* requires that we exercise discernment born of critical reasoning *(bsam byung gi shes rab),* the medium of which is discursive thought *(yid kyi brjod pa).* The precise manner in which this is to be exercised with respect to the objects of study may be summarized with reference to the interpretive keys.

The keys themselves are considered throughout the remainder of the chapter. They fall into the two broad categories of those which are common (*thun mong,* viz. to the interpretation of both sūtras and tantras) and those which are uncommon (*thun mong ma yin pa,* viz. which uniquely pertain to the interpretation of tantras). To the first of these categories belong four sets of rules of thumb, which distinguish: (1) provisional meaning *(drang don)* and definitive meaning *(nges don),* (2) four special intentions *(dgongs pa bzhi)* and four hidden intentions *(ldem dgongs bzhi),* (3) four orientations *(rton pa bzhi),* and (4) four principles of reason *(rigs pa bzhi).* The first three of these groups have been discussed at length elsewhere[7] and will be considered briefly in connection with Mi-pham's work below. The fourth has not, to the best of my knowledge, received extended scholarly attention outside traditional Buddhist circles and our efforts here will for the most part concern it.

Kong-sprul's discussion of the interpretive keys which apply uniquely to the tantras outlines the two sets of rules known as the six parameters *(mtha' drug)* and four modes *(tshul bzhi).* These have also been considered elsewhere and so need not detain us here.[8]

It should be noted that Kong-sprul nowhere seeks to explain the manner in which all these rules are to be applied, or the manner in which they complement, or relate to, one another. Presumably we are to master their use inductively, by discovering in the commentarial literature their actual utilization. This leaves Tibetan hermeneutics in roughly the condition of its premodern western counterpart.[9] This state of affairs is Mi-pham's point of departure.

Kong-sprul's Definitions of the Four Principles of Reason

The four principles of reason are in Sanskrit called the *yukti-catuṣṭayam.*[10] The term *yukti,* which may mean "law, reason, proof, argument; what is correct, right, fit, appropriate,"[11] had been used in connection with the earliest efforts of Indian Buddhists to formulate canons of interpretation.[12] The precise enumeration of four *yukti* appears for the first time, it would seem, in the quintessentially hermeneutical scripture of the Mahāyāna, the *Saṃdhinirmocana-sūtra* (The Sūtra Which Sets Free the [Buddha's] Intention). "The principles of reason," declares the sage, "should be known to be four: the principle of dependence *(apekṣāyukti, ltos pa'i rigs pa),* the principle of efficacy *(kāryakāraṇayukti, bya ba byed pa'i rigs pa),* the principle of valid proof *(upapattisādhanayukti, 'thad pa sgrub pa'i rigs pa),* and the principle of reality *(dharmatāyukti, chos nyid kyi rigs pa).*"[13] Henceforth, this enumeration of the four principles of reason would remain a stable feature of the Indo-Tibetan scholastic tradition. The precise manner in which the four were individually defined and the manner of their interrelation were, however, subject to considerable variation. Kong-sprul's definitions relate rather closely to those given in the *Abhidharma-samuccaya* of Asaṅga and its commentaries.[14] They are as follows:

1. The first is dependent production. It is a principle of reason that in dependence upon the seed the shoot emerges. It is a principle of reason that in dependence upon unknowing *(ma rig pa)* existence-factors *('du byed)* and the other [links in the chain of] dependent origination *(rten 'brel)* emerge. It is a principle of reason that visual consciousness does not emerge by itself *(rang bzhin mi 'byung gi),* but that in dependence upon both the ocular faculty and form as an object it emerges. Such are [examples of] the principle of dependence.

2. The sense faculty, object and consciousness, and so forth act to effect the apprehension of the proper object [of the sense consciousness in question], but do not so effect [apprehension of] other meaningful forms *(don).* It is a principle of reason that when visual consciousness occurs it effects vision directed upon form, but it is not fit *(mi 'os pa)* to hear sound. And the ocular faculty can effect the production of visual consciousness but

cannot produce auditory or other consciousness. Further, it is a principle of reason that a barleycorn produces barley, but it is not a principle of reason for buckwheat, peas, and so forth to be born [from it]. Such is the principle of efficacy.

3. The logic of inference is exemplified by knowing from smoke that there is fire and by recognizing the presence of water from moisture. The logic of direct perception is [exemplified by] the six consciousnesses and the yogin's spiritual vision *(rnal 'byor pa'i sems kyis mthong ba).* The infallible utterances enunciated by the Buddha constitute scriptural authority *(lung).* These form the principle of logic *(tshad ma'i rigs pa),* or the principle of valid proof.

4. It is a principle of reason that water falls downward and not a principle of reason that it falls upward. [The principle here considered] also includes generic properties *(chos spyi)* and individuating characteristics *(rang gi mtshan nyid),* such as the sun's rising in the east, the solidity of earth, the wetness of water, the heat of fire and the motility of air, as well as emptiness and absence of self. These, which are well known as thus abiding by their own natures from all eternity *(thog ma med pa'i dus nas),* are the principle of reality.[15]

The Tibetan *rigs pa,* like its Sanskrit counterpart *yukti,* is a term whose reference may be either extramental or psychological—note the analogy to the English *reason,* when taken to include, for example, "the reason it happened" as well as "his reason for doing it." In passages such as the one given here, it thus appears possible to propose two main approaches to the interpretation of the doctrine: either it may be taken to be a doctrine of natural fitness, that is, one which holds that the world is such that it is in some sense fitting and correct that, for instance, shoots come from seeds and inferences allow us to know certain things; or, to adopt a Kantian tack, it may be a way of describing the a priori conditions for knowledge, such that, for example, it is reasonable to maintain that *x* causes *y* just because we can know the event at hand under no other description than a causal one. I do not believe that Kong-sprul's discussion of the four principles is formulated with sufficient precision to permit an exact determination here. Some clarification will be forthcoming below, especially when we consider Mi-pham's treatment of the principle of reality. But I must confess that this is one of several questions that may be raised in connection with the four principles of reason, for which I have no fully satisfactory answers at the present time.

It should be noted, too, that the four principles of reason differ from the other three groups of rules of thumb listed above in that they are not ostensibly rules for the interpretation of scripture. Kong-sprul tells us nothing regarding their actual role in scriptural interpretation. We must wonder: can their occurrence here be merely a classificatory accident?[16]

Mi-pham's Theory: Sources

Mi-pham sketched out his theory of interpretation in two works: (1) a short verse tract entitled *The Sword of Discernment: An Ascertainment of Meaning (Don rnam par nges pa shes rab ral gri),* written in 1885, his fortieth year;[17] and (2) in the final section of his *Introduction to Scholarship (Mkhas pa'i tshul la 'jug pa'i sgo),* a lengthy scholastic manual intended for more or less elementary instruction, composed in 1900.[18] The four principles of reason, the foundation of his approach, he also treated at some length in his mammoth commentary on the *Mahāyānasūtrālaṃkāra* (The Ornament of the Mahāyāna Sūtras), his last great exegetical work, written in 1911, the year preceding his decease.[19] This last mentioned, being to a great extent dependent on the commentary of Sthiramati[20] and composed primarily to facilitate our understanding of the root-text, does not contribute much to our knowledge of Mi-pham's own theory. It is clear that his conception of the four principles of reason attained much of its final form with his composition of *The Sword of Discernment,* for the exposition in the *Introduction to Scholarship* is little more than a prose restatement of the contents of the former work. Hence, in what follows, my primary aim will be to offer an account of the theory developed in *The Sword of Discernment,* drawing on the *Introduction to Scholarship* and, where relevant, others among Mi-pham's writings, only in order to clarify and fill out the argument. I have also made free use of Mi-pham's own annotations on *The Sword of Discernment,*[21] and of Mkhan-po Nus-ldan's on the *Introduction to Scholarship.*[22] The outline to be followed here is based on the one formulated by Mi-pham himself for the *Introduction to Scholarship,*[23] which is followed, too, by Mkhan-po Nus-ldan. While adhering as closely as possible to the actual words of these texts, I do not offer here a translation, but rather a paraphrase, with occasional digressions and insertions for which I alone am responsible (but which, I believe, are in no case inappropriate or misleading). Of course, it will not be possible in this summary to present and analyze each and every important concept and argument presupposed. My presentation must thus be somewhat elliptical, as is Mi-pham's own.

Mi-pham's Theory: Exposition

1.0. The teaching of the Buddha is profound and vast *(zab cing rgya che),* and therefore hard to understand *(rtogs dka' ba).* Those who wish to savor its meaning require intellectual illumination, which *The Sword of Discernment* is intended to provide.

The Buddha's entire teaching, in all its many dimensions, can be subsumed under two fundamental categories: that teaching which is consistent with the mundane truth which conceals reality *('jig rten kun rdzob kyi bden pa);* and that which reveals the absolutely valuable truth which is reality *(dam pa'i don gyi bden pa).* These two categories are the domains of two fundamental "logics of investigation" *(dpyod pa'i tshad ma),* which are directed upon the two truths respectively. These in turn are wholly subsumed by the four principles of reason.

1.1. *The Principles of Efficacy and Dependence*

Whatever appears in the world comes into being through some cause, this being expressed in the fundamental Buddhist doctrine of dependent origination *(pratītyasamutpāda, rten cing 'brel bar 'byung ba).* Nothing appears independent of its proper causal nexus *(rgyu yi tshogs pa):* lotuses do not merely blossom in space. When a causal nexus is complete it effects the production of its proper result—this is the principle of efficacy. Conversely, whatever is by nature an effect depends upon its proper causal nexus—this is the principle of dependence. The two, of course, are not equivalent: they do not entail that all causes are themselves effects, nor that all effects be causes. We can restate these two principles in the simplest of terms:

1. Principle of efficacy: every cause has an effect.
   $(x)\,(x \text{ is a cause} \supset (\exists y)\,(x \text{ causes } y))$.
2. Principle of dependence: every effect has a cause.
   $(x)\,(x \text{ is an effect} \supset (\exists y)\,(y \text{ causes } x))$.

We will simply assume for the moment that we understand what it means to be a cause, to be an effect, and to cause. Indeed, we function quite adequately in our daily lives without questioning these assumptions. It is the functional utility of these concepts, in fact, that characterizes them as belonging to the logic of the truth which conceals reality.[24] It is on this basis that we undertake or desist from actions in the world, and here we find the root of our technologies, arts, and other branches of learning. That is to say, all practical endeavor is grounded only in our knowledge of the positive and negative contingencies of things *(sthānāsthāna, gnas dang gnas ma yin pa).*[25]

1.2. *The Principle of Reality*

1.2.0. Mi-pham, it will be remarked, has altered the canonical sequence of the four principles of reason. The principle of valid proof, originally and throughout much of the later scholastic tradition third in the list, has traded places with the principle of reality. In this Mi-pham is following the eleventh-century Rnying-ma-pa master Rong-zom Chos-kyi bzang-po,[26] though the arrangements found in both the

Mahāyānasūtrālaṃkāra and Candragomin's *Nyāyālokasiddhi* offer precedents as well.[27] The motive underlying the change of order will become clear below. Mi-pham's discussion divides the principle of reality into two subsections, corresponding to the two truths, viz. conventional reality *(tha snyad kyi chos nyid)* and absolutely valuable reality *(don dam pa'i chos nyid)*.

1.2.1. Conventionally all things, according to their particular essences *(rang rang gi ngo bo nyid kyis),* possess specific individuating characteristics *(rang mtshan)* and possess, too, the generic characteristics *(spyi mtshan)* of the classes to which they belong. Inclusion *(sgrub)* and exclusion *(sel)* determine for any given entity limitlessly many attributes. One way of categorizing these with respect to meaningful forms that are directly apprehended *(mngon sum gyis yongs gzung don)* is to speak of the opposition of substance *(rdzas)* and attribute *(ldog).* The former, as the unique locus of its specific individuating characteristics is a concretum *(rdzas yod),* whose apprehension is nonconceptual *(rtog med).* The latter, attributed to the object in question by a conceptualizing agent *(rtog bcas yid)* which "divides and combines" *(phye zhing sbyor),*[28] is both a generic characteristic and abstractum *(btags yod).* The categories thus elaborated may be multiplied manyfold. Inasmuch as they are conventionally adequate *(tha snyad don mthun)* they unquestionably correspond to reality.

In addition to the categories of substance and attribute, individuating and generic characteristic, concretum and abstractum, which Mi-pham explicitly assigns to conventional reality, his tradition maintains that, for example, what we would term necessary truths are to be classed here as well.[29] The conventional aspect of the principle of reality further plays a foundational role with respect to the concept of causality, as will be indicated below (in paragraph 1.2.3.).

1.2.2. The principles of efficacy, dependence, and reality, as introduced thus far, are all principles belonging to the conventional logic of investigation. The absolute logic of investigation is presented as a second aspect of the principle of reality, but all three of the principles introduced up until now are brought into play again at this juncture.

So far we have taken the concepts of cause, effect, and individual essence as primitives upon which we actually rely in our daily lives, even if we are at a loss to explain them. The "great arguments" *(gtan tshigs chen mo)* of the Madhyamaka[30] are now called upon to demonstrate that there is no causal agent which acts to generate the result,[31] that results do not come to be depending upon such causal agents,[32] and that individual essences are merely convenient fictions.[33] The three gates to liberation *(rnam thar sgo gsum)* are thus thrown open: causes stripped of efficacy are unmarked *(mtshan ma med pa);* results that are not dependent entities can no longer be objects of expectation *(smon pa med pa);* and reality itself cannot be hypostatized through such fancies as individual essence *(ngo bo nyid med pa).*[34]

1.2.3. Returning now to the domain of convention, efficacy and dependence are actual features of the conventional reality of beings *(tha snyad kyi dngos po'i chos nyid).* So, for instance, fire is essentially warm—it is the very nature of the thing to be so. But it is equally the nature of fire to effect the state of being burnt and to depend upon fuel for its own being. Hence, the principles of reason find their limit *(mtha')* in the principle of reality. We cannot ask *why* fire is hot, burns, or depends upon fuel. Such is the way of reality. To seek for further reasons is futile.[35]

It should now be clear that the principle of reality will not permit the sort of very simple formulation advanced above for the principles of efficacy and dependence. It does seem possible, though, to suggest a tentative statement outlining an approach to its precise formulation. Let us assume that for all x, where x is an individual, fact, or state of affairs, there is some (possibly infinite) set of individuating and generic properties $\{P_1, P_2, \ldots P_n \ldots\}$, such that being x entails instantiating all and only $\{P_1, P_2, \ldots P_n \ldots\}$. Let us call $\{P_1, P_2, \ldots P_n \ldots\}$ "the complete concept of x," and further assume that the complete concept of x will include as a subset the causal properties of x, viz. those which are subsumed in the principles of efficacy and dependence. We may assert, then, that a complete definition (or analysis or explanation) of x is one in which the properties entailed by those mentioned in the *definiens* (or *analysans* or *explanans*) are all and only those that are constitutive of the complete concept of x. The conventional aspect of the principle of reality, taken metaphysically, would amount to the principle that the reality of a thing is exhausted in its complete concept; and, taken epistemologically, it would amount to the assertion that a thing is known when one attributes to it some set of properties that constitute a complete definition of that very thing. The absolute aspect of the principle of reality would then be a negative thesis to the effect that the complete concept of a thing neither involves, nor entails, the intrinsic being of that thing. (This formulation can apply only to the absolute *qua* denotation, on which see paragraph 1.3.3 below.)

1.2.4. Thus, we see that Mi-pham subsumes the two logics of investigation within the three principles of reason considered so far; and these he subsumes within the single principle of reality. The metaphysical character of these principles and also their role in the guidance of thought he affirms in these words:

> Because it is appropriate *('os)* and reasonable *(rigs pa nyid)* that the nature of things which are objects of knowledge should so abide, one speaks of

"principles of reason." Or, one speaks of "principles of reason" with reference to judgment that accords with that *(de dang mthun par gzhal ba).*[36]

1.3. *The Principle of Valid Proof*

1.3.0. Having grouped together the principles of efficacy, dependence, and reality as fundamentally metaphysical principles, which pertain by extension to the adequate judgment, Mi-pham turns to treat the remaining principle of reason. From the *Saṃdhinirmocana* onward this principle had always been taken to subsume the topics dealt with in Buddhist logic and epistemology *(pramāṇa, tshad ma),*[37] and so Mi-pham accordingly elaborates here a terse, but remarkably complete, treatise on this subject. As we shall see below, there is a clear sense in which Buddhist logic is essentially hermeneutical. As a result it is impossible to cut material from Mi-pham's presentation without losing much that is important for his theory as a whole. At the same time, limitations of space require that rather severe abridgments be made at this point. So I will have to assume that readers presuppose here the inclusion of the Dignāga-Dharmakīrti theory of direct perception *(pratyakṣa, mngon sum),* inference *(svārthānumāna, rang don rjes dpag),* and argument *(parārthānumāna, gzhan don rjes dpag).*[38] The remarks which follow (in paragraphs 1.3.1–4) are intended only to indicate some interesting points of emphasis in Mi-pham's discussion.

1.3.1. If the determinations *(sgro 'dogs gcod pa)* made with respect to one's own mental states *(rang sems)* were similar to those made with respect to physical forms experienced through direct perception, there would be another awareness of that, *ad indefinitum.* Therefore, self-reference must be distinguished from awareness cognizing an object. This self-clarification *(rang gsal)* is self-presenting awareness *(rang rig).* All that is experienced through other modes of direct perception is ascertained *as* direct perception through self-presentation. If that were not the case, direct perception would in effect be epistemically unfounded *('grub mi 'gyur te).* Inference is rooted in direct perception. Direct perception is made certain by self-presentation. After arriving at this, the experience of one's own mind, with respect to which there can be no error *(ma 'khrul blo yi nyams myong),* there can be no further proof *(sgrub byed).*[39]

1.3.2. Having grasped objects as general objectives *(don spyi),* one associates them with words and they become conceptualized *(ming dang bsres te rtog byed);* conceptual thought then multiplies various conventions. Even among persons who do not know the signs (e.g. preverbal infants), it is the general objective that appears to the mind. Through concepts which are possibly such as to be associated with words *(ming dang 'dres rung rtog pa),* they enter into or desist from actions with respect to objects. Without the conceptualizing intellect, there could be no conventions of refutation and proof, and so none of the topics of inference and learning could be communicated. Concepts permit us to ponder and to undertake future objectives, and so forth, even though these are not directly evident.[40] If there were no inferences, which involve concepts, everything would be as if one were just born. (That Mi-pham, as a representative of a spiritual tradition that places much emphasis on the transcendence of conceptual states of mind, insists here on the value of conceptual processes is illuminating. His exposition reveals that the nonconceptual intuition to which the Buddhist practitioner aspires cannot be correctly regarded as a regression into preconceptual chaos.)

1.3.3. In *The Sword of Discernment,* but not the *Introduction to Scholarship,* Mi-pham introduces a way of subdividing the two logics of investigation, conventional and absolute, that is worth noting owing to the emphasis he placed upon it in other works,[41] and the emphasis placed upon it by his successors.[42] The conventional is divided into an impure realm of what is perceived as being on hand in the ordinary world *(ma dag tshu rol mthong ba)* and a pure realm of supramundane visionary experience *(dag pa'i gzigs snang).* The absolute is divided into the absolute *qua* denotation *(rnam grangs kyi don dam)* and the absolute *qua* undenotable *(rnam grangs ma yin pa'i don dam).*[43] The former division is required in order that our logic and epistemology be rich enough to embrace both mundane *and* visionary experience, and their objects, without reducing one to the other (as our behaviorists do when they attempt to describe, e.g., the believer's sense of divine presence). The latter division prevents us from confusing discourse about the absolute with its ineffable realization, in which the dichotomy of the two truths is transcended in their coalescence. This realization may be spoken of as the sole truth of nirvāṇa. The pristine cognition *(ye shes)* of enlightenment and its embodiment *(sku)* here converge: the noetic agent *(shes byed)* and its object *(shes bya)* are undivided.

1.3.4. It may be objected that, because the first three principles of reason already subsume the categories which apply to our understanding of the world and the arguments which conduce to receptivity to absolute value, the elaboration of this last principle of reason is quite unnecessary, being largely redundant. In replying to this Mi-pham asks that we consider two ways in which the objection might be construed. First, it may be taken as asserting that we do not need to be epistemologists in order to know, that we need not have studied formal logic in order to reason correctly. This, of course, is perfectly true, but it does not establish any redundancy here. The objection thus taken involves a confusion between the act of knowing and the inquiry into what it is to know, the act of inferring and the study of the principles of sound argument.[44] Alternatively, the objector may be suggesting that our foregoing consideration of the absolute should have already led us to conclude that the distinctions made here are not ultimately valid, and so should be dispensed with even conventionally. But this leads to great absurdity: even in our daily affairs we would then be incapable of distinguishing between a thing and its opposite. For one who has been in this manner misled by the notion of absolute realization—a realization in which all affirmation and denial have been utterly transcended—so that he now *affirms* utter nonsense, the principle of valid reason should be hardly considered unnecessary.

1.4. *The Four Orientations*

1.4.0. When one has achieved certainty with respect to the two truths by means of the four modes of reasoning, that is, has freed one's intellect from ignorance *(ma rtogs),* misunderstanding *(log rtogs),* and doubt *(the tshom),* four changes of orientation are automatically realized *(shugs kyis 'byung)* with respect to the intention of the Buddha's doctrine. That is to say, the philosophical insight previously cultivated has now contributed to the formation of a preunderstanding that is appropriate to the task of correctly interpreting the Tathāgata's liberating message.

1.4.1. One orients oneself to the dharma, and not to persons *(gang zag la mi rton, chos la rton).* For it is the path which liberates, not its propounder. The latter may appear in any guise: it is taught that the Sugata himself, for example, according to the requirements of those to be trained, once emanated as a butcher. And even if he who propounds the doctrine appears to be otherwise excellent, it is of no benefit if the content of his teaching contradicts the Mahāyāna: Māra, for instance, emanated in the guise of the Buddha.

1.4.2. Having oriented oneself to the dharma, one orients oneself to its content, and not to its verbal conventions *(tshig la mi rton, don la rton).* Because the motivation for utterance *(brjod 'dod)* is to convey some content, then, so long as a given concatenation of signs gives rise to such understanding, further verbal elaboration is unnecessary: it is like seeking an ox that has been already found. There is no limit to the possible analysis of objects, and so forth, associated with even a single phrase like "Fetch the wood!" But if the utterance of that phrase alone permits of understanding, then the purpose of the verbalization is exhausted.

1.4.3. In penetrating the content, having come to know provisional meaning and definitive meaning, one orients oneself to definitive meaning, and not to provisional meaning *(drang don la mi rton, nges don la rton).* The omniscient one taught the sequence of vehicles as the rungs of a ladder in accord with the predispositions, faculties, and attitudes of his disciples. There are statements which he has purposefully made with an intention *(dgongs pa)* directed to a given intended stratum of meaning *(dgongs gzhi),* but which a critical analysis calls into question if taken literally *(sgra ji bzhin pa).* These are exemplified by the four special intentions and four hidden intentions. Thus, regarding the four philosophical systems and the culminating Vajrayāna, that part of the teaching not clearly disclosed in a lower system is elucidated by a higher one. It is by seeing what both accords with scripture and is proven by reason that one grasps definitive meaning. In the case of the Vajrayāna, whose teachings are "sealed" by the six parameters and four modes, reason can establish the intended content only in association with the precepts transmitted by the appropriate lineage.[45]

1.4.4. If one is to assimilate the definitive meaning of the doctrine, then one must orient oneself to nondual pristine cognition, and not to (mundane) consciousness *(rnam shes la mi rton, ye shes la rton).* The latter is that mind which apprehends objects *(gzung 'dzin sems),* and is entangled in word and concept *(sgra rtog rjes 'brangs).* That mind's very being is objectification *(dmigs pa can gyi bdag nyid),* which is embodied in the dichotomy of apprehended objects and the apprehensions of them, acts which are all nonveridical *(rdzun)*[46] and so cannot touch reality. Attitudes which objectify may grasp their objects as beings *(dngos por dmigs),* nonbeings *(dngos med dmigs),* the conjunction of being and nonbeing *(dngos dngos med gnyis su dmigs),* or the negation of both being and nonbeing *(gnyis med dmigs).*[47] But these objectifications are all equally said to be "Māra's range of activity" *(bdud gyi spyod yul).*[48] The process of objectification is not terminated by refutation or proof; for only when one sees what is as it is, without refutation or proof, is one freed.[49] Released from all apprehended objects and apprehensions, self-emergent and self-luminous, pristine cognition unfolds.

1.5. *The Eight Treasures of Brilliance*

The realization of immediate insight into the nature of reality brings with it the emergence of spiritual faculties that contribute to a profound ability to convey to others the significance of the Buddha's message. These faculties are spoken of in the *Lalitavistarasūtra*[50] as "treasures of brilliance" *(spobs pa'i gter),* and are said to be eight in number: (1) the treasure of mindfulness, so that forgetfulness is overcome; (2) the treasure of intellect, whereby one remains critical; (3) the treasure of realization, which is here specifically the comprehension of the entire corpus of Buddhist scripture; (4) the treasure of retention, which is distinguished from mindfulness in that retention has as its specific objects the topics of formal study; (5) the treasure of brilliance, here the ability to satisfy the needs of others by means of eloquent speech; (6) the treasure of dharma, whereby one acts to preserve the doctrine; (7) the treasure of an enlightened spirit, so that one maintains a constant affinity with the three jewels of the Buddhist religion; and (8) the treasure of actual attainment, for one is now fully receptive to unborn reality. Endowed with these treasures one upholds the doctrine, reveals to others what is to be undertaken and what is to be abandoned, and in the end one comes to realize for oneself the enlightenment of a Buddha.

Some Contemporary Reflections

We began this inquiry considering Buddhist hermeneutics to be the explicit theory guiding Buddhist scriptural interpretation, and we have followed its course as it has merged with Buddhist philosophy as a general theory of exegesis and practice. Turning now to our western traditions of hermeneutical thought, what might be derived from their juxtaposition with Mi-pham's contribution? A comprehensive answer to this question cannot be hastily formulated. I will content myself to consider briefly two related problems that have come to my attention in the course of this research. These concern the dichotomy of explanation and understanding, and the conflict of fundamentally ontological with fundamentally epistemological orientations. Mi-pham, of course, knew nothing of western philosophy. I therefore make no claim to represent here the manner in which he might have treated these issues in their contemporary context.

Hermeneutical philosophy since Dilthey has generally affirmed there to be two distinct scientific methodologies: a methodology of *explanation* which is appropriate to the natural sciences, and a methodology of *understanding (Verstehen)* which is appropriate to the human sciences. This was advocated against the view of the positivist tradition, which maintained that the methods of the human sciences could be reduced to those of the natural sciences. In recent philosophy this monomethodological view has been powerfully asserted in Hempel's covering law theory,[51] which has occasioned a debate within the analytic tradition through the challenges framed by disciples of Wittgenstein such as Anscombe and von Wright.[52] The last mentioned, in particular, has explicitly related his own insistence upon an irreducible distinction of "two great process categories"—causation and intentional agency, which are respectively the objects of the operations known as explanation and understanding—to the work of thinkers associated with the continental hermeneutical tradition. At the same time, philosophers within the hermeneutical tradition, especially Ricoeur, and within the analytic tradition, such as Davidson and Searle, have in various ways questioned the validity of the distinction, though without wishing to resurrect Hempel's program in its particulars.[53] The controversy thus bridges the gulf between two major philosophical traditions which until very recently seemed to be incapable of constructive interaction. Let us now inquire into the manner in which the dispute reflects upon certain features of Mi-pham's thought.

We are concerned here, of course, with the principles of efficacy and dependence, especially in the light of Mi-pham's assertion that these are the basis for our undertaking or desisting from actions in the world. This suggests that Mi-pham would have denied that there is any absolute gulf separating the realm of intentional undertaking from that of causation. It thus appears *prima facie* that his thought is in conflict with the views of those who insist on a thoroughgoing dualism here. Does this point up a fundamental defect in Mi-pham's system?

Before we can answer this question, we should note that many of the contemporary causalists have conceded a major point to philosophers such as von Wright: they have abandoned the program of the logical positivists to rely on causality to explain away the intentional features of human action. But they insist that intentional attitudes may themselves function causally. This von Wright, for instance, would deny. I believe Buddhist thought in general, and Mi-pham in particular, would support some version of the causalist approach to the problem. In his treatment elsewhere of the fundamental doctrine of dependent origination *(pratītya-samutpāda, rten cing 'brel bar 'byung ba),* Mi-pham recalls the distinction between an *inner causality (nang gi rten 'brel)* and an *outer causality (phyi yi rten 'brel).*[54] The former is embodied in the traditional Buddhist scheme of the twelve links of dependent origination, beginning with ignorance and ending in old age and death, and the latter describes natural processes such as the growth of a plant from the seed. I take this distinction to be at least analogous to von Wright's distinction between two great process categories. But, Mi-pham, like Davidson, parts company from von Wright by maintaining both processes to be causal, though it is important to note that this is established without seeking to reduce one category to the other. A detailed analysis of the relevant Buddhist doctrines in Mi-pham's formulation of them cannot be undertaken here. Suffice it to say, however, that in the absence of such an undertaking it is by no means obvious that Buddhist thought is lacking in the conceptual richness required to deal adequately with the conflicting claims of causation and agency. If Mi-pham's theory is defective at this point (as it may yet prove to be), more than a general objection to causalism will be necessary to show wherein a supposed fault may lie.

With regard to the problem of the conflict between ontological and epistemological orientations, it may be said that western philosophy since Kant has moved between two poles, which assert respectively the primacy of being and, in line with Kant's "Copernican revolution," the primacy of knowing. The distinction complements, in some respects, that which obtains with respect to the two process categories. When we emphasize an epistemological and agent-centered orientation to the exclusion of the ontological and causalist, we tend toward idealism; and when we adopt an opposite orientation, we swing in the direction of positivism. And other orientations have also been realized with respect to these fundamental divisions. But this problem of conflicting orientations does not seem to exist for Mi-pham. In the following brief remarks I will offer one explanation for this, without committing myself to any opinion on its implications for contemporary western philosophical investigations.

Mi-pham's most novel contribution to the discussion of the four principles of reason was his reduction of the principles of efficacy and dependence to that of reality. As we have seen, this is where why-questions must reach their end. At the same time, in elaborating the principle of valid proof, he sought the ultimate foundations for his epistemology in the phenomenon of self-presentation. We thus have two fundamental grounds, the first of which is ontological and the second epistemological. What I wish to suggest here is that no tension arises between them because Mi-pham never seeks to reduce one to the other, but rather holds that without such reduction the two foundations nonetheless converge. That they do so ultimately is, of course, entailed by Mi-pham's conception of the absolute as involving the coalescence of noetic agent and object. But it is significant, too, that even within the domain of convention they are not to be thought of as being wholly disparate.[55] For self-presentation confronts us in all our conscious moments with the unity of being and knowing. How does being in pain allow me to know that I am in pain? It just does. No further answer is required. Being and knowing are here no different. And it is characteristic of Rnying-ma-pa thought to find in our ordinary states of awareness *(rig pa)* a subtle but abiding link with the ineffable truth of enlightenment.

Buddhism as a Hermeneutical Endeavor

Mi-pham's theory of interpretation clearly ramifies beyond the apparent limits of scriptural interpretation plain and simple. In concluding this presentation of it, I wish to consider a few of the implications of Mi-pham's work for our general conception of Buddhist hermeneutics.

It will be observed that Mi-pham's discussion is divided into three main phases. First, the four principles of reason are taught so that we might comprehend the fundamental doctrine of Mahāyāna metaphysics, namely that of the two truths. Armed with this insight we set out to transform certain basic orientations in the second phase. And finally, realizing the fruit of this transformation, we gain the endowment of the eight treasures of brilliance. This seems to bear more than accidental resemblance to the systematic teaching of the doctrine according to the categories of ground *(gzhi),* path *(lam),* and result *('bras-bu).* Let us note, however, that with the sole exception of the eight treasures all the major categories employed by Mi-pham are those expounded in the earlier scholastic tradition in particular association with the problems of textual interpretation. It thus would seem to be the case that for Mi-pham the principles of interpretation are really no different from the principles of Buddhist philosophy overall. I believe that this is as it should be.[56]

Vasubandhu, in a frequently cited verse, divided the teaching into the two great domains of transmitted doctrine *(āgama)* and realization *(adhigama).* No English translation can convey the resonance of these technical terms, which are both derived from the same Sanskrit root. (In Tibetan, too, this is lost.) Perhaps we can suggest it by saying that the transmitted doctrine is that which *comes down* to us, while realization is that which *comes through* when the transmission is rightly understood. Vasubandhu associated these two domains with two sorts of spiritually meaningful activity: exegesis and practice. Jointly, they guarantee the continuing integrity of the Buddha's teaching in the world. Now, what I wish to propose here is that we regard both of these activities to be fundamentally interpretive. In the first, receptivity and acumen must open us to the descent of the teaching, for that only occurs when we are capable of understanding the Buddha's intention. In the second, we similarly open ourselves to the realization of reality *qua* absolute value, for that cannot come through to us until we comprehend the real order of things. Clearly a Buddhist theory of interpretation must in the final analysis embrace both domains, for it is through the interpretive act that scripture on the one hand and reality on the other are in fact comprehended.

In developing Buddhist theory of interpretation in this manner Mi-pham was not, of course, undertaking a radical program; he was no revolutionary breaking with tradition in order to explore previously undiscovered pathways in Buddhist thought. Like most Buddhist philosophers, he was engaged in the ongoing process of unpacking the contents of the received tradition. The very inclusion of the four principles of reason among the rules of thumb for interpretation was already indicative of the inseparability of Buddhist hermeneutics from Buddhist logic and metaphysics.[57] The hermeneutical character of the Dignāga-Dharmakīrti system, too, had been clearly enunciated long before Mi-pham's time, for example by Karma-pa VII Chos-grags rgya-mtsho (1454–1506), who introduced his monumental exposition of that system with these words:

> The Buddha, that transcendent lord, who embodies logic . . . set in motion the wheel of the doctrine which is infallible with respect to both provisional and ultimate meaning, so that the genuinely significant, which had been previously unknown, might be clearly known without error. And that [doctrine], according to the faculties of individual disciples, abides in various forms, to whit, provisional meaning, definitive meaning, literal, metaphorical, having special intention, and having a hidden intention. Seeing that its meaning is thus hard for disciples to understand, that great soul Dignāga well established all the scriptures of the Sugata by means of three logics, so that they could be easily understood through the science of logical argument, and so that ignorance, misunderstanding, doubt, and so forth might be removed.[58]

It will not be possible to explore this theme in greater detail here. It will be enough to affirm that there is a fundamental sense in which Buddha-dharma is a hermeneutical endeavor and that this is revealed certainly in our consideration of Mi-pham. Buddhism is hermeneutical in that it demands that we confront and come to understand the message of the Sugata; it is hermeneutical in that it requires a reinterpretation of the world within which we find ourselves and equally a redefinition of ourselves within that world; and it is hermeneutical in that it will not allow us to remain silent, but demands that we enunciate, that is, interpret for others, the message and the reality with which we have struggled.

Notes

I am grateful to several individuals for advice and criticism in connection with this research. The topic for this paper was suggested, and the relevant writings of Mi-pham brought to my attention, by Mkhan-po Sangs-rgyas bstan-'dzin Rin-po-che of Ser-lo dgon-pa, Nepal. Mkhan-po Dpal-ldan shes-rab, currently residing in New York City, indicated to me the important contributions of Candragomin and Rong-zom-pa, and their influence on Mi-pham and the later adherents of his school. The participants in the Buddhist Hermeneutics conference all must be acknowledged for the stimulus they provided. Among them, I wish to thank Michael Broido, Luis Gómez, Jeffrey Hopkins, and Tom Kasulis in particular for their generous comments on specific issues raised here. I am indebted, too, to Professor Philip Quinn, Department of Philosophy, Notre Dame University, for his indications regarding the philosophical content of several passages.

1. For a useful introduction to the life and contributions of this master, see Steven D. Goodman, "Mi-pham rgya-mtsho: an account of his life, the printing of his works, and the structure of his treatise entitled *Mkhas-pa'i tshul la 'jug pa'i sgo*," in Ronald M. Davidson, ed., *Wind Horse,* vol. 1 (Berkeley: Asian Humanities Press, 1981), 58–78.

2. The circularity that seems to me to be problematic here is not a feature of the so-called hermeneutic circle in general. According to Dilthey's conception of the latter, the interpreter is not expected to (and indeed cannot) exclude as

irrelevant all elements of his preunderstanding which have their origins outside the particular text under consideration. The concept of the hermeneutic circle tells us that we cannot understand the text without already understanding the text *in part.* But the circularity to which I here object arises when we insist that to understand the text we must refer only to the text, and nothing more.

3. My reservations with respect to implicit hermeneutics stem from the following considerations: Let us suppose that an individual *a* has interpreted a text *b* and that his interpretation is represented by some body of conclusions *C*. Let us further suppose that there is some theory *T* such that if *b* is read in the light of *T* one would conclude *C*. These suppositions *do not* jointly entail *a*'s having interpreted *b* in the light of *T*. Given these bare bones there is in fact *nothing whatsoever* that can be said of *a*'s implicit hermeneutic. These considerations notwithstanding, I do not disagree with Robert Gimello and David Tracy in their insistence that Buddhist hermeneutics will often require our extending our inquiry to implicit principles of interpretation if we are to investigate Buddhist hermeneutics at all. In such instances we will, of course, have more than bare bones upon which to base our hypotheses. Lest there be some misunderstanding about this, my point here is simply to indicate something of the theoretical limits of this process, and to define my own investigations in terms of those limits.

4. Kong-sprul and Mi-pham were among the closest disciple-colleagues of nineteenth-century Tibet's greatest visionary, 'Jam-dbyangs Mkhyen-brtse'i dbang-po (1820–1892). The best survey to date of these masters and their intellectual and spiritual milieu remains E. Gene Smith's introduction to Lokesh Chandra, ed., *Kongtrul's Encyclopedia of Indo-Tibetan Culture* (New Delhi: International Academy of Indian Culture, 1970). Kong-sprul was, in fact, one of Mi-pham's teachers, but available information on his instruction to him leaves unclear whether he influenced Mi-pham with respect to the present subject matter. On their relationship see Bdud-'joms Rin-po-che 'Jigs-bral-ye-shes-rdo-rje, *Gangs ljongs rgyal bstan yongs kyi phyi mo rnga 'gyur rdo rje theg pa'i bstan pa rin po che ji ltar byung ba'i tshul dag cing gsal bar brjod pa lha dbang gYul las rgyal ba'i rnga bo che'i sgra dbyangs,* in *Collected Writings and Revelations of Bdud-'joms Rin-po-che,* vol. 1 (Delhi, 1979), 697. Translated in G. Dorje and M. Kapstein, *Fundamentals and History of the Nyingmapa Tradition of Tibetan Buddhism* (London: Wisdom Publications, forthcoming).

5. The original Dpal-spungs edition of this work is reproduced in Lokesh Chandra, *Kongtrul's Encyclopedia.* Citations in the present paper, however, refer to Kong-sprul Yon-tan rgya-mtsho (Blo-gros mtha'-yas), *Shes bya kun khyab,* 3 vols. (Beijing: Minorities Press, 1982).

6. It is this aspect of Tibetan hermeneutics that has perhaps received the most attention from Tibetan thinkers themselves, e.g., in Tsong-kha-pa's *tour de force,* the *Drang nges legs bshad snying po,* a complete translation of which is now available in Robert Thurman, *Tsong Khapa's Speech of Gold in the Essence of True Eloquence* (Princeton: Princeton University Press, 1984).

7. Among recent contributions see, for example, Kennard Lipman, "*Nītārtha, Neyārtha,* and *Tathāgatagarbha* in Tibet," *Journal of Indian Philosophy* 8 (1980): 87–95; Robert A. F. Thurman, "Buddhist Hermeneutics," *Journal of the American Academy of Religion* 46 (1): 19–39; and Michael M. Broido, "Abhiprāya and Implication in Tibetan Linguistics," *Journal of Indian Philosophy* 12 (1984): 1–33.

8. See especially the contributions of Broido and Thurman to the present volume and the references therein.

9. Cf. Josef Bleicher, *Contemporary Hermeneutics* (London: Routledge and Kegan Paul, 1980), 14: "The limitation of the pre-Schleiermacher effort consisted . . . in the lack of reflection that transcended merely methodological considerations—which themselves did not reach any systematic formulation and remained on the level of ad hoc insights that were forthcoming from interpretative practice."

10. S. Bagchi, ed., *Mahāyānasūtrālaṃkāra,* Buddhist Sanskrit Texts 13 (Darbhanga: Mithila Institute, 1970), xix.45d. Elsewhere the Sanskrit phrase is *catasro yuktayaḥ;* e.g., Nathmal Tatia, ed., *Abhidharmasamuccayabhāṣyam* (Patna: K. P. Jayaswal Research Institute, 1976), p. 99, no. 125.

11. Cf. Monier Monier-Williams, *A Sanskrit-English Dictionary* (Oxford: Clarendon Press, 1899), 853.

12. The Pali equivalent *yutti* represents a basic category of scriptural analysis in both the *Nettipakaraṇaṃ* and the *Peṭakopadesa.* See Bhikkhu Ñāṇamoli, trans., *The Guide* (London: Luzac and Company, 1962), 36ff.; and idem., *The Pitaka-Disclosure* (London: Luzac and Company, 1965), 116ff. *Yutti* is here translated as "a construing." I am grateful to George Bond for calling these sources to my attention through his presentation to the conference on Buddhist hermeneutics. Cf., also, the concept of *yukti* as it occurs in the *Tattvārtha* chapter of the *Bodhisattvabhūmiḥ,* edited by Nalinaksha Dutt (Patna: K. P. Jayaswal Research Institute, 1978), 25ff.; and the translation by Janice Dean Willis, *On Knowing Reality* (New York: Columbia University Press, 1979), 150.

13. Étienne Lamotte, *Saṃdhinirmocana Sūtra: L'Explication des Mystères* (Louvain: Université de Louvain, 1935), chap. 10, 7.4. 7° (text and translation). Lamotte mistook *rigs pa* in this context to be a translation of the Sanskrit term *nyāya* rather than *yukti.* His attempt to translate the lengthy and difficult passage which adumbrates the four principles of reason he qualifies with these words: "Cet exposé de logique bouddhique étant très special, nous avons cru bien faire de conserver les termes techniques sanscrits dans notre traductions." The present writer has made a new translation of the entire passage, and intends to include it with other materials he has gathered in a forthcoming historical study of the development of the four principles.

14. Pralhad Pradhan, *Abhidharma Samuccaya of Asaṅga* (Santiniketan: Visva-Bharati, 1950), 81; Nathmal Tatia, *Abhidharmasamuccayabhāṣyam.* For a translation of the former see Walpola Rahula, *Le Compendium de la Super-Doctrine d'Asaṅga* (Paris: École française d'Extrême-Orient, 1971), 136. This, however, is seriously flawed in the passage here cited: Rahula has without explanation read *sākṣātkrīyāsādhanayukti* for Pradhan's entirely correct reading of *upapattisādhanayukti.*

15. Kong-sprul, *Shes bya kun khyab,* 3.11–12.

16. Neither do the doxographers of the other Tibetan traditions offer us much assistance at this point. For example, the Dge-lugs-pa scholar Lcang-skya Rol-pa'i rdo-rje (1717–1786), in his *Grub pa'i mtha'i rnam par bzhag pa gsal bar bshad pa thub bstan lhun po'i mdzes rgyan* (Sarnath, U.P.: The Pleasure of Elegant Sayings Press, 1970), 151, says that "relying on these four principles of reason, too, one penetrates the significance of the Jina's scriptures." But this is rather uninformative.

17. *Don rnam par nges pa shes rab ral gri,* modern xylograph from Ser-lo mgon-pa, Nepal, based on the Rdzong-sar edition, 10 folios.

18. *Mkhas pa'i tshul la 'jug pa'i sgo* (Tashijong, H.P.: Sungrab Nyamso Gyunphel Parkhang, 1964), fols. 148b–161b. For a general introduction to this work

see Goodman, "Mi-pham rgya-mtsho"; and Leslie S. Kawamura, "An Analysis of Mi-pham's *mKhas-'jug,*" in Davidson, *Wind Horse,* 112–126.

19. *Collected Writings of 'Jam-mgon 'Ju Mi-pham rgya-mtsho,* vol. A (Gangtok: Sonam Topgay Kazi, 1976), 667–668.

20. Sthīramati, *Sūtrālaṃkāravṛttibhāṣya,* vol. 2 (Rumtek, 1976), 403–410.

21. *Don rnam par nges pa shes rab ral gri mchan bcas,* in *Collected Writings of 'Jam-mgon 'Ju Mi-pham rgya-mtsho,* vol. PA (Gangtok: Sonam Topgay Kazi, 1976), 787–820.

22. *Mkhas pa'i tshul la 'jug pa'i sgo'i mchan 'grel legs bshad snang ba'i 'od zer* (Delhi: Lama Jumre Drakpa, 1974), 653–694.

23. *Mkhas 'jug gi sa bcad mdor bsdus pa pad dkar phreng ba* (Tashijong, H.P.: Sungrab Nyamso Gyunphel Parkhang, 1965), 20b–22b.

24. Dharmakīrti's definition of absolute reality, i.e. efficacy, is here taken as the mark of veridical being in the domain of the concealment of the absolute. See Swami Dwarikadas Shastri, ed., *Pramāṇavārttikam* (Varanasi: Bauddha Bharati, 1968), 100: "What is capable of effecting a result is here [defined as] absolute being." Cf., also, Esho Mikogami, "Some Remarks on the Concept Arthakriyā," *Journal of Indian Philosophy* 7 (1979): 79–94.

25. Goodman, "Mi-pham rgya-mtsho," 71, translates this term as "what is possible and what is impossible"; and Kawamura, "An Analysis of Mi-pham's *mKhas-'jug,*" 114, gives "what is inevitable and what is impossible." The latter is certainly incorrect and the former somewhat inaccurately suggests that both logical and empirical possibility are to be included here. But Mi-pham himself, *Mkhas pa'i tshul la 'jug pa'i sgo,* 23a1 ff., makes it quite clear that this topic concerns only empirical possibility. Accordingly, "positive contingencies" *(gnas)* refers here to natural processes—e.g., a rice-stalk growing from a rice-seed—and "negative contingencies" *(gnas ma yin pa)* to empirically impossible processes—e.g., a cat growing from a rice-seed.

26. See his *Gsang sngags rdo rje theg pa'i tshul las snang ba lhar bsgrub pa Rong zom chos bzang gis mdzad pa,* in *Selected Writings of Roṅ-zom Chos-kyi-bzaṅ-po,* Smanrtsis Shesrig Spendzod, vol. 73 (Leh: S. W. Tashigangpa, 1973), 125–151.

27. The Sanskrit title of the text last mentioned is also given as *Nyāyasiddhāloka,* P 5740, translated by Śrīsiṃhaprabha and Vairocana, although it is not listed in the early ninth century *Ldan dkar dkar chag* as given by Marcelle Lalou, "Les Textes Bouddhiques au Temps du Roi Khri-sroṅ-lde-bcan," *Journal Asiatique* 241, no. 3 (1953): 313–353. The text is noted, but not analyzed, by Satis Chandra Vidyabhusana, *A History of Indian Logic* (Delhi: Motilal Barnarsidass, 1971), 336. Vidyabhusana assigns the author to "about 925 A.D.," but if the attribution of translators is correct he would have been active over a century earlier.

28. Cf. the distinctions made by St. Thomas Aquinas, *Aristotle: On Interpretation,* translated by Jean T. Oesterle (Milwaukee: Marquette University Press, 1962), 17: "There is a twofold operation of the intellect. . . . One is the understanding of simple objects, that is, the operation by which the intellect apprehends just the essence of the thing alone; the other is the operation of composing and dividing. There is also a third operation, that of reasoning, by which reason proceeds from what is known to the investigation of things that are unknown. The first of these operations is ordered to the second, for there cannot be composition and division unless things have already been apprehended simply. The second, in turn, is ordered to the third, for clearly we must proceed from some known truth to which the intellect assents in order to have certitude

about something not yet known." Cf., also, Aristotle, *De Anima,* bk. 3, chap. 6. For Mi-pham's indications concerning the passage from the operation of division and combination to that of reasoning, see below, paragraphs 1.3.1–2.

29. I am indebted to Mkhan-po Dpal-ldan shes-rab for having clarified this point. By now it will be obvious to readers familiar with recent western philosophy that "conventional" is not used here with the same meaning it has in the philosophy of science since Poincaré. For even the necessary truths of logic and mathematics, which may be known a priori, are here termed "conventional" *(sāṅketika, tha snyad pa).* But "conventional" in its Buddhist uses should not be taken to imply "freely chosen from a given set of alternatives," and much less "arbitrary." It refers, rather, to all language and propositional knowledge, and to the principles to which they conform and to their objects; for none of these is or directly points to that absolute reality whose realization is spiritual liberation. That absolute, of which not even the categories of the one and the many or of being and nonbeing can be affirmed, wholly transcends the familiar conventions of logic, experience, language, and thought.

30. For the four major arguments traditionally enumerated in the scholastic treatises of the Madhyamaka school see David Seyfort Ruegg, *The Literature of the Madhyamaka School of Philosophy in India* (Wiesbaden: Otto Harrassowitz, 1981), 112. A detailed account of their exposition according to the Dge-lugs-pa tradition is found in Jeffrey Hopkins, *Meditation on Emptiness* (London: Wisdom Publications, 1983), pt. 2, "Reasoning into Reality." Here I follow Mi-pham's own discussion, as given in *Mkhas pa'i tshul la 'jug pa'i sgo,* 133b–140a. The enumeration of three arguments in the passage which follows, rather than the traditional four, is explained by the fact that the fourth, the "Great Interdependence Argument" *(rten 'brel chen po),* is held to apply equally to the analysis of cause, result, and essence.

31. The argument applied to causes, called "Diamond Fragments" *(rgyu la dpyod pa rdo rje gzegs ma),* proceeds from the assumption that if an individual thing comes into being as the result of some cause, then that cause must either be the thing itself or something other. The supposition that it is the thing itself leads to an infinite regress, whereas the assumption that the cause is other cannot be sustained owing to the absence of any intrinsic relationship between the supposed cause and its result. Having denied these two alternatives nothing is gained by supposing that their conjunction might explain causation; and their joint negation leads to the absurdity of things coming into being causelessly. The argument is intended to demonstrate that the concept of cause is radically defective, i.e. empty.

32. The reality of the result is challenged by the "negation of the coming into being of an existent or of a nonexistent" *('bras bu la dpyod pa yod med skye 'gog).* Whatever comes into being, it is supposed, must be something that exists, does not exist, conjoins existence and nonexistence, or neither exists nor does not exist. Following an argumentative strategy similar to that of the critique of cause, one is led to conclude that the concept of result (i.e. of something that is brought into being) is also defective.

33. The argument employed here intends to reduce to absurdity the notions of the one and the many *(ngo bo la dpyod pa gcig du bral),* with the result that the concept of individual essence is overthrown. As applied to material bodies the argument is similar to Kant's second antinomy. But in the case of spiritual substance it depends on the denial of the unity of consciousness, both through appeal to an assumption of temporal parts and in the light of Humean consider-

ations with respect to the variegation of consciousness. Mi-pham analyzed this argument *in extenso* in his commentary on Śāntarakṣita's *Madhyamakālaṃkāra,* the *Dbu ma rgyan gyi rnam bshad 'jam dbyangs bla ma dgyes pa'i zhal lung,* in *Collected Writings of 'Jam-mgon 'Ju Mi-pham rgya-mtsho,* vol. 12 (Gangtok: Sonam Topgay Kazi, 1976), 1–359.

34. Cf. Étienne Lamotte, *L'Enseignement de Vimalakīrti* (Louvain: Publications Universitaires, 1962), 148 n. 16.

35. Despite the peculiarities of diction, Mi-pham's point here seems to be similar to that made by Aristotle in *Metaphysics,* bk. 7, chap. 17, 1041[a] (trans. W. D. Ross):

> Now "why a thing is itself" is a meaningless inquiry (for [to give meaning to the question "why"] the fact or the existence of the thing must already be evident—e.g. that the moon is eclipsed—but the fact that a thing is itself is the single reason and the single cause to be given in answer to all such questions as "why the man is man, or the musician musical," unless one were to answer "because each thing is inseparable from itself, and its being one just meant this" . . .).

Cf., also, *Posterior Analytics,* bk. 2, chaps. 4–7. For a recent discussion of related issues, see Harry V. Stopes-Roe's observations on "terminal quests," in his "The Intelligibility of the Universe," in Stuart C. Brown, *Reason and Religion* (Ithaca: Cornell University Press, 1977), 53–67.

36. *Mkhas pa'i tshul la 'jug pa'i sgo,* 150a6–b2.

37. The presentation found in the *Saṃdhinirmocana* thus has the distinction of being one of the earliest Buddhist presentations of these topics. They are listed there as falling under three categories: direct perception, inference, and scriptural authority. Later Buddhist logicians tended to refrain from enumerating the last of these as a separate epistemic authority, but recall Kong-sprul's remarks above.

38. The most complete account of this system remains Theodore Stcherbatsky's dated opus, *Buddhist Logic* (reprint ed., New York: Dover, 1962), 2 vols. While there is no comprehensive bibliography for the many contributions made in recent years to the primary and secondary literature on this subject, useful lists of sources are found in Geshe Lobsang Tharchin, *The Logic and Debate Tradition of India, Tibet, and Mongolia* (Freewood Acres, N.J.: First Kalmuk Buddhist Temple, 1979), 237–270; and Ernst Steinkellner, *Dharmakīrti's Pramāṇaviniścayaḥ,* Teil II—Übersetzung und Anmerkungen (Vienna: Verlag der Österreichischen Akademie der Wissenschaften, 1979), 10–19.

39. The issues raised in this passage are of central importance to contemporary epistemology, and require much further study in their Buddhist formulations. The epistemic primacy of self-presentation *(svasaṃvittiḥ)* was sharply contested by those within the Buddhist tradition who maintained this concept to be fundamentally incoherent, like the notion of the sword being used to cut itself. Cf. Śāntideva, *Bodhicāryāvatāra,* chap. 9, v. 18. Also problematic was the precise nature of the chain leading from discrete self-presentations through sensory perceptions to inferential knowledge of the world. For contemporary philosophical discussions of these and related questions see Roderick M. Chisholm, *Theory of Knowledge* (Englewood Cliffs, N.J.: Prentice-Hall, 1966). The connection between the Buddhist notion of *svasaṃvittiḥ* and recent investigations of self-presentation appears to have been first explicitly noted by Paul M. Williams, "On *rang rig,*" in Ernst Steinkellner and Helmut Tauscher, eds., *Contri-*

butions on Tibetan and Buddhist Religion and Philosophy, Proceedings of the Csoma de Körös Symposium Held at Velm-Vienna (Vienna, 1983), 2:321–332. I thank Michael Broido for calling this interesting article to my attention. (Williams, it should be noted, uses "self-consciousness" where I prefer "self-presentation.")

40. One interesting question that can be raised here is whether Buddhist philosophers regarded future states of affairs as having determinate truth-value.

41. See especially his *Nges shes rin po che'i sgron me,* published in a lithographic edition with the commentary of Mkhan-chen Kun-bzang dpal-ldan (Clement Town, U.P.: Nyingma Lama's College, n.d.).

42. Particularly noteworthy here is Bod-pa sprul-sku Mdo-sngags bstan-pa'i nyi-ma's *Lta grub shan 'byed* and its autocommentary, on which see Kennard Lipman, "What Is Buddhist Logic?" in S. D. Goodman and R. Davidson, eds., *Tibetan Buddhism: Reason and Revelation* (Albany: SUNY Press, forthcoming).

43. On this distinction see Ruegg, *Literature of the Madhyamaka School,* 64 and 88.

44. In point of fact this very confusion has been an obstacle to the study of the development of Indian logic. See, e.g., Vidyabhusana, *A History of Indian Logic,* 500 n. 1.

45. Note that it is here that Mi-pham situates most of the interpretive rules of thumb enumerated in the standard scholastic manuals. Cf. the section on "The Scholastic Background" above and the articles referred to in nn. 7 and 8.

46. Nonveridical, that is, in the absolute sense, which does not preclude their being *conventionally* veridical.

47. From a philosophical perspective it is of supreme interest that while Mi-pham considers, e.g., the conjunction of being and nonbeing to be a metaphysical absurdity, he nonetheless maintains that it can be in some sense *objectified.* This merits comparison with certain of the proposals of Alexius Meinong as detailed in his "The Theory of Objects," translated in Roderick M. Chisholm, ed., *Realism and the Background of Phenomenology* (Glencoe, Ill.: Free Press, 1960). A lucid introduction to Meinong's theory may be found in Leonard Linsky, *Referring* (London: Routledge and Kegan Paul, 1967), chap. 2.

48. This is so because the conventional dichotomy of subject and object is a fundamental aspect of the unknowing which is the root of saṃsāric entanglement. For the precise formulation of this in accord with the cosmology of the Rnying-ma-pa school, see Bdud-'joms Rin-po-che 'Jigs-bral-ye-shes-rdo-rje, *Gsang sngags snga 'gyur rnying ma ba'i bstan pa'i rnam gzhag mdo tsam brjod pa legs bshad snang ba'i dga'i ston* (Kalimpong: Dudzom Rinpochee [sic], 1967), 4b6 ff. Translated in G. Dorje and M. Kapstein, *Fundamentals and History of the Nyingmapa Tradition of Tibetan Buddhism.*

49. Cf. E. H. Johnston, ed., *Ratnagotravibhāga* (Patna: Bihar Research Institute, 1950), 1.154, p. 76; and *Abhisamayālaṃkāra,* 5.21, in P. L. Vaidya, ed., *Aṣṭasāhasrikā,* Buddhist Sanskrit Texts 4 (Darbhanga: Mithila Institute, 1960), 523.

50. P. L. Vaidya, ed., *Lalitavistara,* Buddhist Texts Series 1 (Darbhanga: Mithila Institute, 1958), 317. The sūtra refers to them merely as the "eight great treasures" *(aṣṭau mahānidhānāni).*

51. Carl G. Hempel, "The Function of General Laws in History," in Herbert Feigl and Wilfred Sellars, eds., *Readings in Philosophical Analysis* (New York: Appleton-Century-Crofts, 1949), 459–471.

52. G. E. M. Anscombe, *Intention* (Ithaca: Cornell University Press, 1957); Georg Henrik von Wright, *Explanation and Understanding* (Ithaca: Cornell University Press, 1971). An introduction to the domain in which analytic philosophy and hermeneutics intersect is provided by Roy J. Howard, *Three Faces of Hermeneutics* (Berkeley: University of California Press, 1982).

53. For a concise presentation of Paul Ricoeur's view here see his *Hermeneutics and the Human Sciences,* ed. and trans. John B. Thompson (Cambridge: Cambridge University Press, 1981), chap. 5 ("What Is a Text? Explanation and Understanding"). Ricoeur does not seek to deny that explanation and understanding are distinct operations, but refuses to accept Dilthey's absolute bifurcation of their respective domains. In sum (p. 157), ". . . it will be upon the same terrain, within the same sphere of language [*langage*], that explanation and interpretation will enter into debate." By contrast, analytic critics have tended to focus upon the supposed dichotomy between the two process categories of natural causation and intentional agency. See Donald Davidson, *Essays on Actions and Events* (Oxford: Clarendon Press, 1980); and John R. Searle *Intentionality* (Cambridge: Cambridge University Press, 1983), chap. 4 ("Intentional Causation"). One philosopher who has systematically examined both the causation-agency and the explanation-understanding dichotomies is R. M. Chisholm. In the *Person and Object* (La Salle, Ill.: Open Court, 1979), 69–72 ("The Agent as Cause"), he denies that there is any "unbridgeable gap" between the members of the former pair, whereas in *The Foundations of Knowing* (Minneapolis: University of Minnesota Press, 1982), chap. 7 ("Verstehen: The Epistemological Question"), he concludes that the latter distinction is indeed a significant one. Implicit in Chisholm's work, therefore, is the important observation that strict parallelism between these two distinctions need not be presupposed. At the time of this writing I have no clear sense of how Buddhist epistemologists would have treated the notion of *Verstehen.*

54. *Mkhas pa'i tshul la 'jug pa'i sgo,* sec. 4.

55. Cf. Edmund Husserl, *Recherches Logique,* trans. Hubert Élie et al. (Paris: Presses Universitaires de France, 1962), vol. 2, pt. 2, sec. 5, p. 174: "There are not two things . . . which are present in the experience; we do not experience the object and, beside it, the intentional experience which relates to it. . . ."

56. When we survey the history of western hermeneutics since Schleiermacher we find also theory of interpretation becoming fused with more general aspects of epistemology, metaphysics, and the philosophy of language. What I wish to suggest at this juncture is that any theory of interpretation which generalizes its concerns beyond the elaboration of rules of thumb required in connection with the study of a given corpus must inevitably undergo some such transformation, for the reason that interpretive acts and their objects, when considered in general and not specified, are none other than rational and linguistic acts and their objects. If this is so, then hermeneutics as scriptural interpretation will be in essence the conjunction of the appropriate domains of general philosophical inquiry with those rules which are elaborated specifically to link such inquiry with the scriptural corpus under consideration. And this seems to be just what is accomplished by the Buddhist enumerations of interpretive keys. If, in the light of these observations, we turn to western scholastic traditions, I think we will find that logic, theology, rational psychology, etc., are within those traditions hermeneutical in just the same sense that Buddhist philosophy is here claimed to be hermeneutical.

57. It is of interest in this connection that the first western work explicitly

consecrated to interpretation theory was a treatise on logic, Aristotle's *De Interpretatione*.

58. Karma-pa VII Chos-grags rgya-mtsho, *Tshad ma rigs gzhung rgya mtsho* (Thimphu: Topga Tulku, 1973), vol. 1, p. 5, ll. 1–5: *tshad mar gyur pa'i sangs rgyas bcom ldan 'das de nyid kyis . . . chos kyi 'khor lo gnas skabs dang mthar thug gi don la bslu ba med cing sngar ma shes pa'i yang dag pa'i don phyin ci ma log pa gsal bar shes pa'i slad du bskor bar mdzad la/ de'ang gdul bya so so'i dbang gis drang ba'i don dang/ nges pa'i don dang/ sgra ji bzhin pa dang/ ji bzhin ma yin pa dang dgongs pa can dang/ ldem por dgongs pa ci rigs pa'i tshul gyis gnas pa las/ de'i don gdul bya rnams kyis rtogs dka' bar gzigs nas gtan tshigs rigs pa'i sgo nas bde blags tu rtogs par bya ba dang/ ma rtogs pa dang/ log par rtogs pa dang/ the tshom la sogs pa bsal ba'i slad du bdag nyid chen po phyogs kyi glang pos bde bar gshegs pa'i gsung rab ma lus pa tshad ma gsum gyis legs par gtan la phab ste/*

Hermeneutical Phases in Chinese Buddhism

DAVID W. CHAPPELL

In this essay, I argue that each of the major forms of Chinese Buddhism, beginning with the normative tradition (Canonical Buddhism) and its main subtraditions (T'ien-t'ai, Pure Land, and Ch'an), exemplifies at least three different hermeneutical orientations. At various times and in different ways, each of these traditions approaches scripture seeking either (1) to find a subjectively satisfying and crisis-resolving interpretation, or (2) to integrate with the established tradition, or (3) to systematically propagate the new religion.

Hermeneutics has traditionally involved the application of certain techniques or devices for the interpretation of texts, such as a line-by-line analysis or the application of a set of questions or categories to the text. A familiar example of the latter is the medieval quest for a text's literal, moral, allegorical, and mystical meanings. More recently in the West there has arisen a historical consciousness that has revealed that the strangeness between us and the texts we interpret is a problem not simply of the dimness of our knowledge, or of time, or of our soul, but of a different set of values, experiences, and prejudgments *(Vorurteile)* that we bring with us to the text. Thus contemporary Western thinkers often focus on historical issues in textual analysis, because historical consciousness is now a major component of our perspective that was not present for authors writing in other periods. A further refinement of hermeneutical theory has been the questioning of the very process of understanding itself, and how the interpretation of texts relates to that process.[1]

Selecting among these themes, I shall employ a historical approach in examining Chinese Buddhist hermeneutics. Specifically, I will focus on the early phases of translation, exegesis, and canonization that established Buddhism as a major tradition in China. I will then explore the hermeneutical methods used by two sectarian traditions, Pure Land and Ch'an, looking not only for the hermeneutical devices but also for the underlying concerns and values, the preconditions and goals, that motivated and shaped the adoption of particular devices and made them meaningful. However, I will *not* research Chinese Buddhist materials which deal with theories of understanding, although a variety of texts suggest themselves as potentially useful for this line of inquiry.[2]

Even when restricted to early Chinese Buddhism, early Pure Land, and early Ch'an, the range of materials is vast. Accordingly, I will employ as a heuristic device a scheme of *three hermeneutical phases*[3] to assist in analysis and comparison:

1. If we assume that new religions arise in a period of *crisis,* when individuals actively seek a more viable way to resolve conflict and affirm personal worth, the first stage of a new religion involves the discovery of a new interpretation and practice that will resolve the sense of personal crisis in an ultimately satisfying way.

2. Scriptures are used to legitimize the new interpretation and practice, usually in a process of *integration with the established tradition.* As a result a new coherent world view is formed, and the new principles are elaborated and extensively illustrated by scripture. Exegesis in this phase attempts to show how the new interpretation is supported and authenticated by the authoritative tradition.

3. Finally, a phase of *systematic propagation* of the religion begins, in which the new interpretation is streamlined, superfluous or controversial features are omitted or explicitly rejected, catechisms are produced, and programs of practice are institutionalized. This simplification or reductionism takes place out of a concern to indoctrinate new members and to establish the superiority of this new orthodoxy over other paths, rather than showing how they can be integrated.

My objective in proposing this interpretive scheme is not to argue that the three phases are adequate or inclusive, but rather the reverse: namely, that it is not legitimate to argue that any particular Chinese Buddhist tradition had a single hermeneutical method or only one underlying hermeneutical concern. There is no "Buddhist hermeneutic" or even a "Ch'an hermeneutic." Instead we find a variety of approaches at different levels. Any religious movement (or individual) that goes through discernible periods of growth will exhibit different concerns, ask different questions, and therefore exhibit a variety of hermeneutical methods. Thus, the scheme of three hermeneutical phases is at once a critical and a constructive device. Against those who maintain that a tradition can be identified with a specific hermeneutic, I propose that most religious traditions exhibit at least three hermeneutical orientations over time; and, rather than hold that every text, every thinker, and every tradition is so varied that no underlying structure or themes are evident, I would suggest that these three phases are recurring hermeneutical orientations shared by most religious traditions at some time in their history.

Although it would be possible to apply this scheme of three hermeneutical orientations to various parts of Chinese Buddhism, I shall systematically look for them only in the development of the normative tradition (which I call Canonical Buddhism) and then in two subtraditions (Pure Land and Ch'an).

In the case of the T'ien-t'ai tradition, for example, the works of Hui-ssu (515–577) can be identified as expressing the first and second phases of individual affirmation and scriptural legitimation. The writings of Chih-i (538–597) exhibit the concerns of phases two and three by legitimizing and integrating the new ideas and practices with the inherited tradition, and by systematizing new programs of action. Chan-jan (711–782) and later thinkers, who were more concerned with the systematic propagation of T'ien-t'ai, can then be seen as representing the third phase. This analysis suggests that not only a particular school, but even individual thinkers within that school exhibited more than a single hermeneutical concern over the course of their careers. Moreover, some of the exegetical categories devised by Chih-i in particular, such as his five categories of scriptural analysis, continued to be employed at different times by T'ien-t'ai thinkers as well as throughout Chinese Buddhist history.

Canonical Buddhism

The subtraditions of T'ien-t'ai, Pure Land, and Ch'an developed from a shared established tradition which I am calling "Canonical Buddhism" because it was so strongly tied to the Chinese translation, study, and organization of major Buddhist texts. This Canonical Buddhism, which remained normative for all later Chinese Buddhism, had established its major scriptures by the end of the sixth century, was defined and organized by Chinese vinaya masters, had a world view based on the Perfection of Wisdom tradition, and had a standard of practice defined by the Hīnayāna vinaya. The religious paradigm of Canonical Buddhism and its methods of hermeneutics can be shown to have three distinct orientations or phases.

The First Phase

When Buddhism entered China, it came as something foreign that provided relief from the Chinese cultural crisis that prevailed during the decline and collapse of the Han dynasty.[4] To some degree this new Buddhist world was made accessible by being interpreted as a form of Taoism practiced in India. In this interpretation, Buddhism was seen as augmenting the Taoist pantheon and providing a new spiritual technology (rituals, texts, meditations, and various paraphernalia) along with specially trained technicians (priests). Buddha and Lao-tzu were worshipped together and were seen as forms of each other, and strange Sanskrit words and Indian ideas were translated by Taoist terms which were considered to match the Buddhist meanings. This activity has been labeled *ko-i* (matching the meanings), although it seems that this specific phrase originally referred to a more limited practice.[5]

The fact that Buddhism was foreign, on the other hand, was also one of its attractions: its ideas and practices were different enough from those of Chinese society to represent a distinct alternative. By internalizing the new religion through meditation, one could find a new refuge within oneself; and by joining the saṅgha, one could separate oneself from the woes and sufferings attendant with family obligations and participation in Chinese society. Under the leadership of new literati monks from the fourth century on, Buddhism formed a monastic community separate from Chinese society. This refuge attracted a growing following by providing "another world to live in" as an escape from the external crisis in Chinese society.

Chinese Buddhist hermeneutics developed in the fourth century when Chinese literati converted to Buddhism and began to engage in active interpretation and assimilation of Buddhist texts and doctrines.[6] The main problem of interpretation centered on coming to terms with Buddhism as an alternative to traditional moral patterns, as can be seen in the polemical literature of the time, such as the *Mou-tzu.* Intellectually, the various methods that were used to interpret Buddhism all reflected different aspects of the *hsüan-hsüeh* (inner learning) and *ch'ing-t'an* (pure conversation) patterns that were then in vogue.[7] Perhaps as a consequence, the Buddhist texts that dominated thinking in the fourth century were the Perfection of Wisdom scriptures (particularly the 8,000-line and 25,000-line versions) which celebrated the idea of emptiness. Zürcher proposes three reasons for this dominance. First was the "obvious resemblance" between Buddhist theories of emptiness and the themes of *hsüan-hsüeh.* Second, the "chaotic, diffuse and frequently cryptic way" of presenting the idea of emptiness in these Mahāyāna scriptures left room for Chinese thinkers to read their own meanings into the texts. Third, the early translations were often paraphrases that freely used traditional Chinese philosophical terms, prompting fourth-century thinkers to correlate Indian and Chinese ideas. In particular, the main concern of Chinese thinkers was whether it was the outside world that was empty, or whether emptiness referred to the mind of the sage—that is, was it an ontological claim or did it refer to a subjective experience that was to be cultivated in the mind of the sage? (Only later did Chinese thinkers appreciate the strength of the Buddhist criticism of this dualistic distinction.)[8]

The Second Phase

A major turning point occurred in 401 when the great Central Asian translator Kumārajīva was brought to China to translate Indian Buddhist texts in a more authoritative way. Under his expertise, it soon became apparent that the Chinese understanding of Buddhism had been far from correct. Taoism was very different from Buddhism, and the earlier collaboration with Taoist-minded monks turned into internal debate and division.

As more Indian scriptures were translated, educated Buddhist monks began to feel increasingly insecure in their understanding of their new religion. Based on the firm belief that if they looked deeply enough, the truth was to be found in the vast reservoir of Buddhist texts, Buddhist intellectuals of the fifth century initiated a great wave of activity in translation and textual study. It is worth noting here that Buddhism's success at the popular level, especially among the aristocracy, ensured it ample support for what amounted to a major research effort to discover authentic Indian Buddhism.

In contrast to the first phase of Chinese Buddhist hermeneutics, when Buddhism was interpreted from a Taoist frame of reference, the second phase attempted to think purely within the language and concepts provided by Indian Buddhist texts. As a consequence, the validity of these foreign texts as a new authoritative tradition became the subject of controversy. The largest collection of debates on this matter was made by Seng-yu (445–518) in his *Hung-ming chi* (Collection Expanding on and Clarifying [Points of Buddhist Doctrine]). Based on Seng-yu's summary of the six topics dealt with in the collection, we can see that four are related to the status of Buddhist texts as different from the Chinese classics:

> The first of their [i.e., the Buddhists' opponents] doubts is that the doctrines of the sūtras are sweeping, wild, vast, and cannot be verified. The second is that when man dies, his soul perishes, so that there is no such thing as the three ages [of past, present, and future]. The third is that no one has seen the genuine Buddha, and that the rule of the country derives from him no benefit. The fourth is that anciently there was no Buddhist teaching, and that it appeared only recently during the Han era. The fifth is that the teaching belongs to barbarian lands, and does not accord with our Chinese customs. The sixth is that the Buddhist doctrine was unimportant [in China] during the Han and Wei [dynasties], and became flourishing only with the Chin. Because of these six doubts, the mind of faith cannot be established.[9]

The concern of the Chinese Buddhist elite to clarify and systematize the Buddhist scriptures is reflected in the first *Biographies of Eminent Monks (Kao-seng-chuan),* compiled by 530 by Hui-chiao (497–554), which contains 257 biographies in 10 categories. Over half of the monks are listed either as translators or exegetes: translators (35), exegetes (101), wonder workers (20), meditators (21), vinaya experts (13), self-immolators (11), sūtra reciters (21), creators of merit (14), sūtra masters (11), and chanters (10).[10]

This extensive activity devoted to translation resulted in the creation of a number of textual traditions focused on particular scriptures. In the fifth century in South China, the most important texts included Kumārajīva's translations of the *Lotus, Vimalakīrti, Perfection of Wisdom,* and *Daśabhūmika* scriptures, the Sarvāstivādin vinaya, and the *San-lun* and *Ch'eng-shih lun* philosophical treatises. Their popularity was also shared with the *Nirvāṇa Scripture, Heart of Abhidharma Treatise,* and *Queen Śrīmālā Scripture.* In the sixth century southern monks took up the *Compendium to Mahāyāna Treatise (She ta-sheng lun,* abbrev. *She-lun)* and the *Abhidharmakośa.*

In North China in the sixth century, attention focused on three scriptures—the *Nirvāṇa Sūtra, Hua-yen Sūtra,* and *Bodhisattvabhūmi Sūtra*—the Dharmaguptaka vinaya, and two treatises, the *Commentary on the Sūtra of Ten Stages of the Bodhisattva (Shih-ti chin lun)* and the *Commentary on the Perfection of Wisdom Sūtra (Ta chih-tu lun).*

Certain general features can be observed throughout this activity. First, there was a concern to avoid Taoist concepts and to establish a consistent Buddhist vocabulary—here Kumārajīva's translations played a major role. Second, there was a growing tendency to specialize on a specific text, both to gain authoritative knowledge of at least one text or tradition, and to provide a standpoint from which to interpret all other texts. Third, the underlying theme or essence of a text was usually identified in a form of commentary called a *hsüan* or *tsung;* with that understanding as a basis, related texts could then be organized around it. Finally, this practice led to the development of elaborate *p'an-chiao* schemes which classified and listed hierarchically the texts and doctrines of the various schools. What these various hermeneutical methods shared in common was an underlying concern to establish an authoritative understanding of the word of the Buddha, and to integrate that understanding with all authenticated Buddhist scriptures.[11]

The Third Phase

The effort to systematize the Chinese understanding of the Buddhist tradition for the purpose of safeguarding the true teaching and propagating it to others constitutes the third and definitive hermeneutical phase of Canonical Buddhism. A variety of textual schools and *p'an-chiao* systems[12] had attempted to establish themselves as normative for specific themes and texts, but not until the organization of T'ien-t'ai Chih-i (538–597) did any specific school achieve widespread acceptance. Before this happened, however, Canonical Buddhism achieved enduring form in the more inclusive, objective, and historically critical biographies, histories, and dictionary of Seng-yu (445–518) and his disciple Pao-ch'ang, Hui-chiao (497–554), Wei Shou (506–572), and Ching-ying Hui-yüan (523–592).

Among all the traditions, it was the vinaya masters who were most fastidious in trying to maintain the purity of Canonical Buddhism and to construct adequate safeguards. Accordingly, it is not surprising to find that the earliest lists showing the line of transmission of a teaching occur in two vinaya texts. The Mahāsaṃghika *Vinaya* (*T* 22.492c–493a), translated into Chinese in 416–418 by Fa-hsien and Buddhabhadra, has a list of twenty-seven names beginning with Upāli, while the Chinese commentary to the Theravādin *Vinaya* (*T* 24.684b–685a), which was translated by Sambhabhadra, has a list of twenty-four names beginning with Upāli. Otherwise, the lists are completely different.[13]

Seng-yu can serve as a paradigm figure for this phase. He was primarily considered a vinaya specialist, and most of his writings consist of careful collections to preserve and transmit the tradition. Nonextant works include one on Buddhist cosmology *(Shih-chieh chi),* a history of Buddhism *(Fa-yüan tsa-yüan yüan-shih chi),* an explanation of the Sarvāstivādin vinaya *(Shih-sung i chi),* a history of the masters of the Sarvāstivādin school *(Sa-p'o-to-pu),* and a collection of inscriptions *(Fa-chi tsa-chi-ming).* Works of Seng-yu that do survive are a biographical study of Gotama and his relatives (*Shih-chia p'u, T* 50.1–84), a collection of debates about Buddhist doctrine (*Hung-ming chi, T* 52.1–96), and a comprehensive bibliography of Buddhist texts translated into Chinese, including a collection of prefaces and twenty-seven biographies of the transmitters (*Ch'u san-tsang chih-chi, T* 55.1–114). In accordance with his aim of establishing authoritative scriptures and a systematic account, Seng-yu commented on the authenticity of the texts and included references to his sources.

The earliest transmission list from the meditation tradition is found in the *Ch'u san-tsang chi chi* (Collection of Notes on the Translation of the Tripiṭaka), compiled by Seng-yu about 515. It has two lists with over fifty names (*T* 55.89a–b and 89c–90a).[14] This device of establishing a lineage[15] was adopted by both T'ien-t'ai and Ch'an as a method of asserting their orthodoxy, and later bibliographies build on Seng-yu's collection and his method—an influence culminating in this century with the twelve-volume bibliographical dictionary by Ono Gemmyo entitled *Bussho kaisetsu daijiten.* Of course, another manifestation of this concern for comprehensive knowledge of authentic scriptures was the publication of the entire set of Buddhist scriptures with the advent of printing in China.

Biographical collections of eminent Buddhists provided another method of defining and teaching the norms of the new tradition. The classic work of this genre is of course the *Kao-seng-chuan* (Biographies of Eminent Monks), compiled about 530 by Hui-chiao (497–554). Hui-chiao lists eighteen Buddhist histories and biographical collections in his preface, suggesting that his work is not the beginning but the culmination of a long process of historiographical writing. Nevertheless, Arthur Wright observes that Hui-chiao rejected the conventions of Indian hagiography and also turned away from the colorful stories emphasizing morals and the miraculous popular during his time. Indeed, it is striking that Hui-chiao does not mention by name the large biographical collection *Ming-seng chuan,* by Pao-ch'ang, a disciple of Seng-yu, which contained 425 Buddhist biographies. Although this collection is no longer extant, we know that 290 of the monks treated by Hui-chiao were also included in Pao-ch'ang's collection, and Hui-chiao's ten categories of monks seems to be a refinement of Pao-ch'ang's eighteen.[16] Hui-chiao specifically rejects a concern for recording the lives of the famous *(ming),* who may be "men of slight virtue who happen to be in accord with their times," and instead favors those men of real achievement who are eminent *(kao)* but who may hide their brilliance. This is not only a criticism of the *Ming-seng chuan,* but also an attempt to meet the prevailing standards for secular literary and historical writing in order to impress the nobles and the literati with the high standards and discipline of Buddhism. "Miracles punctuate but do not dominate the sequence of events" in the biographies, and are "no more frequent than in many secular biographies of the period." Arthur Wright further comments that a major motive of Hui-chiao was "to rescue Buddhist biography from the limbo of the exotic, the bizarre, and give to the lives of the monks a place of honor in the cultural history of China."[17]

In the *Kao-seng-chuan,* earlier biographies were streamlined by omitting accounts of the miraculous and supplemented by historical data (of family name, birthplace, chronological sequence). In addition, Hui-chiao emphasized relationships between monks and contemporary political and literary leaders to confirm their acceptance within the Chinese upper class. This concern for the active propagation of Buddhism also served to redefine Buddhism from within. Similar but less ambitious motives may have prompted Pao-ch'ang when he compiled the biographies of sixty-five nuns in his *Pi-ch'iu-ni chuan,* which focuses on the moral and religious attainments of the nuns somewhat in the style of the *Lieh-nü-chuan* (Biographies of Exemplary Women) written in the first century B.C.[18]

An interesting anomaly that occurred about this time was the appearance of the *Shih lao chih* (Treatise on Buddhism and Taoism), which is the 114th and final chapter of the *Wei-shu* (History of the Wei Dynasty [399–550]) by Wei Shou (506–572). It is the only chapter in any official dynastic history of China to give a history of Buddhism. The growing acceptance of Buddhism within Chinese intellectual and political circles led to efforts by the Sui ruling house (589–618) to have T'ien-t'ai Chih-i (538–597) write comprehensive treatises integrating Buddhist doctrine and practice. This concern on the part of both the state and the saṅgha to provide a comprehensive, systematic, and normative account of the history and sources of Buddhism was perhaps best expressed in the works of Tsang-ning (d. 1001), under the Sung dynasty.[19] Of course, the convergence of interests between the state and the saṅgha can be seen not just as a quest for consistency and rationality, but also as a concern for institutional control. As a hermeneutical motive this concern regularly appears, and can be seen at certain points in Pure Land and Ch'an.

One method of integrating Buddhist doctrines and practices while asserting the primacy of one's own viewpoint—that of the *p'an-chiao* or hierarchical classification scheme—has been well described, particularly by Leon Hurvitz and Robert Thurman.[20] A few observations should be made here. These *p'an-chiao* schemes began in India when different vehicles, methods, and teachings were found to be mentioned in the *Lotus, Saṃdhinirmocana,* and *Nirvāṇa* scriptures. Careful line-by-line and section-by-section exegesis was supplemented from early times by creative reflection on the purpose, method, and context for each scripture. The use of *p'an-chiao* schemes, however, was not characteristic of vinaya masters of Canonical Buddhism, who tried to treat all texts equally. Nor was it a mark of the Pure Land and Ch'an traditions, which made no claim to comprehensiveness. Rather, *p'an-chiao* systems were popular principally among thinkers in the fifth and sixth centuries, and later among T'ien-t'ai and Hua-yen exegetes, who endeavored to incorporate all texts within an inclusive interpretive scheme. The fundamental argument of the *p'an-chiao* systems involved (1) an appeal to the notion of an underlying sameness of all teachings and texts of the Buddha, which was (2) expressed differently because of the different capacities of listeners, or (3) because of different phases in the teaching career of the Buddha, or (4) because of different methods of teaching (such as sudden, gradual, or indeterminate), or (5) because of different events or circumstances.

By adopting these principles to explain the variations among different scriptures, interpreters could evaluate each text in terms of a wide variety of categories. For example, Chih-i wrote two different commentaries on the *Lotus Sūtra,* the line-by-line *wen-chü* and the more interpretive *hsüan-i.* A basic scheme within the *hsüan-i* (which became very popular for all of later Buddhism) involved five categories of analysis: explaining the title of the scripture *(shih-ming),* discussing the essence *(pien-t'i),* clarifying the distinctiveness of its teaching *(ming-tsung),* discussing the function of the text *(lun-yung),* and classifying the doctrine *(p'an-chiao).* The latitude that this scheme gave a commentator is shown in the fact that Chih-i's *Fa-hua hsüan-i* uses 110 of its 165 pages of text just to discuss the implications of the title of the *Lotus.*[21] Moreover, Chih-i's *hsüan-i* was totally interpretive and did not follow the individual chapters at all —a very different hermeneutical orientation from that of the textual exegesis that had been the dominant method of Canonical Buddhism in the fifth and sixth centuries when the central aims were accuracy, authenticity, and comprehensiveness.

More representative of the vinaya approach to scripture was the careful *Lotus* commentary by Fa-yün (467–529), or the faithful exegetical works by Ching-ying Hui-yüan (523–592), which are scaled in proportion to the contours of the text being analyzed. The responsibility that Hui-yüan felt toward the tradition is also shown in his compilation of a dictionary of basic Buddhist terms *(Ta-ch'eng ta-chang).* While bibliographies, dictionaries, and other textual aids may not appear as exciting as innovative interpretations, they played a crucial role in organizing and establishing the canonical tradition, which constituted a widely accepted basis for all later developments. Also, it should be noted that the various bibliographies, biographies, histories, and dictionaries that we have mentioned were not the earliest in Chinese Buddhism, but they are the earliest that survive. They became the models for later generations to emulate, and they were the first enduring comprehensive compilations before the split of Chinese Buddhism into various subtraditions. As a consequence, they achieved a normative status within Chinese Buddhism and any new hermeneutical methods (such as the *hsüan-i* approach of T'ien-t'ai Chih-i) had first to justify themselves in terms of, or over against, this established canonical tradition.

Having surveyed the hermeneutical issues that arose during the six centuries when Canonical Buddhism became established in China, we may now examine specific developments in the two schools that effectively survived the persecution of 845, Pure Land and Ch'an.

The Pure Land Tradition

"Pure Land" *(ching-t'u)* was a phrase invented in China to refer to Sukhāvatī, the land of bliss created in the western regions by Amitābha, the Buddha of Infinite Light and Infinite Life, for the purification and enlightenment of beings. Mahāyāna Buddhists believed that all Buddhas had spheres of activity (Skt. *kṣetra* 'lands') but Amitābha's land, based on his vow that ordinary people could be reborn there through simple devotion and thereby attain a speedy, painless, and certain enlightenment, was the most popular.

Pure Land devotionalism began in China as early as A.D. 179, when the *Pan-chou san-mei ching,* which recommended the visualization of Amitābha as a meditation practice for bringing a Buddha into one's presence, was translated into Chinese. In the third century more Amitābha scriptures were translated, and by the fourth century there are reports of the first Chinese Pure Land devotees (Ch'üeh Kung-ts'e and his disciple Wei Shih-tu), the first Pure Land lectures (by Chu Fa-kuang), and the first construction of images and pictures of Amitābha and his Pure Land.

In 402 in South China, the meditation master Lu-shan Hui-yüan (334–416) formed a devotional group which centuries later was called the original White Lotus Society. It consisted of Hui-yüan and 123 laity and clergy who sought to support each other in visualizing and making offerings to Amitābha to facilitate rebirth in the Pure Land. After the death of Hui-yüan and his immediate disciples, little is heard of Pure Land practices in the south for the next few centuries.

The First Phase

What was to become a Pure Land sectarian movement did not begin until the late sixth century in North China as a response to war, famine, and the uncertainties of religious life. T'an-luan (c. 488–c. 554) and Tao-ch'o (562–645) were the pioneers of the new devotional movement located at the Hsüan-chung monastery in the remote hills of the Ping-chou area of Shansi province, far removed from the influence of Hui-yüan. The most important Indian Pure Land scriptures had been translated into Chinese by the sixth century, including the *Amitābha Scripture,* the *Wu-liang-shou ching,* the *Kuan wu-liang-shou ching,* and the *Wang-sheng lun* attributed to Vasubandhu.

T'an-luan's spiritual biography vividly illustrates the crisis that Buddhism was experiencing at that time. He was well educated in the literature of his day, as can be seen from the fact that in his major work, the *Wang-sheng lun-chu,* he quotes from at least fifteen non-Buddhist writings (Confucian, Taoist, and official histories) and forty Buddhist scriptures and treatises. However, his biography tells us that "when reading the *Ta-chi ching* [*Mahā-samnipata-sūtra*], he was greatly disturbed by the complexity of the terminology and sentences which were so hard to understand. Thus, he set out to write a commentary on this sūtra." Since the *Ta-chi ching* is a collection of a variety of Buddhist scriptures lacking in any internal unity, it is no wonder that T'an-luan had difficulty. This intellectual dilemma reached the point of crisis when T'an-luan became very sick and had to abandon his work in order to seek a cure. After a miraculous vision of heaven he was healed of his illness, but realized that his textual studies had been of no benefit. The textual preoccupations of contemporary Buddhist intellectuals had left him defenseless in the face of sickness and death. Accordingly, T'an-luan began to seek desperately for a better way of understanding.

In his quest, T'an-luan is said to have read various Taoist texts which offered medical cures and "occasionally some immortals appeared to him." Having traveled halfway across China, he explained in an audience with Emperor Wu of Liang that he "desired to study the dharma of Buddha, but I felt my life was very short, and therefore I made this long journey in the quest of immortality." Indeed, T'an-luan became so proficient in Taoist alchemy that he was remembered in the T'ang dynasty histories as a Taoist sage.[22] Nevertheless, his Taoist quest was cut short by an encounter with the Buddhist translator Bodhiruci, who rejected Taoism with the retort: "Even if you should retain youth and live forever, you would still be within the realm of saṃsāra." Then he gave T'an-luan a Pure Land scripture and recommended practice based upon it with the aim of being reborn in Amitābha's sublime Pure Land.

The profound sense of helplessness he had felt in the face of sickness and death became interpreted for T'an-luan in the Pure Land scriptures. These texts state that enlightenment is difficult in this age because of the five afflictions *(wu-cho):* war and natural disasters, deluded ideas, greed and hatred, infirmity of body and mind, and shortness of life. According to T'an-luan, this description matched his existential situation and made him realize that the compassionate aid of Amitābha was necessary for salvation through rebirth in his Pure Land.

In his major work, the *Wang-sheng lun-chu,* T'an-luan divides Buddhism into two paths: the difficult and the easy. The difficult path involves all traditional Buddhist practices based on self-effort. Later, Tao-ch'o (562–645) called it the path of sages and proclaimed that such practices were doomed to failure because this age was the period predicted by the scriptures when true Buddhism would disappear *(mo-fa,* Jp. *mappō).* The easy path is based on a radical hermeneutical principle which relegates all texts and practices to a secondary position during this crisis period, when only Pure Land scriptures are relevant.

T'an-luan was traditional enough, however, to justify and support his radical departure by two devices. The first was to write a scriptural commentary on the *Wang-sheng lun* using a careful, line-by-line, exegetical study to establish an authoritative source. Second, he interpreted the teachings of the text in terms of the most sophisticated philosophical understanding of his day, so that "rebirth" into the Pure Land of Amitābha became equivalent to "no-birth" and nirvāṇa.[23] In this way the new, selective practice of Pure Land devotionalism became integrated with the authoritative tradition.

The sense of inner crisis and personal need did not end with T'an-luan, and was relived in the experience of Tao-ch'o. Having experienced famine, war, and attacks upon the saṅgha, he piled image upon image to express the desperation of his times, punctuated with his own personal cry: "As for me, I live in a world aflame and bear a sense of dread within."[24] Tao-ch'o asserted the hermeneutical principle that the Buddha's teaching should be made *relevant* to the circumstances of one's own time, and quoted a passage from the *Cheng-ta-nien ching* to this effect: "When devotees single-mindedly seek the way to enlightenment, they should always consider the expedient means of the times *(shih fang-pien).* If they do not grasp the times, then they do not have any expedient means, and it becomes a losing effort. Why is it called a disadvantage? It is like using damp wood to try to make fire. You will not get fire, because it is not timely. If you try to get water from dry wood, you cannot, because you are ignorant."[25]

Tao-ch'o then argued that his age is the period of *mo-fa,* far removed from the time of the Buddha and requiring a special means of salvation: namely, devotion to Amitābha and rebirth in his Pure Land. The majority of the *An-lo-chi,* his only surviving writing, is devoted to quoting scriptures which support Amitābha devotionalism, and to integrating the practice with the prevailing scriptures and philosophy of his time.

The *An-lo-chi* claims to be based on the *Kuan Wu-liang-shou ching,* but unlike T'an-luan, Tao-ch'o did not employ the style of careful exegesis. Rather he rambled from topic to topic and quoted from a wide variety of sources, much in the style of an evangelist. His aim was to persuade, not necessarily to be clear. In fact, one cannot tell from his writing that his major breakthrough in practice consisted in the endless repetition of the name of Amitābha and the use of beans or beads as counters.

The Second Phase

Both T'an-luan and Tao-ch'o were concerned to legitimate and integrate their devotional practices with the accepted orthodoxy of their day. For example, in his *An-lo-chi,* Tao-ch'o includes quotations from at least 45 sūtras, 1 vinaya, and 11 treatises and commentaries. Yamamoto Bukkotsu conservatively compiled a chart of 150 quotations from all sources,[26] while in an independent study Hashimoto Hōkei found 161 quotations from 56 sources, not including the many quotations from two works by T'an-luan.[27] When these sources are listed, Yamamoto found that 28 quotations come from the four main Pure Land scriptures, whereas a total of 31 quotations are from the *Nirvāṇa Sūtra* and the *Ta-chih-tu-lun.*[28]

The Third Phase

The concern to systematize and propagate Pure Land devotionalism is certainly a strong characteristic of both T'an-luan and Tao-ch'o. However, the flavor of their writings does not suggest a well-developed and secure pattern of thought and practice. Instead their main concern was to apply the Pure Land teachings to the crises they experienced and to justify this application by appeal to the accepted philosophy and scriptural traditions of their day. We find a different preoccupation when we turn to the writings of the next generation of disciples, Chia-tsai and Shan-tao (613–681).

Writing in the preface to his *Ching-t'u lun,*[29] Chia-tsai expressed a concern to clarify the disorganization manifested by Tao-ch'o in his *An-lo-chi.* Accordingly, he carefully developed a set of key scriptural passages in support of Pure Land devotionalism and listed the biographies of twenty Pure Land devotees (six monks, four nuns, five laymen, and five laywomen). The *Ching-t'u lun* marks the beginning of a series of Pure Land biographical collections which demonstrate not only the amazing extent of devotion by some, but also the miraculous manifestations that occurred during their deaths as a sign of their welcome by Amitābha into the Pure Land. Clearly this genre of writing represents a consolidation and celebration of Pure Land practice which also served to disseminate the teaching to new disciples.

About 150 years after Chia-tsai compiled his *Ching-t'u lun,* another biographical collection, compiled by Wen-shen and Shao-k'ang, appeared in 805.[30] A similar collection, the *Ching-t'u wang-sheng chuan,* was compiled by Chieh-chu in 1064.[31] These biographical collections, which have continued down to the present day in the Pure Land tradition, represent a different kind of interpretation since they have no concern to integrate their biographies with the larger Buddhist or Chinese cultural tradition, as well as no concern with the context of the lives presented. In seeking to present only those biographical details that reveal some Pure Land practice or spiritual manifestation, they demonstrate a hermeneutic of self-sufficiency.

Shan-tao (613–681) also represents a dramatic change from the writings of T'an-luan and Tao-ch'o. We find no sense of crisis or conflict in his life, and no trace of the sudden conversion in midlife that occurred for both T'an-luan and Tao-ch'o. Rather, as a youth he was apparently converted to Pure Land devotion upon seeing a picture of the Pure Land,[32] and it seems characteristic of Shan-tao's self-confidence that he does not acknowledge any debt to his predecessors. He does not go to great lengths to justify Pure Land ideas and practices in terms of śūnyatā and the theory of the two truths as did Tao-ch'o, and he thinks it harmful even to discuss such things.[33] Whereas Tao-ch'o made 150 references to other texts in his two-fascicle *An-lo-chi,* among the nine fascicles of Shan-tao's writings Kishi Kakuyū found only 126 references, and almost all of these were to Pure Land texts.[34]

Although skilled in art and textual exegesis, Shan-tao's place in history was achieved by using these gifts to firmly organize Pure Land thought and practice in such a way as to serve ordinary people of average capacities. This is shown by the more than three hundred pictures of the Pure Land that he distributed for popular edification. Also, his renown as a popular preacher was complemented by the widespread use of his liturgical writings, such as the *Fa-shih tsan,* the *Pan-chou san-mei tsan,* and the *Wang-sheng li-tsan-chi.* In particular, we can see this emphasis most clearly in his most important work, the *Kuan Wu-liang-shou ching shu.* Unlike the earlier commentary by Ching-ying Hui-yüan, Shan-tao insists that the instructions given in the *Kuan Wu-liang-shou ching* are meant for common laity and that its heroine, Queen Vaidēhī, was not a sage or bodhisattva in disguise, but was an ordinary person. Scriptural support was important to Shan-tao, and in his list of five correct practices *(wu-cheng-hsing)* he revises the five devotional gates found in the *Wang-sheng lun* by inserting the chanting of Pure Land scriptures as the first. However, this is a method of consolidation within Pure Land circles, and does not appeal to a larger interpretive framework.

More examples of self-sufficiency and self-promotion are found in the Pure Land polemical texts which began to appear in the eighth century. For example, the *Lüeh chu-ching-lun nien-fo fa-men wang-sheng ching-t'u chi* (A Collection Outlining Various Scriptures and Treatises Regarding Methods of Contemplating the Buddha and Rebirth in the Pure Land) by Tzu-min Hui-jih (680–748) originally included not only a compendium of Pure Land materials, but also an extensive and harsh attack against Ch'an.[35] The *Nien-fo ching* (A Mirror of Devotion to [Amitābha] Buddha) has a special section refuting six rival schools of Buddhism: the Three Stages sect, Maitreya devotionalism, Sitting Ch'an, scholars, the vinaya tradition, and those who cultivate the six perfections of a bodhisattva.[36] This text fails to treat these options seriously and doesn't try to integrate them with Pure Land practice, but instead simplifies them into easily dismissible stereotypes. This is a long way from the consideration given to Seng-chao by T'an-luan, or to the *Ta-chih-tu-lun* by Tao-ch'o. Other examples are such texts as the eighth-century *Ching-t'u shih-i lun,* which is falsely attributed to T'ien-t'ai Chih-i);[37] the *Shih Ching-t'u ch'ün-i lun* of Huai-kan (d. 701);[38] and the *Lüeh-lun An-lo Ching-t'u i* (which is falsely attributed to T'an-luan).[39]

There were other texts of the eighth century that attempted to integrate Pure Land devotionalism with the new movements of that time, such as Fei-hsi's *Nien-fo san-mei pao-wang lun,* written in 742.[40] These later texts are not devoid of an experimental dimension, and in that sense they echo the concerns of T'an-luan and Tao-ch'o, who tried to integrate Pure Land devotionalism with the concerns of their contemporaries. But if we restrict ourselves to the polemical texts of the eighth century whose intent is to defend and also indoctrinate Pure Land devotionalism, we find in them a very different quality from the conciliatory nature of Fei-hsi and the sixth and early seventh century, when the history of Pure Land theory and practice was less established. In particular, since the catechisms and polemical treatises of the eighth century had the advantage of drawing on earlier writings, they are both more focused in their topics and answers and more concerned with exposing their competitors' errors and inadequacies.

Since there were texts like those by Fei-hsi or later by Ssu-ming Chih-li (960–1028) which tried to relate Pure Land practice to that of other major schools of Buddhism, we must acknowledge that not only was there pluralism in the different schools, but there were also different levels and hermeneutical orientations among later practitioners. Thus, to some degree the first and second phases were repeated for some members of the tradition in each generation. The Pure Land tradition was able to maintain itself as a tradition insofar as later generations found meaningful experiences within the scope of the inherited theories and practices, albeit with some degree of reinterpretation or adaptation.

The Ch'an Tradition

In spite of Ch'an's reputation as an iconoclastic movement and its later fame for teaching "a special transmission outside the scriptures," its combined literary production was far larger than that of any other school of Chinese Buddhism. The textual history of Ch'an has been especially interesting to study because of the recovery in this century of early texts from the Tun-huang caves which have not only provided us with many new materials, but also shown that some of the most important traditional assumptions were based on heavily redacted texts. Accordingly, our present analysis of the early literary history of Ch'an must be considered tentative, since the relevant texts may have been subjected to significant revision.

The earliest texts that are associated with the Ch'an tradition are:

1. The *Treatise on the Two Entrances and Four Practices (Erh-ju ssu-hsing lun,* or *EJSHL),* attributed to Bodhidharma

2. The *Teachings on the Essential Expedient Means for Entering the Path and Pacifying the Mind (Ju-tao an-hsin yao fang-pien fa-men,* or *JTAHY),* attributed to Tao-hsin (580–651)
3. The *Treatise on the Essentials of Cultivating the Mind (Hsiu-hsin yao lun,* or *HHYL),* compiled as a collection of the teachings of Hung-jen (600–674) by his students
4. The epitaph for Fa-ju (638–689)
5. The *Treatise on Contemplating the Mind (Kuan-hsin lun),* by Shen-hsiu (606?–706)
6. The *Treatise on Perfect Illumination (Yüan-ming lun),* attributed to Shen-hsiu
7. The *Five Expedient Means (Wu fang-pien),* attributed to Shen-hsiu
8. The *Annals of the Transmission of the Dharma-treasure (Ch'üan fa-pao chi),* by the layman Tu Fei (by 710)
9. The *Records of the Masters and Disciples of the Laṅkāvatāra (Leng-ch'ieh shih-tz'u chi,* or *LCSTS),* by Ching-chüeh (ca. 714)

For the purposes of this essay, I shall follow the majority of modern scholars in accepting these nine texts as the oldest surviving writings of Ch'an, even though debate over their authenticity continues.

The First Phase

The shorter *EJSHL*[41] by Bodhidharma quotes two lines from the *Vimalakīrti Sūtra* as an illustration. Bodhidharma is also said to have handed a copy of the *Laṅkāvatāra Sūtra* to his disciple, and is thus placed at the head of a *Laṅkāvatāra* exegetical lineage covering four generations. Since none of the texts from this lineage survive, it is difficult to speculate about the hermeneutical methods that were used. However, we can observe that the style of the *EJSHL* is the opposite of the exegetical approach. Instead of relying on line-by-line commentary, in the *EJSHL* Bodhidharma teaches on the authority of his own experience. Although the themes that the text summarizes are classic topics in Mahāyāna, the style is simple and direct, without linguistic flourishes or any appeal to outside authorities, earlier masters or lineages, or extraordinary powers.

From the very beginning and throughout most of its development, Ch'an texts emphasize both the personal, experiential nature of practice and a straightforward and direct style of teaching this practice to disciples. The *JTAHY* attributed to Tao-hsin (580–651) and the *HHYL* attributed to Hung-jen (601–674) continue this attitude of the *EJSHL,* but with important new additions. For the first time, we see scriptural quotations sprinkled throughout the text as illustrations and proof texts. In addition, both treatises employ the question-and-answer format that had been developed as a means of conveying Buddhist teachings that were theoretical or philosophical in nature. Zürcher notes that this format was a legacy of the *ch'ing-t'an* or "pure conversation" style used by the educated elite in rhetorical contests and philosophical debate, and that from the fourth century on "practically all Buddhist apologetic and propagandistic treatises have the form of a dialogue between the author (the 'host') and an imaginary opponent (the 'guest'), in which both parties alternately formulate their views and objections, the 'opponent' finally declaring himself vanquished and convinced."[42]

The dialogue form was also used in Pure Land writings to interpret and convey their teachings, but to a lesser degree than in Ch'an. For example, when T'an-luan felt it necessary to raise important points that were not addressed directly by his text, the *Wang-sheng lun-chu,* he duly interrupts his exegesis with a set of eight questions and answers.[43] In later Ch'an writings, of course, the quality of the dialogue changes when the actions as well as the words are seen as revealing the teaching. This development led to the creation of the distinctive Ch'an literature called *yü-lu,* in which were recorded the sayings and activities of Ch'an masters beginning in the eighth century with Ma-tsu (709–788). The uniqueness of the *yü-lu* texts derives from the assumption that enlightenment is best revealed not only in the explicit teachings but also in the daily activities and encounters of enlightened masters. The transmission lineages, representing the second phase, legitimize these methods, and in the third phase the *yü-lu* encounter literature is further edited and systematized into *kung-an* (Jp. *kōan*) collections for the purpose of systematic propagation.

While the *yü-lu* literature emphasizes the activities of Ch'an masters, it also includes their recorded sayings as well, thus exhibiting a strong continuity with earlier Ch'an treatises such as the *JTAHY* and the *HHYL,* which employ dialogues, and with the *EJSHL,* which is informal enough to count as a summary of the personal teaching of Bodhidharma. The development of this personal, informal style—communicating Buddhist teaching directed at immediate experience rather than scholastic discourse—may thus be taken to predate the *yü-lu* literature and is to be found at the beginning of Ch'an.

As I have suggested, texts intended to meet personal religious needs is characteristic of the earliest literature of a new movement. What is unusual is the continuing production and popularity of this kind of literature at the heart of the Ch'an tradition. Indeed, following the *yü-lu* documents, the *kung-an* collections were also used and interpreted precisely as tools for a personally efficacious practice, rather than merely as literary anthologies or historical records.[44]

The earliest substantial body of writings by a Chinese Ch'an master are the works attributed to Shen-hsiu (606?–706), principally the *Kuan-hsin lun* (Treatise on Contemplating the Mind), *Yüan-ming lun* (Treatise on Perfect Illumination), and *Wu fang-pien* (Five Expedient Means).[45] The *Yüan-ming lun* slightly revises T'ien-t'ai categories for classifying Buddhist texts and divides Buddhism into three types of teaching: gradual, sudden, and perfect. When explaining the gradual teaching, Shen-hsiu says:

> The understanding of ignorant people is completely dependent on the scriptures. Although the scriptures are without error, they must be understood according to one's disposition, which does not [necessarily] match the enlightenment of other people.[46]

For the unenlightened, then, Shen-hsiu recognizes that there would be differences in the interpretation of scriptures. However, when explaining (in a question-and-answer format) the ten aspects of the perfect teaching, he proposes that for those who are enlightened:

> There is only the practice of non-substantiality and the salvation of beings, but no additional intention whatsoever. . . . You must make effort for many a day, dispensing with conventional toils and sitting quietly in meditation *(ching-tso ssu-wei).* You cannot understand the principle of this through an [insight] into a text [gained] during recitation. There is no mutual relationship [between that kind of insight and the realization referred to here]. This is an understanding [based on something] other than one's own efforts. This is a practice [based on something] other than one's own practice. By meditating thus you will avoid errors.[47]

This is an unusually clear statement illustrating the discontinuity of understanding derived from intimate personal experience and the normal scholastic activity of exegesis. As such it illustrates the concerns associated with the first phase of a religion. Moreover, the passage points directly to the fundamental hermeneutical principle of Ch'an: texts can be interpreted adequately only by enlightened masters. It is on this basis that Ch'an makes its claim of penetrating to the "cardinal meaning" of a text,[48] a recurring phrase used by Ch'an masters.

The Second Phase

In spite of Chan's claim of basing its teaching authority on personal experience, from the beginning Ch'an teachings were also interpreted with some reference to the established scriptures. This concern for legitimation through integration with the inherited tradition becomes even more pronounced when later texts actively create lineages claiming authenticity of descent from a line of enlightened teachers.

In the western tradition, Gnostic hermeneutics urged that seekers should rely on spiritual inspiration as being superior to the truth transmitted in written texts or by human authorities. Accordingly, Gnosticism was seen as a major threat to the institutional church, and it was purged from existence. Ch'an, however, was not so radical. All its early texts are related to some scriptural source, or to a lineage of enlightened masters. Also, it is important to remember that most Ch'an masters adhered to the monastic system, even when they were questioning meditation practices, experimenting with scriptural usage, or devising new bodhisattva precepts. Thus the Ch'an tradition continued to possess the basic heritage of Canonical Buddhism in common with other schools of Chinese Buddhism.

The earliest associations with particular Indian scriptures are the quotation in the *EJSHL* from the *Vimalakīrti Sūtra* and Bodhidharma's connection with the *Laṅkāvatāra Sūtra.* The *EJSHL* legacy was transmitted through Bodhidharma's disciple T'an-lin, and the *Vimalakīrti* continued to play a major role for the Ch'an tradition both as a text and as a role model.[49] Of equal importance in the early period of Ch'an was the place of Bodhidharma at the head of a *Laṅkāvatāra* exegetical lineage that included his disciple Hui-k'o, followed by Master Na, his disciple Hui-man (589–642), and finally Fa-ch'ung (587?–665?). In Fa-ch'ung's biography[50] there are twenty-eight people associated with this exegetical line, twelve of whom had written commentaries totaling seventy fascicles.

This lineage of Bodhidharma became formalized when it acquired the name of the One Vehicle school, based on the doctrine of the one vehicle found in the *Laṅkāvatāra Sūtra:* namely, that the enlightened do not discriminate, for there is no grasping and nothing grasped, but only abiding in suchness.[51] A second theme from the *Laṅkāvatāra* that assumed major importance for early Ch'an was the doctrine of an esoteric teaching transmitted outside of written and verbal forms.[52] We do not find this idea in the *JTAHY* or *HHYL,*[53] and the earliest appearance of it in connection with Ch'an is in the epitaph to Fa-ju (d. 689).[54] Nevertheless, based on the brief summary in Fa-ju's epitaph, and the later use of the *Laṅkāvatāra* by Ch'an masters, we can surmise that Bodhidharma's *Laṅkāvatāra* lineage probably did not adopt the line-by-line exegetical method, but instead was more interpretive in its treatment of scripture, perhaps with even more freedom than that shown by T'ien-t'ai Chih-i's *Fa-hua hsüan-i.* As a hermeneutical device, the doctrine of an esoteric teaching was used (1) to justify the role of the enlightened master, (2) to allow a certain measure of freedom from scholasticism and the literal interpretation of texts, (3) to support the idea that each text had a "cardinal meaning," and (4) to protect the central article of faith that the underlying meaning was the *same* in all authentic Buddhist writings.

Another important early Ch'an tradition was based on the use of the Perfection of Wisdom teachings contained in texts such as the *Vimalakīrti Sūtra, Heart Sūtra, Diamond Sūtra, Wen-shu shuo po-jo ching,* and the like. Although the *JTAHY* quotes the *Laṅkāvatāra Sūtra* once, it quotes the *Vimalakīrti Sūtra* and other Perfection of Wisdom texts ten times, constituting over one-third of the scriptural references in the text. Most prominent is the *Vimalakīrti Sūtra,* which is quoted five times, and the *Wen-shu shuo po-jo ching,* representing the basic paradigm for the whole *JTAHY.* Similarly, the *Vimalakīrti Sūtra* is the most frequently quoted text in the *HHYL,* although the *Lotus* and *Nirvāṇa* are quoted almost as often. (In the Tun-huang text of the *Platform Sūtra* we also find the *Vimalakīrti Sūtra* prominent with five quotations.)

These citations are consistently used as proof texts for the particular practice and teaching that is being advocated. There is no concern to be true to the text as a whole, or to survey every part. Furthermore, the sections that are quoted frequently are used to fortify the idea of the inadequacy of words or conceptualizations as a vehicle for conveying the truth. As a consequence, the tradition is used to transcend the tradition: that is, selected quotations are drawn from the scriptures in order to legitimize ignoring the rest of the scriptures. Instead, reliance is placed on individual practice and inner realization of the truth. Interpretative distinctions are to be applied to *people,* not to texts. According to Ch'an, the texts have the same fundamental meaning but are seen as different because of our different levels of attainment.

The one possible exception to this generalization is the exegesis presented in Shen-hsiu's *Wu fang-pien* (Five Expedient Means), which, as the most systematic classification of scriptures found in early Ch'an texts, echoes the approaches of other Chinese Buddhist schools.[55] However, as the study of this text by Robert Zeuschner shows,[56] the primary concern of the *Wu fang-pien* is with the spiritual development of the practitioner, not with the internal characteristics of the scriptures that are discussed.

Specifically, the *Wu fang-pien* begins with a liturgical outline of vows and questions-and-responses, followed by five sections called the five "expedients" *(upāya).* The first section is based on the *Awakening of Faith,*[57] the second is summarized by a quote from the *Lotus Sūtra,*[58] and the third is almost a line-by-line commentary on selected dialogues from the *Vimalakīrti.*[59] The fourth section opens with a quotation from the *Sūtra of the God Ssu-i,*[60] and the last section uses two short quotations from the *Avataṃsaka Sūtra.*[61] Robert Zeuschner points out that while Shen-hsiu says that these texts should be studied in order to lead people to enlightenment, he makes no comment on the relationship between the texts or the distinctiveness of their contents.[62] Nevertheless, it is interesting to note that even in nonsectarian biographies, Shen-hsiu is credited with the practice of checking newly translated scriptures to verify their Ch'an meaning.[63]

The classic Ch'an patriarchal line of Bodhidharma to Hui-k'o to Seng-tsan to Tao-hsin and to Hung-jen first appears in Fa-ju's epitaph, written around 689. This lineage and its transmission of an elitist and esoteric teaching of the Buddha based on the *Awakening of Faith* and the *Laṅkāvatāra* tradition became formalized in the early eighth century in the *Ch'üan fa-pao chi* (Annals of the Transmission of the Dharma-treasure).[64] In spite of the Ch'an emphasis on mind and nonreliance on any external authority, the role of the enlightened master and the importance of an explicit line of transmission were used in this text to form a substitute structure of authority and legitimacy. Although such lineages were usually developed in retrospect during the early period,[65] they were a natural development from the hermeneutical principle that true teachings are determined only by enlightened masters who have actualized the truth of the teachings.

A major legitimizing device from the eighth century on was the "transmission of the lamp" histories of mind-to-mind transmission from enlightened masters. Indeed, the recorded sayings and activities of these enlightened masters came to constitute the largest literary collection of any school of Chinese Buddhism. Although Ch'an lineages did provide a method of legitimation, much like the earlier vinaya lineages,[66] they generally did not involve an integration with Buddhism as a whole but functioned in competition with those of other groups. Moreover, Ch'an writers often redacted the biographies composed by Tao-hsüan in his *Hsü Kao-seng chuan* to fit the needs and interests of Ch'an propagation, making the Ch'an "transmission of the lamp" collections conform to the characteristics we have associated with the third hermeneutical phase.[67]

The Third Phase

When Ch'an began to systematize itself, its two primary concerns were organizing its spiritual genealogies into lineages and reducing the *yü-lu* to more compact episodes which eventually formed the *kung-an* collections.[68]

Obviously when a lineage is constructed, it not only legitimizes those who have inherited the line but also simplifies Buddhist history by ignoring those teachers who are not part of the true line. Moreover, it propagates its teachings with the assertion that those who want to attain the truth should adhere to this true lineage. Thus, a lineage is also a method of interpretation, segregation, and control.

The classic example is the encyclopedic *Ching-te ch'üan-teng lu* (Transmission of the Lamp), composed in 1004. Besides compiling and redacting the biographies of numerous Ch'an masters, it begins with the lives and teachings of the seven Buddhas of the past and the twenty-eight Indian patriarchs and ends in the line of transmission from Bodhidharma to Hui-neng. Instead of trying to embrace the whole range of Buddhist leaders (preachers, vinaya masters, exegetes, wonder workers, etc.) in the style of the sixth-century *Kao-seng chuan* and its later emulators, it only considers Ch'an masters who had experienced the transmission of true enlightenment to represent Buddhism; the rest are regarded as examples of unenlightenment and failure. As a consequence, some very specific hermeneutical principles guide its redaction of historical materials. As John McRae writes:

> The transmission histories, like all other Ch'an works, were intended to function as catalysts for the enlightenment of the readers by exposing them to examples of true religiosity and perfected behavior. In addition to this lofty goal, these texts had two other purposes of a propagandistic and quasi-historical nature: (1) to glorify the sages of the past and thereby legitimize the status of their living disciples and (2) to rationalize the origins and existence of the Ch'an School itself.[69]

Not only did the "transmission of the lamp" biographies alter historical details, but even some of the earlier *yü-lu* were redacted for the purposes of propagation. This process is clearly illustrated in an episode from the *Ma-tsu yü-lu,* the earliest of the *yü-lu.* In the encounter of Wu-yeh with Ma-tsu, he is said to have asked Ma-tsu, "What is the meaning of the patriarch's coming from the west and transmitting the mind seal?" Ma-tsu responded by saying that there was too much commotion, so he should leave and return at a later time. But as Wu-yeh was leaving, Ma-tsu called out to him. When Wu-yeh turned his head, Ma-tsu asked "What is it?" Thereupon Wu-yeh was enlightened.[70] This event is also recorded in the *Sung Kao-seng chuan,* which is based on the historically reliable memorial of Wu-yeh himself,[71] and from its account a less abrupt and more understandable event emerges. In this version, Wu-yeh is enlightened after a straightforward discussion in which Ma-tsu teaches him that the way is not separate from ordinary living beings, and that Buddhahood is not external. Rather, it is like the hand making a fist while still remaining a hand. In the *yü-lu,* not only is discussion rejected, but after his enlightenment Wu-yeh is described as bowing to Ma-tsu, who dismisses him with the words "You fool! Why thank me?" In the earlier account Wu-yeh is reported as saying:

> It has always been maintained that the Buddha-path is long and far, and that it can only be realized after a great number of kalpas of effort and suffering. Today I know for the first time that the true reality of the Dharma-

> kāya is actually perfectly present in myself. All dharmas arise from the mind; they are only ideas and shapes and not reality.[72]

Ma-tsu approved of this statement, and added, "The nature of all dharmas neither arises nor ceases. All dharmas are fundamentally empty and quiet. In the scriptures it is said that all dharmas are originally and always appearances of nirvāṇa."[73]

Ch'an's radical rejection of a conceptual approach to enlightenment and the scriptures is also vividly present in the story of Ma-tsu's encounter with the exegetical master Liang.[74] In this encounter Ma-tsu rejects Liang's claim to be able to interpret scriptures with the mind, since it is so unreliable and contentious. Liang counters with the rhetorical question "What else could one use, empty space?" And Ma-tsu affirms the idea. Liang leaves in protest, but once again Ma-tsu calls out just as Liang is going down the steps, and he turns and is enlightened. Upon returning to his home temple, Liang confesses that although he had thought he was supreme in his interpretation of the scriptures, with one question Ma-tsu had taken his achievements and melted them like ice and crumbled them like pottery. Thereupon he left for the western mountains and was never seen again.[75]

In later periods the major hermeneutical problem for Ch'an was how to interpret the vast literature Ch'an itself had generated so that the teaching could be transmitted and understood by succeeding generations. Specifically, the problem was how to use the collected *yü-lu,* the biographies in the sacred lineage, and the *kung-an* collections. As Wu-men says about the remarks made by the former masters Kan-feng and Yün-men in case forty-eight of the *Wu-men men,* when he examines them "with the true eye, neither of the old masters knows where the way is."[76] Thus, even *kung-an* that had been redacted and commented upon by earlier masters were perceived as inadequate. All props are taken away and no texts or hermeneutical methods are left, except for recourse to religious practice under an enlightened master. In this way, the use of scripture, transmission lineages, *yü-lu,* and *kung-an* collections is relegated to a secondary level, as hermeneutical variations on the recurring Ch'an challenge to seek enlightenment oneself through a face-to-face encounter with a Ch'an master.

Conclusion

When we examine early Canonical Chinese Buddhism, early Pure Land, and early Ch'an literary history from the standpoint of the three hermeneutical phases, certain functional differences and similarities become clear. In all cases the new movements began by interpreting

Buddhist scriptures in a personally meaningful and relevant way. Early Chinese Buddhist literary movements were easily related to *hsüan-hsüeh* ideas, and "matched meanings" with Taoist terms. Meditation, moreover, was introduced as a means of relief from the socio-political woes of the time. When validation came to be sought from the authority represented by Buddhist scriptures, great attention was given to translating and compiling the full corpus of Indian Buddhist texts.

The Pure Land devotional tradition began for T'an-luan as a response to his impotency in the face of sickness and death. It became a popular movement with Tao-ch'o (562–645), who saw it as a means of relief from the chaos of war, famine, and the disestablishment of the Buddhist monasteries.[77] Since the staggering demands of mastering Indian Buddhist ideas, texts, and practices had become a burden rather than a source of relief, Pure Land leaders opted for the simple and accessible practice of appealing to Amitābha's compassionate power for rebirth in his Pure Land. The literal details and authority of the Pure Land scriptures became very important for sanctioning the setting aside of other scriptural demands, and as a guide for the interpretation of validating miracles. By contrast, Ch'an offset the demands of the new orthodoxy of Indian Buddhist scriptures by placing its trust in the personal authority of enlightened masters.

Pure Land thinkers legitimized their outlook, values, and practices by appeal to history and to direct scriptural quotation. Since certain scriptures argued that the teachings must be related to the times, Pure Land scriptures were accordingly chosen as the appropriate ones for this age and all other texts were downgraded. Ch'an emphasized reliance on one's own inner experience to authenticate the validity of the teachings, but also appealed to specific texts such as the *Laṅkāvatāra Sutra* to justify its special orientation and dismissal of scholasticism. In the end, both sectarian movements legitimized themselves (1) by reference to the sacred tradition, and (2) through the example of the lives of their spiritual masters. However, Pure Land and Ch'an relied on different scriptures, different principles, and different personal experiences for their validation. These methods undoubtedly appealed to different kinds of people, and were used to justify their departure from the larger Canonical Chinese Buddhist tradition. Supported by an appeal to selected scriptures, the establishment of a line of enlightened masters was crucial for Ch'an whereas biographical collections reporting supernatural occurrences served to authenticate faith in Amitābha and rebirth in his Pure Land.

The methods of systematized propagation were quite different. Pure Land produced many devotional and ritual manuals, as well as catechisms in the question-and-answer format. Pure Land ritual texts appeared as early as the first hermeneutical phase of the movement in practices devised by Lu-shan Hui-yüan, T'an-luan, and Shan-tao. By comparison, texts for ritual practice do not occur in early Ch'an except as sections of the teachings of Shen-hsiu. However, the encounter with the enlightened master became its own ritual, which later was hallowed and preserved in *kung-an* collections.

The example of T'ien-t'ai doctrinal history serves as a warning that the hermeneutics of a diverse religious community cannot be schematized into exclusive phases or time periods. T'ien-t'ai Chih-i did not advocate a "five period" scheme (based on the five periods of the Buddha's life) for organizing Buddhist texts, but used a "five flavor" scheme, implying variations but not exclusive ones—the categories are more suggestive than they are definitive. Moreover, those who have a keen sense of taste can find all five flavors subtly present in each, so that any one flavor can serve as a vehicle for the whole truth when properly perceived.[78]

Similarly, the three hermeneutical phases described in this essay are a heuristic device and do not always correspond to historically separate periods either in the life of a religious tradition or in the life of an individual. Any religious community must embody all three phases to some degree. Those that never get beyond the first phase will not be perpetuated, just as those that remain in the third phase will wither and die. In contrast to the Chinese claim that there is one essence *(t'i)* and many functions *(yung),* the scheme of three hermeneutical phases analyzes different religious groups in terms of shared functions *(yung),* which assume a variety of methods or forms *(hsiang),* while leaving unanswered the question of their essence *(t'i).* Also unanswered is the modern hermeneutical question regarding Chinese Buddhist theories of understanding, where the focus is not on motives and methods for interpreting texts but on the nature of human understanding and the role of sacred texts in this process.

Notes

1. See John Maraldo, "A Review of Some Approaches to Hermeneutics and Historicality in the Study of Buddhism," *Shin Buddhist Comprehensive Research Institute Annual Memoirs,* 1985: 1–26.

2. In particular, Yogācāra texts would probably be useful in analyzing the processes of understanding. For example, see Diana Paul, *Philosophy of Mind in Sixth Century China* (Palo Alto, Calif.: Stanford University Press, 1985).

3. The scheme of three phases that I use for my analysis of Chinese Buddhist hermeneutics is derived from observations made by Kenelm Burridge in his study of the rise of millenarian religions among smaller societies, as reported in his *New Heaven New Earth: A Study of Millenarian Activities* (New York: Schocken

Books, 1969). Burridge proposed three phases in the development of millenarian movements:

> 1. An individual sense of disenfranchisement from the mainstream of power precipitates a search of the inherited world of knowledge, especially classical scriptures in a literate society, in order to find principles concerning redemption that are more fundamental than those in contemporary institutions. This is "essentially an attempt to explain and comprehend the fact of disenfranchisement." Then there "must be some way of gaining an acknowledged integrity." This is followed by a sharing among other alienated individuals until a new common ground is found which evolves into a new kind of social being (pp. 105–107).
>
> 2. The second phase is a testing of the tentative conclusions through external organization and legitimation: "their activities will remain disorganized until a prophet appears. . . . Whatever the cultural idiom, the message is taken to be beyond man's wit to devise. It is a divine revelation. It transcends the capacities of a man acting alone" (p. 111).
>
> 3. The third phase involves the use of organizational skills to deploy the new assumptions either into the mainstream or separately as a new sect, or else the cycle begins again.

4. The most exhaustive and reliable history of the first four centuries of Buddhism in China is E. Zürcher's *The Buddhist Conquest of China* (Leiden: Brill, 1959). See chap. 1, where he surveys the surviving literature and discusses the major problems.

5. See ibid., 184, for a discussion of this term.

6. Buddhism had entered China in the first century A.D. and the first translations of Buddhist texts began in the second century, but it was not until nearly the beginning of the fourth century that Chinese literati began to convert to Buddhism. Following Zürcher, we can date the beginning of Chinese Buddhist hermeneutics as the moment when Buddhism first attracted the attention of the learned class: the reported cases in both Buddhist and secular literature "of contact between the clergy and the Chinese cultured upper class before 290 A.D. is negligible, whereas in the biographies of late third and fourth century monks such facts are mentioned in ever increasing numbers" (ibid., 71).

7. Ibid., 86–95, gives a review of these intellectual movements.

8. Ibid., 100–102.

9. Translation by Derk Bodde, *A History of Chinese Philosophy,* vol. 2 (Princeton: Princeton University Press, 1953), 285.

10. See Arthur Wright, "Biography and Hagiography Hui-chiao's *Lives of Eminent Monks,*" in *Silver Jubilee Volume of the Zinbun-Kagaku-Kenkyū-syo* (Kyoto, 1954), 383–432.

11. See Leon Hurvitz, *Chih-i (538–597), Mélanges chinois et bouddhiques* 12 (1960–1962): 214–229, for an excellent summary of the early *p'an-chiao* schemes. For their interpretation within the history of Buddhist hermeneutics, see Robert A. F. Thurman, "Buddhist Hermeneutics," *Journal of the American Academy of Religion* 46, no. 1 (1978): 19–39.

12. For an overview of these various *p'an-chiao* systems, see Hurvitz, *Chih-i,* 214–229.

13. See John R. McRae, *The Northern School and the Formation of Early Ch'an Buddhism,* Studies in East Asian Buddhism, no. 3 (Honolulu: University of Hawaii Press, 1986), 79–80 and 298 n. 197.

14. Ibid., and 299 n. 198.

15. The most important statement concerning the T'ien-t'ai lineage was made by Kuan-ting in his preface to the *Mo-ho chih-kuan* by Chih-i, *T* 46.1a–b. This list was based on the *Fu-tsang yin-yüan chuan (History of the Transmission of the Dharma-store)* translated into Chinese in the latter half of the fifth century. See McRae, *The Northern School,* 82–83 and 299–300 n. 205; and Neal Donner, "The Great Calming and Contemplation of Chih-i, Chapter One: The Synopsis" (Ph.D. diss., University of British Columbia, 1976), 36–39.

16. See Wright, "Biography and Hagiography," 410–412.

17. Ibid., especially 384–394.

18. See Kathryn A. A. Cissell, "The *Pi-ch'iu-ni chuan:* Biographies of Famous Chinese Nuns from 317-516 C.E." (Ph.D. diss., University of Wisconsin, 1972), 47.

19. See the study of Albert Dalia, "The 'Political Career' of the Buddhist Historian Tsan-ning," in David Chappell, ed., *Buddhist and Taoist Practice in Medieval Chinese Society,* Asian Studies at Hawaii, no. 34 (Honolulu: University of Hawaii Press, 1987), 146–180.

20. See Hurvitz, *Chih-i,* 183–271. Thurman summarizes the highpoints in "Buddhist Hermeneutics," 29–31.

21. The total size of the *Fa-hua hsüan-i* may be gauged from the fact that it occupies pages 681–814 in vol. 33 of the Taisho edition, out of which pages 691a–779a are devoted to different aspects of the title of the *Lotus.*

22. See Roger Corless, "T'an-luan: Taoist Sage and Buddhist Bodhisattva," in Chappell, *Buddhist and Taoist Practice in Medieval Chinese Society.*

23. See *T* 40.827b.26 and 838c.16f.

24. *T* 47.12b.8–9.

25. *T* 47.4a.26f.

26. Yamamoto Bukkotsu, *Dōshaku kyōgaku no kenkyū* (Kyoto: Nagata bunshōdō, 1957), 77–83.

27. Hashimoto Hōkei, "*Anrakushū* no honshitsu to sono dentō ni kansuru ichi kōsatsu," *Indogaku bukkyōgaku kenkyū* 11, no. 2 (March 1963): 26–32. The many more references listed by Hashimoto in comparison to Yamamoto can be attributed to the fact that he lists not just quotations from texts but also references to them as well.

28. Although the *Nirvāṇa Sūtra* is often quoted, since it was very popular, and Tao-ch'o had been its advocate early in his life, in the *An-lo-chi* it only serves as a negative example. By contrast, Tao-ch'o uses the Perfection of Wisdom philosophy of emptiness as a basis for his thought, much like T'an-luan. T'an-luan emerges as the dominant influence in the *An-lo-chi,* since Yamamoto found fifteen direct quotations of T'an-luan in the *An-lo-chi* and an additional thirty-four phrases and ideas.

29. A three-fascicle work, *T* 47.93–104.

30. *Wang-sheng hsi-fang ching-t'u jui-ying (shan) chuan,* *T* 51.104–108.

31. *T* 51.108–126.

32. *T* 51.105b.

33. *T* 37.351.1–2.

34. Kishi Kakuyū, *Zoku Zendō kyōgaku no kenkyū* (Yamaguchi, Mie, Japan: Kishi Zenji Sangōkai, 1966), 7–8.

35. See my study of Tzu-min Hui-jih, "From Dispute to Dual Cultivation," in Peter N. Gregory, ed., *Traditions of Meditation in Chinese Buddhism,* Studies in East Asian Buddhism, no. 4 (Honolulu: University of Hawaii Press, 1986).

36. See *T* 47.126c–130a.
37. *T* 47.77–81. See the study and translation by Leo Pruden, "The Ching-t'u Shih-i-lun (Ten Doubts Concerning the Pure Land)," *The Eastern Buddhist,* n.s. 6, no. 1 (May 1973): 126–157.
38. *T* 47.30–76.
39. *T* 47.1–4a. See Ishida Mitsuyuki, *Jōdokyō shiri* (Kyoto, 1962), 62.
40. See a review of this text in Chappell, "From Dispute to Dual Cultivation," 175–179.
41. I am referring to the short form of this text which is found both in Tunhuang manuscripts and also in the *Hsü Kao-seng chuan* of Tao-hsüan. For a translation and study of this text in its long form, see John Jorgensen, "The Long Scroll: The Earliest Text of Ch'an Buddhism" (M.A. thesis, Australian National University, 1979).
42. Zürcher, *Buddhist Conquest of China*, 93.
43. *Wang-sheng lun-chu, T* 40.833c.20–834c.27.
44. Even though this was the purpose of the *kung-an,* as collections were written down and made available it became a persistent temptation to treat them as literature or history. See Isshū Miura and Ruth Fuller Sasaki, *The Zen Kōan* (New York: Harcourt, Brace & World, 1965), 11–12.
45. John R. McRae's *The Northern School,* 149–196, provides a study of these treatises and includes complete translations of the *Yüan-ming lun* and *Wu fang-pien*.
46. McRae, *The Northern School,* 151.
47. Ibid., 159.
48. See Michael Pye's insightful article "Comparative Hermeneutics in Religion," in Michael Pye and Robert Morgan, eds., *The Cardinal Meaning: Essays in Comparative Hermeneutics: Buddhism and Christianity* (The Hague: Mouton, 1973), for a discussion of the conflict between those who argue for the "essential meaning" of a religious tradition in contrast to historians who notice that the meaning of a religious tradition changes over time and in different contexts.
49. See Richard Mather's article on the early enthusiasm of the Chinese for the *Vimalakīrti Sūtra,* entitled "Vimalakīrti and Gentry Buddhism," *History of Religions* 8 (1968): 60–73.
50. *T* 50.666a–c.
51. *T* 16.497b.5–9
52. *T* 16.506c.
53. However, the *JTAHY* and *HHYL* might not have been in the *Laṅkāvatāra* line, even though Tao-hsin and Hung-jen are listed by Fa-ju and are inserted into the *Leng-ch'ieh shih-tzu chi* (A Record of the Masters and Disciples of the *Laṅkāvatāra*) in the early eighth century.
54. See the text reprinted in Yanagida Seizan, *Shoki Zenshū shisho no kenkyū* (Kyoto: Hozokan, 1967), 487.
55. See the fivefold classification of scriptures by the T'ien-t'ai school in Hurvitz, *Chih-i,* 214–244.
56. Robert Zeuschner analyzes the use of scriptures in the *Wu fang-pien* in his "Methods of Awakening in Northern Ch'an," in Chappell, *Buddhist and Taoist Practice,* 87–97.
57. See Y. S. Hakeda, *The Awakening of Faith* (New York: Columbia University Press, 1967).
58. See Leon Hurvitz, *Scripture of the Lotus Blossom of the Fine Dharma* (New York: Columbia University Press, 1976).

59. For a comparison of the Tibetan and Chinese versions, see Étienne Lamotte, tr., *L'Enseignement de Vimalakīrti* (Louvain: Publications Universitaires, 1962), recently rendered into English by Sara Boin as *The Teaching of Vimalakīrti,* Sacred Books of the Buddhists, vol. 32 (London: The Pali Text Society, 1976).

60. *T* 15.36b–c.

61. See Thomas Cleary, *The Flower Garland Scripture,* 3 vols. (Boulder, Colo.: Shambhala Press, 1984, 1986, and 1987).

62. Zeuschner, "Methods of Awakening."

63. See the *Sung Kao-seng chuan,* compiled in 988, *T* 50.724c.

64. For a study and translation of this text, see McRae, *The Northern School,* 86–88, 255–269.

65. See Philip Yampolsky, *The Platform Sūtra of the Sixth Patriarch* (New York: Columbia University Press, 1967), 6–23.

66. See above, "Canonical Buddhism, The Third Phase."

67. See McRae, *The Northern School,* chap. 5 ("Development of the 'Transmission of the Lamp' Histories").

68. See Miura and Sasaki, *The Zen Kōan,* for a history of the earliest development of the *kung-an* collections in China.

69. McRae, *The Northern School,* 75.

70. *Hsü Tsang Ching,* vol. 119 (Hong Kong: Fo-ching liu-t'ung ch'u, 1967), 407d.

71. *T* 50.772.

72. Quoted from the translation by Julian Pas of Bavo Lievens, *Ma-tsu De Gesprekken* (Bussum: Het Wereldvenster, 1981), msp. 81.

73. Ibid.

74. *Ma-tsu yü-lu,* in *Hsü Tsang Ching,* 119:408a.

75. A similar example of the burning of scriptural commentaries after experiencing enlightenment is found in case 28 of the *Wu-men men, T* 48.296–c.

76. *T* 48.299a.1–11.

77. See my "Tao-ch'o (562–645): A Pioneer of Chinese Pure Land Buddhism" (Ph.D. diss., Yale University, 1976), 46–57 and 121–126.

78. See David W. Chappell, ed., *T'ien-t'ai Buddhism: An Outline of the Fourfold Teachings* (Tokyo: Daiichi-Shobō, 1983), 36–39.

Glossary

Chan-jan 湛然
Chih-i 智顗
Ching-te ch'üan-teng lu 景德傳燈錄
ching-tso ssu-wei 靜坐思惟
ching-t'u 淨土
Ching-t'u lun 淨土論
Ching-t'u shih-i lun 淨土十疑論
Ching-t'u wang-sheng chuan 淨土往生傳
Ching-ying Hui-yüan 淨影慧遠
ch'ing-t'an 清談
Ch'u san-tsang chih-chi 出三藏記集
Ch'üan fa-pao chi 傳法寶紀
Erh-ju ssu-hsing lun 二入四行論
Fa-ch'ung 法沖
Fa-hua hsüan-i 法華玄義
Fa-ju 法如
Fei-hsi 飛錫
hsiang 相
Hsiu-hsin yao lun 修心要論
hsüan-hsüeh 玄學
Hui-chiao 慧皎
Hui-ssu 慧思
Hung-jen 弘忍
Hung-ming chi 弘明集

Ju-tao an-hsin yao fang-pien fa-men 入道安心要方便法門
Kao-seng chuan 高僧傳
ko-i 格義
Kuan-hsin lun 觀心論
Kuan Wu-liang-shou ching shu 觀無量壽經疏
kung-an 公案
Leng-ch'ie shih-tz'u chi 楞伽師資記
Lüeh chu-ching-lun nien-fo fa-men wang-sheng ching-t'u chi 略諸經論念佛法門往生淨土集
Lüeh-lun An-lo Ching-t'u i 略論安樂淨土義
Lu-shan Hui-yüan 盧山慧遠
Ma-tsu 馬祖
Ma-tsu yü-lu 馬祖語錄
Ming-seng chuan 名僧傳
mo-fa 末法
Nien-fo ching 念佛鏡
Nien-fo san-mei pao-wang lun 念佛三昧寶王論
Pan-chou san-mei ching 般舟三昧經
p'an-chiao 判教
Pao-ch'ang 寶唱
Pi-ch'iu-ni chuan 比丘尼傳
Seng-yu 僧祐
Shan-tao 善導
Shen-hsiu 神秀
Shih-chia p'u 釋迦譜
Shih Ching-t'u ch'ün-i lun 釋淨土群疑論
shih fang-pien 時方便
Shih lao chih 釋老志
Ta-chi ching 大集經
T'an-luan 曇鸞
Tao-ch'o 道綽
Tao-hsin 道信
t'i 體
T'ien-t'ai 天台
Tsan-ning 贊寧
tsung 宗
Tzu-min Hui-jih 慈愍慧日
Wang-sheng lun-chu 往生論註
Wei-shou 魏收
wu-cheng-hsing 五正行
wu-cho 五濁
Wu fang-pien 五方便
yü-lu 語錄
Yüan-ming lun 圓明論
yung 用

What Happened to the "Perfect Teaching"? Another Look at Hua-yen Buddhist Hermeneutics

PETER N. GREGORY

The major hermeneutical framework that Chinese Buddhists devised to harmonize the diffuse and often divergent body of scripture that they revered as the sacred word of the Buddha is frequently referred to by its Chinese appellation, *p'an-chiao,* a term that simply means "doctrinal classification."[1] The underlying rubric around which the various systems of doctrinal classification were articulated within the different sectarian traditions of Chinese Buddhism was the cardinal Mahāyāna teaching of upāya *(fang-pien).* Simply put, this hermeneutical principle meant that the Buddha's teachings were context bound. Hence, in order to understand them properly, it was first necessary to know the context in which they were preached, and that context was determined by the intellectual presuppositions and spiritual capacity of the audience to which any particular teaching was delivered. Some teachings were intended for the most simple, while others, for the more perspicacious. The teachings could thus be classified according to their different degrees of profundity. Of course, any such arrangement was in some sense quite arbitrary, as the principle of upāya itself offered no basis upon which such judgments could be determined. The criterion according to which any such hierarchically structured classification was made depended upon the scripture or scriptural corpus that any given thinker or tradition deemed as expressing the most exalted vision of the Buddha. And the basis upon which such a judgment was made involved a complex mix of doctrinal, historical, psychological, and other factors. In any event, whatever the underlying factors, the structure of *p'an-chiao* defined the rules within which the different sectarian traditions of Chinese Buddhism asserted their individual claims to represent the true, orthodox, ultimate, or most relevant interpretation of the meaning of the Buddha's enlightenment. Even the claim of Ch'an Buddhists to be recipients of a direct, mind-to-mind transmission of the Buddha's enlightenment outside the scriptures is only intelligible historically as a reaction against the pervasive acceptance of *p'an-chiao* as the principal means by which the already established traditions had legitimated their authority.

This chapter will discuss a problem in the doctrinal classification system of one of the most important of the scholastic traditions in Chinese Buddhism, Hua-yen. That tradition took its name from the *Hua-yen (Avataṃsaka) Sūtra,* upon which it staked its authority. Chih-yen (602–668), whom the subsequent tradition recognized as its second "patriarch," followed Hui-kuang (468–537) in classifying the *Hua-yen Sūtra* as the perfect, or complete, teaching *(yüan-chiao),* a designation that implied that its superiority lay in the harmonious manner in which all opposites were comprehensively sublated within it. This classification was taken over by Fa-tsang (643–712), whose elaboration of his *p'an-chiao* in the *Treatise on the Five Teachings (Wu-chiao chang)* is often accepted as expressing the orthodox Hua-yen interpretation in such matters.

The specific hermeneutical issue I wish to address concerns the classification system of Kuei-feng Tsung-mi (780–841),[2] a figure posthumously honored as the fifth Hua-yen patriarch. Despite the stamp of orthodoxy that such recognition by the subsequent tradition implies, when the *p'an-chiao* system that Tsung-mi articulates in his *Inquiry into the Origin of Man (Yüan-jen lun)* is compared with that of Fa-tsang (see the diagram on the following page), one of the most striking differences is that Tsung-mi does not include the perfect teaching as a classificatory category, an omission all the more remarkable considering the identification of the perfect teaching with the *Hua-yen Sūtra,* the very scripture upon which the tradition asserted its identity. How could Tsung-mi, a Hua-yen patriarch no less, not have included the perfect teaching, the teaching taken by the tradition as embodying the most profound insight of the Buddha, in his classification system? I will seek to answer this question by examining some of the hermeneutical issues in Hua-yen thought in the historical context of the time in which Tsung-mi wrote.

The Perfect Teaching and the *Hua-yen Sūtra*

The Hua-yen tradition's claim that the teaching of the *Hua-yen Sūtra* represents the ultimate teaching of the Buddha is based on the wholly unique circumstances in which it was believed to have been preached. According to Fa-tsang's statement in his *Treatise on the Five Teachings* (*T* 45.482b; Cook, 188ff.), the infinite dharma-gate *(shih-shih fa-men)* of the *Hua-yen Sūtra* was taught by the Buddha under the bodhi tree during the second week after he had attained enlightenment while he was in the samādhi of oceanic reflection *(hai-in ting).*[3] It is therefore superior to all

Comparison of the *P'an-chiao* Systems in Fa-tsang's *Treatise on the Five Teachings* and Tsung-mi's *Inquiry into the Origin of Man*

Fa-tsang		Tsung-mi
		(1) Men and gods
(1) Hīnayāna	→	(2) Hīnayāna
(2) Elementary Mahāyāna		
(a) Fa-hsiang/Yogācāra	→	(3) Analysis of phenomenal appearances
(b) Mādhyamika	→	(4) Negation of phenomenal appearances
(3) Advanced Mahāyāna	→	(5) Reveals the nature
(4) Sudden		
(5) Perfect		

other teachings because it directly expresses the content of the Buddha's enlightenment. It is, as Fa-tsang says, the prime teaching in accordance with the truth *(ch'eng-fa pen-chiao),* as opposed to the derivative teaching adapted to the capacity of beings *(chu-chi mo-chiao).* In other words, the preaching of the *Hua-yen Sūtra* revealed the truth as the Buddha experienced it under the bodhi tree, making no concession whatsoever to the limited capacity of beings to comprehend it. Borrowing a metaphor from the sūtra itself (*T* 9.616b14–16; cf. *T* 10.266b3–6), Fa-tsang compares it to the first rays of the rising sun which only illumine the peaks of the highest mountains. It is thus qualitatively different from all other teachings of the Buddha, a fact that Fa-tsang indicates by referring to it as the one vehicle of the special teaching *(pieh-chiao i-sheng).*[4]

Although the samādhi of oceanic reflection *(hai-in san-mei,* Skt. *sāgaramudrā samādhi)* does not play a consequential role within the sūtra itself, it was taken up by its Hua-yen exegetes as one of the principal symbols in terms of which the central meaning of the scripture was interpreted. As the samādhi in which the Buddha preached the sūtra, it represented the state of mind in which the Buddha was immersed immediately after his experience of enlightenment. The *Hua-yen Sūtra,* then, is nothing but the unfolding of the vision of reality that the Buddha realized while in the state of oceanic reflection. Its centrality as the hermeneutical key to the sūtra for the tradition is indicated in the opening words of the *Treatise on the Five Teachings,* where Fa-tsang identifies it with the meaning of the teaching of the one vehicle.

As a metaphor of the Buddha's enlightened awareness, the samādhi of oceanic reflection expresses the totalistic vision in which the harmonious interrelation of all phenomena is simultaneously perceived, just as if the entire universe were reflected upon the surface of the ocean. As Fa-tsang writes in his *Reflections on the Dharmadhātu (Hua-yen yu-hsin fa-chieh chi):*

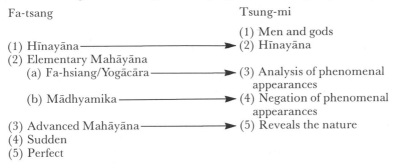

> It is like the reflection of the four divisions [of a great army] on a vast ocean. Although the reflected images differ in kind, they appear simultaneously on [the surface of] the ocean in their proper order. Even though the appearance of the images is manifold, the water [that reflects them] remains undisturbed. The images are indistinguishable from the water, and yet [the water] is calm and clear; the water is indistinguishable from the images, and yet [the images] are multifarious. . . . It is also described as "oceanic" *(hai)* because its various reflections multiply endlessly and their limit is impossible to fathom. To investigate one of them thoroughly is to pursue the infinite, for, in any one of them, all the rest vividly appear at the same time. For this reason, it is said to be "oceanic." It is called "reflection" *(in)* because all the images appear simultaneously within it without distinction of past and present. The myriad diverse kinds [of images] penetrate each other without obstruction. The one and the many are reflected in one another without opposing each other. . . . [It is called] "samādhi" because, although [the images within it] are many and diverse, it remains one and does not change. Even though myriads of images arise in profusion, it remains empty and unperturbed (*T* 45.646b–c).[5]

The vision of reality seen in the samādhi of oceanic reflection is that which the subsequent tradition, following Ch'eng-kuan's (737–838) theory of the fourfold dharmadhātu,[6] characterized as the dharmadhātu of *shih-shih wu-ai,* that is, the realm of the unobstructed interrelation of each and every phenomenon. And it is this vision that is unique to the perfect teaching.

In the *Treatise on the Five Teachings,* Fa-tsang defines the perfect teaching as being represented by what he refers to as *fa-chieh yüan-ch'i,* the conditioned origination of the dharmadhātu, which he regards as the crowning insight of the *Hua-yen Sūtra* (485b7–9; Cook, 223). As elaborated in the final chapter of the *Treatise on the Five Teachings, fa-chieh yüan-ch'i* means that, since all phenomena are devoid of self-nature and arise contingent upon one another, each phenomenon is an organic part of the whole defined by the harmonious interrelation of all of its parts. The character of each phenomenon is thus determined by the whole of which it is an integral part, and the character of the whole is determined by each of the phenomena of which it is comprised. Since the whole is nothing but the interrelation of its parts, each phenomenon can therefore be regarded as determining the character of all other phenomena as well as having its own character determined by all other phenomena.

As the culmination of his description of the perfect teaching, Fa-tsang makes use of the so-called ten profundities *(shih-hsüan),* first formulated by his teacher Chih-yen, to elaborate the implications of *fa-chieh yüan-ch'i.*[7] The infinite interpenetration *(hsiang-ju)* and mutual determination *(hsiang-chi)* of all phenomena described in the ten profundities can be illustrated by the metaphor of Indra's net, the fourth profundity Fa-tsang discusses in the *Treatise on the Five Teachings.* According to this metaphor, the universe is represented by a vast net which extends infinitely in all directions, and the manifold phenomena of which it is comprised, by resplendent jewels suspended at each point of intersection. Each jewel both reflects and is reflected by every other jewel. Each jewel thus reflects each and every other jewel's reflection of its simultaneous reflecting of and being reflected by every other jewel on the net. In this way the process of mutual reflection multiplies endlessly *(ch'ung-ch'ung wu-chin),* just as all phenomena of the universe interrelate without obstruction (see 506a13–b10; Cook, 509–513).[8]

Shih-shih Wu-ai Versus *Li-shih Wu-ai*

In addition to defining the perfect teaching in terms of *fa-chieh yüan-ch'i* in his *Treatise on the Five Teachings,* Fa-tsang also includes nature origination *(hsing-ch'i)* under its heading as well (485b10–11; Cook, 223–224). Although this term derives from the title of the thirty-second chapter of Buddhabhadra's translation of the *Hua-yen Sūtra,* its meaning in Hua-yen thought owes far more to the *Awakening of Faith in Mahāyāna (Ta-sheng ch'i-hsin lun),* the primary text upon which Fa-tsang bases his account of the advanced teaching of the Mahāyāna. In his commentary on the *Awakening of Faith* (*T* 44.243b27), Fa-tsang characterizes this teaching in terms of the conditioned origination from the tathāgatagarbha *(ju-lai-tsang yüan-ch'i),* a doctrine that he describes as elucidating the "harmonious interaction of the absolute and phenomenal without obstruction" *(li-shih jung-t'ung wu-ai)* (243c1). This characterization of the tathāgatagarbha echoes throughout his other works as well and, as *li-shih wu-ai,* became standard within the terminology of the tradition, just as *shih-shih wu-ai* did for *fa-chieh yüan-ch'i.*

In both his *Treatise on the Five Teachings* (484c29–b2; Cook, 218–222) and *Reflections on the Dharmadhātu* (644a1–3), Fa-tsang explains the unobstructed interaction of the absolute and phenomenal in terms of the two aspects of the one mind taught in the *Awakening of Faith.* He identifies the absolute *(li)* with the mind as suchness *(hsin chen-ju)* and the phenomenal *(shih)* with the mind subject to birth-and-death *(hsin sheng-mieh).* Their unobstructed interaction is manifested as the ālayavijñāna, which the *Awakening of Faith* defines in terms of "the interfusion of that which is subject to neither birth nor death with that which is subject to birth-and-death in such a way that they are neither one nor different" (*T* 32.576b8–9). The ālayavijñāna is but another term for the tathāgatagarbha as it responds to conditions *(sui-yüan)* to give rise to all mundane and supramundane dharmas. Just as the ālayavijñāna harbors both the capacity for enlightenment *(chüeh)* and nonenlightenment *(pu-*

chüeh), so too the tathāgatagarbha is the basis for both saṃsāra and nirvāṇa. Even though the tathāgatagarbha as the ālayavijñāna responds to conditions to generate all phenomena, it is, at the same time, identical with the dharmakāya and therefore remains forever untainted. Fa-tsang characterizes this aspect of the tathāgatagarbha as its immutability *(pu-pien).* Moreover, he identifies these two aspects of the tathāgatagarbha—its responding to conditions and its immutability—with the one mind as seen from the point of view of conventional *(su-)* and ultimate truth *(chen-ti).*

For Fa-tsang nature origination, understood in terms of *li-shih wu-ai,* points to the dynamic functioning of the mind *(li)* in the generation of the phenomenal realm *(shih).* All phenomena are thus manifestations of the mind, and, since this mind is intrinsically pure and immutable, the entire realm of phenomena is thereby validated. In this way *li-shih wu-ai* provides the ontological structure in terms of which Fa-tsang articulates his vision of *shih-shih wu-ai.* Nevertheless, the significance of *li-shih wu-ai* becomes eclipsed in his elaboration of the meaning of *shih-shih wu-ai* in the last chapter of the *Treatise on the Five Teachings.*

In his study of Fa-tsang's metaphysics, Liu Ming-Wood has argued that there is a tension between *hsing-ch'i* and *fa-chieh yüan-ch'i*—or *li-shih wu-ai* and *shih-shih wu-ai*—in Fa-tsang's thought, represented by the presence of elements of the advanced teaching within the perfect teaching. Even though Fa-tsang tends to talk as if the advanced teaching had been wholly transcended in the perfect, he cannot do so without also undermining its ontological base—for the perfect teaching *(shih-shih wu-ai)* cannot be established independent of the advanced teaching *(li-shih wu-ai).* Liu thus criticizes Fa-tsang's account of the perfect teaching as inherently unstable. He also points out that the advanced teaching of the Mahāyāna plays a far greater role in Fa-tsang's thought than his classification of it as merely the third teaching within his fivefold scheme would suggest.[9]

Although Ch'eng-kuan follows Fa-tsang in regarding *shih-shih wu-ai* as representing the supreme teaching of the Buddha, he nonetheless emphasizes *li-shih wu-ai* over *shih-shih wu-ai* in his exposition of Hua-yen teachings. Whereas *li-shih wu-ai* tends to vanish into *shih-shih wu-ai* in Fa-tsang's writings, Ch'eng-kuan focuses on the importance of *li-shih wu-ai* in making *shih-shih wu-ai* possible.

> The dharmadhātu of the nonobstruction of phenomena and phenomena constitutes the cardinal teaching of the [*Hua-yen*] *Sūtra.* . . . The reason that each phenomenon is different from every other phenomenon and yet is unobstructed by all other phenomena is that the absolute permeates phenomena. . . . Because phenomena are formed on the basis of the absolute, the one and the many arise in dependence upon one another. . . . It

> is only as a result of the nonobstruction of the phenomenal and the absolute that the nonobstruction of phenomena and phenomena is made possible. . . . Were phenomena not identical with the absolute, they would not be formed from the absolute and phenomena would then obstruct one another. However, because they are identical with the absolute, they are unobstructed. . . . Since phenomena are formed from the absolute, they are included in one another without obstruction (*T* 36.9a28–b7).

Tsung-mi's supplanting of the perfect teaching (i.e., *shih-shih wu-ai*) with that of the tathāgatagarbha (i.e., *li-shih wu-ai*) in his classification of Buddhist teachings can thus be seen as an extension of a trend already evidenced by his teacher Ch'eng-kuan. Moreover, Tsung-mi's primary exposure to Hua-yen thought was through Ch'eng-kuan. The only work of Fa-tsang's that we can say for sure Tsung-mi read was his commentary on the *Awakening of Faith,* which served as the basis on which Tsung-mi composed his own abridged commentary.[10] Fa-tsang's commentary, however, is concerned with explicating the conditioned origination of the tathāgatagarbha and has nothing to say about *shih-shih wu-ai.*

The legacy of Hua-yen teachings to which Tsung-mi was heir thus did not accord the prominence to the teaching of *shih-shih wu-ai* that it had enjoyed in Fa-tsang's writings. But Tsung-mi also went much further than his teacher Ch'eng-kuan in subordinating *shih-shih wu-ai* to *li-shih wu-ai,* as witnessed most dramatically in his exclusion of the perfect teaching as a category within his *p'an-chiao* scheme. The difference between Ch'eng-kuan and Tsung-mi in this regard can also be seen by comparing their comments on the last section of Tu-shun's *Meditation on the Dharmadhātu (Fa-chieh kuan-men),* that of the "Meditation on Total Pervasion and Accommodation" *(chou-pien han-jung kuan).* Ch'eng-kuan interprets the ten meditations enumerated in this section in terms of the ten profundities, which he characterizes as the paradigmatic expression of *shih-shih wu-ai* (*T* 45.683a3–11). Tsung-mi, by contrast, merely observes that the ten meditations correspond to the ten profundities, which he does not even bother to list (*T* 45.692b4–5). Again, in his subcommentary to Ch'eng-kuan's commentary to the chapter on the practice and vows of Samantabhadra from the new translation of the *Gaṇḍavyūha* done by Prajña in 798 (*Hua-yen ching hsing yüan p'in shu ch'ao, ZZ* 1/7/5.399c), Tsung-mi only mentions, but does not discuss, the ten profundities which Ch'eng-kuan had subjected to a detailed analysis in his commentary (*Hua-yen ching hsing yüan p'in shu, ZZ* 1/7/3.246a–d).

Not only does Tsung-mi give scant attention to the ten profundities in precisely those places where we would expect him to devote sustained discussion to them, he eschews the whole vocabulary of *li* and *shih* which Ch'eng-kuan had used to formulate his theory of the fourfold dharmadhātu. Where he does make reference to the fourfold dharmadhātu,[11] he refers to a passage from Ch'eng-kuan's *Hua-yen ching hsing yüan p'in shu* (*ZZ* 1/7/3.249c11–d2) that emphasizes the one true dharmadhātu *(i-chen fa-chieh)* as the essential reality from which the fourfold dharmadhātu derives.[12] Most significantly for Tsung-mi, that passage identifies the one true dharmadhātu with the one mind *(i-hsin)* that wholly embraces manifold existence *(tsung-kai wan-yu).* Tsung-mi identifies the one true dharmadhātu with the tathāgatagarbha, the central doctrine of the teaching that he ranks highest in his classification system. It is also in terms of the one true dharmadhātu that he elaborates his discussion of nature origination in his *Hsing yüan p'in shu ch'ao.*

The Teaching That Reveals the Nature

Within the doctrinal classification scheme that he outlines in his *Inquiry into the Origin of Man,* Tsung-mi accords pride of place to the teaching of the tathāgatagarbha, which he refers to as "the teaching that reveals the nature" *(hsien-hsing chiao).*

> The teaching of the one vehicle that reveals the nature holds that all sentient beings without exception have the intrinsicallly enlightened true mind. From [time] without beginning it is permanently abiding and immaculate. It is shining, unobscured, clear and bright ever-present awareness. It is also called Buddha-nature and it is also called tathāgatagarbha. From time without beginning deluded thoughts cover it, and [sentient beings] by themselves are not aware of it. Because they only recognize their inferior qualities, they become indulgently attached, enmeshed in karma, and experience the suffering of birth-and-death. The great Enlightened One took pity upon them and taught that everything without exception is empty. He further revealed that the purity of the numinous enlightened true mind is wholly identical with that of all Buddhas (*T* 45.710a11–16).

Like Fa-tsang, Tsung-mi turns to the *Hua-yen Sūtra* to support his interpretation of the meaning of the Buddha's enlightenment, but in so doing, he chooses a passage with a thrust quite different from Fa-tsang's vision of the unobstructed harmonious interaction of all phenomena. He quotes the following passage from the *Hua-yen Sūtra,* one that was especially valued in the Ch'an tradition as it was believed to have contained the first words uttered by the Buddha after his enlightenment.

> O Sons of Buddha, there is no place where the wisdom of the Tathāgata does not reach. Why? Because there is not a single sentient being that is not fully endowed with the wisdom of the Tathāgata. It is only on account of their deluded thinking, erroneous views, and attachments that they do not succeed in realizing it. When they become free from deluded thinking,

the all-comprehending wisdom, the spontaneous wisdom, and the unobstructed wisdom will then be manifest before them. . . . At that time the Tathāgata with his unobstructed pure eye of wisdom universally beheld all sentient beings throughout the dharmadhātu and said, "How amazing! How amazing! How can it be that these sentient beings are fully endowed with the wisdom of the Tathāgata and yet, being ignorant and confused, do not know it and do not see it? I must teach them the noble path, enabling them to be forever free from deluded thinking and to achieve for themselves the seeing of the broad and vast wisdom of the Tathāgata within themselves and so be no different from the Buddhas" (*T* 10.272c4–7 and 272c25–273a2).[13]

The significance of this passage for Tsung-mi lay in the fact that it established that the Buddha's enlightenment consisted in his realization that all sentient beings already fully possess the enlightened wisdom of the Buddha and are therefore fundamentally identical with all Buddhas. The defilements which appear to obscure this wisdom are merely adventitious. Buddhist practice should thus be directed toward uncovering the original enlightenment that is the fundamental nature of all beings. Enlightenment is a matter of becoming aware of that which has always been present from the very beginning.

Tsung-mi's account of the teaching that reveals the nature in his *Ch'an Preface (Ch'an-yüan chu-ch'üan-chi tu-hsü)* adds that this teaching is exemplified in those sūtras that expound the tathāgatagarbha, such as the *Hua-yen, Ghanavyūha, Yüan-chüeh, Śūraṅgama, Śrīmālā, Tathāgatagarbha, Lotus,* and *Nirvāṇa,* as well as in śāstras such as the *Awakening of Faith, Buddha Nature (Fo-hsing),* and *Ratnagotravibhāga* (*T* 48.405a24–26; K, 132).

As both his quotation of the *Hua-yen Sūtra* as canonical authority for the teaching that reveals the nature and his inclusion of it within his enumeration of scriptures which exemplify that teaching make clear, Tsung-mi regards the principal teaching of this scripture as the tathāgatagarbha, not its vision of the unobstructed interrelation of all phenomena. He does, however, include the latter within the teaching that reveals the nature in the *Ch'an Preface* (see *T* 48.407c7–12; K, 185), suggesting that he would have seen the perfect teaching as contained within the teaching that reveals the nature.

The *Scripture of Perfect Enlightenment*

One of the scriptures that Tsung-mi lists among those exemplifying the teaching that reveals the nature is the *Yüan-chüeh ching* or *Scripture of Perfect Enlightenment.* Despite his appropriation within the fold of Hua-yen patriarchs, Tsung-mi's primary exegetical activity was devoted to this text, and not the *Hua-yen Sūtra.* Although it purports to have been translated into Chinese by Buddhatrāta in 793, modern scholars agree that it was in all likelihood authored in China sometime around the beginning of the eighth century and that its teaching is based on the *Śūraṅgama Sūtra* and *Awakening of Faith.*[14]

Tsung-mi's esteem for this work was a direct result of his personal experience: it was his encounter with this text that precipitated his first enlightenment experience. As he describes the event in his subcommentary to his preface to his commentary on the scripture, sometime after he had become a novice monk under the Ch'an master Tao-yüan in Sui-chou in 804, he participated in a maigre feast at the home of a local official and lay patron, Jen Kuan. There, when the scripture chanting was over, he came across a copy of the *Scripture of Perfect Enlightenment* for the fist time. After reading only two or three pages, he had an awakening, an experience whose intensity so suddenly overwhelmed him that he found himself uncontrollably dancing for joy (*ZZ* 1/14/3.223a). His disciple and biographer P'ei Hsiu adds that when he later reported what had happened to Tao-yüan, the master confirmed his experience, remarking, "You will greatly spread the perfect and sudden teaching. The Buddhas preached this scripture just for you" (Preface to Tsung-mi's *Yüan-chüeh ching lüeh-shu, T* 39.523c7).

Not only did this text play a crucial role in Tsung-mi's own spiritual development, he also regarded its straightforwardness as better suited to the needs of the times than the grandiose scale of the *Hua-yen Sūtra.*

> If you want to propagate the truth, single out its quintessence, and thoroughly penetrate the ultimate meaning, don't revere the *Hua-yen Sūtra* above all others. Ancient and modern worthies and masters of the Tripiṭaka in both the western regions and this land have all classified it as supreme, as fully related in [Ch'eng-kuan's] introduction to his commentary. Yet its principles become so confused within its voluminous size that beginners become distraught and have difficulty entering into it. . . . It is not as good as this scripture, whose single volume can be entered immediately (*Yüan-chüeh ching ta-shu ch'ao, ZZ* 1/14/3.226a10–14).

Given the fact that Tsung-mi revered this scripture above the *Hua-yen Sūtra* and that he classified it under the teaching that reveals the nature, it should hardly be surprising that he would have been reluctant to posit the perfect teaching, identified exclusively with the *Hua-yen Sūtra,* as a still higher category within his *p'an-chiao.*

In a passage from his introduction to his commentary on the *Scripture of Perfect Enlightenment (Yüan-chüeh ching ta-shu)* discussing how that scripture, within its brief compass, includes a wide variety of ideas, Tsung-mi comments that, within its single fascicle of only twenty-eight pages, the *Scripture of Perfect Enlightenment* fully embodies the ideas expressed in the advanced and sudden teachings and the teaching traditions of emptiness and the analysis of phenomenal appearances (*k'ung-tsung* and *hsiang-tsung,* i.e., Fa-tsang's elementary Mahāyāna), as well as containing those of the Hīnayāna and perfect special teachings (110c8–11). In his subcommentary to this passage, he explains that, even though it contains the ideas of the Hīnayāna and perfect teachings, they are still not its cardinal principle *(tsung)* (234d16–16). This passage indicates that Tsung-mi regarded the *Scripture of Perfect Enlightenment* as fully expressing the content of the the advanced and sudden teachings and only partially that of the perfect teaching. Again, at the end of the section discussing the classification systems of previous scholars *(ch'üan-shih tui-pien)* in his introduction to his commentary (116b5–12), Tsung-mi indicates how that scripture would be classified according to Fa-tsang's five categories of teaching.

1. It is wholly included within, but only partially includes, the perfect teaching. Tsung-mi goes on to explain that the *Perfect Enlightenment Scripture* cannot be said to include the entirety of the perfect teaching because it does not teach the unobstructed interpenetration and mutual determination of all things. It does, however, "directly reveal the essence of the one true dharmadhātu" *(i-chen fa-chieh),* which is included within the perfect teaching of the *Hua-yen Sūtra.*
2. It includes, but is not included within, the first two teachings within Fa-tsang's *p'an-chiao,* those of the Hīnayāna and elementary Mahāyāna, because it includes the two *nairātmya* whereas they do not include the tathāgatagarbha.
3. It both includes and is included within the advanced teaching of the Mahāyāna "because this scripture is also based on the tathāgatagarbha." Tsung-mi adds that it is also referred to as "the Mahāyāna of the sudden teaching."

This passage is especially significant because it reveals precisely that aspect of the perfect teaching that the *Scripture of Perfect Enlightenment* contains as well as that which it lacks: it contains the *Hua-yen Sūtra's* teaching of the one true dharmadhātu but not its teaching of interpenetration and mutual determination. To put it in terms that Tsung-mi does not use, it contains the Hua-yen teaching of *li-shih wu-ai* but not that of *shih-shih wu-ai.*

In addition to identifying the *Scripture of Perfect Enlightenment* with the advanced teaching, Tsung-mi also identified it with the sudden teaching, and his discussion of how it fits within that latter rubric further reveals the way in which he saw it as differing from the *Hua-yen Sūtra.*[15]

In his subcommentary to the *Scripture of Perfect Enlightenment* (*ZZ* 1/14/3.218b7–15), Tsung-mi distinguishes between two different types of sudden teaching: the first he terms *hua-i-tun* (the sudden teaching as a method of exposition) and the second, *chu-chi-tun* (the sudden teaching that was expounded in response to beings of superior capacity). The first refers solely to the *Hua-yen Sūtra,* which was taught immediately after the Buddha had attained enlightenment, whereas the second refers to those scriptures—such as the *Śrīmālā, Ghanavyūha, Chin-kang san-mei, Tathāgatagarbha,* and *Yüan-chüeh*—which, preached to beings of superior capacity, "reveal the one true enlightened nature."

Tsung-mi's discussion of the sudden teaching shows that its content is identical to that of the advanced teaching. His teaching that reveals the nature thus also includes that which Fa-tsang had listed, under a separate category, as the sudden teaching. His claim that the *Scripture of Perfect Enlightenment* contains part of what was taught in the *Hua-yen Sūtra,* moreover, indicates that the teaching that reveals the nature also partially includes the perfect teaching. Finally, Tsung-mi regarded that aspect of the perfect teaching—*shih-shih wu-ai*—that was not included within the teaching that reveals the nature as of so little significance as not to merit the status of a separate category in his classification system. Since this was the aspect that the previous tradition had claimed epitomized the most profound teaching of the Buddha, Tsung-mi's revalorization of Hua-yen teachings marks a radical shift in Hua-yen hermeneutics, a point that belies the claim of one authority on the dharmadhātu theory in the Hua-yen tradition that "it is difficult to find any new development" in Tsung-mi's idea of the dharmadhātu.[16]

The One True Dharmadhātu

As has already been noted, Tsung-mi regarded the one true dharmadhātu as being that aspect of the teaching of the *Hua-yen Sūtra* contained within the teaching that reveals the nature. He discusses the one true dharmadhātu in the fourth section of his introduction to both his commentary and abridged commentary to the *Scripture of Perfect Enlightenment,* "Analyzing the Mysterious and Profound" *(fen-ch'i yu-shen),* in which he outlines his understanding of the central content of the scripture in terms of five stages of phenomenal evolution—a "cosmogony" based on the *Awakening of Faith.* Not only does Tsung-mi consider this cosmogonic process as fundamental to the message of the *Scripture of Perfect Enlightenment,* it is also one of the primary elements within the overall structure of his thought. He discusses it again in the second part of the third section of his introduction to his commentary to the *Awakening of Faith*—a context that emphasizes the crucial role that it played within his understanding of Buddhism, as it is one of the two places wherein his commentary diverges in substance from that of Fa-tsang, on which it is based.[17] This five-stage theory of phenomenal evolution is the subject of the concluding section of his *Inquiry into the Origin of Man.* It also figures prominently in the final section of the *Ch'an Preface.* Its importance in these two works again underlines its centrality within Tsung-mi's thought as a whole. Both works are later than his commentaries and reflect a more mature intellectual position. Moreover, in neither case is their form dictated by the conventions of a commentary format, the set categories and fragmentary nature of which discourage the innovative expression of systematically developed thought.

Tsung-mi's five-stage theory explains how the world of delusion and defilement, the world in terms of which beings experience themselves, evolves out of a unitary ontological principle that is both intrinsically enlightened and pure. It is, in effect, Tsung-mi's theodicy.

In both his discussion of this theory of phenomenal evolution in his commentary and subcommentary to the *Scripture of Perfect Enlightenment,* as well as in his commentary to the *Awakening of Faith,* Tsung-mi elucidates the fundamental basis of this process by linking it to Ch'eng-kuan's description of the one true dharmadhātu. This is a particularly significant hermeneutical move that indicates a marked shift in the fundamental valence of Hua-yen thought. The fourfold dharmadhātu theory was the primary framework within which Ch'eng-kuan interpreted Hua-yen thought and represented his principal contribution to the development of Hua-yen hermeneutics. Tsung-mi's recasting of the significance of the dharmadhātu in terms of the *Awakening of Faith* not only pushes Hua-yen thought toward a much more explicitly ontological metaphysical position, but also makes room for traditional Chinese cosmological preoccupations within the field of Buddhist discourse.

The following composite summary of Tsung-mi's theory of phenomenal evolution is based on his commentary and subcommentary to the *Scripture of Perfect Enlightenment* (see *ZZ* 1/14/2.116c16–117c4 and 1/14/3.264a16–267b5) and his commentary to the *Awakening of Faith* (14v):

1. The one mind alone constitutes the ultimate source: Tsung-mi identifies the ultimate source *(pen-yüan)* with the one mind of the *Awakening of Faith,* the wondrous mind of perfect enlightenment of the *Scripture of Perfect Enlightenment,* and the one true dharmadhātu of the *Hua-yen Sūtra*—all of which are thus synonymous with one another, as well as serving as different expressions for the tathāgatagarbha. Tsung-mi writes, "Even though there are four types of dharmadhātu within Hua-yen, the commentary on that scripture [by Ch'eng-kuan] says, 'In all there is just one true dharmadhātu. It wholly embraces manifold existence and is identical with the one mind.' " Tsung-mi uses this passage from Ch'eng-kuan to

equate the one true dharmadhātu with the mind of sentient beings in the *Awakening of Faith,* quoting the passage from that text that states: " 'Dharma' means the mind of sentient beings. That mind embraces all mundane and supramundane dharmas" (575c21–22).

2. Based on the one mind, two gates open up: this stage corresponds to the two aspects of the one mind described in the *Awakening of Faith.* The first is the mind as suchness *(hsin chen-ju men),* which refers to that which is neither born nor dies. The second is the mind that is subject to birth-and-death *(hsin sheng-mieh men),* which refers to the ālayavijñāna, in which the tathāgatagarbha and that which is subject to birth-and-death are interfused. Tsung-mi quotes Ch'eng-kuan's statement in regard to the dharmadhātu to characterize the former aspect: "Its essence transcends being and nonbeing; its defining characteristic is that it neither arises nor perishes. Since none can probe its beginning or end, how could its center or periphery be perceived?" (249c13–14). Ch'eng-kuan's statement—"If one understands it, he is greatly enlightened; if one is deluded about it, he transmigrates without cease" (249c15)—is then quoted to characterize the latter aspect.
3. Based on this consciousness (i.e., the ālayavijñāna), its two meanings are explained: the first is enlightenment *(chüeh),* which refers to the essence of the mind's transcending of thoughts, etc. The second is unenlightenment *(pu-chüeh),* which refers to the fact that, because beings do not truly recognize the oneness of the dharma of suchness, mental activity unconsciously arises, etc.
4. Based on the latter aspect (i.e., unenlightenment) the three subtle phenomenal appearances are born—viz., activation, perceiving subject, and perceived object. Tsung-mi explains these three terms derived from the *Awakening of Faith* (see 577a8–12) in terms of the *Ch'eng wei-shih lun's* explanation of the bifurcation of the ālayavijñāna into subjective and objective modes *(chien-fen, darśanabhāga* and *hsiang-fen, nimittabhāga).*
5. Based on the last subtle phenomenal appearance, the six coarse phenomenal appearances are born—viz., discrimination, continuation, attachment, symbolic representation, generating karma, and experiencing suffering. This final stage in the process of phenomenal evolution describes how the epistemological dualism that emerged in the last leads to attachment to objects *(fa-chih, dharmagrāha)* and self *(wo-chih, ātmagrāha),* whose inevitable consequence "entails the ensuance of existentiality."[18]

This process can be represented diagrammatically as follows:

The Process of Phenomenal Evolution

(1) Ultimate source: ONE MIND

(2) Two gates: MIND AS SUCHNESS — MIND SUBJECT TO BIRTH-AND-DEATH (ālayavijñāna)

(3) Two aspects: ENLIGHTENED — UNENLIGHTENED

(4) Three subtle phenomenal appearances:

(a) Activation
(b) Perceiving subject
(c) Perceived object

(5) Six coarse phenomenal appearances:

(a) Discrimination
(b) Continuation
(c) Attachment
(d) Symbolic representation
(e) Generating karma
(f) Experiencing suffering

Nature Origination

Tsung-mi's adoption of the one true dharmadhātu as the first principle in a five-stage cosmogonic scheme was already suggested by Ch'eng-kuan's opening words in his preface to his *Hsing yüan p'in shu:* "How great the true dhātu *(ta-tsai chen-chieh)*! The myriad dharmas owe their inception to it *(wan-fa tzu-shih).*" This proclamation, as Tsung-mi points out in his subcommentary, derives from the comments on the first hexagram, *ch'ien* ("the Creative" in the Wilhelm/Baynes translation), in the *Classic of Change (I ching) ("Ta-tsai ch'ien-yüan. Wan-wu tzu-shih").*[19] Whatever the underlying intent behind Ch'eng-kuan's use of this allusion,[20] Tsung-mi took its implications seriously, and it is in his discussion of these words that he provides us with his fullest account of nature origination.

After elucidating the allusion, Tsung-mi defines the "true dhātu" as the "dharmadhātu of suchness *(chen-ju fa-chieh).*" He goes on to say, "Although the varieties of dharmadhātu are of many types, when its overall character is disclosed, there is just the one true dharmadhātu, the pure mind which is the source of Buddhas and sentient beings" (399b5–6). The true dhātu refers to the nature of the essence *(t'i-hsing)* of the mind of the one dharmadhātu *(i fa-chieh hsin),* whereas the myriad dharmas which owe their inception to it refer to the phenomenal appearance of its essence *(t'i-hsiang)* (399b15–17). Tsung-mi continues, "There is not a single dharma that is not a manifestation of the original mind. Nor is there a single dharma that does not conditionally arise from the true dhātu" (399c1–2).

Tsung-mi then distinguishes between two modes of causality according to which "the mind of the one dharmadhātu brings all dharmas to completion." The first of these is nature origination *(hsing-ch'i);* the second, conditioned origination *(yüan-ch'i).* In regard to the first, "nature" corresponds to the true dhātu and "origination," to the myriad dharmas. Tsung-mi says that nature origination thus means that "the entire essence of the dharmadhātu as the nature arises *(ch'i)* to form all dharmas" (399c6). "Since all mundane and supramundane dharmas originate wholly from the nature, there is no other dharma outside of the nature. That is why Buddhas and sentient beings are inextricably interconnected and the pure and defiled lands harmoniously interpenetrate" (399c11–12).

Conditioned origination, on the other hand, refers to the process by which both delusion and enlightenment unfold and, accordingly, is discussed in terms of its impure and pure aspects (see 399d3–400d17). While Tsung-mi's analysis of the various dimensions of conditioned origination becomes more complex, what is worth noting here is that the two directions in which it can move derive from the two aspects of the ālayavijñāna. Delusion is derived from its unenlightened aspect and unfolds according to the three subtle and six coarse phenomenal appearances Tsung-mi appropriates from the *Awakening of Faith.* Its ultimate basis consists in being deluded about the fundamental ground of phenomenal reality, the one true dharmadhātu. Enlightenment corresponds to the process by which beings become aware of that fundamental ground and extirpate the deeply rooted unconscious attitudes and habitual behavior patterns sown by their delusion. Tsung-mi interprets this process as that which the *Awakening of Faith* refers to as "experiential enlightenment" *(shih chüeh)* and outlines it in terms of ten stages in his *Ch'an Preface.*[21] His casting of conditioned origination in terms of the processes of delusion and enlightenment—rather than in terms of a realm in which phenomena interpenetrate without obstruction—makes clear the soteriological thrust animating his ontology. It is only by gaining an insight into nature origination, which reveals the ultimate basis of phenomenal appearances, that one can begin to extricate oneself from the meshes of residual impure conditioning and finally actualize the full potential of the enlightenment that is the birthright of all beings.

Nature origination for Tsung-mi thus explains how the tathāgatagarbha can serve as the ontological ground for Buddhist practice. Expressed in traditional Hua-yen categories, *li-shih wu-ai* offered Tsung-mi a far more effective soteriological prospect than did *shih-shih wu-ai.*

Tsung-mi's Ch'an Background

The most obvious reason that can be given for Tsung-mi's excision of the perfect teaching from his *p'an-chiao* scheme in the *Inquiry into the Origin of Man* is that it was simply irrelevant to his investigation, whose ontological theme is indicated in its title. The progression of teachings that Tsung-mi outlines in that work is arranged according to the degree to which each succeeds in probing the ultimate origin of man. Since enlightenment consists in the realization of this fundamental source, the order of the teachings can thus be taken as describing the process of soteriological progress. Tsung-mi's avowed objective in writing this essay was, after all, soteriological. His omission of the perfect teaching is thus related to his understanding of enlightenment.

The soteriological thrust in Tsung-mi's ontology reveals his intimate involvement with Ch'an. Clearly one of the most significant developments within Chinese Buddhism in the period of almost a century and a half that separated Tsung-mi from Fa-tsang was the rise of Ch'an. In addition to his association with the Hua-yen tradition, Tsung-mi was also deeply involved with the Ch'an of his day, being reckoned as the fifth "patriarch" in the Ho-tse lineage of Southern Ch'an founded by Shen-hui. The perspective from which he appropriated Hua-yen teachings was informed by his prior Ch'an training. It was only in 810, after six years of Ch'an discipline, that he discovered Hua-yen through the writings of Ch'eng-kuan. One of the reasons Tsung-mi seems to have been drawn to Hua-yen was that its teachings provided a solid ontological rationale for Ch'an practice. His reevaluation of traditional Hua-yen teachings accordingly has to be understood in terms of his Ch'an background—particularly his reaction against some of the more radical Ch'an movements of the eighth and ninth centuries.

Of the different Ch'an lines that he discusses in his *Ch'an Chart (Chung-hua ch'uan-hsin-ti Ch'an-men shih-tzu ch'eng-hsi t'u),* Tsung-mi's most sustained criticism is directed against that of Hung-chou, represented by the teachings of Ma-tsu Tao-i (709–788). As I have argued elsewhere,[22] his criticism of that line of Southern Ch'an focuses on its apparent failure to penetrate to the ultimate source of phenomenal appearances—and for Tsung-mi such failure meant that its practice of "simply allowing the mind to act spontaneously" *(tan jen-hsin wei hsiu)* could be interpreted in an antinomian fashion. In other words, Tsung-mi's uneasiness with this brand of Ch'an lay in his perception that, since it lacked solid ontological bearings, its behavioral import was apt to veer in ethically dangerous directions. Tsung-mi's ethical critique of the Hung-chou teaching thus focuses on its ontology. He charges that it merely recognized the nature's functioning-in-accord-with-conditions *(sui-yüan yung),* which it proclaimed as the "total functioning of the Buddha-nature," without also acknowledging the functioning of the self-nature *(tzu-hsing yung),* upon which such conditioned functioning was based. Tsung-mi compares this position to merely recognizing the changing images reflected on the surface of a mirror without also acknowledging the luminous reflectivity *(ming)* of the mirror that makes such reflections possible.

Ma-tsu, like Tsung-mi, hailed from Szechwan. As Yanagida Seizan has suggested in his perceptive study of the background of the *Li-tai fa-pao chi,*[23] just as Ma-tsu's teaching can be seen as a development out of trends within the Szechwanese Buddhist milieu from which he came, so Tsung-mi's can be seen as a reaction against them. In either case, it was the Ch'an movements in Szechwan that formed the context out of which, or against which, each later articulated his own teaching. The most radical of these movements was that of Pao-t'ang, whose fabrication of its own history is preserved in the *Li-tai fa-pao chi.* As Yanagida has shown, this school of Ch'an extended Shen-hui's teaching of no-thought *(wu-nien)* to its logical conclusion by discarding all forms of traditional Buddhist ethical practice and ritual observance. Wu-chu (714–

774), the founder of this school, often held large public meetings in which he preached his radical message to the masses. Tsung-mi, as we would expect, was highly critical of Pao-t'ang Ch'an, derogatorily referring to its practice as one of "extinguishing consciousness" *(mieh-shih).* In any case, it is likely that it was Tsung-mi's acquaintance with this school that shaped his perception of the Hung-chou line of Ch'an taught by Ma-tsu and his successors, and that sensitized him to the antinomian dangers inherent in some of the more radical Mahāyāna doctrines espoused in Ch'an.

Although Tsung-mi does not make the connection, it is tempting to speculate that he may have felt a similarity in the ethical import of the teachings of the Hung-chou line of Ch'an and the Hua-yen teaching of *shih-shih wu-ai.* Behind Tsung-mi's discussion and evaluation of various teachings, whether Buddhist or non-Buddhist, there is a keen sensitivity to their ethical implications that is always evident. One of the reasons Tsung-mi valued the tathāgatagarbha so highly was that it provided a firm ontological ground for Buddhist practice. As expressed in his interpretation of nature origination *(hsing-ch'i),* this doctrine meant that all phenomenal appearances *(hsiang)* only had reality insofar as they were seen to be manifestations *(ch'i)* of the nature *(hsing).* When taken as real in and of themselves, however, phenomenal appearances are the basis of deluded attachment. Only when they are seen to be empty can their true reality be grasped. The doctrine of nature origination can be seen as an elaboration of the meaning of *li-shih wu-ai.* Tsung-mi equates *shih* (phenomena) with *hsiang* (phenomenal appearances). The Hua-yen teaching of *shih-shih wu-ai* thus refers to the intricate web of interconnections that obtain among phenomenal appearances. They are that which —in the context of his criticism of the Hung-chou line of Ch'an—he refers to the functioning-in-accord-with-conditions, merely the ever-changing images reflected on the surface of the mind.

If the criticism that Tsung-mi levels against the Hung-chou teaching can thus be applied against *shih-shih wu-ai,* it further clarifies why, to employ the traditional Hua-yen categories used throughout this chapter, he valued *li-shih wu-ai* over *shih-shih wu-ai* and therefore also why he omitted the perfect teaching from his doctrinal classification system in the *Inquiry into the Origin of Man,* ceding its place to that of the tathāgata-garbha.

Notes

Work on this chapter was supported by a research grant from the Joint Committee on Chinese Studies of the American Council of Learned Societies and the Social Science Research Council, with funds provided by the Andrew W. Mellon Foundation.

1. Both the general nature of *p'an-chiao* as well as its specific character within the Hua-yen tradition have already been well documented in English-language scholarship. A good general discussion of *p'an-chiao* can still be found in Leon Hurvitz's *Chih-i (538–597): An Introduction to the Life and Ideas of a Chinese Buddhist Monk, Mélanges chinois et bouddhiques* 12 (1960–1962), although much of what he has to say about Chih-i's system has been corrected by Sekiguchi Shindai's more recent researches. For a revised and more accurate discussion of T'ien-t'ai doctrinal classification in light of Sekiguchi's findings, see David W. Chappell's "Introduction to the *T'ien-t'ai ssu-chiao-i,*" *The Eastern Buddhist,* n.s. 9, no. 1 (1976): 72–86; reprinted in Chappell et al., *T'ien-t'ai Buddhism: An Outline of the Fourfold Teachings* (Tokyo: Daiichi shobō, 1983). For a discussion of the early Chinese Buddhist classificatory schemes, see Ōchō Einichi, "The Beginnings of Tenet Classification in China," *The Eastern Buddhist,* n.s. 14, no. 2 (1981): 71–94. Liu Ming-Wood's "The *P'an-chiao* System of the Hua-yen School in Chinese Buddhism," *T'oung Pao* 67 (1981): 10–47, provides a generally excellent overview of the "classical" system articulated by Fa-tsang. For a translation of Fa-tsang's *Wu-chiao chang,* see Francis Cook's "Fa-tsang's *Treatise on the Five Doctrines,* An Annotated Translation" (Ph.D. diss., University of Wisconsin, 1970). See also my "Chinese Buddhist Hermeneutics: The Case of Hua-yen," *Journal of the American Academy of Religion* 51, no. 2 (1983): 231–249.

2. This chapter forms the third in a series discussing the differences between Fa-tsang's and Tsung-mi's classificatory systems. See also "The Teaching of Men and Gods: The Doctrinal and Social Basis of Lay Buddhist Practice in the Hua-yen Tradition," in Robert M. Gimello and Peter N. Gregory, eds., *Studies in Ch'an and Hua-yen,* Studies in East Asian Buddhism, no. 1 (Honolulu: University of Hawaii Press, 1983), 253–319, and "The Place of the Sudden Teaching within the Hua-yen Tradition: An Investigation of the Process of Doctrinal Change," *Journal of the International Association of Buddhist Studies* 6, no. 1 (1983): 31–60.

3. The translation of *hai-in* as "oceanic reflection" is that of Thomas Cleary; see his *Entry Into the Inconceivable: An Introduction to Hua-yen Buddhism* (Honolulu: University of Hawaii Press, 1983). For a discussion of this term, see Kamata Shigeo's "Kaiin zammai no sekai" in his *Chūgoku bukkyō shisōshi kenkyū* (Tokyo: Shunjūsha, 1967), 403–425.

4. Of course this metaphor could be interpreted otherwise. In the T'ien-t'ai tradition it is cited to "prove" that the teaching of the *Hua-yen Sūtra* is actually inferior to that of the *Lotus Sūtra,* precisely because it only illumined the highest peaks—that is, was accessible only to the most advanced bodhisattvas. Its "special" *(pieh)* character thus indicated its exclusivity. The *Lotus,* on the other hand, was truly universal, and hence superior, because it employed a panoply of expedient devices geared to reach the varying spiritual capacities of *all* the Buddha's followers.

5. I have adapted the translation of Liu Ming-Wood, "The Teaching of Fa-tsang: An Examination of Buddhist Metaphysics" (Ph.D. diss., University of California, Los Angeles, 1979), 122–123.

6. Sakamoto Yukio has pointed out that Ch'eng-kuan adopted the terminology for the fourfold dharmadhātu theory from Hui-yüan (ca. 673–743), although Ch'eng-kuan's explanation of its meaning differed from that of Hui-yüan; see his "Hokkai engi no rekishi teki keisei," in Miyamoto Shōson, ed., *Bukkyō no konpon shinri* (Tokyo: Sanseidō, 1957), 902–903.

The term "dharmadhātu" has a wide range of meanings throughout Buddhist thought, a good survey of which can be found in Kang Nam Oh, "A

Study of Chinese Hua-yen Buddhism with Special Reference to the *Dharmadhātu (fa-chieh)* Doctrine" (Ph.D. diss., McMaster University, 1976), 11–35. Fa-tsang indicates some of the ways in which it could be interpreted in his discussion at the beginning of his commentary on the "Entering the Dharmadhātu Chapter" *(Ju fa-chieh p'in, Gaṇḍavyūha)* of the *Hua-yen Sūtra* in his *T'an-hsüan chi* (*T* 35.440b11ff.—cf. *T* 44.63b18–21). He points out that in the compound "dharmadhātu" *(fa-chieh),* "dharma" *(fa)* can have three meanings: (1) that which upholds *(ch'ih),* (2) that which serves as a norm *(kuei-tse),* and (3) mental object *(tui-i).* "Dhātu" *(chieh)* likewise has three meanings: (1) the cause *(yin)* (upon which the noble path is realized), (2) the nature *(hsing)* (upon which all dharmas are based), and (3) the differentiated *(fen-ch'i)* (since all conditionally originated phenomena are distinct from one another). According to the first and second senses of "dhātu" *(chieh),* dharmadhātu refers to either the cause for the realization of the noble path or the underlying nature of phenomenal reality. In either case, its meaning is closely related to that of "tathāgatagarbha," and, indeed, in tathāgatagarbha texts such as the *Ratnagotravibhāga (Pao-hsing lun)* the two terms are used synonymously. When dharmadhātu is thus interpreted in line with tathāgatagarbha theory, *fa-chieh yüan-ch'i* can be understood in terms of nature origination *(hsing-ch'i).* In the third sense of "dhātu" *(chieh),* however, Fa-tsang ponts out that "dharma" *(fa)* is equivalent to "dhātu" *(chieh);* dharmadhātu can thus also be understood to refer to differentiated phenomena. In this case *fa-chieh yüan-ch'i* refers to the unobstructed interrelation of phenomena *(shih-shih wu-ai)*—and it is in this sense, Liu Ming-Wood concludes, that Fa-tsang uses the term in his *Treatise on the Five Teachings* (see "The Teaching of Fa-tsang," 391–396). Tsung-mi, in his emphasis on nature origination, interprets "dharmadhātu" strictly in terms of the tathāgatagarbha doctrine.

7. The ten profundities *(shih-hsüan)* were first elaborated by Chih-yen in his *Ten Profound Gates of the Hua-yen* [*Sūtra*] (*Hua-yen shih-hsüan men;* see the translation by Cleary in *Entry Into the Inconceivable,* 126–146). These were adopted by Fa-tsang in his *Treatise on the Five Teachings* without modification, other than in their order (see *T* 45.505a12ff.; Cook, "Fa-tsang's *Treatise on the Five Doctrines,*" 496ff.). Fa-tsang's enumeration of the ten profundities in his *T'an-hsüan chi,* however, replaces two of Chih-yen's categories with two new ones (see *T* 35.123a28–b4). Significantly, one of those deleted by Fa-tsang in this version is "creation through the transformation of the mind alone." Kamata has suggested that this change marked a shift in Fa-tsang's thought away from the tathāgatagarbha doctrine of the *Awakening of Faith* toward a greater emphasis on *shih-shih wu-ai* (see *Chūgoku kegon shisōshi no kenkyū* [Tokyo: Tōkyō daigaku, 1965], 553).

8. Fa-tsang's most detailed explanation of this metaphor can be found in his *Yu-hsin fa-chieh chi* (*T* 45.647a17ff.), translated in Liu, "The Teaching of Fa-tsang," 190.

9. See "The Teaching of Fa-tsang," especially the concluding chapter.

10. Tsung-mi does quote from the *Wang-chin huan-yüan kuan* in his *Hsing yüan p'in shu ch'ao* (399c15–17). Although this work is often attributed to Fa-tsang, Kojima Taizan has argued convincingly against the likelihood of Fa-tsang's authorship. See his "*Mōjin gengen kan* no senja o meguru shomondai," *Nanto bukkyō* 49 (1982): 13–31.

11. See *Chu Hua-yen fa-chieh kuan-men, T* 45.684b24–c1; *Yüan-chüeh ching ta-shu, ZZ* 1/14/2.106d3–6; and *Ta-sheng ch'i-hsin lun shu,* 14v2–3.

12. The phrase *"t'ung* [Mathews no. 6641] *wei i-chen fa-chieh,"* which Tsung-mi claims to be quoting from Ch'eng-kuan, does not occur in Ch'eng-kuan's

Hsing yüan p'in shu. Ch'eng-kuan does, however, use the phrase "*tsung* [Mathews no. 6912] *wei i-chen wu-ai fa-chieh*" in the beginning of his commentary on the "Entering the Dharmadhātu Chapter" in his commentary on the *Hua-yen Sūtra* (see *T* 35.908a16).

13. The chapter of the *Hua-yen Sūtra* from which this passage is quoted seems to have originally circulated as an independent scripture, the **Tathāgatatotpatti-sambhavanirdeśa,* which was translated into Chinese as the *Ju-lai hsing hsien ching* (*T* no. 291) by Dharmarakṣa in the late third century. Significantly in the present context, it seems to have played a seminal role in the development of the tathāgatagarbha doctrine. According to Takasaki Jikido's reconstruction of the development of the tathāgatagarbha doctrine, this passage served as the model for a similar passage in the *Tathāgatagarbha-sūtra* (*Ju-lai-tsang ching*) (see *T* 16.457b28–c10), the first scripture to expound the tathāgatagarbha doctrine explicitly (see *A Study of the Ratnagotravibhāga, Serie Orientale Roma* 33 [1966], 35–36). The importance of this passage from the *Hua-yen Sūtra* for the tathāgatagarbha doctrine is further indicated by its quotation in full in the *Ratnagotravibhāga* (see *T* 31.827a29–c1; Takasaki, 189–192).

14. See Kamata, *Chūgoku kegon shisōshi no kenkyū,* 579–580.

15. See my essay "The Place of the Sudden Teaching" for a more detailed discussion.

16. See Oh, "A Study of Chinese Hua-yen Buddhism," 199. The same opinion is repeated in his "*Dharmadhātu:* An Introduction to Hua-yen Buddhism," *The Eastern Buddhist,* n.s. 12, no. 2 (1979): 86.

17. See Yoshizu Yoshihide, "Shūmitsu no *Daijōkishinronshū* ni tsuite," *Indogaku bukkyōgaku kenkyū* 30, no. 2 (1982): 796–800. Tsung-mi's commentary can be found in case 31, vol. 8, division 5, and part 2 of the *Dai Nippon kōtei daizōkyō.*

18. To borrow the concluding catena of James Joyce's parody of the twelve-linked chain of conditioned origination: "In the ignorance that implies impression that knits knowledge that finds the nameform that whets the wits that convey contacts that sweeten sensation that drives desire that adheres to attachment that dogs death that bitches birth that entails the ensuance of existentiality." See *Finnegans Wake* (New York: Viking Press, 1967), 18.

19. See Z. D. Sung, *The Text of the Yi King,* reprint ed. (Taipei: Ch'eng Wen Publishing Co., 1971), 3.

20. Ch'eng-kuan often claimed to borrow the words from the Chinese religious classics without thereby also adopting their meaning; see *T* 36.2b9, for example.

21. See my essay "Sudden Enlightenment Followed by Gradual Cultivation: Tsung-mi's Analysis of Mind," in Peter N. Gregory, ed., *Sudden and Gradual: Approaches to Enlightenment in Chinese Thought,* Studies in East Asian Buddhism, no. 5 (Honolulu: University of Hawaii Press, 1987), 290–298.

22. "Tsung-mi and the Single Word 'Awareness' *(Chih),*" *Philosophy East and West* 35, no. 3 (1985): 249–269.

23. See Yanagida Seizan, "The *Li-tai fa-pao chi* and the Ch'an Doctrine of Sudden Awakening," trans. Carl W. Bielefeldt, in Lewis Lancaster and Whalen Lai, eds., *Early Ch'an in China and Tibet* (Berkeley: Berkeley Buddhist Studies Series, 1983), 13–49.

Glossary

Ch'an 禪
Ch'an-yüan chu-ch'üan-chi tu-hsü 禪源諸詮集都序
chen-ju fa-chieh 眞如法界
chen-ti 眞諦
ch'eng-fa pen-chiao 稱法本教
Ch'eng-kuan 澄觀
Ch'eng wei-shih lun 成唯識論
chien-fen 見分
Chih-yen 智儼
Chin-kang san-mei ching 金剛三昧經
chou-pien han-jung kuan 周遍含容觀
chu-chi mo-chiao 逐機末教
chu-chi-tun 逐機頓
Chu Hua-yen fa-chieh kuan-men 註華嚴法界觀門
ch'üan-shih tui-pien 權實對辨
chüeh 覺
ch'ung-ch'ung wu-chin 重重無盡
Chung-hua ch'uan-hsin-ti Ch'an-men shih-tzu ch'eng-hsi t'u 中華傳心地禪門師資承襲圖
fa-chieh 法界
Fa-chieh kuan-men 法界觀門
fa-chieh yüan-ch'i 法界緣起
fa-chih 法執
Fa-tsang 法藏
fang-pien 方便
fen-ch'i yu-shen 分齊幽深
Fo-hsing lun 佛性論
hai-in san-mei 海印三昧
hai-in ting 海印定
Ho-tse 荷澤
hsiang 相
hsiang-chi 相即
hsiang-fen 相分
hsiang-ju 相入
hsiang-tsung 相宗
hsien-hsing chiao 顯性敎
hsin chen-ju 心眞如
hsin chen-ju men 心眞如門
hsin sheng-mieh 心生滅
hsin sheng-mieh men 心生滅門
hsing 性
hsing-ch'i 性起
Hsing yüan p'in shu 行願品疏
Hsing yüan p'in shu ch'ao 行願品疏鈔
hua-i-tun 化儀頓
Hua-yen 華嚴
Hua-yen ching 華嚴經
Hua-yen ching hsing yüan p'in shu 華嚴經行願品疏
Hua-yen ching hsing yüan p'in shu ch'ao 華嚴經行願品疏鈔
Hua-yen yu-hsin fa-chieh chi 華嚴遊心法界記
Hui-kuang 慧光
Hung-chou 洪州
i-chen fa-chieh 一眞法界
i fa-chieh hsin 一法界心
i-hsin 一心
Jen Kuan 任權
ju-lai-tsang 如來藏
ju-lai-tsang yüan-ch'i 如來藏緣起
Kuei-feng Tsung-mi 圭峯宗密
k'ung-tsung 空宗
li 理
Li-tai fa-pao chi 歷代法寶記
li-shih jung-t'ung wu-ai 理事融通無礙
li-shih wu-ai 理事無礙
Ma-tsu Tao-i 馬祖道一
mieh-shih 滅識
ming 明
p'an-chiao 判敎
Pao-t'ang 保唐
P'ei Hsiu 裴休
pen-chüeh 本覺
pen-yüan 本源
pieh-chiao i-sheng 別敎一乘
pu-chüeh 不覺
pu-pien 不變
Shen-hui 神會
shih 事
shih-chüeh 始覺
shih-hsüan 十玄
shih-shih fa-men 十十法門
shih-shih wu-ai 事事無礙
su-ti 俗諦
sui-yüan 隨緣
sui-yüan yung 隨緣用

Ta-sheng ch'i-hsin lun 大乘起信論
Ta-sheng ch'i-hsin lun shu 大乘起信論疏
ta-sheng chung-chiao 大乘終教
ta-tsai chen-chieh 大哉眞界
ta-tsai ch'ien-yüan 大哉乾元
tan jen-hsin wei hsiu 但任心爲修
Tao-yüan 道圓
t'i-hsiang 體相
t'i-hsing 體性
tsung 宗
tsung-kai wan-yu 總該萬有
Tsung-mi 宗密
tsung wei i-chen wu-ai fa-chieh 總唯一眞無礙法界
Tu-shun 杜順
t'ung wei i-chen fa-chieh 統唯一眞法界
tzu-hsing yung 自性用
wan-fa tzu-shih 萬法資始
wan-wu tzu-shih 萬物資始
wo-chih 我執
Wu-chiao chang 五教章
Wu-chu 無住
wu-nien 無念
yüan-ch'i 緣起
yüan-chiao 圓教
Yüan-chüeh ching 圓覺經
Yüan-chüeh ching ta-shu 圓覺經大疏
Yüan-chüeh ching ta-shu ch'ao 圓覺經大疏鈔
Yüan-chüeh ching lüeh-shu 圓覺經略疏
Yüan-chüeh ching lüeh-shu ch'ao 圓覺經略疏鈔
Yüan-jen lun 原人論

Ch'an Hermeneutics: A Korean View

ROBERT E. BUSWELL, JR.

The Concerns of Ch'an Hermeneutics

The Ch'an contributions to the hermeneutical debate in East Asian Buddhism present the scholar with a unique set of interpretive problems. The Ch'an tradition has always claimed to be a "separate transmission outside the scriptures"[1] focusing on direct spiritual experience rather than philosophical analysis. Indeed, when scriptures were dismissed as inferior conceptualization and the nonverbal expression of truth was considered to be the paramount level of discourse, it is hardly surprising that Ch'an discussions skirted most of the major issues confronted by text-based Buddhist hermeneuts, such as the *nītārtha/neyārtha* problem. In a process somewhat paralleling the evolution of hermeneutic philosophy in the West, such as some of the work of Heidegger and Ricoeur, Ch'an hermeneutical considerations can be seen evolving toward gnoseological and ontological concerns.[2]

Ch'an hermeneutics directly confronts two of the most fundamental problems in Buddhist spiritual culture: first, what is the process through which enlightenment is achieved, and second, what is the precise content of enlightenment? As we will see, the examinations of these two questions undertaken by Ch'an exegetes were intended to prove their own claim that Buddhist religious development culminated in Ch'an, and not in the scholastic schools *(chiao,* Kor. *kyo)* as their Hua-yen and T'ien-t'ai rivals had contended. Hence hermeneutical principles were developed that would help to distinguish Ch'an's descriptions of practice and enlightenment from seemingly parallel descriptions in the sūtras, and thereby corroborate its claim of being a unique system. Ch'an hermeneutics developed in direct response to pressures from polemicists in the scholastic schools, and by examining the interaction between these rivals, we may adduce much about the ways in which the Ch'an school selectively employed sacred texts in order, first, to uphold its own sectarian position and, second, to counter aspersions cast on it by its rivals. At the same time, however, Ch'an explicitly subordinated this hermeneutic of control to a hermeneutic of recollection, and the school's perspectives are as much a theory of understanding as a system of interpretation. Rather than remaining complacent with a hermeneutic that described the principles by which truth was to be explained, Ch'an adepts insisted on taking the extra step to a direct, personal experience of that truth. In their description of precise techniques by which that realization was to be effected, Ch'an hermeneutics takes on a larger significance, as yet only glimpsed in western treatments of the topic. Hence, a study of the Ch'an approach to the discipline will contribute many new perspectives and significant data for a general theory of hermeneutics.

In this inquiry into Ch'an hermeneutics, I intend to focus on the exegesis given in the Korean Ch'an school (there, known as Sŏn), and specifically on the analysis of Chinul (1158–1210), who presented one of the most provocative and comprehensive examinations of Ch'an hermeneutics found anywhere in East Asia. At the outset, it is worthwhile to point out that treating the Korean approach as emblematic of Ch'an as a whole does not lead to a distortion of the greater tradition as one might suspect. As the successors to a vigorous critical tradition in Chinese Ch'an Buddhism, one that produced the likes of Kuei-feng Tsung-mi (780–841) and Yung-ming Yen-shou (904–975), the Koreans provide trenchant synopses and cogent critiques of the contributions of many of the seminal thinkers of the East Asian Buddhist tradition. From the Korean vantage point, then, we have a ready overview of the entire hermeneutical debate within the East Asian Ch'an school. The Korean hermeneutical system forged by Chinul, in particular, presents a graphic example of the ways in which a hermeneutic of control was designed to culminate in a hermeneutic of recollection. Hence, by examining Chinul's treatment of this topic, as supplemented by other relevant material from Chinese and Korean sources, we should be able to make fairly precise assessments of the presuppositions underlying the Ch'an hermeneutical debate, the challenges it faced in establishing its perspective, and the insights arrived at by the Ch'an hermeneuts.

The Treatment of Ch'an in Hua-yen Hermeneutics

Since the time of Tsung-mi, a fundamental concern in Ch'an hermeneutics was the effort to counter the placement of Ch'an in the doctrinal taxonomy of the rival Hua-yen school. Beginning with Fa-tsang (643–

712), Chinese Hua-yen exegetes developed an interpretive system in which the most simplistic form of Buddhist doctrine was identified as the kataphasis, or "radical pluralism,"[3] of the Hīnayāna (specifically the Sarvāstivāda) school *(Hsiao-sheng chiao).* This approach was considered to be superseded by the apophasis of the Mahāyāna inception teaching *(Ta-sheng shih-chiao),* including both the idealist perspective of Hsüan-tsang's variety of Chinese Yogācāra, which did not accept the existence of the Buddha-nature in all beings, and the Madhyamaka doctrine of śūnyatā. This apophasis was countered by the Mahāyāna final teaching *(Ta-sheng chung-chiao),* founded upon the tathāgatagarbha doctrine of the *Awakening of Faith (Ta-sheng ch'i-hsin lun),* which combined the preceding two partial teachings in a comprehensive fusion of absolute and phenomenal *(li-shih wu-ai).* Implicit in the final teaching, however, was a conceptual bias that in its turn was overcome by the sudden teaching *(tun-chiao),* which "revealed" *(hsien)* rather than verbalized the teaching.[4] This approach was exemplified by Vimalakīrti's celebrated silence, offered as his answer to the meaning of nonduality.[5] The last and culminating phase of the doctrinal progression outlined by the Hua-yen school was of course the complete, or perfect, teaching *(yüan-chiao)* of the *Avataṃsakasūtra,* which reaffirmed without qualification the importance of each individual element of existence in creating and sustaining the universe *(shih-shih wu-ai).* As Peter Gregory has demonstrated, in Hua-yen hermeneutics "we thus see a move from a naive kataphasis through a thoroughgoing apophasis to a new and higher kataphasis."[6]

The major failing of this elaborate taxonomical system lay in its treatment of the so-called sudden teaching. As Hui-yüan (fl. 673–743) first pointed out, the sudden teaching that Fa-tsang described was not an innovative interpretation of doctrine but instead a more advanced method of instruction; as far as content was concerned, it was identical to the Mahāyāna final teachings and did not deserve a separate classification.[7] Since subitism in this scheme clearly referred to a method of exposition, it was not consistent with the other categories of Fa-tsang's taxonomy of the teachings, which were all classified according to their content. This inconsistency between the description of suddenness as involving a style of instruction *(hua-i chiao)* and suddenness as a unique doctrinal category *(hua-fa chiao)* was also noted by the T'ien-t'ai reformer Chan-jan (711–782) and reiterated by Tsung-mi and later Chinul.[8]

It was Ch'eng-kuan (738–840), traditionally regarded as the fourth patriarch of the Hua-yen school, who attempted to answer Hui-yüan's critique of this conception of the sudden teaching. The distinguishing feature of Fa-tsang's characterization of the sudden teaching was its focus on the calm and extinguished noumenal nature of the mind *(chi-mieh li-hsing)* and on nonconceptual descriptions of that principle. While both the inception and final teachings of Mahāyāna are gradual in that they are concerned with successive stages of development, Fa-tsang considered that "as far as the sudden teaching is concerned, [it involves] such [descriptions as] 'words and speech are suddenly cut off,' 'the noumenal-nature suddenly manifests,' 'understanding and conduct are suddenly perfected,' and 'if one thought does not arise, that is Buddhahood.' "[9] Despite the apparent similarities to the language of Ch'an in these descriptions, Fa-tsang himself seems to have had in mind such teachings as were found in the *Vimalakīrtinirdeśasūtra* and *Laṅkāvātarasūtra* in defining this class of doctrine; there is no evidence that he was at all aware of the nascent Ch'an movement. Nevertheless, the Ch'an parallels were quick to be noted by Fa-tsang's successor in the Hua-yen school, Ch'eng-kuan, the first Chinese exegete who attempted to incorporate the Ch'an tradition into a doctrinal classification scheme. Ch'eng-kuan, who seems to have had considerable associations with the Ch'an tradition of his time,[10] proposed that the sudden teaching actually referred to Ch'an:

> The mind-to-mind transmission of Bodhidharma corresponds precisely to this teaching. If one does not point to this one word [the mind] and therewith directly explain that mind is Buddha, then how else would [that mind] be transmitted? Therefore, they speak *(yen)* while relying on the ineffable, and directly verbalize *(ch'üan)* that principle which is separate from verbalization. This teaching is also clear. Therefore, the Southern and Northern schools of Ch'an are indistinguishable from the sudden teaching.[11]

However this interpretation might have helped in Ch'eng-kuan's attempt to vindicate Fa-tsang's description of the sudden teaching,[12] its placement of the Ch'an teachings as inferior to the complete teachings of Hua-yen created a sometimes bitter and always prolix sectarian controversy between later Ch'an and Hua-yen exegetes.

As Ch'an burgeoned in China and then throughout all of East Asia, Ch'eng-kuan's equation of all of Ch'an with the sudden teaching came to be seen as a drastic oversimplification. Ch'an had become a complex tradition propounding a variety of conflicting approaches to practice and enlightenment. Relating Ch'an to any one teaching was no longer tenable. Ch'eng-kuan's own successor in the Hua-yen school, Tsung-mi, summarily rejected this treatment of the Ch'an tradition. In his *Yüan-chüeh ching ta-shu ch'ao* (Autocommentary to the *Complete Enlightenment Sūtra*), Tsung-mi explicitly refers to seven major Ch'an schools popular during his day, and there are passing references to still more schools in his other works.[13] In addition to his Hua-yen affiliations, Tsung-mi was also considered to be the fifth patriarch of the Ho-tse school of Ch'an, a middle Ch'an school founded by Shen-hui (684–758) with close ties to the so-called Southern school of Ch'an. Given the inherent antipathy between his own lineage and the Northern school of Shen-hsiu (606?–706), it is difficult to conceive that Tsung-mi would have permitted a classification in which the Southern and Northern lineages were treated identically. Moreover, Tsung-mi's own eclecticism, which prompted him to look for parallels between Ch'an and the scriptural teachings, would have precluded any assertion that there were qualitative differences between the Ch'an and scholastic schools of his time.[14]

Because of these factors, Tsung-mi rejected Ch'eng-kuan's interpretation of the sudden teaching and proposed instead two complementary interpretations of its meaning: first, he reverted to Chan-jan's description of the sudden teachings as referring to a method of exposition *(hua-i)* rather than to a distinctive doctrinal viewpoint; second, he saw Ch'an as a teaching specifically adapted to the spiritual propensities of the superior cultivator.[15] Going back to earlier *p'an-chiao* precedents,[16] Tsung-mi classified the *hua-i* sudden teaching as a complete and sudden teaching *(yüan-tun chiao),* involving such stereotypically Hua-yen doctrines as the perfect interpenetration of all phenomena.[17] This expansion of the scope of the sudden teaching would prove to be of considerable importance in the exegeses of later Ch'an commentators, such as Yen-shou and Chinul.

Chinul, as is so often the case in his thought, attempts to respond to some of the specific problems which the interpretations of his Chinese predecessors had created for the Ch'an tradition. First of all, Tsung-mi's syncretic perspective, in which explicit correspondences had been drawn between specific scholastic doctrines and the teachings of certain Ch'an schools,[18] left little room for Ch'an's claim of being a unique tradition distinct from the teachings of the sūtras. Second, Tsung-mi's prominent bias in favor of the Ho-tse school of Ch'an, which died out soon after his death, came at the expense of the Hung-chou lineage and it left Tsung-mi's arguments open to attack by the numerous apologists of the burgeoning new schools deriving from that latter line, especially in the Lin-chi school, who felt betrayed by Tsung-mi's analyses.[19] It became Chinul's aim to resurrect whatever was of value to Ch'an practitioners in Tsung-mi's syncretism while merging it with what Chinul regarded as the consummate Ch'an approach of Ta-hui Tsung-kao (1089–1163). Hence, by employing the correspondences Tsung-mi had observed between Ch'an and *chiao,* Chinul attempted to prove that Ch'an was not simply a variety of sudden teaching but instead had explicit parallels with the complete teaching of Hua-yen, the pinnacle of the scholastic doctrine. At the same time, however, Chinul did not stop short with demonstrating the points of convergence between Ch'an and the teachings, as Tsung-mi had done; he also tried to prove the inherent superiority of the Ch'an school over the scholastic schools, on the basis not only of descriptive concerns such as the mode of doctrinal expression but also of soteriological issues such as the higher quality of its religious practice. Hence, in Korean Buddhist hermeneutics, it was Ch'an, and not Hua-yen, that emerged as the only "true" complete and sudden teaching, because its practice resulted in the consummation of the complete teaching, but through a process of sudden, not gradual, realization.

Distinguishing Ch'an from the Sudden Teaching

The seeming parallels we have observed between the Ch'an approach and the Hua-yen description of the sudden teaching were a constant source of irritation to Ch'an theorists. These correspondences implied, of course, that Ch'an was inferior to the complete teaching, the fifth of the five teachings. Moreover, in the Hua-yen description Ch'an emerges as a system solely concerned with the speed at which enlightenment is achieved, rather than with the full perfection of all the phenomenal aspects implicit in the state of Buddhahood. Because such perfection in the phenomenal realm was the goal of the Hua-yen school, as epitomized in its teaching of *shih-shih wu-ai,* Hua-yen would loom superior in any comparisons with Ch'an.

To vindicate Ch'an from these claims of inferiority, there were two approaches that could be followed. First, and most directly, the differences between the description of the state of enlightenment achieved through Ch'an practice and that which was attained via the sudden teaching could be explicated, thereby attacking the reputability of the sudden teaching's gnoseology and demonstrating the distinctiveness of Ch'an. Second, following the Chinese penchant for the rectification of names *(cheng-ming),* the sudden teaching could be redefined in order to refute Fa-tsang's description of its content. Ch'an exegetes could thereby prove that, even if Ch'an were identical to the sudden teaching, the sudden teaching was in fact the ultimate approach to Buddhist spiritual cultivation. As we shall see, Chinul and the Korean school adopted both approaches in their attempt to vindicate the Sŏn orientation.

The Differences Between Ch'an and the Sudden Teaching

To demonstrate the uniqueness of the Ch'an lineage, it was first incumbent on the Koreans to disprove all presumed parallels between the sudden teaching, as it was conceived by the scholiasts, and Ch'an. The fundamental point of difference they focused upon was the inadequacy of the description of the state achieved through the sudden teaching's soteriology. The abandonment of all thought, which the sudden teaching described as the state of Buddhahood, was said to be "merely the Buddhahood achieved through realization of the noumenon; it can be called the undeveloped dharmakāya."[20] While such a state brings about proleptic awareness of the noumenal essence of Buddhahood—that is, the inchoate potentiality of Buddhahood—it does not result in any understanding of the fundamental identity between that noumenal essence and the phenomenal realm. Accordingly, there could be no development of any of the capabilities of that noumenon to adapt expediently to the relative, conceptual sphere. In such an interpretation, the sudden teaching would actually emerge as inferior even to the Mahāyāna final teaching in the quality and content of its understanding.

In contrast to the apophatic one-sidedness of this conception of the sudden teaching, Ch'an makes use of meditative topics such as the *kung-an* (Kor. *kongan*) and the *hua-t'ou* (Kor. *hwadu*) as well as of radical techniques such as shouting and beating in order to bring about a personal realization. Through investigating the *hua-t'ou,* for example, an existential doubt *(i-hsin,* Kor. *ŭisim)* is created that ultimately leads Ch'an adepts to a sudden understanding of the dharmadhātu.

> That the doubt about the *hwadu* is broken and in an instant he activates one moment of realization means that he has a personal realization of the unobstructed *dharmadhātu (muae pŏpkye)*. . . . If they suddenly activate one moment of realization, then the *dharmadhātu* which is perfectly interfused by nature and completely endowed with meritorious qualities is clearly understood. As the patriarch of Ts'ao-ch'i explained: "The self-nature contains the three bodies; / Its discovery perfects the four wisdoms."[21]

Ch'an, therefore, is not simply an approach that exposes the quiescence of the noumenon; instead, it reveals all the unfathomable qualities immanent in that essence by penetrating to the suchness that is the unifying stuff of noumenon and phenomena. This correspondingly opens to the student the ability to use all the phenomenal, adaptable qualities of Buddhahood, as is the case for Ch'an adepts who "have investigated the word [the *hwadu*], broken the doubt, had a personal realization of the one mind, displayed prajñā, and engaged in wide propagation of the teachings of Buddhism."[22] The Ch'an stress on seeing the nature, therefore, is in no way deficient in regard to the complementary aspect of function (*yung,* Kor. *yong*). "If, due to one word of a master, a person looks back on the radiance of the self-nature and suddenly forgets words and understanding, the differences in the conditionally arisen secondary and primary karmic aspects throughout the ten realms will all appear brilliantly in the mirror of his own mind. There the *dharmadhātu's* unimpeded conditioned origination can be perceived."[23]

There are many accounts in Ch'an literature which indicate the fullness of the realization brought about through Ch'an meditation. We see this in a well-known story concerning Hung-chou Shui-liao (fl. eighth century), a student of Ma-tsu Tao-i (709–788).

> While they were out gathering rattan, Master Shui-liao asked Ma-tsu, "What is the real meaning of Bodhidharma's coming from the west?"
>
> Ma-tsu replied, "Come closer and I'll tell you."
>
> When Shui-liao was quite close, Ma-tsu kicked him in the chest, knocking him to the ground. In a daze, Shui-liao got up, clapping his hands and laughing loudly.
>
> Ma-tsu asked, "What insight did you have that has made you laugh?"
>
> Shui-liao said, "Hundreds of thousands of approaches to dharma *(fa-men)* and immeasurable sublime meanings *(miao-i)* are on the tip of one hair; today I have completely understood their source."[24]

A careful comparison of descriptions of the state of enlightenment achieved through Ch'an practice with Hua-yen accounts of the interfusion of the dharmadhātu yield some remarkable similarities. One of the best-known examples of the type of realization brought about through Ch'an techniques—which, despite being apocryphal, is no less telling—is the exchange between the sixth patriarch Hui-neng (638–713) and Yung-chia Hsüan-chüeh [alt. Chen-chüeh] (665–713), which catalyzed the latter's enlightenment.

> When the Great Master Yung-chia Chen-chüeh arrived at Ts'ao-ch'i carrying a gourd bottle and wearing a bamboo hat, he circumambulated the master's seat three times, struck his walking staff down once, and remained standing arrogantly before him. The Sixth Patriarch said, "Śramaṇas must keep the three thousand deportments and the eighty thousand minor rules of conduct. From where does the venerable one come that he is so conceited?"
>
> Chen-chüeh replied, "The matter of birth and death is great; impermanence [death] is fast closing in."
>
> The patriarch asked, "Why don't you experience the unborn and understand that which is not swift?"
>
> Chen-chüeh answered, "The experience is the unborn; understanding is originally without swiftness."
>
> The patriarch said, "That's right. That's the way it is." After a moment Yung-chia took leave, and the patriarch asked, "Aren't you leaving a little too fast?"
>
> Chen-chüeh replied, "Originally I am unmoving; so how can it be fast?"

> The patriarch asked, "Who knows that he is unmoving?"
> Chen-chüeh answered, "It's you who gives rise to such discriminations."
> The patriarch said, "You have understood well the meaning of the unborn. Stay over for one night."[25]

Chinul interprets this story in the following manner.

> . . . the Great Master Yung-chia Chen-chüeh broke straight out of the barrel[26] simply by hearing the Sixth Patriarch ask, "Why don't you experience the unborn?" He suddenly had a realization of the *dharmadhātu* and only answered, "The experience is the unborn; understanding is originally without swiftness." All this accords with the fact that at the point of realization there is no need for an excess of words. . . . In this sort of experience there is an awakening to the original mind which produces, in the mirror of one's mind, a perception of the inexhaustible *dharmadhātu* which is like the multilayered net of Indra. Such experiences are so common in the biographies and records of the Sŏn school that they cannot be counted. Deluded people do not know the source of these experiences. . . . Consequently, when they hear a Sŏn adherent explain that mind is the Buddha, they assume that this means nothing more than the Buddhahood of the nature's purity. . . . From these statements [of Hsüan-chüeh], we know that the Sŏn transmission which is beyond thought is the sudden realization of the *dharmadhātu*. It is certainly not the same as the sudden teachings. The sudden teachings do not explain the characteristics of dharma and advocate that the mere perception of the true nature where one thought does not arise is Buddhahood. . . . This is utter foolishness.[27]

The next morning, after leaving Ts'ao-ch'i, Hsüan-chüeh is said to have composed the celebrated ode *Ch'eng-tao ko* (Song of Enlightenment). Hsüan-chüeh sings of his experience:

> The shining of the mirrorlike mind is unimpeded in its brightness.
> Its bright luster radiates throughout worlds as numerous as grains of sand.
> All the phenomena in creation reflect within it;
> In the one ray of perfect light there is neither inside nor outside.
> One nature completely penetrates all natures,
> One dharma fully contains all other dharmas.
> One moon universally appears in all bodies of water,
> All the moons appearing in those waters are merged in that one moon.
> The dharmakāya of all the Buddhas enters into my own nature,
> And my nature reunites with that of all the Tathāgatas.[28]

Chinul comments on the realization expressed in Hsüan-chüeh's song:

> Then, once outside the temple gate, he broke out in song about his state of realization and said, "One nature completely penetrates all natures. . . ." Thus we know that this master's universal-eye state showed all phenomena to be in perfect interfusion. Sentient beings and Buddhas were perfectly interfused. All the stages of the bodhisattva path were perfectly interfused. The eighty-four thousand approaches to dharma were perfectly interfused. In this manner, the *dharmadhātu's* inexhaustible qualities and functions were brought to complete accomplishment in a snap of the fingers.[29]

As Chinul explains, Ch'an practice is not simply concerned with the removal of the discriminative processes of thought; it also involves the positive reinforcement of wholesome qualities of mind, which can then be applied in the conditioned realm for the benefit of all sentient beings. Hence, Ch'an meditation purports to overcome limited perspectives concerning the absolute realm of the dharmadhātu and, at the same time, to produce both the capacity to transfer the merit deriving from one's understanding to other beings as well as the ability to use the power inherent in that merit as an expedient means of guiding others.[30] Simply because the mind-nature perceived through investigating the *hwadu* is originally tranquil, inherently divorced from conceptual discrimination, and free from relative signs does not mean that it is identical to the undifferentiated noumenon that the sudden teaching calls Buddhahood. Hence, any intimation on the part of the scholiasts that Ch'an is nothing more than the inferior sudden teaching was summarily rejected by the Koreans, and Ch'an's affinities with descriptions found in the complete teaching of Hua-yen were explicitly pointed out.

Redefining the Sudden Teaching

Simultaneous with disproving the affinities between the traditional outlook concerning the sudden teaching and Ch'an, the Korean Sŏn exegetes attempted to redefine the fundamental purport of the sudden teaching. As mentioned above, if Fa-tsang's contention were correct—i.e., that the sudden teaching involved simply the realization of the noumenal-nature which was separate from thought—then the content of the sudden teaching would be comparable to the even more inferior Mahāyāna inception teachings. A convenient foil for a refutation of this contention was found in the *Ta-sheng ch'i-hsin lun,* which proposed:

> The suchness of the mind is the essence of the teaching of the great general characteristic *(ta-tsung hsiang)* of the one *dharmadhātu:* that is to say, it is the mind-nature which neither arises nor ceases. It is only due to deluded thoughts that all dharmas are differentiated. If one leaves behind the

> mind's thoughts, then all the signs of the sense-spheres are nonexistent. For this reason, since the beginning all dharmas have been separate from the signs of words and speech, . . . and, ultimately, are undifferentiated, immutable, and indestructible. They are only the one mind. Therefore it is called suchness.[31]

In this passage, no-thought is said to result in a realization not merely of the quiescence and nondiscrimination of the noumenon, but also of the general characteristic—that is, the totality—of the dharmadhātu. Once that characteristic is realized, there is no longer any need to maintain a condescending attitude toward relative objects, because all objects would then be understood to be the sublime functioning *(miao-yung,* Kor. *myoyong)* of the essence of the dharmadhātu. Hence, the sudden teaching can be seen as an expedient expression of the need to give up attachment to all relative signs—whether skillful or unskillful, defiled or pure—and was intended for cultivators who grasped at characteristics that were ultimately empty. As I shall discuss in more detail below, through the state of no-thought engendered by this teaching, the student achieves the access to realization *(chŭngip)* which the Koreans, following the exposition of Hua-yen doctrine found in the *Hsin Hua-yen ching lun* (Exposition of the New [Translation] of the *Avataṃsakasūtra*) by Li T'ung-hsüan (635–730), have considered to be equivalent to the first abiding-stage (the formal inception of the bodhisattva path) achieved after the completion of the ten levels of faith.[32] Through the realization-awakening *(chŭngo)* achieved on that first abiding-stage, the student is finally able to leave behind his initial understanding of the emptiness of all things and enter into suchness. Hence, although the achievement catalyzed through the sudden teaching "is called the Buddhahood achieved through realization of the noumenon, this suchness is . . . the nature of all dharmas as well as the fountainhead of the manifold supplementary practices [of the bodhisattva] *(manhaeng).*"[33] In this way the Ch'an tradition sought to define the content of the sudden teaching not in terms of the Mahāyāna inception teaching, but in relation to the complete teaching of Hua-yen.

Distinguishing Ch'an from the Complete Teaching

As we have seen, one of the major premises of Ch'an hermeneutics was that its gnoseology had more in common with the synthetic doctrines of the complete teaching than with the radical apophasis of the sudden teaching. At the same time, however, if the uniqueness of Ch'an was to be upheld, its apologists also had to distinguish Ch'an from that pinnacle of the scholastic doctrine and ultimately prove its own unassailable superiority. The logic used by Ch'an exegetes to demonstrate this claim was much shakier than that employed to refute the school's affinities with the sudden teaching. As outlined above, the Ch'an enlightenment experience was analyzed as being closely allied to that of the unimpeded interfusion of the dharmadhātu as taught in the complete teaching. Another evocative element was that the initial level of Ch'an discourse, which I will discuss in detail below, used explanations similar to those found in the Hua-yen school to instruct beginning students in Ch'an practice. Given these admitted parallels, it was not the content of the complete teaching that was called into question—the approach Ch'an scholiasts had followed in refuting the validity of the sudden teaching—but its inferiority as a vehicle for spiritual cultivation when compared to Ch'an. Thus, while clarifying the points of correspondence between Ch'an and Hua-yen doctrines and practices, the Koreans attempted to demonstrate that, despite their affinities, there were indeed specific distinguishing features that could not be overlooked in assessing these schools. Ultimately, when all the evidence had been weighed, Ch'an was to be considered superior to the complete teaching because its approach brought it closer to the absolute itself at all stages of the mārga.

The key to the analysis of the relationship between Ch'an and the complete teaching was provided by Li T'ung-hsüan's exegesis of Hua-yen doctrine. In Li's assessment, which became the standard interpretation of the Korean tradition after Chinul's time, the essence of the dharmadhātu, namely, the one mind,[34] is realized by awakening to the fundamental wisdom of universal brightness *(p'u kwang-ming chih).*[35] Since it was posited that all plurality derives from that perfect essence, its realization brings in turn the consummation of the unimpeded interpenetration between all phenomena *(shih-shih wu-ai),* the raison d'être of the Hua-yen teachings.[36] Ch'an advocates saw a close affinity between Li's interpretation of this wisdom of universal brightness and the penchant in Ch'an practice to remain always focused on the one mind, as the following passage from Chinul's writings demonstrates:

> From the stage of an ordinary man, therefore, until he first gives rise to the *bodhicitta,* practices the bodhisattva path, and finally reaches the stage of fruition, all of Vairocana Buddha's great compassion, wisdom, and vows, as well as each and every thought, each and every action, each and every dharma, each and every moment, and each and every place, are all the operation of his own mind's wisdom of universal brightness.[37]

For Chinul, however, the crucial flaw in Li T'ung-hsüan's outline of practice was its inherently conceptual nature. While Li's system aims to present a viable analysis of the process of spiritual development, it neglects to describe the import of this experience from the standpoint of the person who is actually engaged in the practice. Purely theoretical descriptions are therefore denounced by Sŏn exegetes as being ultimately a hindrance to the meditator, because, rather than helping the student to abandon intellectual knowledge and to experience the mind-essence directly, such descriptions vitiate the real essence of that truth by enclosing it within a framework that merely provides more grist for the mind's conceptualizing mill. Hence, in the development of its students, the complete teaching of Hua-yen relies on acquired knowledge *(śrutamayīprajñā)* and conceptual understanding *(cintamayīprajñā)* rather than on direct meditative experience *(bhāvanāmayīprajñā).*

The inadequacies of this approach are apparent when the state preceding enlightenment is examined. According to the Korean interpretation of Li T'ung-hsüan's and Tsung-mi's analyses of the process of enlightenment, the first moment of awakening is catalyzed by an understanding-awakening *(haeo),* which is the initial comprehension of the fundamental identity between the individual's ignorance and the Buddhas' wisdom. This understanding is said to take place at the first of the ten stages of faith *(ch'osim-chi),* preliminary to the formal entrance to the bodhisattva path itself. But, after continuing to "infuse their learning and training with the Hwaŏm explanation of the unimpeded conditioned-origination of the *dharmadhātu,* then on the level of the ten faiths, their minds are filled with its influence and they perfect both understanding and conduct."[38] At this point, the adept has fulfilled the ten stages of faith and is ready to enter the bodhisattva path formally at the first abiding-stage *(vihāra)* of the arising of the thought of enlightenment *(bodhicittotpāda).* This is accomplished through the access to realization *(chŭngip).* However, as "the access to realization is achieved through thoughtlessness *(munyŏm),* it also involves abandoning words and cutting off thought."[39] The realization-awakening *(chŭngo)* achieved at the first abiding-stage can therefore be achieved only after the student has been established in no-thought. By implication, only after the knowledge and conceptualization inherent in the descriptions of the complete teaching of Hua-yen are transcended—thereby obviating the need for those teachings—can the meditator attain the state of no-thought and thus gain true realization. Hence, the approach of Hua-yen "is vitiated by acquired understanding via words and meaning, so its adherents have not yet attained the undiscriminative wisdom *(mubunbyŏl-chi).* These people must first pass through their views and learning, their understanding and conduct; only then can they enter into realization. At the time of this access to realization, their experience will correspond to the no-thought of the Sŏn approach."[40]

Of course, masters in the Ch'an school sometimes employed descriptions that parallel those found in the complete teaching—an incongruency from the standpoint of the Ch'an adage that the school "does not establish words and letters." Some of the more syncretic Ch'an schools, like the Fa-yen, even adapted Hua-yen terminology such as "unimpeded interfusion" in order to explain the enlightenment experience of Ch'an. Nevertheless, despite the apparent similarities between the descriptions used in the two schools, Ch'an exegetes maintained that there was a fundamental point distinguishing them. Hua-yen was concerned with a theoretical explication of the truth while the Ch'an accounts were intended solely to catalyze awakening—that is, to bring about direct, personal experience of that state of interfusion. Not only were the Ch'an descriptions terser (Ch. *sheng-lüeh,* Kor. *saengnyak*) than the prolix explanations of Hua-yen, they also were expedient expressions propounded with a completely different purpose in mind—immediate realization. Hence, the Ch'an descriptions are actually much closer to the ultimate nonconceptual reality. As Chinul says:

> From the evidence, we can see that, compared with the [ten] mysterious gates in the scholastic schools, the theory of Sŏn is much broader and its realization-wisdom more encompassing. . . . Consequently, the Sŏn approach values only the breaking of grasping and the manifestation of the source; it has no use for a profusion of words or the establishment of doctrines. . . . We should know then that the doctrine of unimpededness as explained by masters of the Sŏn school might be identical to that in the complete teachings, but their descriptions are more concise. Consequently, they are nearer to the actual access to realization.[41]

Resolving Misconceptions about Ch'an

In the preceding sections, I have attempted to show that the three primary thrusts of Ch'an hermeneutics were, first, to distinguish Ch'an from the sudden teaching; second, to demonstrate the affinities between the Ch'an enlightenment experience and the doctrine of the unimpeded interpenetration of the dharmadhātu as found in the complete teaching of Hua-yen; and third, to corroborate Ch'an sectarian claims that the school was finally superior even to that apex of the scholastic teachings. Having set forth these principles, I will now examine some of the misconceptions fostered in previous scholarly treatments of Ch'an which distort the true place of Ch'an within the East Asian hermeneutical tradition.

One misconception has been that Ch'an is somehow closely akin to the Indo-Tibetan Prāsaṅgika-Madhyamaka school,[42] which the East Asians would have classified as part of the Mahāyāna inception teaching. As we have seen, Ch'an hermeneutics began as a response to the evaluation of Ch'an as an inferior teaching by Hua-yen, and is a development on, rather than a radical departure from, the perspectives of the indigenous East Asian tradition. Perforce, Ch'an has stronger affinities with the kataphatic hermeneutics of the Chinese tradition as a whole and the Hua-yen school in particular than with the apophasis that characterized the Chinese perception of the Madhyamaka approach. A fundamental difference between Ch'an practice and that of the Mahāyāna inception teaching is Ch'an's orientation toward instilling in its students not so much an understanding of śūnyatā as a realization of the unimpeded interpenetration of the dharmadhātu. This point is brought out most clearly in the quintessentially Ch'an *Ch'eng-tao ko* by Yung-chia Hsüan-chüeh, which I have quoted from earlier. While some Ch'an descriptions in the *kung-an* collections and the discourse-records *(yü-lu)* of the patriarchs, when taken in isolation, can be construed as being allied in intent and method with those used by the Madhyamakas,[43] such parallels are consistently rejected by exegetes within the Ch'an school, who frequently vilify the latter's doctrine of emptiness.[44] The underlying ontological and soteriological purposes of Ch'an were in fact considered to be quite distinct from those of Madhyamaka, which most of the mature East Asian schools regarded as an inferior teaching; hence, to equate the two is a fundamental misrepresentation of the doctrinal presuppositions of the Chinese tradition.

A less crucial misconstruction is the implication that Ch'an statements, such as those implying the inherent identity between Buddhas and sentient beings, should be considered equivalent to the Mahāyāna final teaching.[45] This is, in fact, a misrepresentation of the distinction Fa-tsang himself drew between the final and complete teachings: namely, that the final teaching refers to the unity of existence and emptiness while the complete teaching refers to the identity of all elements of the phenomenal world.[46] In sum, Ch'an should be regarded as a synthesis of the nonconceptual emphasis of the sudden teaching and the perfected kataphasis of the complete teaching; indeed it was this synthesis that allowed Ch'an to call itself the only true "complete and sudden teaching."

Ch'an Hermeneutical Devices

Levels of Ch'an Discourse: The Three Mysterious Gates

Having examined the polemical motives prompting the development of Ch'an hermeneutics, we may now turn to specific interpretive tools used in the Ch'an school to uphold its sectarian point of view.

A nascent hermeneutical principle vital to distinguishing the various levels of Ch'an discourse and clarifying their differences from scholastic descriptions is the three mysterious gates *(san-hsüan men,* Kor. *samhyŏn-*

mun).[47] In the three mysterious gates, the basic or entry level of Ch'an discourse is to use theories such as mind-only *(wei-hsin)* or mere-representation *(wei-shih)* in order to explain the principle of the unimpeded interpenetration of all phenomena. At this level, rhetoric that is reminiscent of the complete teaching, such as the fundamental identity of sentient beings and Buddhas, is used to explain the first mystery, the "mystery in the essence" *(t'i-chung hsüan,* Kor. *ch'ejung-hyŏn).* After establishing the student in the kind of all-inclusive, nondiscriminative understanding engendered through such kataphatic teachings, the teacher continues on to the explicitly apophatic approach of *hua-t'ou* (Kor. *hwadu*) investigation, known as the "mystery in the word" *(chü-chung hsüan,* Kor. *kujung-hyŏn).* The process of gradually disentangling the student from the conceptual workings of his mind that the *hua-t'ou* brings about eventually culminates in the "mystery in the mystery" *(hsüan-chung hsüan,* Kor. *hyŏnjung-hyŏn),* involving completely nonconceptual expressions such as striking or shouting, which are intended to remove all of the defects implicit in conceptual understanding *(p'o-ping,* Kor. *p'abyŏng).* However, once this misapprehension is resolved, those very same expressions become not weapons to remove the defects of conceptual understanding, but "complete expressions" of truth *(ch'üan-t'i,* Kor. *chŏnje).*[48] Hence, Ch'an discourse finally culminates in an experientially based kataphasis that authenticates the conceptually based kataphasis of the mystery in the essence. Here we see once again that Ch'an discourse is not intended to be merely an imitation of the Mahāyāna inception or final teachings, but instead mirrors the progression of Chinese hermeneutical structures from naive kataphasis, to radical apophasis, to perfected kataphasis. For this reason, Ch'an discourse is distinguished by a gnoseological perspective that allows it to encompass the whole of Chinese hermeneutics by expanding the narrow exegetical and sectarian interests of the scholastic schools into a larger concern with the spiritual well-being of each individual adept.

Live-word/Dead-word

One of the most distinctive hermeneutical tools developed in Ch'an is that of the "live-word" *(huo-chü,* Kor. *hwalgu)* and "dead-word" *(ssu-chü,* Kor. *sagu).*[49] As these terms are used by Ch'an teachers, any type of theoretical description, whether found in Ch'an or in scholastic writings, would be considered a "dead-word," while any teaching that is intended not to explain but to enlighten would be a "live-word." "In the Sŏn approach, all these true teachings deriving from the faith and understanding of the complete and sudden school which are as numerous as the sands of the Ganges are called dead-words because they induce people to create the obstacle of understanding."[50] The live-word, however, permits no conceptual understanding at which the deluded mind might grasp; as it has been described by Ta-hui Tsung-kao, "This one word is the weapon which smashes all types of wrong knowledge and wrong conceptualization."[51] By the same token, however, if the processes by which this live-word brings about realization were themselves to become the subject of theoretical interpretation, that "live-word" would automatically become instead a "dead-word." To warn his students about this inveterate tendency to reflect on the principles involved in contemplation, Ta-hui said, "Students of Ch'an must investigate the live-word; do not investigate the dead-word. If you stay fixed on the live-word, you will not forget it for an eternity of kalpas; but if you stay fixed on the dead-word, you will not be able to save yourself."[52] If there be any doubt about where Ch'an and Hua-yen expressions fit into this scheme, we need only recall the statement by Chinul's eminent Yi-dynasty successor in the Chogye school, Sŏsan Hyujŏng (1520–1604): "The shortcut approach [of Sŏn] is the live-word; . . . the complete and sudden approach [of Hwaŏm] is the dead-word."[53]

By resorting to the device of the "live-word," Ch'an exegetes justified their use of conceptual ideas—provided of course that such ideas were intended to catalyze awakening—without belying their claim that such descriptions differed fundamentally from those used in the scholastic schools. The distinction between the explicit purposes of Ch'an and scholastic doctrine adumbrated in the live-word/dead-word principle was also drawn by Tsung-mi, in a passage from his *Ch'an-yüan chu-ch'üan chi tu-hsü:* "The teachings of the Buddha are intended to support tens of thousands of generations; hence their principles have been demonstrated in detail. The admonitions of the patriarchs involve an immediate crossing-over to liberation; they aim at producing mysterious penetration."[54]

Tsung-mi's position suggests that Ch'an's claim of being a separate transmission outside the scriptures inevitably relegates the scholastic teachings to an extremely constricted role: the continuity of the ecclesiastical structures of the church and the preservation of its dogma. Ultimately, the scriptures have nothing to do with realization. Even though the Buddha surely must have uttered "live" words, in the sense that they were intended to prompt personal liberation, once those words were recorded and transmitted from generation to generation, they became dead. This caveat would seem to apply as well to the teachings of the patriarchs of the Ch'an school when they came to be recorded in the many and varied anthologies that the school's adepts compiled. Finally, all such transmitted words are dead, because they only serve to sustain the faith of the religious adherents of the Buddhist church; they do not lead to no-thought, which is the access to realization. For

Chinul, the only live-word was the *hwadu,* because it, and not scholastic explanations, helped to break down the conceptualizing tendency of the mind, resulting in no-thought.[55]

Of course, theoretical descriptions of the processes involved in *hwadu* practice, such as Chinul himself made, are themselves dead-words. Nevertheless, Chinul regarded them as vital to the successful development of the vast majority of Ch'an students, for without the correct understanding about his practice and his status on the spiritual path that is engendered by such accounts, it would be the rare student indeed who would be able to make consistent progress in his training. So, while the analysis of Ch'an practice made by Chinul and other exegetes might be "dead," its inculcation in Ch'an students at the inception of their practice is the factor that largely determines their later success in attaining true realization.

I might add, however, that it would seem that even the dead-words of the scriptures can come alive, provided that they are read with the purpose of bringing about realization. Such was the case with Chinul's own enlightenment experiences, which took place while he was reading texts: specifically, the sixth patriarch's *Platform Sūtra,* Li T'ung-hsüan's *Hsin Hua-yen ching lun,* and Ta-hui's *Ta-hui yü-lü.* Chinul, in fact, was one of the few Korean masters who never made the incumbent pilgrimage to study under eminent Chinese Ch'an masters. Moreover, Korean Sŏn during his own time was so degenerate that he was unable to find a master who was competent to teach him about orthodox Sŏn practice. Given those circumstances, Chinul fell back on the only reliable source of instruction available to him: the sūtras attributed to the Buddha and the words of the Ch'an patriarchs.[56] While Chinul never says so explicitly, I am sure he would not deny that those texts were as alive for him as any nonverbal expression of truth, if not in fact brought alive through his "perfect reading" of them.

Circular Graphics

Another hermeneutical device of particular importance in the Ch'an school was that of circular graphics. Such symbols were used to describe different levels of spiritual understanding and practice, but without resorting to the bane of verbalization. This use of circles as an expedient means of teaching in the Ch'an school seems to have begun with Nan-yang Hui-chung (677–744), who is said to have transmitted a set of ninety-seven such forms. The book listing them, however, was destroyed by one of his students, Yang-shan Hui-chi (803–887), cofounder of the Kuei-yang school of the classical Chinese Ch'an tradition. Despite Hui-chi's apparent antipathy toward Hui-chung's symbols, circular graphics became one of the most distinctive features of the Kuei-yang teaching technique. Later Chinese masters who employed such symbolism included Tung-shan Liang-chieh (807–869), whose five rankings are probably the most well known usage, and Kao-feng Yüan-miao (1238–1295), who used circles to represent rational Ch'an, Tathāgata Ch'an, and patriarchal Ch'an.[57]

In Korea, circular symbols were introduced by Sunji (fl. 858), a contemporary of Tung-shan, who studied in China under Hui-chi. Given Sunji's chronological proximity to Hui-chung, it is possible that his graphics closely mirror Hui-chung's own circles, which are no longer extant. Sunji developed several different sets of circles to symbolize various aspects of Buddhist ontology and practice; for example, he used eight symbols in four sets to explain the noumenon and five symbols in four sets to explain the process of spiritual maturation. It is his second group of four symbols in two sets, however, that is explicitly hermeneutical; it is designed to "negate falsity and reveal truth" (see figure 1). Symbol 1a is the logograph for man inside a circle, with the ox-logograph above. This is the sign of "abandoning the doctrine but retaining conceptual thinking." This graphic symbolizes the teaching of the one Buddha vehicle of T'ien-t'ai, which was considered to allow a person to attain some measure of liberation, but without freeing him from his dependence on verbal teachings. The ox-logograph (symbolizing conceptual understanding) remains outside the circle (representing the noumenal wisdom), indicating that while scriptural teachings may provide the support necessary to induce initial awakening, they do not lead to the complete perfection of the noumenal wisdom. Its complement, symbol 1b, has the logograph for man inside a circle, which is the sign of "cognize the root and return to the source." Because conceptual understanding has been transcended and the noumenal wisdom achieved in this sign, the ox-logograph is removed but the man-logograph is retained. This graphic refers to the meditative practices of Sŏn as well as to the teachings found in the *Vajrasamādhisūtra* (*T* no. 273). Symbol 2a is the man-logograph inside a circle with the ox-logograph underneath; this is the sign for "losing one's head and recognizing only one's shadow." This refers to Pure Land adherents who do not have faith in their own innate Buddhahood, but instead seek rebirth in some distant Pure Land where they believe it will be easier for them to attain enlightenment. By seeking externally for enlightenment rather than looking for the Pure Land that is within their own minds, such people only sustain their own delusion. The complement to this, symbol 2b, is again the man-logograph inside a circle, representing the sign "turning one's back on one's shadow and recognizing one's head." In this sign, one reflects internally on the light emanating from the source of the mind, as would the Sŏn adept, and realizes that the Buddha and the Pure Land are innate in one's own mind.[58]

While circular graphics seem to have been neglected after Sunji's

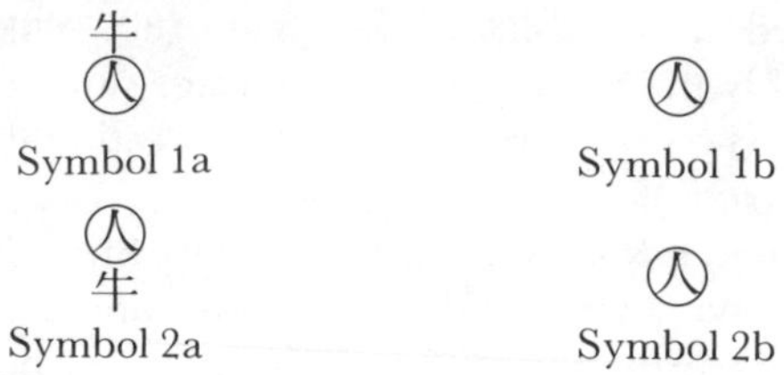

Figure 1. Sunji's Circular Graphics

time and were not employed by Chinul, they enjoyed a resurgence of popularity in Korea during the Yi dynasty and found numerous explicators, including Hamhŏ Tŭkt'ong (1376–1433) and Paekp'a Kŭngsŏn (d. 1852). The explanations of the meaning of the symbols used by Sunji and other Sŏn adepts drew heavily upon Hwaŏm (Hua-yen) teachings, and exemplify the affinities that existed between the hermeneutical approaches of the two schools.

The Value of Ch'an to a General Theory of Hermeneutics

From the preceding discussion, it should be clear that the Ch'an school developed interpretive approaches that employed unique hermeneutical principles. While these principles pertained implicitly to scriptural interpretation, they were more fundamentally concerned with ordering the broad range of spiritual experience, and then with catalyzing direct realization of those levels of experience. This orientation suggests that there is a pronounced soteriological thrust to Buddhist, and especially Ch'an, hermeneutics that is not found in the interpretive methods developed, for example, in the Judeo-Christian tradition.

The live-word/dead-word notion and the use of circular graphics provide an approach to Ch'an interpretation that allows greater fidelity to the historical and doctrinal contexts of that tradition than would the inevitably culture-bound concepts of western hermeneutics. At the same time, however, such alternate approaches to hermeneutics provide interesting material for a comparison of exegetical principles, which should offer significant input toward developing a truly cross-cultural theory of religious interpretation.[59] Indeed, in any development of a general theory of hermeneutics, we cannot afford to ignore the unique contributions that Ch'an has made to the discipline.

Notes

1. According to a famous gnome on Ch'an practice attributed by the tradition to Bodhidharma: "A separate transmission outside the scriptures, / No reliance upon words and letters, / Directly pointing to the human mind, / See

the nature and achieve Buddhahood." For the textual history of this passage, see the discussion in D. T. Suzuki, *Essays in Zen Buddhism,* vol. 1 (1927; reprint ed., London: Rider and Co., 1958), 176.

2. I am thinking specifically of Martin Heidegger's *Being and Time,* trans. John MacQuarrie and Edward Robinson (New York: Harper and Row, 1962), and Paul Ricoeur's "Existence and Hermeneutics," in *The Conflict of Interpretations* (Evanston: Northwestern University Press, 1974), 11–24.

3. Theodore Stcherbatsky, *The Central Conception of Buddhism and the Meaning of the Word "Dharma"* (1923; reprint ed., Delhi: Motilal Banarsidass, 1979), 73; this analysis has been accepted by most subsequent Buddhologists. For a critique, however, see David J. Kalupahana, *Causality: The Central Philosophy of Buddhism* (Honolulu: University Press of Hawaii, 1975), 69–88.

4. See Peter N. Gregory, "Chinese Buddhist Hermeneutics: The Case of Hua-yen," *Journal of the American Academy of Religion* 51 (1983): 238, quoting Fa-tsang, *Hua-yen i-sheng chiao-i fen-ch'i chang* (alt tit. *Wu-chiao chang*), *T* 45.495b5.

5. *Wei-mo-chieh so-shuo ching (Vimalakīrtinirdeśasūtra)* 2, *T* 14.551c23–24; Robert A. F. Thurman, trans., *The Holy Teaching of Vimalakīrti* (University Park: University of Pennsylvania Press, 1976), 77; Gregory, "Chinese Buddhist Hermeneutics," 246 n. 5.

6. Gregory, "Chinese Buddhist Hermeneutics," 239. For general surveys in English of the Hua-yen doctrinal taxonomies, see Junjirō Takakusu, *The Essentials of Buddhist Philosophy* (Honolulu: University of Hawaii Press, 1947), 114–117; Liu Ming-wood, "The *P'an-chiao* System of the Hua-yen School in Chinese Buddhism," *T'oung Pao* 67 (1981): 18–47; Gregory, "Chinese Buddhist Hermeneutics," 238–245.

7. Hui-yüan, *Hsü Hua-yen lüeh-shu k'an-ting chi, ZZ* 1/5/12a4–6; quoted in Liu, "*P'an-chiao* System of Hua-yen," 33; Gregory, "Chinese Buddhist Hermeneutics," 239, and Peter N. Gregory, "The Place of the Sudden Teaching within the Hua-yen Tradition: An Investigation of the Process of Doctrinal Change," *Journal of the International Association of Buddhist Studies* 6 (1983): 39.

8. See Robert E. Buswell, Jr., *The Korean Approach to Zen: The Collected Works of Chinul* (Honolulu: University of Hawaii Press, 1983), 355 n. 125, which also includes other relevant references; this volume is hereafter cited as *KAZ.* See also discussions in Gregory, "Sudden Teaching," 52, and Gregory, "Chinese Buddhist Hermeneutics," 239–240. For the treatments by Tsung-mi and Chinul, see *KAZ,* 291–294.

9. *Wu-chiao chang* 1, *T* 45.481b16–18; see *KAZ,* 241, 244. See also Liu, "*P'an-chiao* System," 34, and Gregory, "Sudden Teaching," 34.

10. See Gregory, "Sudden Teaching," 57 n. 24, summarizing the research of Kamata Shigeo, who suggests that the Ox-head (Niu-t'ou) school of middle Ch'an exerted the most influence over Ch'eng-kuan's thought.

11. *Ta-fang kuang fo hua-yen ching sui-shu yen-i ch'ao, T* 36.62b1–4. See Liu, "*P'an-chiao* System," 34, and Gregory, "Sudden Teaching," 42.

12. See Gregory's discussion in "Sudden Teaching," 42–43.

13. See *KAZ,* 90–91 nn. 184, 185; the relevant passages from Tsung-mi's works are excerpted in Jan Yün-hua, "Tsung-mi: His Analysis of Ch'an Buddhism," *T'oung Pao* 58 (1972): 41–50. See also the discussion in the introduction to *KAZ,* 39, and nn. 183–185.

14. See summary in Gregory, "Sudden Teaching," 44–45.

15. *Ch'an-yüan chu-ch'üan chi tou-hsü* 3, *T* 48.407b–408a; excerpted by Chinul in *Pŏpchip pyŏrhaengnok chŏryo pyŏngip sagi,* in *KAZ,* 292; see also Chinul's discussion in *KAZ,* 292–304.

16. Compare Gregory's "Sudden Teaching," 49–50.
17. *Ch'an-yüan chu-ch'üan chi tou-hsü* 3, *T* 48.407c6–12; Gregory, "Sudden Teaching," 48–49.
18. For these links see Gregory, "Sudden Teaching," 45.
19. See, for example, the searing criticism of Tsung-mi by Chüeh-fan Hui-hung (1071–1128), the noted Sung historiographer and third-generation master in the Huang-lung lineage of the Lin-chi school, in his *Lin-chien-lu;* translated in *KAZ,* 347–348 n. 69. Note also the traducement of Tsung-mi by Le-t'an K'o-wen (alt. Chen-ching) (1025–1101), who called Tsung-mi "a rank-smelling guy who brings ruin on ordinary men" *(p'o fan-fu sao-ch'ou han);* quoted with approval by Ta-hui in *Ta-hui yü-lü* 30, *T* 47.941a3–4.
20. *KAZ,* 241.
21. *KAZ,* 249, and 242; quote is from *Liu-tsu t'an ching* (Platform Sūtra of the Sixth Patriarch) *T* 48.356b; and cf. *KAZ,* 242–243, where the dharmadhātu is equated with the one mind. For a full discussion of this process see *KAZ,* 247–249, and Robert E. Buswell, Jr., "Chinul's Synthesis of Chinese Meditative Techniques in Korean Sŏn Buddhism," in Peter N. Gregory, ed., *Traditions of Meditation in Chinese Buddhism,* Studies in East Asian Buddhism, no. 4 (Honolulu: University of Hawaii Press, 1986).
22. *KAZ,* 252–253.
23. *KAZ,* 217.
24. *Ching-te ch'uan-teng lu* (Transmission of the Lamp, Compiled During the Ching-te Reign-period) 8, *T* 51.262c; quoted in *KAZ,* 247.
25. *Liu-tsu t'an ching, T* 48.357c.; quoted in *KAZ,* 247.
26. "Barrel" refers to the "lacquer barrel" (Ch. *ch'i-t'ung,* Kor. *ch'ilt'ong*), an expression first used by Hsüeh-feng I-ts'un (822–908). It is used as a symbol for ignorance, which is like a black-lacquer barrel that allows no light to enter. Breaking the lacquer barrel is enlightenment. See *Pi-yen lu* (Blue Cliff Record) 1, case 5, *T* 48.144c.
27. *KAZ,* 248, and 213–214.
28. *Ch'eng-tao ko, T* 48.396a–b; quoted in *KAZ,* 212–213, and 162, 172, 248.
29. *KAZ,* 248.
30. See Chinul's discussion in *KAZ,* 249.
31. *Ta-sheng ch'i-hsin lun, T* 32.576a; cf. Yoshito S. Hakeda, trans., *The Awakening of Faith in Mahāyāna* (New York: Columbia University Press, 1967), 32–34. Quoted in *KAZ,* 243.
32. See *KAZ,* 241–242; and cf. *KAZ,* 295–296, and my discussion at *KAZ,* 358–359 n. 143, for Tsung-mi's view.
33. *KAZ,* 244.
34. *KAZ,* 203.
35. "Universal brightness . . . is the essence of the fruition wisdom of the dharmadhātu." *Hsin Hua-yen ching lun* 7, *T* 36.762b3.
36. Note Chinul's summary: "We know that the sea of characteristics of the ten bodies of Vairocana Buddha, the perfected fruition wisdom, is entirely the Buddha of the mind's own wisdom of universal brightness. According to what an individual's faculties can bear, it manifests what appear to be external characteristics; the regalia of his world and his person are, however, originally not external things. Since the measure of the mind's own wisdom of universal brightness is equal to the *dharmadhātu* and the whole of space, that wisdom's forms and functions are by nature free: they may be one or many, great or small, sentient beings or Buddhas. . . ." *KAZ,* 208.
37. *KAZ,* 208.

38. *KAZ,* 241.

39. *KAZ,* 242; and note Li T'ung-hsüan's comment: "First, enter in faith through acquired understanding; later, unite [with the unimpeded *dharmadhātu*] through thoughtlessness." *Hsin Hua-yen ching lun* 17, *T* 36.834b, quoted in *KAZ,* 242, 250.

40. *KAZ,* 249–250.

41. *KAZ,* 251, and 213. See also Chinul's discussion at *KAZ,* 321–322.

42. See Robert A. F. Thurman, "Buddhist Hermeneutics," *Journal of the American Academy of Religion* 48 (1978): 35–37. Calling the Mahāyāna inception doctrine apophatic does not of course mean that the Chinese portrayed Prāsaṅgika-Madhyamaka doctrine correctly. Indeed, a solid case might be made that Indo-Tibetan Prāsaṅgika places as much emphasis upon kataphatic affirmation *(mahākaruṇā)* as it does upon absolute negation (śūnyatā). Within all Chinese doctrinal taxonomies, however, any such parallels between the Mahāyāna inception teaching and Hua-yen or Ch'an would have been summarily rejected, and to claim otherwise is a distortion of the primary thrust of the East Asian Buddhist tradition. David Kalupahana's related claim (*Buddhist Philosophy: A Historical Analysis* [Honolulu: University Press of Hawaii, 1976], 170–176) that Ch'an Buddhism developed under the influence of the Hīnayāna teachings of the Chinese *Āgamas* may, for similar reasons, be ignored.

43. See, for example, the samples of Ch'an dialogue cited by Thurman, "Buddhist Hermeneutics," 36–37. Perhaps the prime exemplar of a "Madhyamaka" approach to Ch'an would be Niu-t'ou Fa-jung (594–657); for his records, see Chang Chung-yuan, *Original Teachings of Ch'an Buddhism: Selected from The Transmission of the Lamp* (New York: Pantheon Books, 1969), 17–26. I should note, however, that for the purposes of this essay, I am discussing Ch'an as it has been covered in theoretical treatments by Ch'an exegetes, not according to the teachings of the *kung-an* collections and discourse-records. Given the style of these latter genres of Ch'an literature, they can support virtually anything one might wish to claim about Ch'an when taken out of their traditional praxis context.

44. Ta-hui criticizes the doctrine of emptiness as involving "interpretations based solely on maintaining the void-calmness of indifference—that is, to teach people to rest until they attain a nescience wherein they are like earth, wood, tile, or rock." *Ta-hui yü-lü* 19, *T* 47.891a; quoted in *KAZ,* 337.

45. This misconstruction is found in Liu ("*P'an-chiao* System," 35), who does acknowledge elsewhere the parallels between Ch'an and the complete teaching.

46. *Hua-yen yu-hsin fa-chieh chi, T* 45.650b19–23; this passage is quoted in Liu ("*P'an-chiao* System," 39) and should have cautioned him about the difficulties inherent in his earlier statement.

47. The "three mysterious gates" were methods of instruction first used by Lin-chi I-hsüan (d. 866) and subsequently adopted by Fa-yen Wen-i (885–958), Yün-men Wen-yen (862?–949), and Fen-yang Shan-chao (947–1024). See *Lin-chi lu, T* 47.497a19–20; Ruth Fuller Sasaki, trans., *The Record of Lin-chi* (Kyoto: Institute for Zen Studies, 1975), 6; and Lin-chi's biographies in *Ching-te ch'uan-teng lu* 12, *T* 51.291a14 and 300b24. For their use by Fen-yang Shan-chao, see *Ching-te ch'uan-teng lu* 13, *T* 51.305a17, and *Hsü ch'uan-teng lu* 1, *T* 51.469b20. For Fa-yen and Yün-men, see *KAZ,* 250. For their treatment by Chinul, see *KAZ,* 214–215, 244–245.

48. See *KAZ,* 240–241 for discussion of these two aspects of *hwadu* investigation.

49. The terms "live-word" and "dead-word" are attributed to Tung-shan

Shou-ch'u (d. 990), a disciple of Yün-men Wen-yen (862?–949); see Chang, *Original Teachings,* 271. The terms are also used by Ta-hui, from whom Chinul and the later Korean tradition adopted them; see, for example, *Ta-hui yü-lü* 14, *T* 47.870b et passim; note also Chinul's discussion at *KAZ,* 240. For a Vajrayāna version of the live-word/dead-word notion, see Michael Broido, "Does Tibetan Hermeneutics Throw Any Light on *Sandhābhāsa?*" *Journal of the Tibet Society* 2 (1982): 16–20.

50. *KAZ,* 240.

51. *Ta-hui yü-lü* 26, *T* 47.921c; quoted also in *KAZ,* 338.

52. *Ta-hui yü-lü* 14, *T* 47.870b; quoted in *KAZ,* 252.

53. Sŏsan Hyujŏng, *Sŏn'ga kugam* (Guide to the Sŏn school), trans. Pŏpchong (Seoul: Chŏngŭmsa, 1976), 41. See also the discussion by Yŏndam Yuil (1720–1799), *Pŏpchip pyŏrhaengnok chŏryo kwamok pyŏngip sagi* (Taehŭng-sa xylograph, dated 1916, in the Tungguk University archives), fol. 29a12–29b6.

54. Tsung-mi, *Ch'an-yüan chu-ch'üan chi tou-hsü* 1, *T* 48.400a; quoted in *KAZ,* 251, 321–322. Note also the distinction between scholar and meditator monks *(ganthadurassa bhikkhu* and *vipassanadhurassa bhikkhu)* in the Pali commentarial tradition; Michael Carrithers, *The Forest Monks of Sri Lanka: An Anthropological and Historical Study* (Delhi: Oxford University Press, 1983), 168–169.

55. Robert Gimello's hypothesis ("Li T'ung-hsüan and the Practical Dimensions of Hua-yen," in Robert M. Gimello and Peter N. Gregory, eds., *Studies in Ch'an and Hua-yen,* Studies in East Asian Buddhism, no. 1 [Honolulu: University of Hawaii Press, 1983], 346–350) that Chinul may have intended to include Li T'ung-hsüan's writings in the second mystery because he "used language in just such a way as to inspire the transcendence of language" (p. 349) is something of an overstatement of Chinul's generous attitude toward Li; actually, Chinul valued Li's thought principally for the support it lent to orthodox Ch'an soteriological methods. According to Chinul's tripartite division of Ch'an discourse, even the words of this highly regarded commentator would have been relegated to the first mysterious gate because they still involved conceptualization; thus they could not establish the student in thoughtlessness (the access to realization), which occurred through the second gate, the "mystery in the word." This is not, however, to deny Gimello's primary thesis in his essay: "that it was the merit of Li T'ung-hsüan's thought to have preserved the insights of Hua-yen in forms that would allow their integration into religious contexts quite unlike those in which Hua-yen was born" (p. 149).

56. For Chinul's enlightenment experiences and the role of texts in bringing them about, see the introduction to *KAZ,* 20–29.

57. These different usages of circular graphics in Chinese Ch'an and Korean Sŏn are outlined in Kyung-bo Seo (Sŏ Kyŏngbo), *A Study of Korean Zen Buddhism Approached Through the Chodangjip* (cover title: *Han'guk Sŏn pulgyo sasang*) (Seoul: Poryŏn'gak, 1973), 253–312.

58. Sunji's different sets of circles are discussed in his biography in *Chodang chip,* fasc. 20; I have summarized the gist of Sunji's biography in a plain narrative in Peter H. Lee, ed., *Sources of Korean Tradition* (New York: Columbia University Press, forthcoming). The "translation" of Sunji's chapter in *Chodang chip* made by Seo in *Korean Zen Buddhism* is filled with errors and should be consulted only in conjunction with the original Chinese text. The section has also been summarized with somewhat greater success in Han Kidu, *Silla sidae ŭi Sŏn sasang* (Iri: Wŏn'gwang University Press, 1974), 90–100.

59. See Ninian Smart's comments concerning the role of tradition-specific theories of interpretation in the development of a general theory of herme-

neutics, in his essay "Comparative Hermeneutics: An Epilogue about the Future," in Michael Pye and Robert Morgan, eds., *The Cardinal Meaning: Essays in Comparative Hermeneutics: Buddhism and Christianity,* Religion and Reason 6 (The Hague: Mouton and Co., 1973), 195–199.

Glossary

Chan-jan 湛然
Ch'an-yüan chu-ch'üan chi tou-hsü 禪源諸詮集都序
ch'ejung-hyŏn 體中玄
Chen-chüeh 眞覺
Ch'eng-kuan 澄觀
cheng-ming 正名
Ch'eng-tao ko 證道歌
chiao 教
ch'ilt'ong 漆桶
chi-mieh li-hsing 寂滅理性
Ching-te ch'uan-teng lu 景德傳燈錄
Chinul 知訥
ch'i-t'ung 漆桶
Chodang chip 祖堂集
chŏnje 全提
ch'osim-chi 初心地
ch'üan 詮
ch'üan-t'i 全提
chü-chung hsüan 句中玄
Chüeh-fan Hui-hung 覺範慧洪
chŭngip 證入
chŭngo 證悟
fa-men 法門
Fa-tsang 法藏
Fa-yen 法眼
Fa-yen Wen-i 法眼文益
Fen-yang Shan-chao 汾陽善昭
haeo 解悟
Hamhŏ Tŭkt'ong 涵虛得通
Ho-tse 荷澤
Hsiao-sheng chiao 小乘教
hsien 顯
Hsin Hua-yen ching lun 新華嚴經論
Hsü Hua-yen lüeh-shu k'an-ting chi 續華嚴略疏刋定記
hsüan-chung hsüan 玄中玄
hua-fa chiao 化法教
hua-i 化儀
hua-i chiao 化儀教
hua-t'ou 話頭
Hua-yen i-sheng chiao-i fen-ch'i chang 華嚴一乘教義分齊章
Hua-yen yu-hsin fa-chieh chi 華嚴遊心法界記
Hui-neng 慧能
Hui-yüan 慧苑
Hung-chou Shui-liao 洪州水潦
huo-chü 活句
hwadu 話頭
hwalgu 活句
Hwaŏm 華嚴
hyŏnjung-hyŏn 玄中玄
i-hsin 疑心
Kao-feng Yüan-miao 高峰原妙
kongan 公案
Kuei-feng Tsung-mi 圭峰宗密
Kuei-yang 潙仰
kujung-hyŏn 句中玄
kung-an 公案
kyo 教
kyŏngjŏl-mun 徑截門
Le-t'an K'o-wen [Chen-ching] 泐潭克文[眞淨]
Li T'ung-hsüan 李通玄
Lin-chi I-hsüan 臨濟義玄
Lin-chi lu 臨濟錄
Lin-chien-lu 林間錄
li-shih wu-ai 理事無礙
Liu-tsu t'an ching 六祖壇經
manhaeng 萬行
Ma-tsu Tao-i 馬祖道一
miao-i 妙意
miao-yung 妙用
muae pŏpkye 無礙法界
mubunbyŏl-chi 無分別智
myoyong 妙用
Nang-yang Hui-chung 南陽慧忠
p'abyŏng 破病
Paekp'a Kŭngsŏn 白坡亘璇

p'o fan-fu sao-ch'ou han 破凡夫臊臭漢
p'o-ping 破病
p'u kwang-ming chih 普光明智
Pi-yen lu 碧巖錄
Pŏpchip pyŏrhaengnok chŏryo kwamok pyŏngip sagi 法集別行錄節要科目並入私記
Pŏpchip pyŏrhaengnok chŏryo pyŏngip sagi 法集別行錄節要並入私記
saengnyak 省略
sagu 死句
samhyŏn-mun 三玄門
san-hsüan men 三玄門
Shen-hsiu 神秀
Shen-hui 神會
sheng-lüeh 省略
shih-shih wu-ai 事事無礙
Sŏn 禪
Sŏn'ga kugam 禪家龜鑑
Sŏsan Hyujŏng 西山休靜
ssu-chü 死句
Sunji 順之(支)
Ta pan-nieh-p'an ching chi-chieh 大般涅槃經集解
Ta-fang-kuang fo hua-yen ching sui-shu yen-i ch'ao 大方廣佛華嚴經隨疏演義鈔
Ta-hui Tsung-kao 大慧宗杲
Ta-hui yü-lu 大慧語錄
Ta-sheng ch'i-hsin lun 大乘起信論
Ta-sheng chung-chiao 大乘終教
Ta-sheng shih-chiao 大乘始教
ta-tsung hsiang 大總相
t'i-chung hsüan 體中玄
tun-chiao 頓教
Tung-shan Liang-chieh 洞山良介
Tung-shan Shou-ch'u 洞山守初
ŭisim 疑心
wei-hsin 唯心
wei-shih 唯識
Wu-chiao chang 五教章
Yang-shan Hui-chi 仰山慧寂
yen 言
Yŏndam Yuil 蓮潭有一
yong 用
yüan-chiao 圓教
Yüan-chüeh ching ta-shu ch'ao 圓覺經大疏鈔
yüan-tun chiao 圓頓教
yü-lu 語錄
yung 用
Yung-chia Hsüan-chüeh 永嘉玄覺
Yung-ming Yen-shou 永明延壽
Yün-men Wen-yen 雲門文偃

Truth Words: The Basis of Kūkai's Theory of Interpretation

THOMAS P. KASULIS

It is the early ninth century in Japan. Emperor Kammu has recently moved the capital to Heian (Kyoto). In the mountains of Yoshino adjacent to the old capital areas of Nara and Nagaoka, a young college dropout sits in meditation, envisioning a full moon above the heart of the bodhisattva Kokūzō (Ākāśagarbha). He is chanting a *darani (dhāraṇī)* dedicated to that heavenly personage. What motivates this man to give up his scholastic studies in the city to undergo austerities in the mountains? Why would he turn his back on a comfortable career as a bureaucrat in order to wander half-naked in the cold of Yoshino, going from teacher to teacher, talking with hermit after hermit? What possible benefit from this incantation could outweigh the study of the Chinese classics he enjoys so much and at which he so excels?

However radical a change in life-style this asceticism may superficially suggest, on a deeper level the young man is being consistent with his past, his genius, and his lifelong drive to fathom the depths of his own psyche. The fruit of this particular arduous discipline is not thought to be healing powers, or psychokinetic energy, or interpersonal charisma. Rather, the motivation behind this retreat from books to a life among the rocks and trees is, oddly enough, an *intellectual* quest. That is, based on his reading of a text known as *Kokūzōgumonjihō,* the young man believes that if he takes this ascetic practice to its culmination and chants the *darani* one million times, he will be able to remember and understand all the key passages of every Buddhist work.[1]

The religious name taken by the young man was Kūkai, meaning the "sky and sea" or the "sea of emptiness." Posthumously, he would receive the title of Kōbō Daishi (Great teacher who promulgated the dharma). This episode from his early life exemplifies his profound concern for textual interpretation. It also suggests his fundamental conviction that the text's true meaning is not in the letters written on the page, but in the dynamics between the words and reader. Indeed, his faith in this point was so earnest that, based on something he read, he was willing to abandon temporarily his study of books in order to become a better reader.

To grasp Kūkai's view of interpretation, we must begin with the man himself. His answers were, after all, addressed to his questions, not ours. To understand what he said, we must go back to where and when he said it. In fact, Kūkai himself emphasized the interpenetration of the three mysteries or intimacies *(sammitsu):* body, speech, and mind. To penetrate the meaning of his words, therefore, we must consider the psychological and physical environment in which he lived.

Kūkai was born in 774 as a member of the Saeki clan (a branch of the influential Ōtomo family) in the province of Sanuki on the island of Kyūshū. In the opening of his historical novel about Kūkai, Shiba Ryōtarō discusses the character of this natural setting:

> The province of Sanuki in which Kūkai was born borders on the five inner provinces around the capital, separated from them by the waters of Chinu. The plains are broad, the mountains exceptionally low. Conical hills dot the landscape as though sprinkled here and there across the fields. Probably because the plains are broad, the sky—shining with the light off the sea—is opened up in its terrible expanse. Formed in the shoals, the clouds shift through their variegated forms. Is this not a natural environment that would nurture visions in a man?[2]

Of aristocratic stock, Kūkai was given the education of a young man befitting his station. Schooled in the Chinese classics, it was natural that when he came of age, he was sent to the capital to attend the university *(daigaku).* Yet, as a native of Shikoku, he also grew up removed from the urban sophistication and sinified life-style of the Nara court. So although he eventually became a friend of emperors and was recognized as a cultural celebrity, he always mistrusted urban glitter and preferred mountain spirituality. In a poem of his later years, he expresses this orientation explicitly. We can also note that, like his modern biographer Shiba, Kūkai himself liked to play on the naturalistic references in his name:

Why I Go Into The Mountains

You ask, "Teacher, why do you go into that deep cold—
That difficult place among the deep, steep peaks
Where the climb is painful and the descent dangerous,
That place where the mountain *kami* and tree spirits make their home?"

. . .

"There's no point in staying on and on (in the city).
I must go. I must.
No, no. I cannot stay.
This teacher of the great void *(kū)*, this child of [Shingon's]
milky sea *(kai)*
Does not weary of seeing Mount Kōya's rocks and pines,
And is continually moved by its clear-flowing streams.
Do not take pride in the poison of fame and gain.
Do not be consumed in the fiery world of delusion.
Taking up the secluded religious life, one quickly enters the
realm of the dharmakāya."[3]

This belief in the spiritual superiority of the mountains to the city was reinforced when Kūkai went to the capital to study at around the age of eighteen. The six Nara schools or Buddhist sects certified by the government followed a scholastic approach to the religion, emphasizing in their urban temples the study of texts over religious practices. In fact, the great religious leaders of the capital such as Gomyō (of the Hossō school), Tao-hsüan (of the Ritsu and Kegon), and Dōji (of the Sanron) seem to have gone regularly into the mountains of Yoshino themselves, presumably for religious retreats.[4] Thus, in forsaking the city for the mountains, Kūkai was really not being heretical, just earnest and single-minded.

In any case, after his sojourn in the imperial college, Kūkai did retreat into the mountains, probably for several years. Sometime around the period when he actually dropped out of school, he wrote his first formal critical study, *Aims of the Three Teachings (Sangōshiiki).*[5] This work is important for our understanding of Kūkai's theory of interpretation in several respects. First, there is the issue of genre. It is essentially a work of didactic fiction detailing a discussion among a Confucian, a Taoist, and a Buddhist ascetic. In his preface to the work (apparently written in 797, when he was twenty-four), Kūkai states two purposes for writing it. First, he sees it as an apologia addressed to his relatives, justifying his decision to leave Confucian studies for a life of Buddhist asceticism. Second, since in the work the three sages attempt to convert a young man from his profligate life-style, the preface tells us that Kūkai himself has such a nephew and he hopes this work will have a positive effect on him.

We can make three observations about *Aims of the Three Teachings* as an example of didactic fiction. First, Kūkai was explicit about what he was doing and what he was trying to accomplish by writing the work. His preface to an early draft compares his project with other works of fiction in both China and Japan. It is clear from those comments that fiction is to be evaluated ultimately by its effects on the reader rather than its style or content. So a work with didactic purpose (like his own) is, in the final analysis, a greater contribution than a work which merely tantalizes, stirs certain emotions, or amuses. Here we find an early tendency on Kūkai's part to interpret the meaning of a text in terms of what its words *do* as much as what they say or evoke.

Second, analogous to the point just made, Kūkai (like Plato, especially in his early and middle dialogues) understood religious or philosophical positions in terms of the people who hold them. That is, a major criterion for evaluating a teaching is its effects on the human being who lives according to it. As the title of the work suggests, Kūkai was more interested in the teachings' *aims* than in their content, or perhaps better stated, he saw the aims as inseparable from their content. He saw no sharp distinction between theory and practice.

Third, the work displays Kūkai's early use of imagination as a vehicle for expressing the dharma. To explain the teachings of Confucianism, Taoism, and Buddhism, Kūkai used an artistic device: creating a fictional discussion among proponents of the three life-styles. He would never return to this specific genre again (although he did tinker with the text of *Aims* later in life), but he continued to uphold the centrality of artistic expression, especially art and poetry, as ideal vehicles for conveying the most profound levels of religious truth.

Having briefly discussed the significance of its genre, we turn now to the actual content of the work. First, we notice that all three teachings turn out to be effective means for reforming the young man. The Confucian sage in the book refers to the ideals of duty, filial piety, and loyalty. He claims that if the young man would study the classic virtues and accept his social responsibilities, he would find a personal and social harmony far exceeding any short-term enjoyment derived from his fast and loose life-style. The Taoist, on the other hand, promises self-purification and longevity for anyone practicing the alchemical arts and introspection. The Buddhist, the final speaker, chastises his companions for their emphasis on mundane benefits. After all, the Buddhist ascetic claims, this world of impermanence is permeated with suffering. What is really needed, he said, is the transcendent bliss of nirvāṇa, the ground of universal wisdom and compassion befitting all beings. In short, all three sages show a path out of moral degeneracy. As a cure for the profligate life-style, any of the three would be effective.

Obviously, Kūkai did not take the three teachings to be equals, however. This brings us to our second observation. In *Aims,* Buddhism is deemed superior because its viewpoint is transcendent, more complete, and absolute. In other words, *Aims* establishes a hierarchy of teachings based on their ability to go beyond the ordinary world of experience. In crude terms, the more other-worldly the religion, the better. By this criterion, Confucianism's social harmony is a quantum leap beyond the hedonism of the young man, but is still subordinate to Taoism's search for immortality. Envisioning Buddhism to be the most other-worldly religious tradition, Kūkai ranks it the highest.

Although Kūkai's evaluation of Buddhism as the supreme tradition never changed, it is important to see how he came to view Buddhism as something much more than a world-negating asceticism. To follow this reversal in his thinking, we return to his biography, investigating the nature of the experience that led him not only to leave the mountains, but also to visit the most cosmopolitan and bustling city of the time, the Chinese capital of Ch'ang-an.

Again, it was the reading of a text that changed the course of Kūkai's life. When he was about thirty years old, he came across a copy of *Dainichikyō (Mahāvairocana Sūtra).* We can observe two connections between this work and the earlier scripture that had so affected him, *Kokūzōgumonjihō.* First, both works were translated into Chinese by the same person, Śubhākarasimha (637–735), the first patriarch of esoteric Buddhism in China. In being so deeply influenced by the texts Śubhākarasiṃha had chosen to translate, Kūkai was, in effect, becoming an unwitting disciple of esoteric Buddhism. When Kūkai went to China, therefore, he was able to assimilate the Shingon teachings in a period of just over two years. This was a tribute not only to his genius, but also to the fact that he had been an anonymous Shingon Buddhist for years, practicing the tradition without the benefit of its explicit philosophical and liturgical structure.

The second connection between *Dainichikyō* and *Kokūzōgumonjihō* is more intriguing. As we have seen, Kūkai made his retreat into the mountains because he believed his millionfold incantation of Kokūzō's *darani* would give him the ability to memorize and understand all the critical passages in every Buddhist scripture. Yet, Kūkai found that he could not completely understand many key sections of *Dainichikyō.* Since no one in Japan could help him with his questions, Kūkai resolved to study at the source itself by visiting the Chinese capital.

The interesting issue here, however, is why the failure of the Kokūzō practice to deliver its promised exegetical omniscience did not discourage Kūkai from following the tradition further. Indeed, to the contrary, Kūkai risked his life on the hazardous journey to China. One explanation might be that Kūkai found he could understand the ideas in the text, but not its ritualistic references. Since there could be no dichotomy between theory and practice, he realized that his knowledge had to be grounded in esoteric practices, practices as yet unknown in Japan at the time. This, in itself, would have justified Kūkai's trip to China.

But going further, perhaps Kūkai saw in the text the promise of something more than another interpretation of reality. Perhaps he saw at least the germ of a *theory* of interpretation itself, a hermeneutic that would make sense of the two, as yet unintegrated, forces in his life: a faith in texts as revealing truths that can transform the person and a conviction that the truth is lived through practice, not the philosophical study of texts. As an individual, Kūkai felt himself pulled in two opposing directions. Part of him was only at home in the solitude and ritualistic closeness to nature found in the mountains. Another part of him was only at home in the world of words, texts, and cultural accomplishment. Somehow he had to integrate the mountains and the city: the indigenous Japanese awe for the natural, animistic, and shamanistic as well as the imported Chinese reverence for scholarship, learning, and moral virtue. It was probably this inner conflict on both the personal and cultural levels that led Kūkai to venture his life in order to understand an obscure Buddhist text.

In any case, Kūkai went to China and returned two and a half years later as the eighth patriarch of esoteric Buddhism. Not accidentally, his tradition is known as *Shingon* Buddhism. Historically, *shingon* serves as one of the Sino-Japanese renderings for *mantra* or sacred incantation. Hence the term itself suggests ritualistic practice. Ideographically, the two characters of *shingon* actually mean "truth word."

Kūkai's personal quest, as we have seen, can be understood in terms of his search for the truth of words. Both these aspects, the ritualistic structure and the question of truth, are intimate parts of the Shingon theory Kūkai inherited and then developed. To understand Kūkai's theory of interpretation, we shift our focus from biographical to more philosophical issues and begin by considering each aspect in turn.

At the heart of Kūkai's hermeneutic is a theory about the nature of words. From the Shingon standpoint, each and every thing in the universe is an "expressive symbol" *(monji)* of the dharmakāya. In fact, the universe as a whole is the "symbolic embodiment" *(sammayashin)* of the dharmakāya as the Buddha, Dainichi. In this respect, contrary to exoteric schools of Buddhism which understand the dharmakāya to be the *abstract* identification of the Buddha with reality itself, Shingon maintains that the identification between Buddha and reality is *concrete* and *personal.* To understand the impact of this teaching, it is useful to talk about Shingon theory as operative on three levels: what we shall call the cosmic, the microcosmic, and the macrocosmic.

On the cosmic or supersensible level, the world is just Dainichi Nyorai's act or function *(yū).* As an enlightened person, Dainichi is in a meditative state, mentally envisioning reality (maṇḍala), verbally intoning the sacred sounds (mantra), and physically enacting the sacred gestures (mudrā). From this perspective, we are all part of the mental, verbal, and bodily activity of Dainichi's enlightenment, the so-called "three mysteries" or "three intimacies" *(sammitsu)*. Since Dainichi is fully enlightened, there is nothing hidden. Each entity is, therefore, a direct manifestation of Dainichi's self-expression for Dainichi's enjoyment *(jijuyū sammai)*. In this sense, everything is an intimation of the three intimacies.

From the microcosmic perspective, this activity of Dainichi's enlightenment is manifest as subperceptible resonances *(kyō)*. These resonances in turn coalesce into structural configurations such as the five physical elements (earth, water, fire, wind, and space), the five mental wisdoms (and the five Buddhas associated with each), and the five configurations of sound at the basis of all languages. In respect of the latter, we can say that foundationally (that is, at the subperceptible level) every word is a true word *(shingon)* in that it is a surface (macrocosmic) manifestation of a microcosmic expression within Dainichi's enlightened activity.

This brings us to the macrophysical level, the realm of perceptible reality or of ordinary human experience. Although in a cosmic sense, the whole universe is the supersensible expression of Dainichi, and although in a microcosmic sense, the universe is constituted by subperceptible resonances manifesting Dainichi's activity, we are ordinarily completely oblivious to those spiritual dimensions. In the macrophysical world, we are generally only aware of everyday things and events. Through Shingon practice, however, we can be aware of the world as being not just the world of things, but also a world of intimation in which each thing expresses Dainichi's enlightened function. Let us examine one aspect of this practice, the one most closely related to the issue of words.

As already mentioned, there are three mysteries or intimacies: that of physical gesture (mudrā), that of meditative thought (maṇḍala), and that of intonation or speech (mantra). For each intimacy, ritual supplies the spiritual context such that one becomes directly aware of the pure physical-mental-verbal *act* of Dainichi. In the linguistic realm, for example, Shingon ritual recognizes five seed mantras: *A, Va, Ra, Ha,* and *Kha*. By intoning these mantras (with the proper physical and mental posture), the practitioner becomes attuned to basic resonances constituting all language. That is, through mantric practice, one knows directly the "truth words" *(shingon)* inaudible to ordinary hearing. This insight enriches experience in two ways. First, one recognizes these microcosmic resonances to be the elemental constituents of the entire universe: the ordinary macrocosmic world is suddenly experienced as the surface structure of a deeper spiritual reality. Secondly, that deeper, microcosmic level is itself seen not as the basic building blocks of an atomistic universe, but rather as the symbolic self-expression or intimation of a *single act* which is none other than the cosmic Dainichi Nyorai.

With this metaphysics of language as a background, we can describe fairly simply Kūkai's theory of verbal truth. On the microcosmic level, all utterances are equally true or genuine since they are surface manifestations of the universal resonances constituting the universe. All sound is, after all, only the intimation of Dainichi *qua* mantra. In this respect, an enlightened Shingon Buddhist could even be aware of the inaudible truth being spoken in lies, for example. This understanding of truth is not philosophically interesting, however, since it is contrasted with, or opposed to, nothing else. Insofar as the universe itself is Dainichi, there can be no falseness.

From the macrocosmic perspective, though, the Shingon theory of verbal truth becomes more interesting, especially since it assumes what we have already said about microcosmic verbal truth. In what sense, for example, can we say that what Kūkai said was more *true* than what a liar says? They are both macrocosmic manifestations of Dainichi's mantra, are they not? Yes, but Kūkai's utterances lead the audience to sense the existence of a microcosmic, spiritual level of reality, whereas a liar's utterances would not. In this regard, we have returned to Kūkai's early emphasis on what words do, rather than what they say.

Shingon Buddhist expressions are designed to make us plumb the macrocosmic level of expression until we reach the depths of the microcosmic. If a set of expressions leads us to think about the spirituality at the foundation of ordinary experience and if, more importantly, it causes us to change our behavior and to undertake Shingon practice, those expressions are *true* in a macrocosmic as well as a microcosmic sense. We could, therefore, make this definition of macrocosmic verbal truth into a hermeneutic criterion for interpreting and evaluating various religio-philosophical theories: the more a theory leads us to recognize the microcosmic and cosmic dimensions of reality, the more true the theory. This is, in fact, the criterion Kūkai applied in a most creative aspect of his philosophical theory: his articulation of the ten states of mind.

To a great extent, what has been said thus far is a theory of language acceptable to many, if not all, Buddhists in the esoteric tradition. In fact, Kūkai probably learned much of this theory while in China. After he returned to Japan, however, he applied the implicit hermeneutic principle to a hierarchical characterization of spiritual insight, correlating each level with various philosophical and religious theories.

It is fairly certain that this classification scheme was of Kūkai's own invention since there is no known parallel in the Chinese tradition. Of course, various *p'an-chiao* classifications existed in China, especially in the T'ien-t'ai and Hua-yen traditions. Furthermore, texts like the *Lotus Sūtra* had much earlier developed the idea that certain teachings were intended for specific audiences as a skill-in-means. Kūkai's system, however, classified states of mind, not teachings. He saw the doctrines as part of discrete world views, ways in which people understood, and lived in, reality. They are, in the final analysis, worlds in which people live, options for being in the world. In this respect, the most obvious parallel is his own *Aims of the Three Teachings,* a work written before he had gone to China and before the Chinese sectarian *p'an-chiao* systems were known in Japan.

Kūkai's system is most fully detailed in his *Ten States of Mind (Jūjūshinron)* and then abridged in his *Jeweled Key to the Secret Treasury (Hizōhōyaku),* both written about 830.[6] The works were a response to an imperial request for a doctrinal summation from each of the recognized Buddhist schools. Kūkai decided to go beyond a mere summary of Shingon and to give a synopsis of all teachings from a Shingon perspective. In effect, he drew up a hierarchy of all the known religious-philosophical traditions in Japan at the time. For each school, he wrote a poem summarizing the teaching, gave a prose description of the teaching, quoted extensively from scriptural sources, and evaluated the strengths and weaknesses of each. Obviously, we cannot summarize this enterprise here, but a bird's-eye view of the structure will be useful in understanding Kūkai's basic interpretive strategy.

One: The Deluded, Ramlike State of Mind[7]

This is a nonreligious, subhuman state in which the person has no sense of ideals by which to act or the ability to regulate one's desires.

Two: The Ignorant, Childlike, but Tempered State of Mind

In this state human ideals are followed in a mechanical, rule-structured way. It is beyond level one insofar as it shows awareness of others and a sense of social responsibility. It is the lowest, most primitive, state of moral consciousness.

(the Confucianist)

Three: The Infantlike, Composed State of Mind

People of this class see the limitations of this world and renounce it in a wish for something transcendent which can serve as a source of serenity and immortality. Like the newborn suckling, such people obliterate this world's turmoils and find peace in something beyond.

(the Taoist)

Four: The State of Mind Recognizing Only Skandhas, Not Ātman as Real

Such people have understood Śakyamuni's teaching about impermanence, recognizing the reality of the psychophysical constituents and, consequently, the emptiness of self. Thus, the pursuit of personal gain sought on levels one to three is overcome in the elimination of ignorance and craving.

(the Śrāvaka)

Five: The State of Mind Free of Karmic Seeds

Without hearing the doctrines of any teacher, these people discover within themselves that the karmic roots of suffering are delusions. Breaking free of ignorance, the person also breaks free of the karmic cycle of birth and death, achieving enlightenment on one's own.

(the Pratyeka-buddhas)

Six: The Mahāyāna State of Mind Concerned With Others

By recognizing that dharmas are manifestations of mind, these people know the emptiness of dharmas as well as the emptiness of self. In this way, they reach the universal compassion of the bodhisattva.

(Hossō [Yogācāra])

Seven: The State of Mind Awakened to the Unborn Nature of Mind

Through the eightfold negations, insight into the two levels of truth, and the acceptance of the logic of the middle, these people recognize that mind in itself is unborn. Therefore, the distinction between mind and nonmind (subject and object, mind and body) is relative, not absolute.

(Sanron [Mādhyamika])

Eight: The State of Mind Following the One Path Without Artifice (or The State of Really Knowing One's Own Mind, or The State of Mind Empty and Objectless)[8]

In this state one rejects the exclusiveness of the logic of the middle, seeing the unity of all approaches. Beyond sheer emptiness, truth is also a skill-in-means which depends on the audience. One mind contains all things.

(Tendai [T'ien-t'ai])

Nine: The State of Mind Completely without Individuated Essence
In this state one recognizes the complete interpenetration of all things and principles. What other states might recognize as a substratum is understood to be all there is. Hence, enlightenment is completely immanent.
(Kegon [Hua-yen])

Ten: The State of Mind Esoteric and Glorious
This state subordinates all exoteric teachings to the immediacy and comprehensiveness of esoteric practice and enlightenment. One does not merely know of the interpenetration of all things—one participates in it through esoteric ritual. The dharmakāya is directly experienced and is no longer a speculative abstraction.
(Shingon)

Let us now consider the criteria used in making this classification. First, we may note that Kūkai's discussion focuses not so much on the philosophical integrity of each level, but more on the type of person produced by each world view. That is why he discusses states of mind, rather than classes of teaching. Certainly the philosophical positions are evaluated according to what they *say* (their internal logic, their completeness, and so forth), but much more weight is given to what they *do* to, or for, people. On the lowest level of the schema, for example, we find positions maintaining that people are primarily driven by instinctual, unconscious forces. Kūkai would hold that such theories are false. His grounds for this judgment would not be empirical evidence, but rather the claim that such theories lead to the lowest type of individual, that is, people who live their lives in an inhuman, animalistic world. Since the theories discussed on levels two through ten all produce humane individuals, they are all inherently more true.

There is a profound psychological insight in Kūkai's approach. His theory suggests that a person's world view is confirmed in that person's own experience. One who is driven by animalistic desires believes all people are so driven. And one who believes human beings are essentially animalistic acts accordingly. In short, one's mind resides in a world fitting one's own theory. This is the fundamental sense of *jūshin*. One can see the limitations of one's world view only when one looks beyond the known world to other states of mind open to further dimensions of human potential. Only then can one see the falseness in one's previous perspective. Being aware of potential beyond one's present state is possible only because of Dainichi's grace *(kaji)*, a spiritual resonance between Dainichi and the individual that makes one conscious of the world as esoteric intimation.

In a parallel fashion, the highest-level teachings, those of Shingon, produce individuals who directly and immediately know through esoteric practices the spirituality inherent at the microcosmic level. They also know of, through symbolic intimation, the cosmic dharmakāya. All religious teachings produce individuals of states two through nine. That is, they are all exoteric teachings operative strictly in the macrocosmic dimension. They are ranked according to how readily their followers can recognize the existence of, and desire to fathom experientially, the microcosmic depths of experience and reality. Let us briefly see how this criterion generates the specific ranking.

The Confucianists, unlike the lowest level of people, recognize the need for moral ideals. Yet, they are only interested in maximizing harmony within the social realm as if there were no other dimension to experience or reality. Hence, the Taoists are placed above them insofar as they at least recognize the possibility of another dimension. Still, their recognition of this other dimension is rather childlike, dreaming of a heaven full of immortals. The Hīnayāna Buddhists (states four and five) are superior to the Taoists insofar as they recognize the universality of impermanence and reject the idea of an immortal self. They recognize the reality of a continuous process underlying the apparent world of substance. Still, they fall short insofar as they try to achieve enlightenment for themselves as if they were somehow separate from the rest of the world. Thus, they recognize the theoretical possibility of a microprocess, but they have not fathomed its universality.

States six through nine represent exoteric Māhayāna teachings. As such, they all accept the principle of universal salvation. This universalistic perspective is a step toward realizing the totality of the microcosmic, the unity of the cosmic, dharmakāya. In Kūkai's scheme, all four Māhayāna states emphasize their own particular form of oneness, the degree of interpenetration increasing as one moves up the hierarchy. Specifically, Hossō stresses the oneness of compassion and wisdom, Sanron the oneness of saṃsāra and nirvāṇa, Tendai the oneness of paths to enlightenment, and Kegon the interpenetration of principle with thing and thing with thing. In this respect, we can see how Kūkai's view of transcendence matured from the time he wrote his *Aims of the Three Teachings*. That is, the Buddhist schools discussed in states six through nine increasingly emphasize the inseparability of transcendence and immanence. The other-worldliness of Buddhism so sharply delineated in the *Aims* is not visible in the higher five levels of the *Ten States*. Viewed in this light, we might surmise that Kūkai, the mature Shingon master, could have viewed the young Kūkai of Yoshino as a level five pratyeka-buddha.

This discussion of transcendence and immanence allows us to see more clearly the qualitative difference between levels eight or nine and level ten—that is, between the exoteric teachings of Tendai or Kegon and the esoteric teachings of Shingon. Kūkai's interpretation was that Kegon (and, to a slightly lesser extent, Tendai) developed the highest level of understanding available through the exoteric approach. That is, strictly through the analysis of the macrocosmic, those states of mind have glimpsed the philosophical necessity for a ground of interpenetration. In a sense, they have discovered the microcosmic as a transcendental, logically *a priori,* reality.

Kūkai claims, however, that Tendai and Kegon lack experiential verification since they lack esoteric practice. Therefore, they can speculate about the microcosmic without truly knowing it. Only esoteric practice, Kūkai maintained, could generate a direct participation in the microcosmic. The Shingon Buddhist uses ritual to effect an experiential, *a posteriori* knowledge of the microcosmic. This epistemic intimacy, this direct contact with mystery, is central to Kūkai's world view. Once one has experienced reality through this world view, one will also see the microcosmic and the macrocosmic as intimations, as "symbolic expressions" *(monji)* of Dainichi's enlightened act.

For this reason, from the true esoteric standpoint, there are in fact no nonesoteric states of mind. Kūkai believes in what we might call a "maṇḍalic hermeneutic"; that is, all the teachings emanate from the dharmakāya itself. In fact, the full title of Kūkai's work is the *Secret Maṇḍala's Ten States of Mind (Himitsu mandara jūjūshinron).* Like the Womb (or Matrix) Maṇḍala with Dainichi Nyorai in the middle and all the diverse realms of existence encircling it, Buddhism is at its core the preaching of Dainichi Nyorai, but as this teaching ranges outward into its many manifestations, it is viewed differently by the different states of mind; it actually takes form not only as different world views, but also as different worlds. The closer one is to the center of the maṇḍala (as in the states of mind represented by the exoteric teachings of Tendai and Kegon), the more one feels the centripetal pull of "grace" *(kaji)*—that is, the more likely one is to make the leap into the intimate understanding available only through esotericism. But, of course, one can begin from any point, making a sudden leap into the center by undertaking Shingon practice and realizing directly the dharmakāya's teaching.

If we do interpret the model of the ten states to be like a maṇḍala, two other aspects of Kūkai's work come more sharply into focus. First, it helps explain why Kūkai would write about other schools when his imperial charge was simply to explain the doctrines of his own school. According to Shingon, all realities and all theories are ultimately manifestations of Dainichi Nyorai's enlightenment. So, Kūkai's *Ten States* and *Jeweled Key* are designed to show how there can be a diversity of world views even though all world views are essentially Dainichi's activity. As a maṇḍala can show all worlds—whether heavenly, infernal, or mundane—to be manifestations of the dharmakāya, Kūkai's treatises show all teachings to be manifestations of the dharmakāya's teaching.

Second, the maṇḍala-related theory of interpretation helps explain why Kūkai's evaluation of the schools so often refers to esoteric texts. Of course, in both the *Ten States* and *Jeweled Key,* Kūkai cites scriptures from the respective exoteric traditions, but the overwhelming preponderance of quotations is from esoteric works. The effect is to remind the reader that all schools can be viewed from the esoteric perspective. Within themselves, all the states have their own consistency, but only the Shingon standpoint reveals how all the discrete positions actually emanate from the single source of everything, namely, Dainichi Nyorai, the dharmakāya.

This brings us to our final comment about Kūkai's theory of interpretation. We can now ask the most general hermeneutic question: how, from Kūkai's point of view, should one read a text to determine its meaning? Since every text, indeed every thing whatsoever, is a symbolic expression of Dainichi, every text must have an esoteric dimension. Thus, the first and most important response is that the reader should be aware of the wondrous presence of the text itself; its verbal content (mind), its sound (intonation), and its very tangibility (body) are all manifestations of the Dainichi's enlightenment. In other words, the dharmakāya expounds the dharma through every dharma. This is essentially the principle of *hosshin seppō* that Kūkai emphasized so strongly.[9] Consequently, Kūkai sought out mantras in supposedly exoteric texts as intimations of the esoteric within them. In his analysis of the *Heart Sūtra,* for example, he focuses on the closing lines. Or, in the case of the *Lotus Sūtra,* he takes the Sanskrit title itself as a mantra and, therefore, the most important part of the whole work.

Secondly, and only secondarily according to Kūkai's view, one should look at the text's exoteric meaning. In what ways does it suggest a dimension beneath the macrocosmic? Do the words point to something outside the ordinary referential world of objects? In a more contemporary vocabulary, do the words *deconstruct* our usual ways of seeing the world? Do the words disassociate themselves from being used as signs for supposedly independently existing realities? From the Shingon standpoint, the verbal and the ontological are inseparable. This is true not only because we see the world through our concepts and words: Even the Hossō (state six) and Sanron (state seven) schools recognized that. Rather, for Shingon, verbalization is itself, in itself, ontological. The world as it is known to the enlightened ones is an intimation, a symbolic expression, of Dainichi's enlightened activity. Hence, the true function of words is to appear on the macrocosmic level with an inherent self-deconstructive tendency. True words on the macrocosmic level dissolve into the inaudible mystery of the resonance *(kyō)* characteristic of the microcosmos.

It is not strange, therefore, that Kūkai often summarized a complex point by writing a poem. The truth of a statement depends not on the status of its referent, but on how it affects us. For the enlightened, of course, the teaching may be expressed through any medium, but for the unenlightened, a medium more suggestive and less explicit might be more effective. Kūkai often favored art over words as the best vehicle for communicating with the ordinary person, maintaining that "all the essentials of the Esoteric Buddhist doctrines are, in reality, set forth therein."[10]

Still, we cannot do without words. Kūkai, a philosopher whose religious quest began with the search for meaning in sacred texts, understood that point very well when he wrote:

> The dharma is beyond speech, but without speech it cannot be revealed. Suchness transcends forms, but without depending on forms it cannot be realized. Though one may at times err by taking the finger pointing at the moon to be the moon itself, the Buddha's teachings which guide people are limitless. . . .[11]

Notes

1. For a concise discussion of this esoteric practice and its place in the mountain cults of the Nara period, see Sonoda Kōyū's essay "Kodai bukkyō ni okeru sanrinshugyō to sono igi" (Mountain Practices and Their Significance in Ancient Buddhism), in Wada Shūjō and Takagi Shingen, eds., *Kūkai* (Tokyo: Yoshikawa Kōbunkan, 1982).

2. Shiba Ryōtarō, *Kūkai no fūkei* (Kūkai's Landscape) (Tokyo: Chūō Kōronsha, 1974), 1:3.

3. *Kōbō daishi zenshū* (Collected Works of Kōbō Daishi) (Kōyasan daigaku mikkyō bunka kenkyūjo, 1978), 3:406–407.

4. See Sonoda, "Kodai," for historical evidence about the use of Yoshino as a retreat area during the Nara period.

5. For a good English translation of this work, see "Indications of the Goals of the Three Teachings," in Yoshito S. Hakeda, *Kūkai: Basic Works* (New York: Columbia University Press, 1972).

6. There is no translation of *Jūjūshinron* into a European language. *Hizōhōyaku,* on the other hand, is translated by Hakeda in *Kūkai: Basic Works* as "The Precious Key to the Secret Treasury."

7. Kūkai took the names of the ten states directly from the *Dainichikyō* and they are virtually the same in both the *Ten States* and the *Jeweled Key.*

8. A footnote in Katsumata Shunkyō, ed., *Kōbō daishi chosaku zenshū* (Tokyo: Sankibō busshorin, 1979), 1:183, remarks that the three titles correspond to the three truths in T'ien-t'ai: the middle, the provisional, and the empty, respectively.

9. *Hosshin seppō* (the dharmakāya preaches the dharma) is contrasted with

the exoteric idea that since the dharmakāya is formless, it cannot teach. Esoteric Buddhists believe that this world itself is the teaching of the dharmakāya. Tamaki Kōshirō has argued that Kūkai's teachings are distinctive for their strong emphasis on the principle of *hosshin seppō* and that this emphasis carried over into Japanese Buddhism at large. See, for example, his *Nihon bukkyō shisōron* (Essays on Japanese Buddhist Thought) (Tokyo: Heirakuji shoten, 1974), vol. 1, especially chap. 1.

10. Hakeda, *Kūkai,* 146.

11. Hakeda, *Kūkai,* 145.

Glossary

daigaku 大学
Dainichikyō 大日経
darani 陀羅尼
Dōji 道慈
Gomyō 護命
Himitsu mandara jūjūshinron 秘密曼荼羅十住心論
Hizōhōyaku 秘蔵宝鑰
hosshin seppō 法身説法
jijuyū sammai 自受用三昧
Jūjūshinron 十住心論
jūshin 住心
kaji 加持
Katsumata Shunkyō 勝又俊教
Kōbō Daishi 弘法大師
Kokūzō 虚空蔵
Kokūzōgumonjihō 虚空蔵求聞持法
Kūkai 空海
kyō 響
monji 文字
p'an-chiao 判教
sammayashin 三昧耶身
sammitsu 三密
Sangōshiiki 三教指帰
Shiba Ryōtarō 司馬寮太郎
Shingon 真言
Sonoda Kōyū 園田香融
Takagi Shingen 高木訷元
Tamaki Kōshirō 玉城康四郎
Tao-hsüan 道璿
Wada Shūjō 和多秀乗
yū 用

Shinran's Proofs of True Buddhism

ROGER TASHI CORLESS

The Problem

Jōdo Shinshū has received a bad press. Its founder, Shinran, tends to come across as a simpleton, such that his Buddhism need not be taken seriously. Arthur Lloyd, for instance, called it "a quasi-Buddhist religion,"[1] Edward Conze said it tended "to cheapen salvation,"[2] and Travers Christmas Humphreys, Q.C., questioned us about it in his best barrister's style, "But is it Buddhism?"[3] Even those who are committed to the Shinshū tradition are somewhat embarrassed at Shinran's apparent eisegesis. The translation team of the Hongwanji International Center observes, in an introduction to their English version of the *Yuishinshō-mon'i:*

> Some historians of Buddhist thought have been highly critical of Shinran, stating that he makes light of the basic texts by quoting from them arbitrarily without the least regard for the context and original meaning.[4]

Their introduction does not counter the criticism directly but attempts to justify it by an appeal to the uniqueness of Shinran's satori. This defense is not very satisfactory, since it may be used to support any viewpoint whatever, unless we know something about what it is that makes Shinran's satori unique.

In this essay I shall first try to expose Shinran's hermeneutic method (and I assume from the outset that he indeed has one) and then ask what kind of hermeneutic it is, and upon what kind of satori it might be based. If both the hermeneutic and the satori, or at any rate their interconnection, turn out to be honest and Buddhist, we may feel we can banish the qualms of Shinshū's cultured despisers.

Hermeneutics in the *Kyōgyōshinshō*

The *Kyōgyōshinshō,* more exactly called *Ken Jōdo Shinjitsu Kyōgyōshō Monrui,* is a collection of sūtric and śāstric passages drawn together by Shinran under topical heads and provided by him with occasional explanatory comments. A thorough analysis of its hermeneutic would require us to make complete translations of each of the many texts to which he refers and then examine how portions of these texts are used by Shinran. In this essay I will attempt something less ambitious.

The major śāstric source for *K* (as I will henceforth call the text) is T'an-luan's *Commentary on the Pure Land Discourse,* commonly known as the *Lun-chu* (Jp. *Ronchu*) found in volume 40 of the Taishō Tripiṭaka (no. 1819). Since I have translated and analyzed this text,[5] I feel I can say something about how Shinran used it. I shall confine myself to the first four chapters of *K,* wherein is the meat of the argument, and compare how T'an-luan and Shinran arrive at their respective understandings of Buddhism. Even here, I shall not be exhaustive, but focus on certain passages which seem to me sufficient to make the point.

A fundamental difference in method at once appears. T'an-luan calls his work a *chu,* that is, commentarial notes, on the existing *lun* or śāstra (which purports to be by Vasubandhu), to which it stays very close. Shinran prepares a *monrui,* which I would suggest means "assembled text" or "proof text."[6] Proof texts are commonly an irritation to the scholar with linear Cartesian presuppositions, for they are *as a rule* quoted out of their original context. I have argued elsewhere[7] that this is indeed a feature of proof texts in all scriptural traditions, and that its intent is to get at the "spiritual" or "deep" meaning behind or within the plain meaning of the letters. Shinran's unconcern for context, then, will not initially disturb us, and we shall inquire later as to what kind of deep meaning he is getting at.

Assembled Texts Proving the True Teaching (kyō)

EXPOSITION

Of the many sūtras which mention the Pure Land teaching, T'an-luan refers chiefly to the *Larger Sukhāvatīvyūha (Daimuryōjukyō),* the *Smaller Sukhāvatīvyūha (Amidakyō),* and the misleadingly retitled *Amitāyurdhyāna Sūtra (Kammuryōjukyō),* which I shall call the *Contemplation Sūtra (Kangyō).* These three have come to be regarded as one, and in Japan are customarily referred to as the *Jōdo Sambukyō.* T'an-luan takes them to be of equal authority, never suggesting that one might contain a higher teaching than another, and at one point indeed he seeks to resolve a contradiction between two of the sūtras not by preferring one over the other but by strict textual analysis:

Question: The *Larger Sukhāvatīvyūha* says, "Those who so wish all go to birth [in the Pure Land]: only those who are guilty of the five abominations and who have vilified the true dharma are excluded." The *Contemplation Sūtra* says, "Those who perform the five abominations and the ten evils, and are replete with everything bad, also go to birth." How can we reconcile these two sūtras?

Answer: One sūtra comprehensively *(chü)* refers to two grave transgressions: first, the five abominations; second, vilifying the true dharma. If one is guilty of *both* these transgressions, one cannot go to birth. The other sūtra only *(tan)* refers to the transgressions of performing the ten evils, the five abominations, and so on, and does not speak about vilifying the true dharma. Therefore, one can go to birth if one has not vilified the true dharma.

(*T* 40.834a14–20)

Shinran, however, makes clear at the outset that the *Larger Sukhāvatīvyūha* has priority for him:

The true teaching is presented *(ken)* in the *Larger Sukhāvatīvyūha.* (*K* 265:4)[8]

The primacy of this sūtra for Shinran is due to the fact that its "main point" *(shū)* is to tell of Amita Tathāgata's primal vow *(hongan)* "and thus that Buddha's name is the essence *(tai)* of the sūtra" (*K* 265:7–8).

This last phrase is a quote from T'an-luan, but in T'an luan the context requires us to read it as a *classification* of the sūtras rather than as a reference to the *content* of *one* of the sūtras (the Chinese text is identical in both T'an-luan and Shinran). T'an-luan says:

Śākyamuni Buddha spoke [twice] in the town of Rājagṛha and [once] in the city-state of Śrāvastī, in the midst of great congregations, on the merits of the adornments of the Buddha Amitāyus. Thus, that Buddha's name characterizes *(t'i)* the [three] sūtras.

(*T* 40.826b12–14)

Since the *Larger Sukhāvatīvyūha* and the *Contemplation Sūtra* were preached at Rājagṛha, and the *Smaller Sukhāvatīvyūha* at Śrāvastī, T'an-luan must be referring to the three sūtras as a unit. But for Shinran, the name and the vow are primary and he sees them as controlling rather than classifying the only sūtra which speaks of both, namely, the *Larger Sukhāvatīvyūha.*

Shinran then authenticates the *Larger Sukhāvatīvyūha* because at its opening the Buddha is seen to be shining with preternatural light, indicating that he had something of supreme importance to say. He supports this with a comment by the Korean master Kyŏnghŭng:

This means his *abhijñā* was being manifested. He is not just out of the ordinary. He is unequalled. (*K* 267:8–9)

T'an-luan authenticates the sūtras by the standard recourse to the observation that

> the sūtras begin with "Thus . . . ," showing them to be trustworthy, so that we may get into them. (*T* 40.844a29)

That is, they have been remembered by Ānanda, and so they must accurately recount the Buddha's words. Shinran quotes this passage at *K* 317:8, translated by D. T. Suzuki as follows:

> The sūtras start with "Thus, I have heard." This testifies to the fact that faith is the agent that introduces us [to things we wish to put to practice].[9]

Again, the Chinese underlying both of these passages is identical, yet Suzuki's translation cannot be faulted, for in the context (the chapter on true faith in *K*) this is clearly how Shinran understands it.

CONCLUSION

T'an-luan, then, regards the three[10] sūtras as a unit and authenticates them according to standard textual authorization categories *(pramāṇa).* Shinran focuses on Amita's name, faith, and vow, and "selects" *(senchaku)* texts which authenticate, or can be made to authenticate, these features.

Assembled Texts Proving the True Practice (gyō)

EXPOSITION

T'an-luan recommends a fivefold practice which he calls the five recollection gates *(wu nien-men):* prostrations to Amita *(li-pai),* chanting Amita's praises *(tsan-t'an),* resolving to be born in the Pure Land *(tso-yüan),* visualizations of the Pure Land *(kuan-ch'a)* (the descriptions of which take up most of his text), and *hui-hsiang,* a phrase which he uses to mean both "turning over" one's merits to others (i.e., *pariṇāmanā*) and "turning back" to saṃsāra when one has reached perfection by birth in the Pure Land. I translate this last as "turning toward" to bring out its ambiguity. These five gates are treated throughout the *Lun-chu* but are summarized at *T* 40.835a20–23. They are derived directly from the śāstra on which T'an-luan is commenting.

Shinran concerns himself with only one practice, that of the *nembutsu,* which for T'an-luan is the second gate. In general, Shinran selects passages dealing with *nembutsu* and ignores everything else. Instead of five recollection gates there is, for Shinran, only "one recollection" that is a "unique moment" when all other practices implode into a "single invocation." (All three of these translation equivalents convey Shinran's understanding of the term *ichinen.*)

> One moment of practice means that the perfection of the specially selected easy practice is manifest in the totality of the invocation. (*K* 292:1–2)

By "the totality of the invocation" Shinran is referring to the controversy over how many times one should invoke Amita's name to do it "completely." The sūtras give the number ten, which T'an-luan says means "perfection":

> When the sūtras speak of "ten invocations" they are clearly referring to the perfection of the work: it is not necessary to know the exact number. As it has been said, "The summer cicada knows nothing of spring and autumn" (*Chuang Tzu,* I). How could such an insect know summertime? (*T* 40.834c20–22)

That is, one just keeps chanting without bothering about beginning or end (which, in my experience, is the only way not to become bored while chanting mantras), just as the summer cicada is born after the spring (which it therefore does not know) and keeps chirping until it dies just before the autumn (which it therefore also does not know) and so, having no reference points, it does not even know "summer."[11]

Shinran construes "the total number" as the all-inclusive "one" and, in a dense passage, piles up identifications between one mind, nondual practice, one recollection, one invocation, right practice, right activity, right recollection, and finally *nembutsu* and *Namu Amida Butsu* (*K* 292:10–12).

EXCURSUS ON THE *San Amida Butsu Ge*

Shinran's exclusion of other practices is most clear in his handling of a liturgical text by T'an-luan, *Tsan A-mi-t'o Fo Chi*[12] (Canticles on Amita Buddha) (*T* 47, no. 1978). Shinran composes a hymn in Japanese using T'an-luan's title (pronounced *San Amida Butsu Ge*) and much of his material, but departs from T'an-luan at significant points. Most notably, he omits T'an-luan's passages confessing transgressions to Amita and the bodhisattvas and requesting their aid for virtuous activity in the future. T'an-luan says:

> Hail, Amita, Buddha of the West! With a full heart I worship you! Mercifully turn and protect me! Cause the holy seed to grow! From this time forth, through subsequent lives, I resolve always to accept that Buddha! May all beings be born in blessed peace! Hail, Avalokiteśvara! . . . Hail, Mahāsthāmaprāpta! . . . Hail, all bodhisattvas of Sukhāvatī! . . . For the sake of my teacher, my parents, my spiritual friends, and all beings of the dharma realm, that they may cast down the three barriers and all be born together in Amita Buddha's land, I now go for refuge and confess my transgressions.

This passage occurs twice in T'an-luan (*T* 47.421b16–27 and 424b7–18) but it is conspicuously absent in Shinran's version, for whom confession and petition smack too much of self-power.

Again, even in passages where the *nembutsu* is featured, Shinran modifies the wording so that any vestige of self-power is removed. T'an-luan says:

> If one should hear Amita's merit-bearing name . . . only once, one obtains the great benefit *(jo wen A-mi-t'o te-hao . . . hsia chih i-nien te ta-li).* (*T* 47.422c3–4)[13]

Shinran makes this mean:

> Hearing Amita Buddha's name . . . is the unique moment of the supremely great benefit *(Amida Butsu no Mina o kiki . . . ichinen dairi mujō nari).*[14]

The difference is subtle but vital. For T'an-luan, hearing the name introduces one to the powerful practice of Amita's invocation; for Shinran, hearing the name is a confirmation of one's assured liberation through Amida's power. The movements are opposite.

CONCLUSION

T'an-luan teaches a fivefold practice obtained directly from his comma (i.e., the text on which he is commenting). Shinran selects the single practice of *nembutsu* from T'an-luan's second gate and implodes all other practices into it. This single practice is not a method for *obtaining* the Pure Land but the natural result of a mind which realizes it *has been given* the Pure Land.

Assembled Texts Proving the True Faith (shin)

EXPOSITION

Faith is an aspect of the practice for T'an-luan, but he does not give it prominence. At one point, however, he discusses faith in the context of the unification of the practice. T'an-luan tells us that reciting Amita's name purifies our minds because its essence *(i)* is infinite wisdom. If this purification does not occur in the practitioner, he explains that it is because one is not practicing in accordance with the correspondence *(hsiang-ing)* of the name *(ming)* Amitābha (i.e., infinite light) and its essence *(i)* (infinite wisdom). Effective invocation requires that it be pure *(shun),* that is, unmixed with other thoughts; definite *(chüeh-ting),* that is, not half-hearted; and continuous *(hsiang-hsü),* meaning without gaps between the repetitions of the phrases.

These three aspects are "completely interdependent" and "therefore the master of the discourse [Vasubandhu] bases himself on the words 'I, with one mind . . .' " (*T* 40.835b18–c2). That is, Vasubandhu begins his essay with the words "I single-mindedly take refuge . . ."[15] and T'an-luan tells us that this means his mind is unified around the faithful *(hsin-hsin)* practice of invoking Amita's name.

Such a bringing of the inner attitude into line with the outer practice is consonant with the Confucian ethic of the rectification of names *(cheng-ming),* in which a person is to live up to, but not beyond, his title or "name" *(ming).* In *Analects* XII:11, for example, Confucius says that good government consists in "the ruler ruling, the minister ministering, the father being paternal, and the son being filial." This produces the cardinal Confucian virtue of genuineness *(hsin).* I suggest that T'an-luan thinks of faithful practice along these lines.

Shinran, however, does not speak of the unification of attitude and practice, or mind and body as we might say, but of the union of the mind with the mind. He has a long definition of faith, extending from *K* 312 to 323, the essence of which is the unification of the three minds (*sanshin*[a]). These three minds are extracted from the eighteenth vow of Dharmākara, which Shinran calls the primal vow *(hongan),* in the *Larger Sukhāvatīvyūha.* The Chinese reads in part (full text at *T* 12.268a26–28; quoted by T'an-luan at *T* 40.844a3–5):

shih-fang chung-sheng chih-hsin hsin-le yü sheng wo kuo nai-chih shih-nien

which seems to mean, in context:

> [May] all beings in the ten directions who sincerely develop joyful faith in me and who, desiring to be born in my land, have recollected me up to ten times [be so born].

This passage from the sūtra is pulled apart by Shinran into what Shinshū has come to call the threefold *shinjin* or *sanshin*[b], consisting of "(1) sincere mind, (2) trust, and (3) aspiration for birth in the Pure Land" *(chih-hsin/shishin, hsin-le/shingyō,* and *yü-sheng/yokushō),* which "Shinran . . . regarded . . . as the manifestations of the working of Other Power, stating that the sincere mind of the Buddha enters the ignorant and deluded mind of man, causing in him the experience of joyful faith and prompting him to aspire for the Pure Land."[16] The three distinct attitudes so isolated are then unified when they are unmixed with *doubt* (*K* 319:8)—a possibility not envisaged by T'an-luan—to become the impenetrable true vajra mind *(kongō shinshin)* which is the true faith *(shinjitsu shinjin),* and *this* is why "the master of the discourse bases himself on the words 'I, with one mind . . .' " (*K* 319:8–10).

CONCLUSION

Faith for T'an-luan is a Confucian genuineness of practice in which the inner attitude and the outer appearance are solidly and effectively unified. Faith for Shinran is a certainty of belief from which all doubt has been expelled by the power of Amita's primal vow.

Assembled Texts Proving the True Attainment (shō)

EXPOSITION

T'an-luan sees the Pure Land attainment as one of gradual perfection as the practitioner proceeds through the five recollection gates, which he also calls the gates of approach *(chin),* the great congregation *(ta hui-chung),* the house *(chai),* the rooms *(wu),* and playing in the gardens and woods *(yüan-lin yu-hsi).* The first four gates are those of entering *(ju)* the Pure Land, and the fifth is that of leaving *(ch'u)* it to serve as a bodhisattva within saṃsāra (*T* 40.843a20–23). The fifth gate is itself dual, for it is a "turning toward" *(hui-hsiang)* with a "going aspect" *(wang-hsiang)* in which one "turns over" *(hui-shih)* one's merit to all beings while still oneself imperfect, and a "returning aspect" *(huan-hsiang)* of turning back to reenter *(hui-ju)* saṃsāra after having become perfected (*T* 40.836a20–27). This mutuality of proceeding into and out of the Pure Land T'an-luan derives, again, more or less directly from his text.

Shinran has no such mutuality. For him there is only one gate and one movement: Amita comes out through the fifth gate and enters saṃsāra.

> Now, I draw a conclusion as to the teaching, practice, faith, and attainment of true Buddhism *(shinshū):* it is a benefit *(li-kai/riyaku)* of the "turning toward" *(hui-hsiang/ekō)* of the Tathāgata's great compassion. Therefore, in both the cause and the effect there is nothing which is not related to the perfection of "turning toward" in Amita Tathāgata's pure vow. The cause is pure, so the effect is pure. Let us realize this. (*K* 349:3–4)

Shinran supports his conclusion by a quotation from T'an-luan concerning "leaving" the Pure Land. T'an-luan says:

> *Leaving through the fifth gate:* Because of "turning toward" in the power of the primal vow, they contemplate the sufferings of beings and, out of great compassion, they show transformation bodies, turning around and entering the gardens of saṃsāra and the woods of the passions, wherein they play by means of the superknowledges, reaching the stage of teaching-and-converting. This is called "leaving through the fifth gate." (*T* 40.843b19–21)

Now, it happens that in the Chinese the subject is not expressed. The context in T'an-luan clearly implies the perfected practitioners, now become mahā-bodhisattvas, as the subject, but Shinran leaves us with the impression that Amita Buddha is to be read as the subject, and indeed D. T. Suzuki supplies this subject in the following remarkable translation of the above passage. (The words in brackets are Suzuki's; the underlying Chinese text is identical to that of T'an-luan translated above.)

> *The Treatise on the Pure Land* reads: "The fifth gate [in which the 'others benefiting' Original Prayer expresses itself as a mode of the turning-over practice or activity] is called the outgoing phase. It consists in the Buddha observing out of his great compassionate heart the extent to which all beings are suffering and being plagued, and of his being induced, thereby, to assume a body of transformation in order to save all beings from their pitiable situation. He thus enters into the field of birth-and-death, into the thicket of the evil passions, where he leads his missionary life in teaching the Dharma and in converting all beings. [In all sincerity,] he displays here miraculous deeds; [he acts effortlessly, leaving no trace, as if] engaged in play. All this comes out of his Original Prayer, which is turned-over to the saving of all beings. This is called the fifth gate [of his activity] and belongs to the outgoing category."[17]

Once again, we cannot fault Suzuki's translation except perhaps for a prolixity wholly absent in the spare structure of the classical Chinese, for at the end of his chapter on attainment, Shinran adds some words of his own which indicate quite clearly that he wishes to be understood just as D. T. Suzuki has taken him:

> Thus, we can fully understand, through the true words of the great holy one, that the attainment of great nirvāṇa is controlled by the "turning toward" power of the vow. It has been demonstrated that the true meaning of the benefit of the "returning aspect" (Ch. *huan-hsiang*) is "benefiting others" (Jp. *rita*). (*K* 358:8)

Shinran is careful to use the compound *rita* (Ch. *li-t'o*) which T'an-luan distinguishes from *t'o-li (tari)* as follows:

> "Others being benefited" *(t'o-li/tari)* and "benefiting others" *(li-t'o/rita)* may be talked of from two sides: speaking from the point of view of the Buddha, we should properly say "benefiting others" *(li-t'o/rita);* speaking from the point of view of beings, we should properly say "others being benefited" *(t'o-li/tari).*
>
> (*T* 40.843c25–27)

By using *rita/li-t'o* Shinran leaves us in no doubt that it is the Buddha's bestowing of benefit which is here in question, and thus D. T. Suzuki is justified in translating the concluding phrase of Shinran's remarks as "[the Nyorai's] true intention to benefit others is revealed."[18]

CONCLUSION

Attainment for T'an-luan is a gradual process of purification within saṃsāra and entry into the Pure Land, consequent upon which the purified practitioner returns to saṃsāra to spread the dharma as a mahā-bodhisattva. For Shinran, there is really no attainment as such; there is the offer of purification as the Buddha Amita comes into saṃsāra to meet us. Again, T'an-luan's hermeneutic is an exegesis of his text while Shinran implodes all progress and attainment into the power of the primal vow entirely directed toward beings.

The Nature of the Hermeneutic

T'an-luan's hermeneutic is relatively conservative, but then so it should be, as a *chu* or commentary *au pied de la lettre*. Shinran's "proof text" hermeneutic is more startling, even distressing. Faith *(shinjin)*, other power *(tariki)*, and the primal vow *(hongan)* are paramount, they *are* true Buddhism *(shinshū)*; texts supporting these features are discovered or reinterpreted until they do support them; *and therefore* faith, other power, and the primal vow are shown to be paramount, they *are* true Buddhism. The impenetrability of this *petitio principii* is no doubt what troubles Shinran's cultured despisers.

The Hongwanji translation team explains Shinran's logic in terms of the inner realization "of Śākyamuni, of Nāgārjuna, Asaṅga, Vasubandhu, and of the great Zen masters. The *Laṅkāvatāra Sūtra* calls it 'the realization of wisdom of self-knowledge' *(svapratyātmāryajñāna)*."[19] But how do we know this? How do we distinguish between Napoleon Bonaparte and a person who sincerely believes himself to be Napoleon Bonaparte, although everyone else calls him Fred Bloggs? What is to prevent me from saying that having studied the *Wall Street Journal* and meditated, I have had a vision of the Great Gum Boo and she has told me that I am an incarnation of the Gross National Product (as a proof of which, I keep getting fatter and more and more in debt)? More simply, is Shinran Buddhist or only "quasi-Buddhist" as Arthur Lloyd believed? The Hongwanji translation team does not answer: they merely *assert* that he "established the Pure Land teaching firmly in the fundamental position of Mahāyāna Buddhism."[20] How can we find out if this is in fact the case?

A distinctive feature of Buddhism in Shinran's time is the breakup of the Tendai synthesis into some of its component parts, each becoming, for the founders of the new lineages so formed, the "one thing necessary," the truly liberating dharma door. For Shinran, this "one thing" was the *hongan,* and it was his experience of the power of the *hongan* that was his particular dharma door. Through it he passed to an experience of śūnyatā that he expressed in new terms, terms that have indeed been misunderstood as a departure from Buddhism, but whose content may be seen as an aspect of nonduality, and therefore quite Buddhist.

A synonym for śūnyatā is nonduality. The *locus classicus* of this teaching is Nāgārjuna's *Mūlamadhyamakakārikāḥ* 25:20:

> Nirvāṇa's limit is the limit of saṃsāra: between these two not even the subtlest something can be discerned.

Nāgārjuna does not say that nirvāṇa and saṃsāra are the same: they are "two." But nor does he say that they are different: nothing can be discerned which separates them. This further implies that they are not somehow mixed together in some sort of "both/and" condition overcoming an "either/or" condition. Nirvāṇa and saṃsāra are neither the same (the incorrect teaching of monism) nor different (the incorrect teachings of dualism and pluralism). They are "empty." To borrow a term from Christian theology which I have found illuminating, nirvāṇa and saṃsāra "co-inhere."[21]

A practical problem with the elegant edifice of Tendai catholicity is the difficulty of seeing the "one thing necessary," the nonduality of saṃsāra and nirvāṇa, in all the liturgical, meditational, and studious goings-on. Those teachers who emerged from Tendai to found new lineages in their own right, memorialized in somewhat garish pictures beside the path leading down from the Enryakuji, each faced a problem in Mahāyāna which no contemporary teacher could solve for them. Each then records a breakthrough: Nichiren saw the *Lotus Sūtra,* the "round and perfect" teaching of Tendai, as the answer to oppression; Dōgen finally understood the *kōan* about dropping off the body and the mind; Hōnen felt the great power of the *nembutsu;* and Shinran discovered who it really was who was saying the *nembutsu*—Amida himself.

Shinran had practiced as a *dōsō* monk on Mt. Hiei for twenty years, chanting the *nembutsu* conscientiously but feeling no nearer liberation. Descending into Kyōto he met Hōnen and something "clicked." He wrote of his dramatic change of heart:

> So I, Gutoku Shaku Shinran, in the first year of Kennin [1201 C.E.] abandoned the miscellaneous practices [i.e., all the other Tendai practices] and allied myself with the primal vow. (*K* 423:10)

This laconic note is packed with the anguish and joy of the death of Shinran's old way of life that had not worked and the birth of his new way of the *hongan,* of absolute other power, which did work.

He calls himself *Gutoku,* "the bald-headed idiot." *Toku* 'baldness' refers to his monastic tonsure, the outward sign of superior wisdom, virtue (there is a homophone meaning "virtue"), and serenity. But he felt none of this—he was *gujin* 'an idiot', *gusō* or *gushaku* 'a stupid monk', that is, a monk who needed instruction (after twenty years!) on how to be a monk, *gu* being also a self-referencing polite prefix (as in *gufu* 'stupid father', i.e., 'my father'). In the extremity of his helplessness, he allied himself with the *nembutsu* teaching of (putative) Vasubandhu *(Tenshin)* and his interpreter T'an-luan *(Donran),* taking the last half of each of their names and calling himself Shinran, the one name among the many which he used by which he has become most commonly known to posterity. He thus signifies how, at a stroke, he abandoned his former life-style and orthodox Buddhism as he knew it. This could not have been an easy decision. It was like the great death of Rinzai Zen as Hakuin describes it:

> After [experiencing the Great Death and] you have returned to life, unconsciously the pure and uninvolved true principle of undistracted meditation will appear before you . . . and at once your body and mind will drop off. The true, unlimited, eternal, perfected Tathāgata will manifest himself clearly before your eyes and never depart, though you should attempt to drive him away. . . . In the Pure Land School [this experience] is to fulfill one's vow for rebirth in Paradise . . .[22]

From now on the presence of Amida's *hongan* was a certainty in Shinran's life. The Shin Buddhist Kakunyo was later to write of this moment, in his *Shūjishō,* in a way that seems explicitly to link the Rinzai Great Death with the Shin One Thought:

> When in accordance with the words of a good master they awaken in their ordinary moments One Thought of trust in Amida, let this be regarded as the last moment, the end of the world, for them.[23]

The particular problem that vexed Shinran was "How can I, so full of defects, recite the *nembutsu* in order to obtain Amida's help unless Amida himself helps me to recite?"—that is, how can the self purify itself or, as it is put in Zen, the knife cut itself? His answer was the discovery of the nonduality of his impure mind and Amida's pure mind, the co-inherence of *his* practice and *Amida's* attainment. This was an authentic experience of śūnyatā by means of the dharma door of the nonduality of the "entering" and "leaving" aspects of the Pure Land practice, just as Dōgen's solution to Ju-ching's *kōan* was an authentic experience of śūnyatā by means of the dharma door of the nonduality of inherent enlightenment *(hongaku)* and manifest enlightenment *(shikaku).* Shinran felt his awakening as the perfection of *ekō,* Amida's leaving the Pure Land to seek beings, co-inherently with the realization of his own need to enter the Pure Land. Then, he compiled his *monrui* to demonstrate *(ken)* this.

The emergence of Shinran's new interpretation of Buddhism is similar to the event Thomas Kuhn calls a paradigm shift in the emergence of a new understanding of science. What he calls "normal science" is a matter of solving puzzles within an accepted framework. Anomalous results are regarded as the product of some deficiency of method. But it occasionally happens that so many anomalous results are obtained, without any defect of method being uncovered, that strain is put on the framework as a whole. If the anomalies cannot be cleared up and they continue to accumulate, the entire discipline is thrown into crisis until someone has a flash of insight which suddenly unifies the data in a new and satisfactory way. Once this new paradigm has itself become "normal," the process of puzzle solving begins again within the revised structure.

Kuhn points out that the method of demonstration of fact within a paradigm is fundamentally different from that between two competing paradigms. Logic will solve a puzzle, but only that mysterious use of language we call persuasion can move us out of an accepted paradigm and into a strange new one. This persuasion uses paradigms to destroy paradigms, and its argument

> is necessarily circular . . . whatever its force, the status of the circular argument is only that of persuasion. It cannot be made logically or even probabilistically compelling for those who refuse to step into the circle.[24]

Shinran's argument is certainly circular, and it seems to be an attempt to *persuade* us to see Buddhism differently than heretofore. He had not been able to solve the puzzles of "normal" Mahāyāna, the Tendai framework went into crisis for him, then it collapsed, and with a flash of insight he entered into the new paradigmatic circle of absolute Other Power. Thus, in order to understand Shinran we have to be willing to step into his circle.

And what is his circle? It is, finally, the very Buddhist view that the universe is not a problem, we do not have to earn happiness, the mind of clear light is already shining within us. We suspiciously question the universe from the prison of our suffering and push frantically at the door of our laboriously constructed ego. But the joke is that the door opens inward, and when we give up, body and mind drop off, the question disappears as the *kōan* dissolves, and we spontaneously shout *Namu Amida Butsu!*

> The happiness coming from faith is the greatest I could enjoy in this life. This is the happiness I am enjoying every day and night . . .[25]

Notes

1. Rev. Arthur Lloyd, *Shinran and His Work* (Tōkyō: Kobunkwan, 1910), 14.
2. Edward Conze, *Buddhism: Its Essence and Development* (Oxford: Cassirer, 1951; reprint, New York: Harper, 1959), 206.
3. Christmas Humphreys, *Buddhism,* rev. ed. (New York: Penguin Books, 1955), 165.
4. *Notes on "Essentials of Faith Alone": A Translation of Shinran's Yuishinshōmon'i* (Kyōto: Hongwanji International Center, 1979), 17f.
5. Roger Corless, "T'an-luan's Commentary on the Pure Land Discourse" (Ph.D. diss., University of Wisconsin-Madison, 1973).
6. I have truculently and imperfectly accepted David Tracy's criticism that the translation "proof texts," given without further explanation, is misleading, for it is used in modern English in a way that apparently denies precisely the

deeper meaning that Shinran's use of *monrui* is designed to affirm. A proof text is claimed to have one and only one meaning, and that is its literal or surface meaning. We observe, however, that proof texts are carefully chosen and may be said to override other passages which are not used as proof texts. Fortuitously, as I was revising this essay for publication, I was called upon by Jehovah's Witness missionaries and had a chance to investigate their hermeneutic method, which is almost entirely that of employing proof texts. The Bible is true, I was told, because archaeology has proved that Noah's flood actually occurred. The writings of other religions are false because they are not God's Word. (Here, an argument actually based upon the *sensus plenior* is presented as if it were an argument *to* the *sensus plenior* from the observed truth of the *sensus litteralis.*) God created Adam and Eve as the first human couple (Gen. 2:7, 21–22). "But, what about Gen. 1:27, where it says that God created all humans all at once?" "That tells us *that* he created them, and Gen. 2 tells us *how* he did it." "Why, in Gen. 2, is the creation of fish not mentioned?" "Because God had already created them in Gen. 1:21." (They had me there!) "So why did God create the beasts and the birds in Gen. 2:19 when he had already created them in Gen. 1:20 and 24?" "I don't question that, *these are God's mysteries*" (my italics). So, it seems that the "clear and distinct, surface meaning" of the proof text is a leg-pull. My persistent visitors *knew* that the Bible was God's Word and *therefore* that it must be inerrant. This is to our modern minds no doubt obscurantist and perverse, but it is nevertheless a descendant of the Thomistic teaching on Biblical inspiration, wherein the human author says more than he knows because God is the true author.

As for *monrui, rui* means a compilation of things of the same class made from an assortment of many classes, as one might collect, say, all the balls of one particular color from a bin containing balls of many different colors. I have been unable to find a satisfactory English equivalent to *rui* but I feel that "assembled" comes nearest to the meaning. "Marshalled" is a little too strict whereas "collected" is too lax. The texts are, however, "assembled" to "prove" Shinran's view of true Buddhism.

7. Roger Corless, "Sacred Text, Context and Proof-Text," in *The Critical Study of Sacred Texts,* ed. Wendy Doniger O'Flaherty, Berkeley Religious Studies Series, no. 2 (Berkeley, Calif.: Graduate Theological Union, 1979), 257–270. To my confusion, I now discover that my understanding of the meaning of the terms *nītārtha* and *neyārtha* in this article is precisely the reverse of the truth. The gentle reader will, therefore, please to emend her copy, descrying that my argument is not thereby endangered.

8. References to *K* are by page and column number in the critical, annotated edition of Hoshino Gempō, et al., Nihon Shisō Taikei, vol. 11 (Tokyo: Iwanami Shoten, 1975).

9. Gutoku Shaku Shinran, *The Kyōgyōshinshō: The Collection of Passages Expounding the True Teaching, Living, Faith and Realizing of the Pure Land,* trans. Daisetz Teitarō Suzuki, and ed. Eastern Buddhist Society (Kyoto: Shinshū Ōtaniha, 1973), 114.

10. That is, the three sūtras which are here under discussion. Shinran uses many more sūtras in compiling *K.* For a list of sūtras quoted by T'an-luan, and their relative frequency, see my "T'an-luan's Commentary," 44.

11. The chirping of the cicada or *semi* resembles the sound of rosary beads being rubbed together while one says mantras, and the Japanese sometimes explain that the *semi,* therefore, is chanting the Buddha's praises.

12. *Chi* is the Buddhist pronunciation of *chieh;* see Mathews 775(a).

13. The great benefit *(ta li)* is, for T'an-luan, that of benefiting oneself by birth in the Pure Land and benefiting others by returning to saṃsāra; see *T* 40.843a20–c8 et passim. Shinran rearranged a similar passage earlier in T'an-luan's text to exclude the first benefit; see *T* 47.421c24 and the Ryūdai edition (see following note), 48).

14. Text from the Ryūdai edition, *The Jōdo Wasan: The Hymns on the Pure Land,* with translation and notes by Ryūkyō Fujimoto et al. (Kyōto: Ryūkoku University, 1965), 5f. My translation.

15. There seems to be a hermeneutical shift from Vasubandhu's "single-mindedness" to T'an-luan's "one mind" consequent upon the movement from a more abstract Sanskrit term *(cittaikāgratā)* to a more reified Chinese term *(i-hsin).* The ease with which the Chinese may be taken as reified then provides the basis for Shinran's even more concrete understanding.

16. *Notes on "Essentials,"* 105–106.

17. *The Kyōgyōshinshō,* 181. Text at *K* 349:7–8.

18. *The Kyōgyōshinshō,* 200.

19. *Notes on "Essentials,"* 18.

20. Ibid., 19.

21. Co-inherence *(perichōrēsis, circumincessio)* is the doctrine that, first, the divinity and humanity of Christ and, secondly, the persons of the Trinity are related in such a way that each fully contains the other so that there is no blending or compromise or dominance of one over the other; in other words, they are neither the same (the Monophysite heresy) nor different (the Nestorian heresy) nor some kind of mixture (the Eutychian heresy). I suggest that a creative resonance exists between the models of perichōrēsis and śūnyatā in my essay "The Mutual Fulfillment of Buddhism And Christianity in Co-Inherent Superconsciousness," in *Buddhist-Christian Dialogue: Possibilities for Mutual Transformation,* ed. Paul O. Ingram and Frederick J. Streng (Honolulu: University of Hawaii Press, 1986), and in a paper entitled "Can Emptiness Will?" delivered at the conference "Paradigm Shifts in Buddhism and Christianity," Honolulu, January 1984.

22. Philip B. Yampolsky, *The Zen Master Hakuin: Selected Writings* (New York: Columbia University Press, 1971), 94f.

23. Translation by Kenshō Yokogawa in D. T. Suzuki, *Collected Writings on Shin Buddhism* (Kyoto: Shinshū Ōtaniha, 1973), 128.

24. Thomas S. Kuhn, *The Structure of Scientific Revolutions,* 2d ed. (Chicago: University of Chicago Press, 1970), 94.

25. *Selected Essays of Manshi Kiyozawa,* trans. Kenji Tajima and Floyd Shacklock (Kyoto: Bukkyō Bunka Society, 1936), 76.

Glossary

Amida 阿彌陀

Amida Butsu no Mina o kiki/ichinen dairi mujō nari 阿彌陀佛の御名をきき一念大利無上なり

Amidakyō 阿彌陀經

chai 宅

cheng-ming 正名

chi 偈

chieh 偈

chih-hsin 至心

chin 近

chu 註

ch'u 出

chü 具

chüeh-ting 決定
Daimuryōjukyō 大無量寿經
Dōgen 道元
Donran 曇鸞
dōsō 堂僧
ekō 廻向
Enryakuji 延暦寺
gu 愚
gufu 愚父
gujin 愚人
gushaku 愚釋
gusō 愚僧
Gutoku Shaku Shinran 愚禿釋親鸞
gyō 行
Hakuin 白隱
Hieizan 比叡山
Hōnen 法然
hongaku 本覺
hongan 本願
hsiang-hsü 相續
hsiang-ing 相應
hsin 信
hsin-hsin 信心
hsin-le 信樂
huan-hsiang 還相
hui-hsiang 廻向
hui-ju 廻入
hui-shih 廻施
i 義
i-hsin 一心
ichinen 一念
jo wen A-mi-t'o te-hao/hsia chih i-nien te ta-li 若聞阿彌陀德號下至一念得大利
Jōdo Sambukyō 浄土三部経
Jōdō Shinshū 浄土真宗
ju 入
Ju-ching 如淨
Kakunyo 覚如
Kammuryōjukyō 観無量寿経
Kangyō 観経
ken 顕
Ken Jōdo Shinjitsu Kyōgyōshō Monrui 顕浄土真実教行証文類
Kennin 建仁
kōan 公案
kongō shinshin 金剛真心
kuan-ch'a 觀察
kyō 教
Kyōgyōshinshō 教行信証
Kyŏnghŭng 憬興
li-kai 利益
li-pai 禮拜
li-t'o 利他
lun 論
Lun-chu 論註
ming 名
monrui 文類
Namu Amida Butsu 南無阿彌陀佛
nembutsu 念佛
Nichiren 日蓮
Nyorai 如來
Rinzai Zen 臨濟禪
rita 利他
riyaku 利益
ronchu 論註
rui 類
San Amida Butsu Ge 讚阿彌陀佛偈
sanshin[a] 三心
sanshin[b] 三信
semi 蟬
senchaku 選擇
shih-fang chung-sheng chih-hsin hsin-le yü sheng wo kuo nai-chih shih-nien 十方衆生至心信樂欲生我國乃至十念
shikaku 始覺
shin 信
shingyō 信樂
shinjin 信心
shinjitsu shinjin 眞實信心
Shinran 親鸞
shinshū 眞宗
shishin 至心
shō 証
shū 宗
Shūjishō 執持抄
shun 淳
ta hui-chung 大會衆
ta li 大利
tai 體
tan 但
T'an-luan 曇鸞
tari 他利

tariki 他力
Tendai 天台
Tenshin 天親
t'i 體
t'o-li 他利
Tsan A-mi-t'o Fo Chi 讚阿彌陀佛偈
toku 德
toku 禿
tsan-t'an 讚歎
tso-yüan 作願
wang-hsiang 往相
wu 屋
wu nien-men 五念門
yokushō 欲生
yü-sheng 欲生
yüan-lin yu-hsi 園林遊戲
Yuishinshōmon'i 唯信鈔文意

Contributors

George D. Bond (Ph.D., Northwestern University, 1972) is an associate professor in the Department of the History and Literature of Religion at Northwestern University. He is the author of *The Word of the Buddha: The Tipiṭaka and Its Interpretation in Theravāda Buddhism* and coeditor of *Sainthood in World Religions.*

Michael M. Broido (Ph.D., Cambridge University, 1967) is Senior Research Fellow in Linguistics at Magdalen College, University of Oxford. His research has included work on Tibetan interpretations of Madhyamaka and Vajrayāna thought, especially in relation to their Indian prototypes. His articles on Indian and Tibetan hermeneutics have appeared in the *Journal of the Tibet Society* and the *Journal of Indian Philosophy.*

Robert E. Buswell, Jr. (Ph.D., University of California, Berkeley, 1985) is an assistant professor in the Department of East Asian Languages and Cultures at the University of California, Los Angeles. He is the author of *The Korean Approach to Zen: The Collected Works of Chinul* and the forthcoming *The Apocryphal Vajrasamādhisūtra and the Origins of Ch'an.*

David W. Chappell (Ph.D., Yale University, 1976) is professor of religion and director of the East-West Religions Project at the University of Hawaii. He is the editor of *T'ien-t'ai Buddhism: An Outline of the Fourfold Teachings* and coeditor of *Buddhist and Taoist Studies,* volumes 1 and 2. He is also founding editor of the journal *Buddhist-Christian Studies.*

Roger Tashi Corless (Ph.D., University of Wisconsin, 1973) is associate professor of religion at Duke University. In addition to articles on East Asian Buddhism, he has published extensively in the area of comparative mysticism, especially Buddhist and Roman Catholic, and is an active participant in Buddhist-Christian dialogue.

Peter N. Gregory (Ph.D., Harvard University, 1981) is an assistant professor in the Program in Religious Studies and Center for East Asian and Pacific Studies at the University of Illinois, Urbana. He is the editor of *Traditions of Meditation in Chinese Buddhism* and *Sudden and Gradual: Approaches to Enlightenment in Chinese Thought,* and coeditor of *Studies in Ch'an and Hua-yen.*

Matthew Kapstein (Ph.D., Brown University, 1986) is assistant professor of Sanskrit in the Department of South Asian Languages and Civilizations at the University of Chicago. He is cotranslator of *The Fundamentals and History of the Nyingmapa Tradition of Tibetan Buddhism* and coeditor of *Soundings in Tibetan Civilization.*

Thomas P. Kasulis (Ph.D., Yale University, 1975) is professor of philosophy and religion at Northland College. He is the author of *Zen Action/Zen Person* and editor and cotranslator of Yuasa Yasuo's *The Body: Toward an Eastern Mind-body Theory.*

Étienne Lamotte (1903–1983) was the preeminent European Buddhologist of the twentieth century. His major publications include *Saṃdhinirmocana Sūtra: L'Explication des Mystères, L'Enseignement de Vimalakīrti, Histoire du Bouddhisme Indien,* and *Le Traité de la Grande Vertu de Sagesse de Nāgārjuna.*

Donald S. Lopez, Jr. (Ph.D., University of Virginia, 1982) is professor of religion at Middlebury College. He is the author of *A Study of Svātantrika* and *The Heart Sūtra Explained: Indian and Tibetan Commentaries,* and coeditor of *The Christ and the Bodhisattva.*

Robert A. F. Thurman (Ph.D., Harvard University, 1972) is professor of religion at Amherst College and president of the American Institute of Buddhist Studies. He is the translator of *The Holy Teaching of Vimalakīrti* and author of *Tsong Khapa's Speech of Gold in the Essence of True Eloquence.*

Index

Production Notes

This book was designed by Roger Eggers. Composition and paging were done on the Quadex Composing System and typesetting on the Compugraphic 8400 by the design and production staff of University of Hawaii Press.

The text typeface is Baskerville and the display typeface is Compugraphic Palatino.

Offset presswork and binding were done by Vail-Ballou Press, Inc. Text paper is Glatfelter Offset Vellum, basis 45.